Epigraphy and Islamic Culture

Architectural inscriptions are a fascinating aspect of Islamic cultural heritage because of their rich and diverse historical content and artistic merit. These inscriptions help us understand the advent of Islam and its gradual diffusion in Bengal, which eventually resulted in a Muslim majority region, making the Bengali Muslims the second largest linguistic group in the Islamic world.

This book is an interpretive study of the Arabic and Persian epigraphic texts of Bengal in the wider context of a rich epigraphic tradition in the Islamic world. While focusing on previously untapped sources, it takes a fresh look into the Islamic inscriptions of Bengal and examines the inner dynamics of the social, intellectual and religious transformations of this eastern region of South Asia. It explores many new inscriptions including Persian epigraphs that appeared immediately after the Muslim conquest of Bengal indicating an early introduction of Persian language in the region through a cultural interaction with Khurasan and Central Asia. In addition to deciphering and editing the epigraphic texts, the information derived from them has been analysed to construct the political, administrative, social, religious and cultural scenario of the period.

The first survey of the Muslim inscriptions in India ever to be attempted on this scale, the book reveals the significance of epigraphy as a source for Islamic history and culture. As such, it will be of interest to students and scholars of Asian Studies, Asian History and Islamic Studies.

Mohammad Yusuf Siddiq is President of the Bangladesh Association for Needy People's Improvement. He has written extensively on the history, civilization and culture of Muslim Bengal, including a dozen entries in the *Encyclopaedia of Islam*.

Routledge contemporary South Asia series

1 **Pakistan**
Social and cultural transformations in a Muslim nation
Mohammad A. Qadeer

2 **Labor, Democratization and Development in India and Pakistan**
Christopher Candland

3 **China–India Relations**
Contemporary dynamics
Amardeep Athwal

4 **Madrasas in South Asia**
Teaching terror?
Jamal Malik

5 **Labor, Globalization and the State**
Workers, women and migrants confront neoliberalism
Edited by Debdas Banerjee and Michael Goldfield

6 **Indian Literature and Popular Cinema**
Recasting classics
Edited by Heidi R.M. Pauwels

7 **Islamist Militancy in Bangladesh**
A complex web
Ali Riaz

8 **Regionalism in South Asia**
Negotiating cooperation, institutional structures
Kishore C. Dash

9 **Federalism, Nationalism and Development**
India and the Punjab economy
Pritam Singh

10 **Human Development and Social Power**
Perspectives from South Asia
Ananya Mukherjee Reed

11 **The South Asian Diaspora**
Transnational networks and changing identities
Edited by Rajesh Rai and Peter Reeves

12 **Pakistan–Japan Relations**
Continuity and change in economic relations and security interests
Aḥmad Rashid Malik

13 **Himalayan Frontiers of India**
Historical, geo-political and strategic perspectives
K. Warikoo

14 **India's Open-Economy Policy**
Globalism, rivalry, continuity
Jalal Alamgir

15 The Separatist Conflict in Sri Lanka
Terrorism, ethnicity, political economy
Asoka Bandarage

16 India's Energy Security
Edited by Ligia Noronha and Anant Sudarshan

17 Globalization and the Middle Classes in India
The social and cultural impact of neoliberal reforms
Ruchira Ganguly-Scrase and Timothy J. Scrase

18 Water Policy Processes in India
Discourses of power and resistance
Vandana Asthana

19 Minority Governments in India
The puzzle of elusive majorities
Csaba Nikolenyi

20 The Maoist Insurgency in Nepal
Revolution in the twenty-first century
Edited by Mahendra Lawoti and Anup K. Pahari

21 Global Capital and Peripheral Labour
The history and political economy of plantation workers in India
K. Ravi Raman

22 Maoism in India
Reincarnation of ultra-left wing extremism in the twenty-first century
Bidyut Chakrabarty and Rajat Kujur

23 Economic and Human Development in Contemporary India
Cronyism and fragility
Debdas Banerjee

24 Culture and the Environment in the Himalaya
Arjun Guneratne

25 The Rise of Ethnic Politics in Nepal
Democracy in the margins
Susan I. Hangen

26 The Multiplex in India
A cultural economy of urban leisure
Adrian Athique and Douglas Hill

27 Tsunami Recovery in Sri Lanka
Ethnic and regional dimensions
Dennis B. McGilvray and Michele R. Gamburd

28 Development, Democracy and the State
Critiquing the Kerala model of development
K. Ravi Raman

29 Mohajir Militancy in Pakistan
Violence and transformation in the Karachi conflict
Nichola Khan

30 Nationbuilding, Gender and War Crimes in South Asia
Bina D'Costa

31 The State in India after Liberalization
Interdisciplinary perspectives
Edited by Akhil Gupta and K. Sivaramakrishnan

32 **National Identities in Pakistan**
The 1971 war in contemporary Pakistani fiction
Cara Cilano

33 **Political Islam and Governance in Bangladesh**
Edited by Ali Riaz and C. Christine Fair

34 **Bengali Cinema**
'An Other Nation'
Sharmistha Gooptu

35 **NGOs in India**
The challenges of women's empowerment and accountability
Patrick Kilby

36 **The Labour Movement in the Global South**
Trade unions in Sri Lanka
S. Janaka Biyanwila

37 **Building Bangalore**
Architecture and urban transformation in India's Silicon Valley
John C. Stallmeyer

38 **Conflict and Peacebuilding in Sri Lanka**
Caught in the peace trap?
Edited by Jonathan Goodhand, Jonathan Spencer and Benedict Korf

39 **Microcredit and Women's Empowerment**
A case study of Bangladesh
Amunui Faraizi, Jim McAllister and Taskinur Rahman

40 **South Asia in the New World Order**
The role of regional cooperation
Shahid Javed Burki

41 **Explaining Pakistan's Foreign Policy**
Escaping India
Aparna Pande

42 **Development-induced Displacement, Rehabilitation and Resettlement in India**
Current issues and challenges
Edited by Sakarama Somayaji and Smrithi Talwar

43 **The Politics of Belonging in India**
Becoming adivasi
Edited by Daniel J. Rycroft and Sangeeta Dasgupta

44 **Re-Orientalism and South Asian Identity Politics**
The oriental other within
Edited by Lisa Lau and Ana Cristina Mendes

45 **Islamic Revival in Nepal**
Religion and a new nation
Megan Adamson Sijapati

46 **Education and Inequality in India**
A classroom view
Manabi Majumdar and Jos Mooij

47 **The Culturalization of Caste in India**
Identity and inequality in a multicultural age
Balmurli Natrajan

48 **Corporate Social Responsibility in India**
Bidyut Chakrabarty

49 **Pakistan's Stability Paradox**
Domestic, regional and international dimensions
Edited by Ashutosh Misra and Michael E. Clarke

50 **Transforming Urban Water Supplies in India**
The role of reform and partnerships in globalization
Govind Gopakumar

51 **South Asian Security**
Twenty-first century discourses
Sagarika Dutt and Alok Bansal

52 **Non-discrimination and Equality in India**
Contesting boundaries of social justice
Vidhu Verma

53 **Being Middle-class in India**
A way of life
Henrike Donner

54 **Kashmir's Right to Secede**
A critical examination of contemporary theories of secession
Matthew J. Webb

55 **Bollywood Travels**
Culture, diaspora and border crossings in popular Hindi cinema
Rajinder Dudrah

56 **Nation, Territory, and Globalization in Pakistan**
Traversing the margins
Chad Haines

57 **The Politics of Ethnicity in Pakistan**
The Baloch, Sindhi and Mohajir Ethnic Movements
Farhan Hanif Siddiqi

58 **Nationalism and Ethnic Conflict**
Identities and mobilization after 1990
Edited by Mahendra Lawoti and Susan Hangen

59 **Islam and Higher Education**
Concepts, challenges and opportunities
Marodsilton Muborakshoeva

60 **Religious Freedom in India**
Sovereignty and (anti) conversion
Goldie Osuri

61 **Everyday Ethnicity in Sri Lanka**
Up-country Tamil identity politics
Daniel Bass

62 **Ritual and Recovery in Post-Conflict Sri Lanka**
Eloquent bodies
Jane Derges

63 **Bollywood and Globalisation**
The global power of popular Hindi cinema
Edited by David J. Schaefer and Kavita Karan

64 **Regional Economic Integration in South Asia**
Trapped in conflict?
Amita Batra

65 **Architecture and Nationalism in Sri Lanka**
The trouser under the cloth
Anoma Pieris

66 **Civil Society and Democratization in India**
Institutions, ideologies and interests
Sarbeswar Sahoo

67 **Contemporary Pakistani Fiction in English**
Idea, nation, state
Cara N. Cilano

68 **Transitional Justice in South Asia**
A study of Afghanistan and Nepal
Tazreena Sajjad

69 **Displacement and Resettlement in India**
The human cost of development
Hari Mohan Mathur

70 **Water, Democracy and Neoliberalism in India**
The Power to Reform
Vicky Walters

71 **Capitalist Development in India's Informal Economy**
Elisabetta Basile

72 **Nation, Constitutionalism and Buddhism in Sri Lanka**
Roshan de Silva Wijeyeratne

73 **Counterinsurgency, Democracy, and the Politics of Identity in India**
From warfare to welfare?
Mona Bhan

74 **Enterprise Culture in Neoliberal India**
Studies in youth, class, work and media
Edited by Nandini Gooptu

75 **The Politics of Economic Restructuring in India**
Economic governance and state spatial rescaling
Loraine Kennedy

76 **The Other in South Asian Religion, Literature and Film**
Perspectives on Otherism and Otherness
Edited by Diana Dimitrova

77 **Being Bengali**
At home and in the world
Edited by Mridula Nath Chakraborty

78 **The Political Economy of Ethnic Conflict in Sri Lanka**
Nikolaos Biziouras

79 **Indian Arranged Marriages**
A social psychological perspective
Tulika Jaiswal

80 **Writing the City in British Asian Diasporas**
Edited by Seán McLoughlin, William Gould, Ananya Jahanara Kabir and Emma Tomalin

81 **Post-9/11 Espionage Fiction in the US and Pakistan**
Spies and 'terrorists'
Cara Cilano

82 **Left Radicalism in India**
Bidyut Chakrabarty

83 **'Nation-State' and Minority Rights in India**
Comparative perspectives on Muslim and Sikh identities
Tanweer Fazal

84 **Pakistan's Nuclear Policy**
A minimum credible deterrence
Zafar Khan

85 **Imagining Muslims in South Asia and the Diaspora**
Secularism, religion, representations
Claire Chambers and Caroline Herbert

86 Indian Foreign Policy in Transition
Relations with South Asia
Arijit Mazumdar

87 Corporate Social Responsibility and Development in Pakistan
Nadeem Malik

88 Indian Capitalism in Development
Barbara Harriss-White and Judith Heyer

89 Bangladesh Cinema and National Identity
In search of the modern?
Zakir Hossain Raju

90 Suicide in Sri Lanka
The anthropology of an epidemic
Tom Widger

91 Epigraphy and Islamic Culture
Inscriptions of the early Muslim rulers of Bengal (1205–1494)
Mohammad Yusuf Siddiq

92 Reshaping City Governance
London, Mumbai, Kolkata, Hyderabad
Nirmala Rao

93 The Indian Partition in Literature and Films
History, politics, and aesthetics
Rini Bhattacharya Mehta and Debali Mookerjea-Leonard

94 Development, Poverty and Power in Pakistan
The impact of state and donor interventions on farmers
Syed Mohammad Ali

95 Ethnic Subnationalist Insurgencies in South Asia
Identities, interests and challenges to state authority
Jugdep S. Chima

96 International Migration and Development in South Asia
Edited by Md Mizanur Rahman and Tan Tai Yong

97 Twenty-First Century Bollywood
Ajay Gehlawat

98 Political Economy of Development in India
Indigeneity in transition in the State of Kerala
Darley Kjosavik and Nadarajah Shanmugaratnam

99 State and Nation-Building in Pakistan
Beyond Islam and security
Edited by Roger D. Long, Gurharpal Singh, Yunas Samad, and Ian Talbot

100 Subaltern Movements in India
Gendered geographies of struggle against neoliberal development
Manisha Desai

101 Islamic Banking in Pakistan
Shariah-compliant finance and the quest to make Pakistan more Islamic
Feisal Khan

102 The Bengal Diaspora
Rethinking Muslim migration
Claire Alexander, Joya Chatterji, and Annu Jalais

103 Mobilizing Religion and Gender in India
The role of activism
Nandini Deo

Epigraphy and Islamic Culture

Inscriptions of the early Muslim rulers of Bengal (1205–1494)

Mohammad Yusuf Siddiq

Routledge
Taylor & Francis Group
LONDON AND NEW YORK

First published 2016 by Routledge

2 Park Square, Milton Park, Abingdon, Oxfordshire OX14 4RN
711 Third Avenue, New York, NY 10017

Routledge is an imprint of the Taylor & Francis Group, an informa business

First issued in paperback 2018

British Library Cataloguing in Publication Data
A catalogue record for this book is available from the British Library

Library of Congress Cataloging in Publication Data
Siddiq, Mohammad Yusuf, author.
Epigraphy and Islamic culture : inscriptions of the early Muslim rulers of Bengal (1205–1494) / Mohammad Yusuf Siddiq.
pages cm. – (Routledge contemporary South Asia series)
Includes bibliographical references and index.
1. Islamic inscriptions–India–Bengal. 2. Architectural inscriptions–India–Bengal. 3. Inscriptions, Arabic–India–Bengal. 4. Inscriptions, Persian–India–Bengal. 5. Bengal (India)–Civilization. 6. India–Civilization–Islamic influences. I. Title.
CN1173.B4S52 2015
729'.19095414 909'.09767–dc23 2015019964

ISBN: 978-0-415-29782-0 (hbk)
ISBN: 978-1-138-32020-8 (pbk)

Typeset in Times New Roman
by Wearset Ltd, Boldon, Tyne and Wear

To
My Parents
Muhammad Mujibur Rahman and Bilqis Begum
who once lived in the village of Dadanchak on the bank of the mighty river Pagla in the past (dried up completely towards the end of the twentieth century as a result of ecological and environmental changes in the area) in Chapai Nawabganj district, not far from the ancient Muslim capitals of Gaur and Pandua, and whose dedication to Arabic and Islamic Studies is always a source of inspiration for me in this epigraphic journey

and to

Jamāl al-Dīn al-Shībī (779–837/1378–1433),
the true founder of the scientific study of inscription and the father of Islamic epigraphy, and a celebrated scholar and mentor at the famous Bengali seminary at Makkah known as al-Madrasa al-Sulṭāniyyah al-Ghiyāthiyyah al-Bangāliyyah (named after its Bengali patron al-Sulṭān Ghiyāth al-Dīn A'ẓam Shāh, the ruler of Bengal), whose meticulous study of tombstones and stelae of Makkah set an unprecedented scholarly standard of epigraphy for the first time in history

Contents

List of figures xv
Sigla xvii
Note on transliteration xviii
Foreword xix
Acknowledgements xxi
List of abbreviations xxiv

Introduction: epigraphy of Muslim Bengal 1

1 **Epigraphy as an important source for Islamic history and civilization** 9
Epigraphy in Islamic tradition 9
Use of inscriptions in Islamic architecture 10
Emergence of Islamic epigraphy 11
Importance of Islamic epigraphy 12
Thematic variety of Islamic inscriptions 13
Use of inscriptions as legal deeds 16
Globalization and cultural continuity of the Islamic world: comparison of some inscriptions of Bengal with those of Andalusia 17
Diversity of materials and features in Bengal inscriptions 21
Comparison of Islamic inscriptions with Sanskrit inscriptions in Bengal 22
Some conclusive remarks 23

2 **The diffusion of Islam in Bengal and the articulation of a new order** 27
The land 27
The advent of Islam and the Bengal hinterland 29
Merchants and the faith: early Islamic contacts with Bengal 31

The Muslim conquest of Bengal and the beginning of Islamic consolidation 34
The emergence of the independent Sultanate and the spread of Islamic culture 37
From syncretistic tradition to Islamic reassertion: the mighty Mughals and the British Raj 39
Royalty and ruling establishment 43
Commerce and maritime activities 44
Mosques: the nucleus of Islamic society 45
The role of 'ulamā' and madrasas in the transmission of knowledge 48

3 Nature, aesthetic perception and mysticism: spiritual dimensions of the Islamic inscriptions of Bengal 58

4 Worldly authority and paradisiacal ambition: diversity of titles in the Islamic inscriptions of Bengal 72
Titles in Islamic culture and their historical importance 73

5 Early Islamic inscriptions 87
Inscriptions of the Khaljī chiefs 87
Inscriptions of the early rulers appointed by the Delhi Sultans 95
Inscriptions of the Balbanī rulers 101

6 Inscriptions of the Sultanate period 120
Inscriptions of the early Ilyās Shāhī rulers 120
Inscriptions of the indigenous Bengali sulṭāns (Sulṭān Jalāl al-Dīn Muḥammad Shāh and his son) 134
Inscriptions of the later Ilyās Shāhī rulers (the restored dynasty) 139
Inscriptions of the so-called Ḥabashī rulers of Abyssinian origin 227

Bibliography 242
Index 255

Figures

I.1 **(Ins. 1)**: The earliest (the first) Islamic inscription of Bengal discovered so far recording the name of Sulṭān 'Alā' Dīn 1
I.2 Early Islamic contact with Bengal 2
2.1 Diffusion of mosques in medieval Bengal 46
2.2 Growth of the madrasa institution in medieval Bengal 49
3.1 The funerary inscription of Nur Quṭb al-'Ālam at his khānqāh in Ḥaḍrat Pandua dated 863/1459 58
3.2 Early khānqāhs, appearance of sufi orders and ḥajj routes, in medieval Bengal 63
4.1 Exuberant titles for Fatḥ Shāh in an inscription in Gaur dated 889/1484 72
6.1 Commemorative inscription (Khānqāh in Pandua, Malda district, West Bengal) 133
6.2 Commemorative inscription (Pandua, Malda district, West Bengal) 134
6.3 Commemorative inscription (the Shrine of Ghazī Pīr, Shibganj Police Station, Nawabganj district) 138
6.4 Commemorative inscription (Gaur in Malda district, West Bengal) 141
6.5 Bridge inscription (Mahdipur High School Museum, Mahdipur Post Office, English Bazar Police Station, Malda district, West Bengal) 165
6.6 Commemorative inscriptions (Nīm Darwāza (halfway entrance) in Gaur, in the police station of Ingrez Bazar in Malda district, West Bengal) 176
6.7 Commemorative inscription (Pichhli Gangarampur village, west of Malda town, West Bengal) 197
6.8 Commemorative inscription (British Museum) 202
6.9 Commemorative inscription (Shrine of Boamaloti in the suburb of Gaur, Malda district, West Bengal) 210
6.10 Commemorative inscription (Mughrapara near Sonārgā'on, district of Dhaka, Bangladesh) 215
6.11 Commemorative inscription (an unidentified Sultanate mosque in Rohanpur near Gaur, Bangladesh) 222

6.12 Commemorative inscription (an unidentified Sultanate monument from the royal citadel in Gaur) 226
6.13 Commemorative inscription (Chapai-Maheshpur village in Gobratala Union, Palsha Post Office, Chapai Nawabganj district, Bangladesh) 227
6.14 Commemorative inscription (Sultanate masjid in Gaur, Ingrez Bazar police station, Malda district, West Bengal) 236

Sigla

The following symbols are used in the epigraphic study in this book:

Italic	Words or letters that are rendered incorrectly by the inscriber in the texts are ***italicized.***
—	**Underlining** a letter or a word indicates that it could not be deciphered satisfactorily because it was either damaged or illegible.
<>	**Pointed brackets** indicate emendation of words or phrases that are incorrect in the inscription.
[ ]	**Square brackets** enclose conjectural restoration of missing parts of the text proposed by the author.
( )	**Parentheses** contain glosses such as addition of words to clarify meaning or references to chapter and verse of Qur’ānic quotations.
{ }	**Braces** are used for conjectural deletion of letters that do not properly belong to the text but have been erroneously added by the inscriber.

Note on transliteration

Foreign words that do not appear commonly in an unabridged English dictionary are transliterated with diacritics. Proper names appear in their English form when a standard English form exists (e.g. Sultanate not Sulṭāni, Chittagong, not Chatgaon or Chottogram). In general, the Library of Congress system of transliteration is used with minor modifications.

Foreword

The Bengal delta region evolved cultural traditions distinct from those of the rest of South Asia from at least the eighth century, when first Buddhist kings of the Pala dynasty (*ca.* 750–1161) and then Hindu kings of the Sena dynasty (*ca.* 1097–1223) held sway. Reflected in literature, architecture or sculpture, these traditions persisted with remarkable tenacity. In the early thirteenth century, when Persianized Turks linked to the Delhi Sultanate (1206–1526) conquered the delta, Islamic culture found distinctive modes of expression as it gradually became rooted in Bengal. This was especially clear after the mid-fourteenth century, when Muslim rulers of the delta became politically severed from their former overlords, the sultans of Delhi. From 1342 down to the Mughal conquest of the delta in the early seventeenth century, a series of independent Muslim dynasties ruled over Bengal, governing mainly from their capital of Guar on the banks of the Ganges River in the region's northwestern sector.

Nowhere was Islamic culture in Bengal expressed more vividly or distinctly than in the region's rich tradition of public inscriptions, recorded either in Arabic or in Persian. Indeed, as Mohammad Yusuf Siddiq makes plain in the present volume, in medieval Bengal ruling authorities carried the art of epigraphy to heights seen nowhere else in the Islamic world. Just as their Pala and Sena predecessors employed black basalt as their preferred medium for carving Buddhist or Hindu images, so too did Bengal's Muslim rulers use that exquisite medium for recording public inscriptions. Most of these appeared on the exterior surfaces of mosques, shrines, tombs, palaces, Sufi hospices and shrines, or on civil structures such as bridges, caravanserais, tanks or wells. In particular, the sultans of Bengal adopted the intricate and stylized form of calligraphy known as the *ṭughrā'* and raised it to a very high aesthetic level. Indeed, the aesthetics of this form was so pronounced that in some inscriptions the writing itself is barely decipherable. Attaining their peak under the Husain Shahi dynasty of kings (1494–1539), inscriptions of the *ṭughrā'* type are distinctive for their elongated shafts formed from Arabic letters like *alef* or *lām*, which rise to the top of a panel in a symmetrical way. These shafts often widen as they approach the top, while other letters like *nūn* or *fī* might sweep across the vertical shafts, appearing rather like swans or boats coursing across the black basalt stone. The appearance of such figures in these inscriptions is perhaps not surprising, as they are intimately associated with the Bengal's lush, riverine landscape. As the author rightly comments, Islam, as these inscriptions reveal, appears to have been 'assimilated into Bengali life and had become part of the natural experience of the land'.

Apart from their aesthetic appeal, however, the many inscriptions reproduced and discussed in this volume also had the practical function of informing the public of significant facts surrounding the construction of prominent structures. These included the identity of the patron, the purpose(s) of the monument in question, the date of its construction and so on. Indeed, these records afford historians with valuable information for reconstructing the socio-political context in which a given inscription was recorded. This information not only supplements what otherwise might be found in contemporary chronicles or coins; in some ways it surpasses such sources in point of accuracy, given their immediate physical proximity to the structures to which they were affixed. For example, from epigraphic evidence we learn that in the reign of the Mughal emperor Aurangzeb (1658–1707) Shi'i migrants settled in Bengal and patronized mosques in the Dhaka region. We also learn that in the same emperor's reign, Bengali Hindus patronized civil projects like building bridges, and that they acquired a taste for the Persian language.

The present volume is unique in being the first study of its kind to discuss inscriptions dating not only to Bengal's Sultanate period, but also to the succeeding Mughal era down to 1707. This scope enables the reader to see the gradual changes in style and subject matter that accompanied the re-uniting of the Bengal delta with upper India that occurred when the delta was annexed by the imperial Mughals in the early seventeenth century.

For all these reasons, academic scholars and the reading public alike owe Dr Siddiq a great debt of gratitude for painstakingly putting together such a comprehensive and lushly illustrated volume respecting one of the noblest legacies of pre-modern Bengal.

Professor Richard M. Eaton
Department of History, University of Arizona, USA

Acknowledgements

In this long epigraphic journey, I received continuous support and encouragement from various people and numerous sources and to all of them I express my sincere gratitude. The present work evolved through various stages. The idea of working on the inscriptions of Bengal took shape in 1981 when I was still a student at Umm al-Qura University in Makkah al-Mukarramah. Thanks to my Professors in Umm al-Qura University, particularly the late Riad Eletre, the late Abdel Rahman Fahmy and Ḥusām al-Dīn al-Samarraie (lately a professor of Islamic history and my colleague at Sharjah University), who not only made me interested in Islamic epigraphy, but also trained me laboriously in this vast, yet extremely interesting field. Still, I could not have ventured to undertake the project on the inscriptions of Bengal had I not received particular encouragement and active support from the late Professor Oleg Grabar (passed away 8 January 2010) when I joined the Aga Khan Program for Islamic Architecture at Harvard University and Massachusetts Institute of Technology (MIT) in 1987 first as a Research Associate, and later on as a Post Doctoral Fellow. Not only did he inspire me to write this book, but he also provided me with many valuable insights throughout this epigraphic mission. I also thank Harvard's Center for Middle Eastern Studies, Center for the Study of World Religions and Islamic Legal Studies Program for extending to me fellowships and providing a much needed sanctuary where I could devote myself to writing.

Acknowledgement is gratefully given to my colleagues and professors at Harvard University, particularly, Annemarie Schimmel (passed away 26 January 2003), Wolfhart Heinrichs (passed away 23 January 2014), Roy Parvez Mottahedeh, William A. Graham and Aron Zysow (formerly a professor of Arabic at the University of Washington, Seattle), without whose unremitting aid and valuable comments, this huge task could not have been completed. I am deeply indebted to Clifford Edmund Bosworth, Professor Emeritus of Manchester University, UK and my colleague at the Center for Middle Eastern Studies at Harvard University in 1993 (passed away 28 February 2015), Mongi ‘Abd al-Nabi (originally from Tunisia, living currently in Damascus and his wife Rim al-Jabi) and Sheikh Abdul Karim (originally from Khulna, Bangladesh, currently Vice President of Sharjah Islamic Bank, UAE) for their kind support at various stages of preparing the manuscript. Both of my special friends and former colleagues (at Zayed University in

Dubai, UAE) Erika Mitchell (currently living in East Calaisi, Vermont) and Seth Frisbie (currently an Associate Professor at Norwich University, Vermont), deserve my special thanks for their interest, encouragement and relentless editorial support while writing this book.

There were various organizations that helped me in my epigraphic research in many different ways. The Fondation Max Van Berchem, Geneva, Switzerland provided me with a generous grant to undertake the whole project of surveying the Islamic inscriptions of Bengal. The Higher Education Commission, Islamabad, Pakistan, and the Faculty of Higher Education and Research of Sharjah University in the United Arab Emirates supported me with necessary funds for further advancement in my epigraphic research. A generous research grant by the Iran Heritage Foundation, London, UK helped me particularly in carrying out a comprehensive study of the Persian inscriptions of the region.

The Department of Archaeology, Bangladesh, in general, and its Chief Photographer, Tauhidun Nabi, in particular, deserve my special gratitude for their continuous help in procuring a large number of epigraphic images used in this book. The Department of Epigraphy of the Archaeological Survey of India as well as the Indian National Museum, Calcutta provided me with a large number of useful photographs from time to time. The Bangladesh National Museum, Varendra Research Museum, the University Museum, Philadelphia and the British Museum, London provided me with all kinds of facilities to photograph Islamic inscriptions of Bengal in their collections.

Margaret Savçenko (passed away in 2002) of the Aga Khan Program for Islamic Architecture at Harvard University read the initial draft of the book painstakingly more than once and suggested many valuable improvements. The Aga Khan Program for Islamic Architecture at Harvard University and Massachusetts Institute of Technology helped me with their remarkable collections of the visual images of the Islamic world. I would like to express my special gratitude to the late Shri Krishna Kamal Sarkar (a former headmaster of Mahdipur High School who passed away in 2013), and the residents of Mahdipur village (adjacent to Gaur, Malda district, West Bengal) for extending to me their kindest hospitality and every possible support during my field work in West Bengal. My colleagues and students both at the University of the Punjab, Lahore (specially Maryam Ahmad, a brilliant PhD student at the Department of Islamic Studies, and my research associate in this research project, who, along with the late Sayyid Qasim Mahmood [a prolific Urdu writer from Lahore] played the most important role in rendering this whole research work into Urdu), as well as from LUMS (Lahore University of Management Sciences) always offered me unrelenting support during my visiting professorship in Pakistan and made me feel at home in every possible way during my stay in Lahore. I am grateful to every member of my family for continuous support and encouragement during this work. All of my children helped me in their own creative ways at different stages of this work. My grandchildren, nephews and nieces put their best efforts to keep me in good humour and cheerful spirits through their playful, joyous and ever happy company.

Lastly, I thank my parents, Professor Muhammad Mujibur Rahman and Bilqis Begum, and my late grandmother Kulthūm who always stood beside me and provided me with every possible comfort and inspiration needed in this long, challenging and sometimes stressful, but yet extremely interesting, epigraphic journey.

This study of the Islamic inscriptions of Bengal was funded by Fondation Max Van Berchem, Geneve, Switzerland, the Iran Heritage Foundation, London, UK and Sharjah University, UAE.

Abbreviations

ASB	Asiatic Society of Bengal (Kolkata, West Bengal, India)
ASI	Archaeological Survey of India
ASR	*Archaeological Survey (of India) Report*
EIAPS	*Epigraphia Indica Arabic and Persian Supplement*
EIM	*Epigraphia Indo-Moslemica*
ins.	inscription
JASB	*Journal of the Asiatic Society of Bengal*
JASBD	*Journal of the Asiatic Society of Bangladesh*
JASP	*Journal of the Asiatic Society of Pakistan*
KBOPL	Khuda Baksh Oriental Public Library, Patna, Bihar
n.s.	new series
PASB	*Proceedings of the Asiatic Society of Bengal*

Introduction

Epigraphy of Muslim Bengal

Figure I.1 **(Ins. 1)**: The earliest (the first) Islamic inscription of Bengal discovered so far recording the name of Sulṭān ʻAlā' Dīn (*ca.* CE 1210–1213), the second Muslim ruler of Bengal and the first one to proclaim himself sultan (author's own image).[1]

In the beginning, I praise and thank God, the One Who in His (divine) wisdom has provided this inn (-like world). At every moment someone is entering into it, while someone else is departing, for no one has the capacity to settle here permanently.

As soon as someone becomes aware of the rapid movement of the cosmos, he soon realizes that there is no other provision for the way [of life] except good deeds. Due to the justice of Sulṭān ʻAlā' Dīn wa Dunyā' shāh-e-jahān (the king of the world), even a lamb does not (need to) hide from a wolf.

Because of his efforts, Islam grows every moment. By the mercy of (God) the Just, this bridge was completed during his reign. This good action is possible only by the one who is day and night continually engaged in acts of benevolence for everyone – the noble as well as the commoner.

أول ثنا وحمد بگويم خدا يرا
كاراست بحكمت خود اين سرايرا
هردم يكى درآيد [و] د يگر برون رود
كس را مجال نيست كه اين جاسكون شود
انكس كه باشد آگه ازين چرخ نشه سير
داند كه زاد راه نباشد دگر چوخير
سلطان علاء دين ودنيا شه جهان
كه زعدل او زگرگ بگشته بره نمان
إسلام را فزايش هردم ز جهد او
از فضل حق تمام شد اين پل بعهد او
اين خير را مخير آنست كومدام
شب روز خير كردي در حق خاص عام

With this Persian inscription of Sulṭān 'Alā' Dīn [wa Dunyā' 'Alī Mardān Khaljī] from Sultanganj (now in Varendra Research Museum, Rajshahi University, Bangladesh), an Islamic epigraphic tradition began around 1210–1213 in the eastern hinterland of the Islamic world, historically known as Bengal. Just a decade before, it had been ruled by the Hindu dynasty of the Senas and, before that, by the Buddhist dynasty of the Pala (see Figure I.2). The mystical verses of this first Islamic epigraph in Bengal, deeply imbued in a profound spiritual message, commemorate construction of a bridge that symbolically connected this newly conquered outpost with the rest of the Islamic world. Though ornamenting a secular structure, the text carries some religious elements: divine presence in every cosmic scheme, praise of God and the transitory nature of life. In a way, this reflects the characteristic Islamic perspective which does not formally separate religious life and everyday worldly activities. Indeed most inscriptions in the Islamic world, even if affixed to secular structures, resonate with religious expressions, constituting in some way or another public statements of faith that serve to remind Muslims of aspects of their Islamic beliefs. In addition, phrases commonly found in these inscriptions often reflect the public, societal or state trends of their time. Therefore, to interpret these texts in their proper contexts

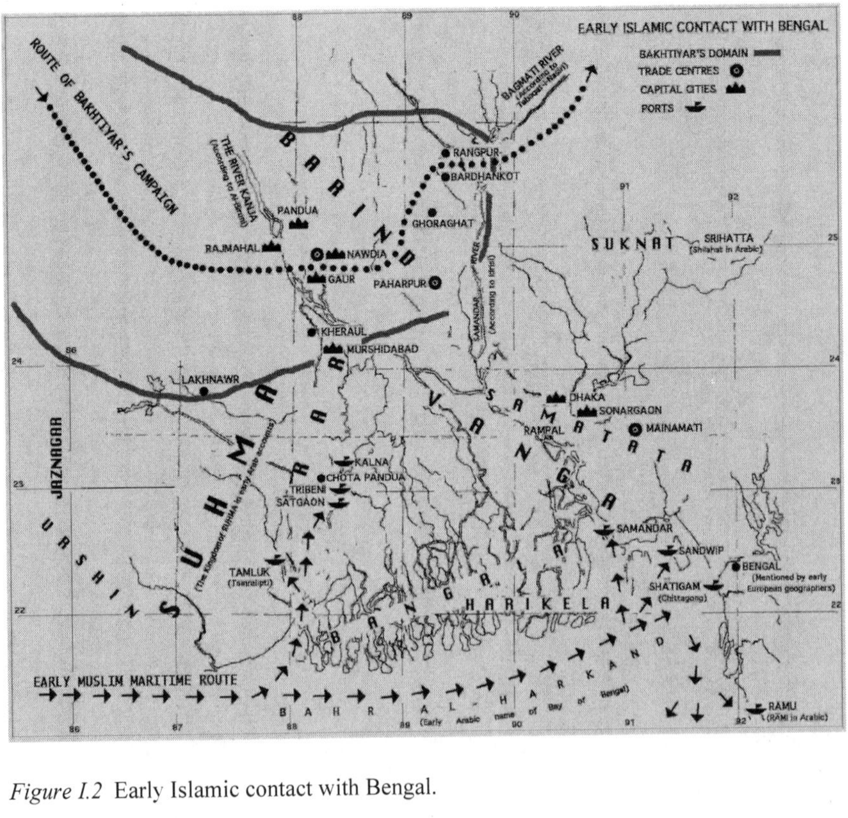

Figure I.2 Early Islamic contact with Bengal.

can be quite a refreshing exercise for the historian, opening up a rich, hitherto untapped, historical source.

The second Islamic inscription from Bengal (from the reign of Sulṭān Giyāth al-Dīn ʻIwaḍ dated 618/1221, discovered in a khānqāh in Sian, Birbhum, West Bengal) commemorates the construction of a khānqāh, a key institution in the spread of the teachings of Islam and its spiritual message (see Figure 3.2). The third Islamic inscription from Bengal (from the reign of Balkā Khān Khaljī, discovered in Naohata, Rahjshahi, Bangladesh, now in Varendra Research Museum, commemorates the construction of a masjid and madrasa complex, two other important institutions of Muslim religious, social and intellectual life (see Figures 2.1 and 2.2). Bengal has an epigraphic heritage extending back to the pre-Islamic period. Inscriptions of various styles are evident in this region, which was once rich in stone carving and sculpture. In the pre-Islamic period, however, artists and craftsmen did not use their skill to exhibit calligraphy as such; Sanskrit and Pali inscriptions are generally informative rather than calligraphic in intent. Inscriptions became more common after the advent of Islam to Bengal and as Bengali Muslim rulers launched into architectural projects. It is difficult to imagine a building of that period without some kind of inscription; it was as if it would have appeared naked or unfinished without. As a result, epigraphic records and inscriptions are plentiful in terms of both artistic accomplishment and historical information.

Historical accounts of the Islamic dynasties in South Asia are numerous, particularly those regarding the central authorities in Delhi. A number of sourcebooks, mostly in Persian, record the deeds of sultans and emperors. Bengal, however, has a very small share of this rich heritage of historical writing. Of whatever might once have existed, very little has survived. One example of a lost source is a Persian manuscript on early Muslim rule in Bengal found by Francis Buchanan Hamilton in a shrine in Pandua in the early nineteenth century and mentioned in his book, *A Geographical, Statistical and Historical Description of the District or Zilla of Dinajpur in the Province or Soubah of Bengal* (Calcutta, 1833). Unfortunately, the manuscript cannot be traced. Several factors, including natural calamities such as flood and fire, may account for the lack of extant sources. The prolonged monsoons and generally humid weather in Bengal pose an additional challenge to the preservation of archives.

Another important factor in accounting for the scarcity of materials on the history of Muslim Bengal was the attitude of imperial chroniclers in Delhi towards this region – very few were keen to record events there because it was so remote from the capital. What was recorded in writing usually reflected the official version of events, such as military expeditions to subdue the region, as there was always a temptation for the governors to rebel. Written in the capital, these texts exhibit not only a generally urban bias, but also the views of central government; thus, they seldom provide reliable information on the region.

Though the epigraphic heritage of Bengal fills many gaps left by earlier historians, its study did not begin until the second half of the eighteenth century, when some Muslim *ulamā* (often known as *Munshī* or *Mawlavī* in traditional

Bengali society) began to take a scholarly interest in deciphering the texts. The first scholar to realize the importance of epigraphic evidence for dynastic history and to use it as a source for dating different historical monuments and architectural remains was Sayed Ghulam Hussein Salim Zayedpuri (d. 1817). He lived in Ingrezbazar (Malda) near Gaur, the ruined early Muslim capital of Bengal which abounded in inscriptions. He was a pioneer of Islamic epigraphy who examined for the first time inscriptions with a great academic interest as early as in the mid-eighteenth century. While compiling *Riyāḍ al-Salāṭīn* – the history of Bengal – (completed in 1788, published in Calcutta by the Asiatic Society of Bengal in 1893), he studied the epigraphic materials of Gaur and used them in constructing a chronology of Bengal's ruling dynasties. However, it was Sayyid Munshī Ilāhī Bakhsh al-Ḥusaynī Awrangzebādī – an indirect disciple of Sayed Ghulam Hussein – who systematically examined a significant number of the Islamic inscriptions of Gaur, Pandua and adjacent areas. In total, he deciphered forty-two inscriptions with astonishing accuracy, most of them for the first time. He used this epigraphic evidence in writing the history of Muslim rule in Bengal, which formed a substantial part of his ambitious project of writing the history of the world. Part of this monumental Persian work – *Khūrshīd-i-Jahān Numā* – covered the history of Muslim rule in Bengal, and was edited and published, with an English translation by Henry Beveridge, in the *Journal of the Asiatic Society of Bengal* in 1895. Interestingly, one of Munshī Ilāhī Bakhsh's students, Abid Ali Khan, also took a great interest in the inscriptions of Gaur and Pandua as is evident in both of his works *Short Notes on the Ancient Monuments of Gaur and Pandua* (Malda, 1913) and *Memoirs of Gaur and Pandua* (edited by H. E. Stapleton, Calcutta, 1931).

Early in the nineteenth century British collectors began to take an interest in these inscriptions, motivated principally by their visual appeal. For many of them, colonizing of lands and peoples also meant colonizing their arts, architecture, archaeological heritage and even interpretation of their history and culture. Most of the private as well as museum collections of this period were built upon works removed from their context and often illegally or improperly acquired. As interest in Oriental antiquities and art objects developed in the West, many Europeans set out to explore ancient sites in search of them. Cities such as Gaur and Pandua attracted a number of such adventurers, many of whom were little more than plunderers, or at best antique collectors. Some, however, left accounts and diaries of their experience, most of them now preserved in the India Office Library in London, which provide a rich source for materials on inscriptions that no longer exist.

Foremost among the British scholars pioneering this field is Sir Henry Creighton who lived in and around Gaur for twenty years (1786–1807), and wrote a book, *The Ruins of Gaur* (London, 1817) illustrated with fabulous sketches and architectural drawings. He often refers to inscriptions he found in the old Islamic monuments of the area. Another celebrated British collector of Oriental antiquities was Major William Franklin, who visited Gaur at the beginning of the nineteenth century. Both of his diaries, *Journal of a Route from*

Rajmahal to Gaur and *The Ruins of Gaur*, preserved in the India Office Library (MSS nos 19 and 285), give a clear description of the archaeological remains in the region and record a number of inscriptions. The collection that he took with him to England consisted of many monumental inscriptions, some of which he gave to the British Museum. The most elegant piece in this collection, however, found its way through antique dealers to the United States, where it ended up in the museum of the University of Pennsylvania in Philadelphia.

Franklin was accompanied on his tour by a local guide named Munshī Shayām Prasād, a scholar of Arabic and Persian. At Franklin's request, he prepared a report on the archaeological remains of the area. It, too, has become a valuable source for the epigraphy of the region (MS 2841 in the India Office Library, later published by A. H. Dani as an appendix to his book, *Muslim Architecture of Bengal*, Dhaka: Asiatic Society of Pakistan, 1961). Another contemporary archaeologist, named Orme, also left a brief report, *The Ruins of Gaur*, now in the India Office Library (MS 65: 25), which describes a few inscriptions. Francis Buchanan Hamilton was another early nineteenth century scholar who noted a number of inscriptions during his tour of the district of Dinajpur in 1807–1808. He mentions some of them in his work *A Geographical, Statistical and Historical Description of the District or Zilla of Dinajpur* (Calcutta, 1833).

In the second half of the nineteenth century, the investigation of the art and archaeology of the region became more scholarly. One of the first studies of this period was by Captain W. N. Lees, who published an Arabic inscription of Sultan Bārbak Shāh in the *JASB* in 1860. Among the important studies of that time is *Gaur, its Ruins and Inscriptions* by J. H. Ravenshaw (London, 1878), which is particularly rich in illustrations and texts. The formation of the Archaeological Survey of India in 1861 brought a revolutionary change to the archaeological study of South Asia. Its first director general, Sir Alexander Cunningham, and his subsequent colleagues, took systematic steps to record all existing inscriptions. Other scholars to discover Islamic inscriptions of Bengal during this period were Dr James Wise, E. Vesey Westmacott, Hili and Walter M. Bourke. Many of the rubbings they collected were sent to the Asiatic Society of Bengal in Calcutta, where scholars such as Henry Blochmann deciphered and published them.

Among other scholars to contribute to this field in the late nineteenth and early twentieth centuries were R. D. Banerji, Henry Beveridge, H. E. Stapleton, S. Aulad Husain, Rahmat Ali Taish, Hamid Allah Khan and Khan Sahib Moulvi Abdul Wali. At the end of the nineteenth century, the Archaeological Survey of India established a separate section for epigraphy and began to publish a journal, *Epigraphia Indica.* With the passage of time, a more specialized series came out under the name *Epigraphia Indo-Moslemica* that was devoted entirely to the Arabic and Persian inscriptions of India. Eminent scholars such as Ghulam Yazdani, Paul Horn, Denison Ross and J. Horvitz either participated in its editing or contributing scholarly articles. Its first volume was published in 1907–1908. After independence from the British, its name changed to *Epigraphia Indica, Arabic and Persian Supplement.* Scholars such as Ziauddin

Desai published a number of inscriptions from Bengal. Two important works were published before the independence of Bangladesh and certainly provided models for a comprehensive epigraphic study of the region. The first was *Bibliography of Muslim Inscriptions of Bengal* by A. H. Dani published as an appendix to *Journal of the Asiatic Society of Pakistan*, vol. 2 (1957), and the other *Inscriptions of Bengal* by an eminent twentieth century epigraphist, Maulvi Shamsud-Din Ahmed (Rajshahi: Varendra Research Museum, 1960). Among recent publications, *Corpus of Arabic and Persian Inscriptions of Bihar* (Patna: Jayaslal Research Institute, 1973), by Qeyamuddin Ahmad, and *Corpus of the Arabic and Persian Inscriptions of Bengal* (Dhaka: Asiatic Society of Bangladesh, 1992), by Abdul Karim, a prominent historian of Bangladesh, are indeed important additions to this genre. Recent publication of two monumental books, the first one in Arabic (*Riḥla ma'a al-Nuqūsh al-Kitābiyya fī 'l-Bangāl*)[2] and the second one in Urdu (*Mashriq men Islāmī Tahzīb ke Athār: Bangāl ke 'Arbī wa Fārsī Katbāt*)[3] are important additions to this field as they contain an elaborate discussion of almost 400 inscriptions. All of these works have enriched the field of epigraphy of the region. However, much still remains to be explored in the history and epigraphy of Bengal, and the task is challenging.

The present work takes a different approach from the previous works in the field as it aims towards an interpretive study of the Arabic and Persian epigraphic texts of Bengal in the wider context of the rich epigraphic tradition of the Islamic world. While focusing on previously untapped sources, the book takes a fresh look into Islamic inscriptions to examine the inner dynamics of the social, intellectual and cultural transformations of this eastern region of South Asia. It explores many new inscriptions including the two earliest Persian epigraphs that appeared within the first three decades of the Muslim rule in the region, indicating an early introduction of Persian language and culture in Bengal under the patronage of Khalji rulers coming from Khurasan. Previously published works did not recognize the importance of some inscriptions from the formative period of Mughal rule in Bengal, particularly during Akbar's era. This present work is the first to discuss a number of inscriptions from the reign of the Mughal emperor Akbar. It also focuses on numerous other previously unnoticed inscriptions from Sultanate as well as Mughal periods that somehow found their way to different newly built mosques in distant remote rural areas of Bangladesh and West Bengal, including the famous Nim Darwaza inscription of Barbak Shah at Miyaneh Dar in Gaur Citadel, dated 871 (1466–1467). In addition to deciphering and editing the epigraphic texts anew, I have analysed the information derived from them in detail in this book to help develop an understanding of the political, administrative, social, religious and cultural setting of that period. In addition, the cursory information available in these inscriptions about the monuments they belonged to has been used to reconstruct the architectural history of the region. The chapter on Islamic calligraphy examines these inscriptions as art in detail. It discusses a few extremely distinctive calligraphic creations through a regional style, namely Bengali *ṭughrā'*, in addition to considering the artistic merit of other popular styles, such as Kufi, *thulth, naskh, riqā', rayḥānī, muḥaqqaq* and Bihārī.

The Islamic inscriptions of Bengal thus provide historical clues about early Muslim rule in the region. The names of quite a few rulers of Bengal during this period can only be established on the basis of epigraphic evidence. These inscriptions also furnish details of the local administration such as the names of revenue collectors, police officers, local army commanders and representatives of the central government in the area and their officials, names that would otherwise be lost to history. While these names can be analysed and interpreted for the historical reconstruction of the past, the titles accompanying them can throw light on the personality of the title bearer and many other contemporary issues.

The Islamic inscriptions of Bengal during the period 1205–1707 number roughly 400. While most of the pre-Mughal inscriptions are in Arabic, Mughal inscriptions are usually in Persian. Most of them belong to religious architecture, recording construction of mosques, madrasas, khānqāhs, shrines, mausoleums etc. Quite naturally, they contain a religious message in the form of verses from the Qur'ān or sayings of the Prophet (*ḥadīth*). These messages can be very helpful in understanding religious trends and transformations in the region. One of the primary goals of the present study is to capture these messages and to interpret them in their proper context. Indeed, Islamic epigraphic texts serve as one of the primary sources for understanding the early spread of Islam in Bengal since they shed new light on the religious and cultural dynamics of a crucial period of Bengal history. With the diffusion of Islam in the region, the use of Arabic and Persian also started spreading in the region, evidence of which we can find in these Islamic inscriptions.

Hence this book not only extends previous research, but it also enhances the understanding of the region's history. It explores the complex history of the consolidation of Islam in a region which, despite having no direct geographical link with the rest of the Islamic world, has a strong Islamic identity and plays an important role in the Islamic world. It also helps us understand the arrival of Islam in Bengal and its gradual diffusion in the region that eventually resulted in a Muslim majority and made Bengali Muslims the second largest linguistic group in the Islamic world.

A well-known French colonial administrator in North Africa once compared the world of Islam to a resonant box: the faintest sound in one corner reverberates through the whole. As elsewhere in the Islamic world, this apt metaphor finds expression also in Bengal, a significant part of which constitutes present-day Bangladesh, which is the third most populous Islamic country in the world. In spite of their distinctive character in artistic expression and textual content, Islamic inscriptions of Bengal form an inseparable part of the epigraphic heritage of the world of Islam. While the aim of this study is confined to the epigraphy of Bengal, it will ultimately contribute to the understanding of larger issues pertaining to the civilization and culture of a region where nearly one-eighth of the Muslim population of the world live today.

Notes

1 For details, please see ins. no. 1 in Chapter 5.

2 Mohammad Yusuf Siddiq, *Riḥla ma'a al-Nuqūsh al-Kitābiyya fī Bilād al-Bangāl: Darasa Tārīkhiyya Haḍāriyya* (Damascus: Dar al-Fikr, 2004); see also its Persian translation by Layla Musazadeh, *Katībah hā* (Tehran: Kelk Simin, 2014).

3 Mohammad Yusuf Siddiq *Mashriq men Islāmī Tahzīb ke Athār: Bangāl ke 'Arbī wa Fārsī Katbāt* (Islamabad: National University of Science and Technology [NUST], 2013).

1 Epigraphy as an important source for Islamic history and civilization

These are the remains that point out to our past
Therefore look for the traces after we are gone.[1]

تلك آثارنا تدلّ علينا
فانظروا بعدنا إلى الآثار (أديب اسحاق الد مشقي)

Epigraphy in Islamic tradition

One of the most interesting intellectual achievements of Islamic civilization and its contributions to the science of historiography is its rich legacy of historical texts. This historical output is not limited to chronicles and books on history (such as the *Ṭabaqāt* [Biographical Dictionaries] of various writers),[2] but has assumed other forms, including inscriptions. Like most other modes of expression in Islamic culture, these epigraphs also reflect in their own ways the Islamic faith. The extraordinary number of epigraphs also underscores the important role that inscriptions played in transmitting Islamic culture. Inscriptions can be found not only on buildings, but also on textiles and rugs, metal and glass objects, ceramics and ornaments, not to mention arms, coins and seals. In some regions, a rich tradition of inscribing on stone existed even before the advent of Islam. Ibn Isḥāq, for instance, mentions a number of Syriac inscriptions which were unearthed while Ka'ba was demolished for reconstruction when the Prophet was about thirty-five years of age.[3] During the Umayyad period, Muḥammad ibn al-Sā'ib al-Kalbī (father of the famous early Muslim historian ibn-Hishām) took great interest in the Lakhmid stelae and funerary inscriptions that he found preserved in the churches in and around Kufa.

The use of archaeological materials for scholarly investigation is encouraged in the Qur'ān. The word *āthār*, which can be found in several places in the Qur'ān, is used in modern Arabic to mean archaeology.[4] Archaeological findings offer many clues to the past; epigraphic studies reveal evidence of rulers who might otherwise have remained unknown. Thus we read in the chapter 'Believers' in the Qur'ān:

> Do they not travel through the earth and see the end of those who had lived before them? They were more numerous than these and superior in strength

and [ancient] remains in the land [where they had once lived]. Yet all that they accomplished was of no profit to them.

(40:82)

Use of inscriptions in Islamic architecture

Inscriptions have been used in Islamic culture since the formative period of Islam. The earliest Islamic inscriptions date from the first/seventh century. They became more common as architectural projects expanded in the Islamic world. It is difficult to imagine a building of the early period without some kind of inscription, as if without one, the building would seem to be incomplete or unfinished. As a result, epigraphic records and inscriptions are plentiful in terms of both artistic merit and historical information. Until the fourth/eleventh century, most appeared on the inside of buildings. After that century, however, inscription began to be used to decorate also the outsides of buildings. During this period, the cursive *naskh* and *thulth*, started to gain in popularity while use of the angular style known as Kūfī (angular) declined.[5]

While these inscriptions conveyed messages as text, their calligraphic expression and aesthetic elements quite often constituted a vibrant decorative appeal in an Islamic building. The use of written messages for architectural decoration may be described as a typical Islamic cultural phenomenon. In some buildings, the calligraphic panels are placed too high to be deciphered,[6] suggesting that their aesthetic impact was more important than the textual message. In fact many early Kūfī inscriptions and some Bengali *ṭughrā'* (a highly intricate and stylized form of calligraphy) inscriptions from the Sultanate period in Bengal are almost indecipherable, again suggesting that aesthetics were more important than content. For those regions influenced by Shiʿism, this development may to some extent have been inspired by its mystical tendency, especially the belief that a hierarchy of knowledge and spiritual development obtains among people so that not all inscriptions may or should be read by ordinary viewers. In a number of Islamic inscriptions, letters are easily confused and uncertainties are created where the logic of the pattern of ornamentation takes precedence over legibility.[7]

However, it is also probable that with many inscriptions, some kind of historical intent was there from the very beginning. Indeed, some inscriptions were intended to be read in the future, perhaps by scholars, or, more particularly, by historians. It is also possible that, being accustomed to the Kūfī style, educated Muslims were quite comfortable with the intricacies of Kūfī patterns, more so than with the cursive styles (like *naskh*) that we today consider easier. Kūfī script enjoyed a higher status than cursive writing in those days. The selection of an appropriate place for an inscription on a monument was also important, since those parts of the monuments that were most easily seen best served the purpose.

In spite of the great importance that Islam attached to reading, writing and learning, the majority of the rural population in much of the Muslim world remained illiterate. However, the viewing of religious inscriptions, especially Qur'ānic ones, was still a source of *baraka* (blessings). For the ordinary literate person, being able to recognize a text, e.g. the Throne Verse from the Qur'ān (2:255) or sayings of the Prophet on the virtues of building a masjid, was the important thing, rather than being able to decipher the text accurately and completely. Quite a few inscriptions therefore served an iconographic function, in place of the figurative imagery used in other traditions. Nevertheless, the vast majority of Islamic inscriptions can be called informative in that they provide some simple information such as the date of construction, the kind of structure, the name of the personage by and for whom it was built, etc. Another common feature is certain reiterated formulas that recur in many Islamic inscriptions, in some cases repeated interminably. Since most of these formulas are phrases of religious import, they consciously reflect the dominant 'meaning' or 'message' with which the monument is intended to be associated.

Emergence of Islamic epigraphy

Inscriptions are found everywhere in the Muslim world from the Iberian Peninsula to the Indonesian archipelago. They were of sufficient interest to draw occasional notices by Muslim historians and writers from quite an early period. Al-Jahshiyāri (d. 331/942), for instance, records a number of Arabic inscriptions on the gates of Acre and Sidon as well as on a treasury building in Azarbayjan.[8] Ibn al-'Athīr tells us that in 630 (1232–1233), he saw in the court of the congregational mosque of Mosul a stone slab with an inscription which contained useful information about the extension of the mosque during the reign of the Abbasid Caliph Mahdī.

Later, fourteenth and fifteenth century Arab scholars, such as Taqī al-Dīn Aḥmad ibn 'Alī al-Maqrīzī (d. 845/1441) and Taqī al-Dīn al-Fāsī (775–832/1374–1428; taught at the famous Bengali seminary in Makkah, al-Madrasa al-Sulṭāniyyah al-Ghiyāthiyyah al-Bangāliyyah) studied inscriptions as an important source for regional history. Al-Fāsī's work was more methodical in dealing with the epigraphs of Makkah as he surveyed the architectural remains of this ancient city and deciphered their inscriptions. He cross-checked the dates appearing in the epigraphic texts with other historical sources to substantiate in a remarkably accurate way his findings about the history of Makkah.[9] Still, the credit for making the study of inscriptions as a distinct discipline goes to Jamāl al-Dīn Muḥammad ibn 'Alī al-Shībī[10] (779–837/1378–1433). His meticulous study of Makkan tombstones and stelae established for the first time a remarkably and unprecedentedly high standard for scholarly epigraphic study. He can truly be considered the father of epigraphy (شيخ دراسة النقوش الكتابية الأثرية). Al-Fāsī used epigraphic evidence to fill the gaps in historical narratives while compiling his monumental work on the history of Makkah; al-Shībī looked at the inscriptions for their own sake, a strictly epigraphic approach. Not only did he painstakingly decipher a great number of tombstones in the graveyard of al-Ma'lā (popularly also known as al-Mu'allā), he also recorded such basic information as style of script, date, etc., exactly as a modern epigraphist would do.

However, approaching Islamic inscriptions in a systematic way with an academic interest began in earnest in the late nineteenth century, when Islamic epigraphy saw some of its rules codified as a result of the dedicated efforts of the famous Swiss orientalist Max Van Berchem (1863–1923), who can be regarded as the pioneer of the science of modern Islamic epigraphy in this age. He established research methodology for the study of Arabic inscriptions, not only as an art form, but also as a scholarly field of considerable importance for Oriental studies in the fields of language, history, art and architecture. Instead of just deciphering, reading and translating inscriptions, a work of considerable skill by itself, he established the methodology of analysing each inscription in its cultural and historical context, often culminating in a whole essay covering its particular time and space as well as the biographical details of the names appearing in the epigraphic text. His pioneering works, such as *Matériaux pour un Corpus Inscriptionum Arabicarum,*[11] certainly paved the way for establishing Islamic epigraphy as a science. Soon after his work, the monumental task of cataloguing the Islamic inscriptions began with the publication of the *Répertoire chronologique d'épigraphie arabe* in 1931. More than 8,000 inscriptions were edited in the first sixteen successive volumes of *Répertoire* (Cairo, 1931–1964) alone, which covered the first eight centuries, and the effort continues to this day. In spite of the fact that *Répertoire* remains incomplete in a number of ways, partly because of the discoveries of a number of new inscriptions that came into light after its publication, it can still be considered one of the most useful inventories and the only existing attempt at a systematic grouping of Islamic inscriptions by year and in an approximately geographical order. Scholars such as Tychsen, Reinaud, J. J. Marcel, George C. Miles, S. Flury, Gaston Wiet, E. Herzfeld, A. Grohmann, Jean Sauvaget, Moritz Sobernheim, E. Lévi-Provençal, and J. Sourdel-Thomine have contributed greatly in the field in Western languages. On the other hand, Ḥasan Mohammed al-Hawary, Ibrahim Jum'a, Hasan al-Basha, Zaki Muhammad Hasan and Abder Rahman Fahmy and many others have contributed much in the Arabic language. A number of valuable works have also been rendered in other languages of the Islamic world, particularly in Persian, Urdu, Turkish, Bengali, Pushtoo, Bahasa Malay and Bahasa Indonesia.

Importance of Islamic epigraphy

Almost every inscription, whether on a milestone, frieze or tombstone, contains useful information. The inclusion of inscribed panels was and remains so common that it is difficult to imagine a building in an Islamic culture without one. In miniature painting, buildings are often shown decorated with inscribed panels. Architectural inscriptions are often large enough to catch the viewer's attention; in this way they interact directly with the aesthetics of their surroundings. The horizontal inscriptional band on the *kiswa* (the decorated black cloth used to veil the Ka'ba) as well as *ṭirāz* (a highly stylized form of embroidered writing on early Islamic textiles) may well have influenced and been influenced by architectural epigraphy.[12]

In many cases when a region came under Islamic rule or influence, for everyday use the local language was often retained, but Arabic was the official, religious, educational and literary medium. In Central and South Asia, Persian was used in the royal courts, but Arabic remained the language of religion and therefore the lingua franca among Muslims. Islamic inscriptions across this vast land used both Arabic and Persian. Rulers used Persian, even though many came from a Turko-Afghan background and some spoke Turkic dialects. In South Asia, inscriptions in Turkish are rare since the conquerors hardly ever used that language for writing. Out of the Indian languages, Sanskrit was used in rare cases both for numismatic and epigraphic purposes. The first coin issued by Ikhtiyār al-Dīn Muḥammad Bakhtiyār Khaljī commemorating his conquest of the Gaur region has inscriptions in both Arabic and Sanskrit. This suggests that the Muslim ruling class patronized the elite culture, perhaps at the cost of the popular one. The first and the third earliest inscriptions in Bengal, executed under the patronage of early Muslim rulers, namely Sultan 'Alā' Dīn 'Alī Mardān (607–610/1210–1213) and Balkā Khān Khaljī (626–28/1229–1231), are inscribed in Persian, while a khānqāh inscription (dated 618/1221) from the reign of Ghiyāth al-Dīn 'Iwaḍ from Sian, Birbhum district, not far from the early Islamic centre of Lakhnawr (see Figure 3.2), dated 618/1221 is rendered in Arabic. Though the first Persian inscription seemingly appeared in the mid-eleventh century (1055–1060) in a tomb in Safid Buland in the northern part of Farghana valley in Uzbekistan, Bengal also seems to be one of the first and earliest regions to have Persian architectural inscriptions. Especially after the establishment of Mughal rule in the region, Persian became the dominant language for inscriptions. That Persian was used as early as the beginning of thirteenth century in the Bengal frontier, so far from both Persia and Central Asia, is intriguing.

Thematic variety of Islamic inscriptions

Inscriptions can be difficult to read, and much of the information in them may appear trivial to the uninitiated. Epigraphic sources rarely package and present information conveniently. Rather, they contain scattered bits of data, which need to be put together coherently with the help of other sources. However, one can gradually develop the skills and sensitivity that make their study both useful and interesting. From the point of view of political history, important data in an epigraphic text can be a date, a place name or the name of the ruler recorded there. A historian can then try to incorporate all this fragmentary information into a historically coherent narrative. Such information can tell us that the area where the inscription was found was indeed under the jurisdiction of the ruler mentioned. If the name of the ruler in the inscription is different from the one usually found in contemporary chronicles, it might mean that some unusual event, such as a rebellion, had taken place there which historians for some reason did not record. One such example is the Baramatyabari inscription of Bengal dated 934/1528, which records Maḥmūd Shāh as being the sultan, even though the ruler of Bengal at that time was in fact Nuṣrat Shāh. The inscription suggests that Maḥmūd Shāh may have proclaimed himself the sultan in defiance of the authority of his brother, the ruling sultan, Nuṣrat Shāh, in 1528, though no such event is recorded in contemporary historical writings. Indeed, many violent events, especially those that went against the interests of the ruling establishment, were not usually recorded by official chroniclers at the imperial court, leaving the reader of the chronicle with the impression that peace and happiness prevailed throughout a ruler's reign. Generally speaking, dates on inscriptions are more reliable than dates in the texts of historical manuscripts, and therefore they provide valuable clues for reconstructing events in local history. While travelling in the famous city of Multan, the famous traveller Ibn Baṭṭūṭa saw an important inscription in an old Islamic edifice. Through this epigraphic text, he came to know that a ruler of the region, Ghazi Malik, fought twenty-nine wars against Mongol invaders. Ibn Baṭṭūṭa also noticed a commemorative inscription on the miḥrāb of the earliest Jāmi‘ Masjid in Delhi, which he deciphered. This inscription helped him to find the exact date of the Muslim conquest of Delhi.[13]

Islamic inscriptions can sometimes provide some invaluable historical clues about the political history of a region. The names of many rulers of the Sultanate of Bengal can only be established on the basis of epigraphic evidence. Quite often, the names of local administrators were not recorded by the imperial chroniclers living far away from the provinces. Inscriptions are sometimes the only source that can furnish details about the local administration such as the names of revenue collectors, police officers, local army commanders and representatives of the central government in the area and their officials, names that would otherwise be lost to history. These names can be quite helpful since they can be analysed and interpreted for the historical purposes. Similarly, older or original names of places or administrative units and divisions in use when the inscription was made can be preserved, as can details bearing on social or religious history. Commemorative inscriptions sometimes tell us why the inscriptions themselves were made. The theme of sovereignty is historically associated with monumental entranceways, for example, because they were thought to be proper places to proclaim the sovereign's power. Epigraphic texts can also help us understand religious trends in a region.

While the content of an individual epigraphic text may vary, one can often sense a common thread of meaning, a unity of message. The inscription over a masjid entrance is apt to contain Qur'ānic verses in praise of God, or other verses or Prophetic sayings that promise divine reward for those who construct and maintain masjids. Inscriptions on miḥrābs often use a verse in which the word *miḥrāb* (in Arabic) itself appears. The calligraphers also find a great source of inspiration, spiritually and aesthetically, in inscribing on religious buildings *al-asmā' al-ḥusnā'* (the beautiful names of God), the *basmala* and sometimes a poetic verse on a spiritual theme (usually in Persian, but sometimes also in Arabic). Sayings of the Prophet (*ḥadīth*) start to appear on inscriptions towards the end of the eleventh century; there is a minbar inscription dated 484/1081 on the tomb of the head of Ḥusayn, grandson of the Prophet, in Ascalon, later moved to the sanctuary in Hebron in Palestine.[14] Mughal emperor Babar mentions in his famous autobiography, *Tuzuk-i-Bābarī* known in Persian as *Bāburnāma*, an elegant inscription that used to decorate the façade of the central Jami‘ Masjid (built by his ancestor, Amīr Tīmūr, next to his famous castle) in Samarqand. It contained an exquisitely written Qur’ānic verse (إذ يرفع إبراهيم القواعد) very popular among mosque inscriptions. Inscribed above eye-level, this monumental inscription was nevertheless so large that, according to Babar, it could be seen from a great distance. Common elements in the inscriptions in different parts of the Islamic world indicate that a silent process of universalization of values and tastes was taking place in that world, along with the flow of merchants, travellers, *ḥadīth* collectors, knowledge seekers and sufis (see Figure 3.2).

Both Qur’ānic verses as well as *ḥadīth* quoted in the epigraphic text can yield historical clues since they were selected for their appropriateness for a particular setting. Quite naturally, they contain some kind of religious message in the form of verses from the Qur’ān or sayings of the Prophet (*ḥadīth*). These messages can be very helpful in understanding religious trends and transformations in the region. The Throne Verse is often and appropriately used for funerary inscriptions and for calligraphy in mosques, as it is considered a source of *baraka*.[15] A particular *ḥadīth* may be selected for an inscription on the same principle of appropriateness. So can names with religious connotations: the appearance of the names of the first four caliphs in an epigraphic text, for example, can be taken as evidence that the patron was a Sunni Muslim. If the patron of the building had been a Shī‘ī, only the name of ‘Alī and the direct descendents of the Prophet (particularly the *pāk panj tan* or five holy bodies, a popular Shī‘ī invocation in South Asia) would appear.[16] If, for example, the epigraphic text contains the terms of *waqf* (endowment),[17] as is the case with an inscription from Nayabari, not far from Dhaka, dated 1003/1595 (see also another *Waqf* inscription of a khānqāh in Sitalmat, Bengal dated 652/1254), then the verse selected may contain messages promising rewards for those who look after the endowment and punishment for those who neglect or vandalize it.

Tombstones and stele can also furnish valuable information; they are sometimes the only authentic evidence we have for ethnic immigration to a particular region, since the surnames, titles and, more particularly, the *nisba* (geographical attribution) of the deceased person on a tombstone will indicate the family’s place of origin and the name of his tribe, such as Kābulī, Shīrāzī or Qāqshāl. In addition, tombstones may mention the profession of the deceased person or his social status, which can be useful for social and genealogical study.[18] Most importantly, it furnishes us with the most authentic date of the death of the person for whom the tombstone was made.

Inscriptions are found on all kinds of structures – mosques, madrasas, khānqāhs, shrines, mausoleums, forts, palaces, tanks, wells and caravanserais (see Figures 0.2, 2.1, 2.2 and 3.2) – and are again often the most authentic record for architectural chronology in Islamic civilization. Consequently, they are an important source for understanding the architectural activities of a particular region. Many are inscribed on a beautifully decorated background, and studying these decorative motifs can itself be rewarding. Sometimes, an inscription plays a central role in architectural decoration (e.g. the gate inscription of Nīm Darwāza at Miyāneh Dar dated 871/1466–1467). Quite often, the effect of Islamic inscriptions can be sensed at the very first sight of a building. The majority of Islamic inscriptions record the circumstances of a building's construction, which allows us to date and to identify buildings and their functions. The calligraphic panels are usually so well blended into the overall decorative programme that they seem to be an integral part of the architecture in many Islamic buildings, especially in Iran (e.g. Masjid-i-Mīr in Mashhad), Central Asia (e.g. the Gur-i-Mīr complex in Samarqand) and Turkey. In Bengal, however, it is somewhat different, as inscriptions are not completely blended into the aesthetic unity of the architecture; rather, they remain distinctive in their appearance.

Diffusion of Islam meant diffusion of the use of Arabic as the primary religious and intellectual language. That a vast majority of epigraphs were inscribed in Arabic suggests that the Arabic language had a strong impact on the cultural life of educated Muslims in general, as it was taught to high levels of proficiency in madrasas and other Islamic institutions in all regions. In Central and South Asia, however, Persian was also widely used. Both languages are accordingly found in the Islamic inscriptions of Bengal. The likeness and affinity in the choice of language, layout, theme, literary style and taste in ornament, found in the Islamic inscriptions, point to a remarkable cultural coherence in the medieval world of Islam.

Use of inscriptions as legal deeds

Before the arrival of Muslims in Bengal (the first Muslim conquest under Ikhtiyār al-Dīn Bakhtiyār Khaljī began in 601/1205), copper and other metal plates in general, and stone slabs in some rare cases, were used to record land grants and endowments in the region. Muslims, in general, preferred paper for writing legal documents. Inscriptions were also used sometimes to record endowment for religious edifices as well as for charity or welfare purposes, known in Islamic culture as *waqf*. A famous early fifteenth century Arab historian Taqī al-Dīn Aḥmad ibn 'Alī al-Maqrīzī (d. 845/1441), for instance, mentioned in details about a *waqf* text inscribed on al-Waṭāṭīṭ well constructed under the patronage of vizier Abū 'l-Faḍl.[19] Quite a few inscriptions of Bengal shed light on the institution of *waqf* in medieval Bengal. In some instances, these epigraphic texts record the very terms of *waqf*,[20] as is the case with an inscription from Nayabari, not far from Dhaka, dated 1003/1595 (see also another *waqf* inscription of a khānqāh in Sitalmat, Bengal dated 652/1254).

Quite often, a particular Qur'ānic verse or a saying of the Prophet is found in these inscriptions that carries a religious message appropriate for that particular *waqf* inscription. The verses selected in these inscriptions often contain messages promising rewards for those who look after the endowment and punishment for those who neglect or vandalize it. The *madad-i-ma'āsh* inscription from Nayabari dated 1003/1595 serves as a good example of how epigraphic panels were occasionally used to record legal documents such as *waqf* (endowment) deeds for mosques and madrasas.[21] This tradition existed in certain parts of the Islamic world until the eighteenth century, no doubt in part because it had the practical advantage that stone slabs are less likely to perish or be stolen. For example, a complete *waqf* is inscribed in a building in Qazwin in Iran.[22] There are a number of such inscriptions in Bengal, such as the Dohar inscription dated 1000/1591 and the Barakatra inscription dated 1052/1642 from Bengal. During the Mughal period, we find the institution *diwān-i-risāla*, which dealt with religious matters, endowments and grants of *madad-i-ma'āsh*, and which was controlled by the *sadr al-sudūr*, who also combined the office of the *qāḍī-i mamālik* or Chief Judge of the realm.

Globalization and cultural continuity of the Islamic world: comparison of some inscriptions of Bengal with those of Andalusia

Two extremely interesting and exquisite inscriptions of Gaur dated 871/1466 that once belonged to two magnificent royal entrances to the Bādshāhī citadel in Gaur (namely, Nīm Darwāza and Chānd Darwāza), deserve special attention as they so closely resemble some fabulous eighth/fourteenth century inscriptions that appeared at the other end of the Islamic world, in the Alhambra Palace in Granada. The literary style of the verses in these inscriptions bear some resemblance in composition to Qaṣīda al-Burda of Imām al-Būṣīrī. But since the purpose of these epigraphic texts is commemorative, exactness of meter (Baḥr al-Basīṭ) in their poetic rhyme is not being observed throughout.

It is striking indeed to note the conceptual and stylistic harmonies between the two inscriptions on royal monuments in Gaur and Granada, capitals of two different Muslim kingdoms thousands of miles apart. Both royal complexes were created over years to serve various functions, private palaces for the royals, mosques, public courts, castles and gardens. Neither of the inscriptions use the local vernacular, but rather a very high quality of rhetorical, poetic Arabic. There is an interesting correspondence in the religious, social and cultural context – both capitals were inhabited largely by Muslims while the majority of the population in adjacent areas were non-Muslims. The grandiosity of the royal palace as well as water cosmology are among the prominent themes in many of the verses in the inscriptions of both Alhambra and Gaur. The river Darro ran alongside side of Granada and a series of irrigation canals watered vast orchards of orange trees in and around Alhambra; several canals, lakes and water pools ornamented the lovely landscape of the royal palace of Gaur, with the old channel of the mighty Ganges flowing to the west of the palace. Reference to these water canals can be found in a verse in the Chānd Darwāza inscription that is written as follows:

A watercourse flows beneath it, like the waters of Paradise,
whose fruits take away need and pain.

نَهْرٌ جَرَىٰ تَحْتَهَاْ كَالسَّلْسَبِيْلِ لَهُ
أَجْنَاْءُ دُرٌّ قَلَتْ بالفَقْرِوالمِحَنِ

Likewise, the verses in the second line of the Nīm Darwāza inscription echo the aesthetic aspects of the Bārbak Shāh's palace, its monumental gate and the fabulous garden around it. The whole setting, compared with the Biblical garden of Eden (جَنَّة عَدنٍ), is an earthly embodiment of the paradisiacal garden or *janna* (الجنة). Perhaps, the idea of *janna* (lit. garden) is more powerfully depicted in the Chānd Darwāza inscription using the exact Qur'ānic term *salsabīl* (السلسبيل) or spring. Excavation by the Archaeological Survey of India on the site during 2002–2005[23] (adjacent to Baisgazi Wall of Gaur) clearly indicates the existence of an elaborate system of water channels, cisterns and aqueducts that criss-crossed the surrounding gardens of the magnificent wooden palace, finally to merge with the river Ganges in the west. One of these canals passes through a hidden interior tunnel, running intricately through the middle of the palace, before it links up to a magnificent jetty of a river port at the back of the palace facing the Ganges.

Interestingly, the concept of gardens with pools and fountains dominates the theme of a number of verses in the inscriptions of the Alhambra palace in Granada. The Court of Lions was embellished with a majestic water-fountain alluded to metaphorically in the verses inscribed within the palace. One of the verses (inscribed on the Hall of Ambassadors written by the Naṣirid vizier lisān al-Dīn al-Khaṭīb, known also with the title Dhū 'l-Wizāratayn), runs in Arabic as follows:

Whoever approaches me complaining of thirst,
I offer him a cool and satisfying drink, unmixed and pure.

مَنْ جَاْءَنِي يَشْكُوْ الظَّمَاءَ فَمَوْرِدِيْ
صِرْفُ الزُّلالِ العَذَبِ دُوْنَ مِزَاْجِ

Similarly, in the verses of ibn Zamrak inscribed on the Fountain of the Lions, we find a comparable metaphor:

Haven't you noticed the rhythm in the gushing water,
that runs creating graceful currents descending from above.

أَلَمْ تَرَ أَنَّ الماءَ يَجْرِيْ بِسَفْحِهَاْ
وَلكِنَّهَا أَبْدَتْ عَلَيْهِ المَجَارِيَا

Water is projected in all these verses as a fascinating aspect of the art that gave these monuments a special meaning. We also find several other metaphors referring to water cosmology in a number of other verses by ibn Zamrak inscribed in different places of Alhambra, such as *al-ibrīq* (الإبريق) or jug and *inā' al-mā'* (إناء الماء) or water vessel. While Burj al-Mā' (برج الماء) or Tower of Water, that used to glorify one of the compounds of Alhambra vanished long ago, Fanā' al-Birka (فناء البركة) or the 'Court of the Cistern' along with the 'Room of the Ship' exist to this day to remind us of the aesthetic beauty of water. Similarly, Bāb al-Sharī'a (باب الشريعة) or the Gate of Justice also carries the same allusion in that *sharī'a* can mean a source of drinking water. The front court of Alhambra, a starting point of the whole complex, was known as Fanā' al-Rayḥān (فناء الريحان) or Rayḥān (lit. basil/mint) Court, where basil and mint plants adorned the view. The term *rayḥān* appears in a verse in the Chānd Darwāza inscription that runs:

> Its gate provides refuge, like fragrant basil to the soul,
> to friends, while to foes it is forbidden and remote.

> بَأْبُهُ رَأْحَةٌ لِلرُّوْحِ رَيْحَأْنَاً
> لِذِيْ الْحَبِيْبِ وَلِلأَعْدَأْءِ كَالشَّطَنِ

The inscriptions of both Miyāneh Dar in Gaur and Alhambra give expression to the basic drive of rulers and ruling classes everywhere and in every age for power and glory, which lose their meaning unless exclusive. Nothing is known about the first line on the upper half of the Nīm Darwāza inscription, which disappeared long ago without trace. But one can easily imagine that it contained verses referring to the unparalleled glory of Sultan Bārbak Shāh's power and his fabulous palace. Indeed, several verses in the Chānd Darwāza inscription as well as in the remaining part of the Nīm Darwāza inscription glorify the majestic rule of the sultan and the exemplary grandiosity of the royal palace. While Chānd Darwāza (lit. 'Moon Gate' in Bengali) was a prominent gate in the Sultanate palace of Gaur; al-Burj al-Qamarī (lit. 'Moon Tower' in Arabic) was an important architectural element in Alhambra. The thematic similarity of the verses in the inscriptions at Miyāneh Dar with a number of verses in Alhambra is striking. For example, we find these verses in Alhambra:

> O son of kings, and of the sons of kings, whose
> power the stars submit when your origins are compared
> When you erect a palace, there is no equal to it; it achieves
> such a glory that all the other glories are subdued by it.

> يَا ابْنَ الملُوكِ وَأَبْنَاْءَ الملُوْكِ وَمَنْ
> تَعْنُوْا النُّجُوْمَ لَهْ قَدْراً إِذا انْتَسَبَ
> إِنْ كُنْتَ شَيَّدْتَ قَصْراً لانَظِيْرَ لَهُ
> حَاْزَ الْعُلَي وَتَمَّتْ مِنْ دُوْنِهِ الرُّتَبُ

A similar theme can be found in the inscription which once decorated the two lion head shaped spouts in the Alhambra bath that end with the following two verses:

Blessed be he who gave the Imām Muḥammad
a mansion which in beauty exceeds all other mansions
Here is the Garden containing wonders of art
the like of which God forbids should elsewhere be found.

تَبَارَكَ مَنْ أَعْطَى الإِمَامَ مُحَمَّداً
مَغَانِيَ زَانَتْ بِالجَمَالِ المغَانِيَا
وإلا فهذا الروض فيه بدائع
أَبَى اللَّهُ أن يَلْقَي لَهَا الحُسْنَ ثَانِيَا

Verses in Chānd Darwāza inscription praising Bārbak Shāh as an unmatched and incomparable king on the earth run as follows:

Is there in the two Iraqs a sultan as generous,
As Bārbak Shāh, or in Syria and in Yaman.
No! There is not unto him in all God's land,
An equal in generosity, for he is unique, unparalleled in time.

هل في العراقين سلطانٌ لهُ كَرَمٌ
كباربكشاهِ وفي الشامِ واليمنِ
كلا فما في بلادِ اللّهِ قَطٌّ لهُ
في البذْلِ مِثْلٌ فهذا واحدُ الزَّمَن

Though use of poetical motifs became common in Persian inscriptions (particularly in Bengal since the advent of the Mughal in the sixteenth century), they were rarely used before this period in Arabic inscriptions. These poems were especially composed to reflect the glamour of royalty, whether in the Alhambra or in the palace citadel of Gaur. We may consider them as topical, as explanatory of the purpose of the buildings, referring not only to specific elements of the palaces (e.g. the monumental gates), but also to their unique settings.[24]

Among the distinctive aspects of these two different epigraphic programmes we notice that the inscriptions of Alhambra are at eye level, for instance around the niches of the walls. Artistically they are well-harmonized with the overall decorative scheme of the building. On the other hand, both the Nīm Darwāza and Chānd Darwāza inscriptions in the Gaur Citadel were placed quite high above eye level making them difficult to read except by special effort by a handful of learned people (e.g. 'ulamā') in the area. While we know the names of those who composed the different verses inscribed in the Alhambra palace, namely, ibn Zamrak (verses on the Rayḥān [Basil] Court), ibn al-Jayyāb (verses on two halls adjacent to the Rayḥān [Basil] Court), and lisān al-Dīn al-Khaṭīb,[25] we know nothing about the poets who composed the beautiful verses either in the Chānd Darwāza or Nīm Darwāza inscriptions. While much of the Alhambra complex is still intact, very little of the Sultanate palace complex in Gaur remains extant.

Diversity of materials and features in Bengal inscriptions

Bengal has a rich tradition of stone carving and sculptures going back to the periods of the Palas (750–1150) and Senas (1095–1300), which was inspired by the religious imagery of Hinduism and Buddhism. In spite of this superb stone-carving tradition, the artists and craftsmen did not in general use their skill for decorative writing in pre-Islamic periods. This changed with the advent of Islam in the early thirteenth century. Representation and sculpture, though they evolved in other traditions as power symbols often associated with divine power, could not acquire any such significance or appreciation in Islamic culture, whose religious message was so firmly aniconic. Instead, Muslims explored other media to express their artistic zeal, and it was in calligraphy that they found the means to do this. Calligraphy accordingly found a new role in Bengal after the Muslim conquest in 1205, when Bengali artists adapted their traditional stone-carving skills to produce some spectacular specimens of Islamic calligraphy in stone, quite a number of which have survived to this day. Calligraphic patterns and styles in the inscriptions of Bengal come in a great diversity, which can be most helpful for determining the period of construction of many monuments whose dates cannot otherwise be ascertained. In addition, they are also a good source for art historical information.

With the passage of time, a special institution, mostly known as *Diwān al-'Inshā'*, became established in the leading Islamic capitals, particularly in the Arab world. Responsible for imperial writing protocol and chancellery script, this was the office which endorsed the formal text of royal inscriptions for state sponsored architecture. Art and architectural activities required a series of interactive processes that necessarily led to interaction between the Muslims and the non-Muslims. In the case of inscriptions, the patrons (e.g. sultans or court nobles) commissioned the work, a local *'ālim* (Islamic scholar) wrote the texts, a calligrapher designed the calligraphic layout to accommodate the text in such a way that it covered the whole surface of the stone slab. Then he outlined it on the stone probably in charcoal or by incising very light and small dots. A very skilled stoneworker then chiselled away the surface of the slab, leaving the lettering and borderlines on all the four sides in relief form. One might wonder about the origin of the scribes, calligraphers, artists and craftsmen who left us such a rich legacy of art and architecture including a vast number of Islamic inscriptions. While the *nisba*s (the place of origin) of the scribes and calligraphers found in a number of epigraphic texts indicate that most of them originally came from Iran and Central Asia, many stoneworkers, masons, craftsmen and artisans were also locally recruited. Not all the commissioned works were fully completed, for we do find some inscriptions where the calligraphic outlines were marked on the stone, but the chiselling process was never completed, perhaps due to some unusual circumstance.[26] Though the epigraphic texts often contained Qur'ānic verses and *ḥadīth*, there is little evidence that anyone was concerned about employing non-Muslim stonecutters to inscribe religious texts.[27]

An inscription can also tell us about the proficiency of the stone engravers and rockcutters at a given time and place.[28] The kind of stone used for the inscription can often provide interesting clues about the stone trade during that period. In Bengal, black basalt was used for inscriptions in most cases. Because of its scarcity throughout Bengal, it had to be imported from neighbouring regions, mostly from Rajmahal in Bihar. In cases when a stone was rare and valuable, it was often used more than once; for that reason stone slabs can be found that have inscriptions on both sides dating from different periods. A stone slab from Sian with an Arabic inscription dated 618/1221 is a good example of such a case: an earlier Sanskrit inscription on the other side was left intact.[29] Sometimes stone slabs were acquired from ruined and deserted buildings and reused without removing the original decorative motifs. In some epigraphic stone slabs in Bengal, we find traces of Hindu figural motifs, suggesting that they were picked up from the ruins of dilapidated temples and monasteries in the area. This was a utilitarian practice with no malign intentions. Even in the construction of mosques, old building materials were reused,[30] in some cases, bought from their previous owners.

Though many inscriptions were made for commemorative purposes, the small amount of space available for the text discouraged unnecessary rhetoric. The messages they contain often give an unadorned account of what happened and thus can be considered a reliable primary source for documentation. Arabic inscriptions are also helpful in guiding us in tracing the palaeographic development of Arabic writing. Very few of the epigraphic texts of Bengal bear the name of the calligrapher. In a way, this reflects the cultural values of the past Islamic societies, where the creation of a work of art was more a social expression of the Muslim *ummah* than an individual creation or an artist's effort to perpetuate his name through his artwork.

Comparison of Islamic inscriptions with Sanskrit inscriptions in Bengal

While pre-Islamic (namely Sanskrit and Proto-Bengali) inscriptions are mostly incised, Arabic and Persian inscriptions in Bengal were in general rendered in relief; it is rare to find any Islamic inscription in incised form. Sanskrit inscriptions quite often provide the primary historical source for many non-Muslim dynasties of the ancient period in South Asia. This is not usually the case for Muslim rule in the region. In the Islamic tradition, historical accounts were normally recorded on paper in the form of chronicles. However, not all the regions share this rich legacy of history writing to the same degree, and calamities could affect the preservation of manuscripts in one region more than another. This is especially true of pre-Mughal Bengal (1205–1538), where chronicles were either not often written or have not survived. Inscriptions fill many gaps in the early history of Muslim Bengal, which is otherwise not well recorded. These inscriptions are, however, not as lengthy as the Sanskrit inscriptions from the region. One reason was that calligraphic considerations for Arabic and Persian inscriptions required more space than, for instance, inscriptions in Sanskrit. Some of the Sanskrit inscriptions from the Pala and the Sena dynasties of Bengal are so lengthy that they include a full genealogy of the rulers. A further reason is that both the Pala and Sena rulers used copper and bronze plate for their inscriptions in addition to stone slabs,[31] whereas the Muslims used only stone slabs for a more monumental effect. The letters in Sanskrit inscriptions are also much more compact than letters in Arabic and Persian inscriptions and their calligraphic output is also restricted. There are some Sanskrit as well as bilingual inscriptions (Arabic and Persian, Arabic and Sanskrit or Persian and Sanskrit) from the Muslim dynasties in Bengal (one example is the Nayabari inscription, dated 1003/1595), but their number is insignificant.

Some conclusive remarks

Inscriptions can be invaluable for historians. They are a distinctive part of the Islamic cultural heritage in particular. Islamic epigraphic texts serve as one of the primary sources for understanding the early spread of Islam in many different regions. They can cast fresh light on the religious and cultural dynamics of different periods of history. They help us, for instance, to understand the complex history of the consolidation of Islam in the Bengal region which, despite having no direct geographical link with the rest of the Islamic world, nevertheless has a strong Islamic identity. Epigraphic study can thus amend the old approaches and bring fresh findings that enhance our understanding of regional history. Islamic inscriptions vary from one region to another both in their artistic expression and literary style, but we may also find a unity that prevails in the Islamic messages that most of them convey. The great diversity that exists historically in the regional cultural expressions in the Islamic world is truly amazing. But one also discovers interestingly a remarkable cultural continuity in these vast regions, as if ideas travelled from one corner of the world of Islam to the other in a literary manner as well as spiritually. With the spread of Islamic civilization, a gradual globalization was taking place in the old world, albeit silently.

Notes

1 Adīb Isḥāq al-Damashqī, *al-Durar*, quoted in *Tarīkh al-Adab al-'Arabī*, ed. Hanna al-Fakhuri (Beirut, n.d.): 1048–49.

2 For instance, Mawlānā Minhāj al-Dīn Sirāj al-Dīn, *Ṭabaqāt-i-Nāṣirī*, ed. 'Abd al-Ḥay Ḥabībī (Kabul, AH 1342), provides much useful information about early Muslim rule in Bengal.

3 Ibn Isḥāq, *Sirat Rasūl Allāh* quoted in Martin Ling's *Muḥammad: His Life Based on the Early Sources* (New York: Inner Traditions International Ltd, 1983): 42.

4 The celebrated Muslim historian Taqī al-Dīn Aḥmad ibn 'Alī al-Maqrīzī also uses the word *āthār* to connote more or less the same meaning in his treatise on the relics and remains of Cairo *al-Khiṭaṭ wa 'l-Āthār* (Cairo, AH 1370).

5 One of the earliest examples of this development can be seen in the Qur'ānic inscriptions on the *tabūt* of al-Ḥusayn made sometime around 550/1155 in Cairo, in which both Kūfī and *naskh* are used; see Caroline Williams, 'The Quranic Inscriptions on the *tabut* of al-Ḥusayn', *Islamic Art* 2 (1987): 3–13. Another example is Quṭb Mīnār in Delhi built in the early thirteenth century.

6 The inscription on the Ẓafar Khān's masjid dated 698/1298 in Tribeni, Hooghly; the Chhoto Sona Masjid inscription in Gaur from the reign of Ḥusayn Shāh and Bagha Masjid inscription in the district of Rajshahi dated 930/1523–1524 are examples of this kind of calligraphic programme, where the inscriptions are placed too high to be easily read.

7 R. Ettinghausen, 'Arabic epigraphy: communication or symbolic affirmation', in *Near Eastern Numismatics, Iconography, Epigraphy and History: Studies in Honor of George C. Miles*, ed. D. K. Kouymjian (Beirut: American University of Beirut, 1974): 297–317.

8 For further details, see *Répertoire chronologique d'épigraphie arabe*, vols 37 and 43 (Cairo).

9 Taqī al-Dīn Muḥammad ibn Aḥmad al-Ḥusaynī al-Fāsī al-Makkī, *al-'Aqd al-Thamīn fī Tārīkh al-Balad al-Amīn*, ed. Muḥammad 'Abd al-Qādir Aḥmad 'Aṭā', vol. 3 (Beirut: Dār al-Kutub al-'Ilmiyyah, 1998): 419 (see also other editions, e.g. edited by Muḥammad Ḥamīd al-Faqī, Cairo: Muḥammad Sarūr al-Ṣabbān publisher, AH 1378, and Beirut edition by Mu'assasa al-Risala [n.d.]). al-Fāsī also surveyed a number of the oldest surviving mosques of his time in Taif and read their existing inscriptions; see, for instance, *Shafā al-Garām bi Akhbār al-Balad al-Ḥarām*, vol. 1 (Beirut: Dār al-Kutub al-'Ilmiyyah, 2002): 122 (see also other editions, e.g. edited by 'Umar 'Abd al-Salām Tadmurī [Beirut: Dār al-Kitāb al-'Arabī, 1405]).

10 Muḥammad ibn 'Alī ibn Muḥammad Jamāl al-Dīn al-Makkī al-Qarshī al-Shībī, *al-Sharf al-A'lā fī Dhikr Qubūr Maqbira Bāb al-Ma'lā*, MS no. 354 s.f. 1179 in King Sa'ūd University Library, MS no. 130/900 in Shaykh 'Arif Ḥikmat Library in Madinah (copied in 1231/1816 by Aḥmad al-Azharī), MS no 18325 in National Library in Tunisia (copied in 891/1486 by Abū 'l-Qāsim ibn 'Alī ibn Muḥammad al-Qaḥṭānī), MS no. 6124 in Berlin Library (copied in 1122/1710 by Muḥammad Sa'īd ibn Ismā'īl al-Makkī). It is interesting to note that the prominent family of Shībī earned fame and respect in Makkah during the fifteenth century through their education and cultural activities. Quite a few of this clan hold various high positions in Makkah such as chief justice, muftī (deliverer of legal and religious verdict) and imām of the Grand Mosque. A number of scholars from this family taught at the famous Bengali religious seminary in Makkah named as al-Madrasa al-Sulṭāniyyah al-Ghiyāthiyyah al-Bangāliyyah after its Bengali patron al-Sulṭān Ghiyāth al-Dīn A'ẓam Shāh, the ruler of Bengal.

11 Max Van Berchem, *Matériaux pour un Corpus Inscriptionum Arabicarum*, in *Mémoires publiés par les Membres de l'Institut Français d'Archéologie Orientale* (*Egypte*, vol. Xix, Cairo 1903; *Jérusalem*, vols, xliii, xlv, Cairo 1920–2; *Syrie du Nord* [in collaboration with E. Herzfield], vols LXXVII–LXXVII, Cairo 1955).

12 One can argue that it was architectural epigraphy which influenced the *Kiswa* as well as the *ṭirāz* tradition in the Muslim world.

13 Ibn-Baṭṭūṭa, *Riḥla* (Beirut; Dār Ṣādir, n.d.), 421.

14 A number of writings by the famous epigraphist Max Van Berchem shed light on these issues. See, for instance, his article: 'Note on the Graffiti of the Cistern at Wady el-Joz', *Palestine Exploration Fund Quarterly Statement* (1915): 85–90, 195–198.

15 The use of the Throne Verse for funerary inscriptions is quite common almost everywhere in the Muslim world. We find it, for instance, in the inscriptions on the *tābūt* of al-Ḥusayn dated 550 (1155) now in the Islamic Museum in Cairo.

16 The Garh Jaripa inscription dated 893/1487, the Ḥusaynī Dālān inscription dated 1052/1642 and the Piyārī Dās Road masjid inscription dated 1109/1697 are good examples of this kind of epigraphic record.

17 A number of such inscriptions have been discovered in Bengal. Of these, a Burarchar inscription and a Dohar inscription both dated 1000/1591 and now preserved in the Bangladesh National Museum, Dhaka, probably belong to the same edifice that is referred to in the Nayabari inscription. Other examples are a Gaur inscription dated

893/1489, now in the British Museum, and a Barakatra inscription dated 1055/1645, in the Bangladesh National Museum.

18 In the Barakatra inscription dated 1055/1645, for instance, Abu 'l-Qāsim al-Ḥusaynī (who endowed the edifice) uses the *nisba* al-Ṭabaṭab'ī al-Sīmnānī (from Ṭabāṭabā and Simnān), and the calligrapher Sa'ad al-Dīn Muḥammad uses the *nisba* al-Shīrāzī (from Shiraz). In a Nayabari inscription dated 1003/1595, Bhāgal Khān, who endowed a masjid, is called Ḥajji (one who has performed pilgrimage).

19 See, for instance, *al-Khiṭaṭ wa 'l-Āthār* (Cairo, AH 1370) for details. This monumental work on the relics and remains of Cairo can truly be considered as a *magnum opus* in the field.

20 A number of such inscriptions have been discovered in Bengal. Of these, a Burarchar inscription and a Dohar inscription both dated 1000/1591 and now preserved in the Bangladesh National Museum, Dhaka, probably belong to the same edifice that is referred to in the Nayabari inscription. Other examples are a Gaur inscription dated 893/1489, now in the British Museum, and a Barakatra inscription dated 1055/1645, in the Bangladesh National Museum.

21 The institution of a *waqf* had certain advantages since *waqf* property could not be confiscated easily, even by those in power.

22 Sourdel-Thomine, 'Inscriptions Seljoukides et salles a couples de Qazwin en Iran', *Revue de Etudes Islamiques* 42 (1974): 3–43.

23 Bimal Bandyopadhyay 'Recent excavation of the area adjacent to Baisgazi Wall of Gaur and scientific clearance at some adjacent areas, District, Malda, West Bengal' *Journal of Bengal Art*, 9–10 (2004–2005, published in 2006): 12–23.

24 For a detailed and in-depth discussion on the meaning and metaphor of verses in Alhambra inscriptions, see Oleg Grabar, *The Alhambra* (Sebastopol, CA: Solipsist Press, 1992): 75–129.

25 James Cavanah Murphy, *History of the Mahometan Empire in Spain* (London, 1816) (see English translation of the Arabic inscriptions of Alhambra in appendix by Shakespeare under the title: 'A Collection of the Historical Notices and Poems in the Alhambra of Granada'); Jules Goury and Owen Jones, *Plans, Elevations, Sections and Details of the Alhambra*, 2 vols (London: 1842–1845); Ṣabīḥ Ṣādiq, 'Qaṣr al-Ḥamrā': Diwān Shi'rī al-Manqūsh 'Alā' 'l-Jidrān', *al-Faysal*, 353 (December 2005): 54–67).

26 The unfinished masjid inscription from Mandra dated 836/1433 presents a visual description about how the calligraphic programme used to be outlined on the slab before it was actually inscribed.

27 We have at least one definite source that informs us about the widespread employment of Muslim craftsmen in sophisticated technology, art and architecture in eastern India including Orissa. See *Baya Chakara*, trans. Alice Boner, Sadasiva Rathasarma and others, in *New Light on the Sun Temple of Konark* (Varanasi: D. Chowkhamba Sanskrit Office, 1972): 57, 68, 93, 116.

28 Hasan al-Basha, 'Ahmiyat Shawāhid al-Qubūr ka Masdarin li Tarīkhi 'l-Jazirah al-'Arabiyyah', *Majallat Darasat Tarīkh al-Jazīrah al-'Arabiyyah* [Riyadh University Press] 1(1) (AH 1399): 81–83.

29 It may be mentioned here that in most areas of the Bengal delta, stone is not easily available, and therefore had to be imported from places such as Jharkhand (i.e. Rajmahal) and Bihar through its vast riverain routes.

30 A stone miḥrab from a ruined Sultanate mosque in Gaur, now in the Varendra Research Museum in Rajshahi, is a good example of reuse of old building materials. Traditional Bengali decorative motives usually found in temple architecture in Bengal cover almost all of the outer façade. The use of old building materials, especially from ruined Hindu temples, for the construction of mosques by the Muslim rulers has led some people to assume that mosques were erected after Hindu temples were destroyed on those sites. These unfounded beliefs have occasionally resulted in communal

tensions and the demolition of places of worship in South Asia, such as the destruction of the Babri masjid in Ayodha in India in 1993.

31 See, for instance, Dinesh Chandra Sarkar, 'Mainamatir Chandra Bangshiyo Tamra Shasantroy', in *Abdul Karim Sahitya Visharad Commemorative Volume*, ed. Mohammad Enamul Hoque (Dacca: Asiatic Society of Pakistan, 1972): i–vii.

2 The diffusion of Islam in Bengal and the articulation of a new order

The land

The name Bengal in its English form – Bangala or Bangal, in Arabic, Persian and Urdu, and Banglā or Bangladesh (as a historical term), in its Bengali version – refers to the territory roughly situated between 27° and 21° latitude and 92.50° and 87° longitude. The eastern parts of the present Dhaka district, the districts of Comilla and Sylhet (Habānaq according to Ibn Baṭṭūṭa, Suknāt in other Islamic sources and Śrihaṭṭa in Sanskrit) in Bangladesh and the state of Tripura in India were known in ancient times as Samataṭa. The northwest part of Bengal, to the west of the river Atrai up to the Ganges, is relatively high land. It was known as Gowḍa (popularly Gau̱r or Gau̱ro, at times referring to the metropolitan area of the region) in the early days, and later on as Barind in Persian writings (according to an early Muslim historian, Mawlānā Minhāj al-Dīn 'Uthmān Sirāj al-Dīn)[1] or Varendra Bhūmī in local Sanskrit and Bengali writings. This was where the Muslim conquerors first settled; they used Lakhnawtī (according to Islamic sources; Lakṣmṇāvatī in Sanskrit and Bengali) and the neighbouring cities of Gaur, Devikot and later on Pandua and Ekdala as their capital. The section lying to the west of the Hugli-Bhagirathi river bore the name of Rā̱dha or Rāḍh (according to the *Ṭabaqāt-i-Nāṣirī* of Mawlānā Minhāj al-Dīn). The northern part of Rā̱dha often served as an entry point for the early Muslim forces coming overland from the north. The famous ancient port city of Tamralipti lay at the southern tip of Rā̱dha.

Southern Bengal (namely, Sundarban and Khulna in Bangladesh and Twenty Four Parganas in West Bengal, India) was usually known as Banga (Vaṅga in Sanskrit), and the coastal land as Harikela (e.g. the Chittagong area in the early period as well as Sylhet in the later period).[2] Muslim geographers called it Harkand from which comes Baḥr al-Harkand, the early Arabic name for the Bay of Bengal. From the early eighth to late tenth centuries, Harikela was an independent state contiguous with Samataṭa and Vaṅga (which included Chandradvipa).[3] The ancient Harikela kingdom once extended to Sundarban. A thick forest on the coastal region of the Gangetic delta (at present mainly in the southernmost part of the present division of Khulna in Bangladesh and in the district of Twenty Four Parganas [Chhabbish Pargana in Bengali] in the Indian state of

West Bengal), Sundarban once extended much deeper into the mainland. It bears traces of early human settlement. Indigenous non-Aryan nomad tribes roamed in this region and gradually came under the influence of Hinduism and Buddhism (through rulers such as Dummanpal around the twelfth century), and finally Islam. In the east of Harikela, a Hindu kingdom, Chandradvīpa (Deva dynasty), emerged in the thirteenth century, which was gradually absorbed in the Mughal empire in the early seventeenth century.[4]

The earliest Islamic sources from before the conquest of Bengal do not refer to this land by the name of Vaṅga or Bangala; they call it the kingdom of Ruhmī,[5] probably a reference to Suhma, an ancient name of the western region of Bengal (see Figure 0.2). There is considerable confusion about its location and its name appeared as Ruhmī,[6] Rahma[7] and Dahum.[8] Of these, the closest to Bengali is Dharma (a spelling used by Sulaymān al-Tājir),[9] a possible reference to a famous Bengali king Dharmapāla (769–801). Sulaymān al-Tājir also noticed correctly Dharmapāla's non-aristocratic, i.e. humble, origin. According to Ibn Khurradādhbih,[10] Ruhmī was a vast kingdom which probably included in its frontiers the Kanja (Ganges) river and Abbina, was bordered by Kāmrūn (Kamrup) not far from Tibet and China, and was bountifully supplied with elephants, buffalo and Indian aloe wood. Its coast, according to Ḥudūd al-'Ālam,[11] included areas such as Nimyās, Samandar, Andrās, Ūrshīn (Orissa) and Harkand (ancient Harikela near Chandradvīpa in South Bengal). The port of Samandar which was presumably located somewhere in the Chittagong coast from Karnafuli estuary to the Choto Pheni estuary[12] (or perhaps near the present port of Chandpur at the mouth of Meghna river), is mentioned by al-Idrīsi, who also refers to a river 'Musla', perhaps the Meghna.[13]

The kingdom of Ruhmī, according to most of these early sources, fought constantly with its neighbours, Ballaharā (Raja Ballahrāya of the Rāṣṭrakūṭa dynasty of the Deccan) and Jurz (Gurjaras of Kanauj). It was particularly famous for its fine cotton cloth, known in the West as muslin. In addition to gold coins, cowrie-shells were used for currency. Trade with the Arabs flourished in the port cities in the south, especially in Shāṭi'-jām (Chittagong) and Samandar. The recent discovery of two Abbasid coins in Bangladesh, one from Paharpur dated 172/788 from the time of Hārūn al-Rashīd (170–193/786–809) and the other from Mainamati minted during the reign of Abū Aḥmad 'Abd-Allah al-Muntaṣir billāh (247–248/861–862), attests to this early Arab-Bengal trade link which undoubtedly accelerated the consolidation of Islam in the region.[14]

The name Vaṅga or Vangāla-deśa is quite old. We find it during the reign of Govinda Chandra (sometime between AD 1021–1023) in the Tirumalai Sanskrit inscription of the Rajendra-Cola dynasty. It also appears in a few other Sanskrit inscriptions of the Chandra dynasty discovered in Mainamati, Bangladesh.[15] The historian Minhāj Sirāj al-Dīn was perhaps the first Muslim writer to refer to the name Bilād-i-Bang. Besides Banga, he also mentions a few other regions (or perhaps sub-regions) in this eastern part of South Asia, namely, Bihār, Bilād Lakhnawti (Gauḍa Deśa), Diyār Suknāt (most likely the Samataṭa region comprising the present Sylhet district)[16] and Kāmrūd (Kamrup).[17] Shahr-i-Nawdia (mistakenly transliterated as Nadia, but unlikely to be the same as the present district of Nadia), the capital of Lakṣmaṇasena (Rāy Lakhmaniyah according to Minhāj) was probably located on the bank of the old channel of the river Jahnabi or Bhagirathi which changed its course westward later on. It may be identified either with the present village of Nawdah[18] on the western bank of the currently dried river Pagla slightly westward of Mahdipur village, or with the village of Nawdapara, an archaeological site near Rohanpur railway station in Chapai Nawabgnaj district, both not far from the city of Gaur. This assumption is further supported by epigraphic evidence, as a number of inscriptions of the early Muslim rulers (including the bridge inscription from Sultanganj from the reign of Sultan 'Alā' Dīn ['Ali Mardān Khaljī] in *circa* 1210–1213 [ins. no. 1] and the masjid-madrasa inscription from Naohata from the reign of Balkā Khān Khaljī in *circa* 1229–1231 [ins. no. 3]) have been discovered in the areas not far from Gaur, but not a single Islamic inscription has thus far been found in the Nadia district.

With the consolidation of Muslim rule in the eastern and southeastern parts of the region and more particularly with the emergence of a new Muslim capital of Sonārgā'on in the area known as Bangal, the name Bangāla gradually became more popular. Sulṭān Ilyās Shāh (740–759/1339–1358), for instance, used the title Shāh-i-Bangāliyān. Many early fifteenth century Arab historians, such as al-Fāsī and al-Shībī, used this name extensively. Thus we find that throughout the medieval Muslim period, Bangāla (sometimes referred as Diyār-e-Bangālah as well)[19] was the widely accepted name for the region. It appears as Ṣūba-i-Bangala (the province of Bengal) in a Sherpur inscription dated 1042/1632, a Churihatta inscription dated 1060/1650 and in a number of other inscriptions after that. The famous Arab Captain Aḥmad ibn Mājid (b. 1440) often refers to 'Bangala' and 'the land of Bang' in his book *al-Fawā'id fī Uṣūl 'ilm al-Baḥr wa 'l-Qawā'id* [A Treatise in Oceanography] compiled in 895/1490. These names are also used by Sulaymān ibn Aḥmad ibn Sulaymān al-Mahrī, an early sixteenth century Omani sea captain, who provides us with amazingly rich details about the Bay of Bengal and its coast in his books (e.g. *The Tale of Fabulous Seas* and *A Manual of Seas*).[20]

Hence 'Bengal' in the historical sense (and particularly in this book) encompasses mainly the areas now known as Bangladesh and West Bengal. Occasionally the term may be extended loosely to cover certain adjoining areas of the neighbouring regions such as Arakan (in present Myanmar [formerly Burma]) and Tripura, Assam, Bihar and Orissa (in present India). Through a long historical process, these areas altogether have formulated a distinctive regional cultural identity within the greater Indo-Muslim cultural sphere that can aptly be called Muslim Bengali culture.

The advent of Islam and the Bengal hinterland

Bengal, once an outpost of the Islamic world, today has the largest Muslim population in South Asia. Linguistically, Bengali Muslims (approximately 150 million in Bangladesh and 40 million in West Bengal, Assam, Tripura and other regions of South Asia and in certain parts of Arakan in Burma) form the second largest linguistic as well as ethnic group in the Islamic world after the Arabs, if not the first. Islam is not only the faith of the majority of the approximately 240 million Bengali-speaking people inhabiting the eastern part of South Asia, but it is also their predominant and primary culture. Although geographically distant from Makkah and Madinah, the heartland of Islam, Bengal has nonetheless played an important role in shaping the history of the Islamic East.

There has been much speculation about the factors that led to the spread of Islam in this region and several intriguing questions remain unanswered. One is why this particular region attained such an overwhelmingly Muslim majority, while many other regions in the central, western and southern or even eastern parts of the Subcontinent did not, though they remained under Muslim rule for a considerable period. There are a number of theories about the consolidation of Islam in Bengal.[21] They can be described mainly as: (1) mass immigration of Muslims into the area; (2) massive conversion of lower-caste Hindus to escape the caste system rigorously imposed by the upper class Hindus; (3) dominance of Islam as the religion of the ruling class and eagerness of the indigenous population to associate themselves with the ruling class; and (4) acceptance of Islam as a more appropriate way of life in the changed circumstances in the rural settings, i.e. from a tribal nomadic system to a settled farming system (e.g. Eaton's theory about the emergence of Islam as the religion of axe and plough in the Bengal delta).[22] It appears that though a large segment of the population in Bengal embraced Islam in a formal sense at various times and for various reasons, consciousness of their Islamic identity and the degree of the intensity of their faith and religious adherence grew gradually over a long period, a process that continues to this day. A sizeable portion of the farming population gradually adopted Islam for practical reasons as if it suited their agrarian life more than the other extant faiths in the region. On the other hand, it seems that Islam did not gain much popularity among certain indigenous castes traditionally engaged in specific professions such as *Dom* (mainly engaged in bamboo handicrafts and various menial jobs), *Chamar* (leather related works, shoemakers), *Napit* (barbers), *Methor* (toilet cleaners), *kamar* (blacksmiths) and *kumar* (pottery manufacturers), etc.

Bengal experienced great prosperity during the rule of the independent Muslim sultans, whose far-reaching welfare works, such as *siqāya* (water tanks and wells particularly mentioned in quite a few Ḥusayn Shāhī inscriptions), helped spread Islam to the furthest corners of the region. Institutions, such as *waqf* and *madad-i-ma'āsh* (endowment and land-grants to support masjid, madrasas and khānqāhs mentioned in a number of inscriptions), benefited the commoners greatly, regardless of their religion. Islam thus appeared in Bengal as the religion of commoners.[23] Bengal's ecological balance and natural harmony left a strong imprint on its popular literature, art, architecture, culture and folklore during the Sultanate and Mughal periods. Islam finally emerged as the faith, as well as the primary culture, of the majority of the population of Bengal. During the Mughal period too, Bengal witnessed sustained growth in the positive utilization of its natural resources without losing its ecological balance and came to be considered the granary of the empire.

There are a number of other issues pertaining to the formation of early Muslim society which remain unresolved. One central question is what was the relationship between the conquering Muslim forces, who must have been exclusively male, and the indigenous population? Minhāj al-Dīn, author of *Ṭabaqāt-i-Nāṣirī*, reports that, when Ikhtiyār al-Dīn Muḥammad Bakhtiyār returned to the capital Devikot in northern Bengal after his defeat in Tibet, in which almost all of his soldiers perished, the wives and the children of those who perished (predominantly Khaljī soldiers) started to wail in the streets, rooftops and corners loudly. The situation was so embarrassing for Bakhtiyār that he could not appear in public after that and he soon died broken-hearted.[24] Does this statement imply that the Muslim army had settled down in this newly conquered land and married into the local population immediately after their arrival? While one cannot rule out the possibility that a limited number of families, particularly spouses, occasionally accompanied the Muslim army to Bengal, this certainly did not happen on mass scale for practical reasons. Female names in epigraphic texts, such as Boa Malati (dated 941/1534–1535), and other bits of social and historical evidence strongly suggest that large-scale inter-marriage between the newly settled Muslim male soldiers and the females from the local population occurred at different stages throughout history. Successive military expeditions by Delhi Sultans against independent Muslim rulers of Bengal brought more and more Muslim soldiers into the Bengali cultural region over centuries. Many of these soldiers settled in the region adding to the numerical expansion of the Muslim population in Bengal.

Epigraphic evidence does not give a clear picture of all these different historical settings nor does it provide complete answers to numerous questions regarding the spread of Islam in Bengal. Still, epigraphs offer many clues. The number of Islamic inscriptions during the Sultanate and early Mughal periods (1204–1707) is fairly large (approximately 400), indicating the gradual spread of Islamic culture into the different spheres of Bengali life.

Merchants and the faith: early Islamic contacts with Bengal

Merchants played a vital role in disseminating religion and culture in the Old World. This is especially true of Islam, as Muslim merchants carried the message of Islam to different corners of Asia and Africa both through overland and maritime trade. In the absence of any organized institution of professional missionaries, trade and commerce played a key role in conversion to Islam. However, the historical experiences as well as the process of this transformation were different in nature when compared with the aggressive proselytization practised by Western Christian missionary institutions. While the missionary activities were viewed by many traditional societies in the East as one of the tools of colonial expansionism, Islam entered these regions in most cases as civilization-making ideology and finally emerged as a primary regional culture.

Although commercial activities played an important role in disseminating Islamic cultural and ideological influences in different regions, expansion of Islam cannot be reduced to commerce, nor can commerce (in the Indian Ocean, for instance) be reduced to mere Muslim mercantile activities. Factors leading to the diffusion of Islam varied from one region to another. While Islamic trade and maritime activities in Southeast Asia and Far East Asia played a key role in the Islamization process in a significant part of the region (e.g. Indonesia and Malaysia), it played a comparatively lesser role in Bengal.

In the first (introductory) phase of Islam in Bengal, Islamic contacts came from different directions, but mainly via the northern and northwestern land route and the southern sea route of the Bay of Bengal (see Figure 0.2) through trade and commerce. Thus, the conquest by Muḥammad Bakhtiyār was not the first contact with Muslims in the region. Bengal had already come into limited contact with Muslim traders, merchants, sailors and sufi shaykhs at a much earlier stage. Minhāj al-Dīn, author of *Ṭabaqāt-i-Nāṣirī*, mentions that when Bakhtiyār appeared before the gates of Nawdia, the capital of the Sena dynasty of Bengal, with only eighteen horsemen, the people guarding the gates of the city mistook them for a party of Muslim horse traders and opened the gates. This certainly suggests that Muslim horse traders were a familiar sight in Bengal before the conquest.

Indian sources also refer to early Muslim contacts with Bengal. A Sanskrit inscription of Ratnapala (third–fourth/ninth–tenth century) mentions 'Tajikas'[25] apparently a reference to the Tajiks of Central Asia. The Chinese form of the word, *Ta-shih,* was also used by Chinese sources to refer to Muslims, and the word seems to have been used with the same meaning in this Indian inscription.[26] In a Sanskrit inscription dated 1206 found near the city of Gauhati in Assam, the name *Turaśka* (people of Turkic origin) is used for the Muslim forces in the area.[27]

It was the coastal areas of the Bay of Bengal where the Muslim traders, saints and sufis came first and introduced Islam much before the Muslim conquest in the north. The possibility of some early Muslim settlement especially in its southeastern coastal region may not be ruled out as Muslim traders had extensive maritime activities in the Bay of Bengal. A number of medieval Muslim maritime accounts provide detailed descriptions of Baḥr al-Harkand (the Bay of Bengal), its tides, waves and currents, wind directions, islands and many other navigational details.

Shipwrecks and other calamities in the Bay of Bengal no doubt led to Muslim voyagers, particularly the Arab seafarers, gradually settling there. Place names, such as Jahaj Bhangar Ghat (meaning the landing stage after shipwreck), in Chittagong coastal areas bear the relics of such incidents in the past. An old Arakanese chronicle, first noticed in the mid-nineteenth century, reports a few Arabs in a village on the coast of Arakan, not far from Chittagong. According to another Arakanese chronicle, about a century-and-a-half later, King Tsu-la-Taing Tsan-da-ya (340–346/951–957) defeated one Thu-ra-tan (Arabic sulṭān) and erected a victory memorial at Tset-ta-going (Chittagong).[28] Evidently, the 'Thu-ra-tan' was a person to be reckoned with and had for some reason or other aroused the jealousy of, or posed a threat to, the Arakanese king, but he is not mentioned in any other source. On the basis of the Arakanese chronicle, the historian Enamul Haq concluded that the Muslim settlers in the Chittagong region gradually grew into a compact and influential community, and eventually organized an independent principality comprising the coastal Chittagong and Noakhali districts. The ruler of this Muslim principality bore the title *sulṭān*.[29]

Chittagong was visited by Ibn Baṭṭūṭa during the reign of Fakhr al-Dīn Mubarak Shāh (739–50/1338–1349), who described it as a port near the mouth of the Ganges, as do the Chinese accounts of the fifteenth century, and Abū 'l-Faḍl, the courtier-historian of Akbar's reign. It may therefore be assumed that Muslim merchants, who went there, referred to it in Arabic as *Shāṭī' al-Gangā* (the bank of the Ganges) or later *Shāṭī-Jām* (e.g. Sulaymān ibn Aḥmad ibn Sulaymān, *'Umdat al-Biḥār*). The expression gradually assumed the local form (of Bengali dialect) Sadkawan, Chitagang or Chatgaon. Through Ibn Baṭṭūṭa, we also know that the sea trade was never limited to Chittagong; rather, traders penetrated through inland waterways deep into the mainland.

There is an admixture of Arabic words, idioms and phrases in the local dialects of the Chittagong and Noakhali districts, a result of the close contacts between Arabs and the local population through the ages. While contacts with Muslims in other parts of Bengal were overland and mainly Turko-Persian, the coastal areas were influenced more by Arab contacts. The first Muslim conquest of Chittagong did not occur until the fourteenth century, in the time of Fakhr al-Dīn Mubārak Shāh of Sunārgā'on (Dhaka), and effective control of the area was not achieved until the early sixteenth century. When the Portuguese merchant Barbosa visited the locality about 924/1518, he found the port, which he describes as the prosperous city of 'Bengala' (see Figure 0.2), inhabited mainly by rich Muslim merchants from Arabia, Persia and Abyssinia. They owned large ships and exported fine cotton cloth, sugar and other valuable commodities to such places as Coromondal, Malabar, Cambay, Pegu, Tennasserin, Sumatra, Malacca and Ceylon. Early tenth/sixteenth century accounts indicate Bengali Muslim merchants spread widely across the ports of the archipelago carrying Muslim Bengali cultural influence with them. As a result, rulers in the peninsula and Sumatra were called sultan like their counterpart in Bengal. Tomé Pires particularly noted that many of the Moorish people of Pase are Bengalis and even the Moorish king is of the Bengali caste.[30] Naturally, the growth of such a prosperous Muslim community must have taken time. Expansion of the Bengali Muslim merchant community and their mercantile activities in the Indian ocean and their role in spreading Islam in Southeast Asia in the medieval age is an important subject in its own right which has yet to be researched properly. Early Islamic maritime literature provides us with valuable information about Baḥr Shalāhaṭ (the Strait of Malacca) and the neighbouring islands such as Jazira al-Ramnī or Jazira al-Rāmī, which was most likely the city of Lāmurī on Sumatra).[31] Jazirat al-Rāmī may also refer to the kingdom of Rame, which is mentioned by the English traveller Ralph Fitch, who visited Bengal in

1585–1586. Its capital was Ramu, which still exists not far from the town of Cox's Bazar, but it is now a small and declining town.

After Islam was introduced in the coastal area of Bengal, it spread into neighbouring Arakan. In the map of Blaves, the area to the south of the river Karnafuli, consisting of the southern Chittagong district and the district of Chittagong Hill Tracts, is designated as 'Codovascam', the name the Portuguese gave to the locality, after Khudā Bakhsh Khān, an administrator of the area who established himself as its ruler towards the end of the Ḥusayn Shāhī period.[32] The Magh rajahs of Arakan often caused much hardship to the Muslim inhabitants as well as to the rulers of Bengal, especially during the early Mughal period. The constant encounter of the Arakanese with the Muslims in Bengal, however, eventually resulted in the strong impact of Islam on their culture. The support of the Muslim rulers of Bengal for the Arakanese king Naramithla in his battles with Ava during ninth/fifteenth century, as appears in some local oral traditions, further indicate this interaction. In the long run, Arakan itself became, and still remains, predominantly Muslim. Thus, the first phase of Islamic contact, predominantly Arab, paved the way for the consolidation of Islam in Bengal and its neighbouring areas. It was, however, limited in nature, as it failed to establish the Arab Shāfi'ī culture that commonly prevailed along the coastal belt in the Indian Ocean perhaps due to its very liberal attitude in day to day matters (for example no restrictions on any kind of seafood). In spite of the continuous European onslaught on Arab maritime activities in the Indian Ocean beginning in the early sixteenth century, Arab ships continued to sail from different ports to the Bay of Bengal, particularly from Oman, trading mostly in the fine Bengali cotton fabric of muslin until the beginning of the eighteenth century.

During the Sultanate period, particularly after the coming to power of the Bengali Muslim sultan Jalāl al-Dīn Muḥammad Shāh (r. 818–836/1414–1433) from the house of Ganesh, economic integration of Bengal with the wider world of Islam provided the region with economic growth. Its market became open to Indian Ocean trade and Bengali agriculture and industrial products found an outlet for maritime export. Thus, Bengal, as well as all of South Asia, became an integral part of the Islamic civilization that dominated the contemporary Old World until the advent of Western colonial powers in the region. After the Mughal emperor Akbar's conquest of the entire region and the establishment of state administration at the grass-roots level even in the low, marshy land of the southern delta, Bengal was integrated further into the world trade and commerce system. Islam, in Eaton's view, entered this delta as a civilization-building ideology.[33]

The Muslim conquest of Bengal and the beginning of Islamic consolidation

Like most of the other regions in the Islamic world, the history of Islam in Bengal begins not with defeat, but with victory; not with fall, but with rise. The pivotal message of the early Islamic inscriptions is of God's help in the total victory, not God as a source of testing (see, for instance, Chehil Ghāzi Masjid Inscription in Dinajpur, dated 865/1460). The first Islamic inscription from the reign of Sultan 'Alā' Dīn 'Alī Mardān asserts that Islam grows every moment due to the effort of the ruler. Even the popular titles of the Muslim rulers of the Bengali Sultanate, such as Abū 'l-Muẓaffar (victorious), convey the same message.

It was on 19 Ramaḍān 601 (10 May 1205)[34] that Ikhtiyār al-Dīn Muḥammad Bakhtiyār, an adventurer from the Turkish Khaljī tribe of mountainous central Afghanistan (known as Khaljistān), defeated Lakhśmana Sena, a Hindu king of the powerful Sena dynasty of Bengal, with just a handful of soldiers and swept over almost the whole terrain of Rāṟa and Barindra in an amazingly short time. This sudden Muslim victory was very surprising since Lakhśmana Sena was considered a powerful king of eastern India who had previously conquered many neighbouring areas and towns such as Kalinga, Kamarupa, Puri (Purushattam-Khśetra in ancient days) and Prayaga. He was, in fact, quite appreciated by a contemporary Muslim historian, Minhāj al-Dīn, who wrote in detail about the early Muslim campaigns in Bengal. Through this military victory, a strong Muslim foothold was established in the eastern part of South Asia which was soon to change the social, cultural, political and demographic makeup of the region. Marshal sports, such horse riding, were never a part of the popular culture of Bengal, nor did cavalry ever play any meaningful role in the defensive strategy of the Bengal army. On the contrary, the military victory of this raiding Muslim army was achieved through the superior tactics and swift mobility of the Muslim cavalry, as depicted in some of the earliest beautifully minted commemorative gold and silver coins of Bakhtiyār and Sultan 'Alā' Dīn 'Ali Mardān Khaljī both at Gaur and Delhi.[35] Another underlying factor contributing to this victory was the failure of the Sena Dynasty to gain popular support, especially from the semi-Hinduized indigenous Buddhist population of Bengal, who had not accepted the rule of the Hindu Sena Dynasty wholeheartedly. Bengal had a rich tradition of Buddhism before the Sena rule. In addition to the Buddhist Pala Dynasty, some of the early Hindu kings were also influenced by it. On a Ramapala Sanskrit copperplate, for instance, we find that a Hindu king, Suvarna Chandra, is described as a follower of Buddha.

Unlike their predecessors the Buddhist Pala Dynasty of Bengal, who were the original inhabitants of Bengal, the Senas were Brahman Kshatriya (one of the highest Hindu castes) and worshippers of Shiva and Shakti. They came probably as fortune seekers from Karnat in South India, a region far away from Bengal. Shortly after their arrival, they were able to establish a fiefdom in Barindra, in northern Bengal.[36] As the Pala Dynasty weakened, the Senas began to emerge as the only powerful rulers of Bengal. Their adherence to the caste system kept them from establishing roots among the local population. The Vedic religion, which the Aryans brought with them, never took strong root in the local people of this region. This might have been one of the factors that led a good portion of the indigenous Mlechcha (a Sanskrit term essentially connoting non-Aryan natives/uncivilized non-Hindu aborigines of India) population (such as the Mech tribe in the north, according to *Ṭabaqāt-i-Nāṣirī*) to cooperate with the Muslim conquerors identified by the Aryan (Vedic) Hindus as *Yavana* (originally Sanskrit word meaning polluted outsiders/aliens, somewhat close to the ancient Greek concept of *Barbarophonoi*). As a counterbalance to the previous ruling class of the Senas, Bakhtiyār tried to woo some non-Aryan indigenous tribes in the region successfully to the extent of building a huge monastery for the Buddhist population of the area.[37] Thus, we notice that the assimilation of the indigenous people with the new immigrant Muslims from Afghanistan and Central Asia started at the very dawn of the Muslim conquest. This factor may have influenced Bakhtiyār to move his seat of rule farther north to Devikot, inhabited mainly by local tribes to this day rather than to Lakhnot or Nawdah (the present Mahdipur village and its adjacent areas), in the heart of the Lakhnawti (Gaur) region.

The earliest recorded conversion to Islam took place among the indigenous tribe of Mech (most likely an abbreviated form of the Sanskrit word *Mlechchha* close to the ancient Greek idea of *Xenos* [ξένος]) inhabiting the foothills of the Himalayas in the north of Bengal.[38] The newly converted Muslim ʻAlī Mech, an influential tribal leader, played a key role in guiding Bakhtiyār Khaljī during his Tibet campaign as well as ensuring a safe return passage for him after the disastrous failure of his Tibetan expedition. It seems that a large segment of the tribal population slowly converted to Islam over a long period as they gradually moved towards a settled agrarian life.[39] Another factor contributing to the diffusion of Islam in this region was the role of religious personalities (e.g. *qādī*s, ʻulamāʼ and sufis) and traders who interacted successfully with the Bengali peasants (see Figures 2.1 and 2.2, below).

The military success of Bakhtiyār Khaljī in Bengal resulted in the creation of a strong Muslim presence in the eastern hinterland of the Subcontinent. It also generated a zeal for further expansion among the new ruling class. Had Bakhtiyār's military adventure in Tibet been successful, the history of Sino-Islamic relations would have been quite different, for Tibet might have entered into the ethos of Islam. In any case, Bakhtiyār's successors continued a policy of expansion in almost all directions, though with limited success. The early rulers, such as Ḥusām al-Dīn ʻIwaḍ Khaljī and Mughīth al-Dīn Ṭughril, led a number of military campaigns in eastern Bengal. In the first half of the fourteenth century, Muslim troops penetrated into Suknāt (Sylhet), Kāmru (Kamrup) and Assam, crossing the Brahmaputra river in the east and northeast, and to Chittagong on the Bay of Bengal in the south.

This second phase of Islam in Bengal proved to be far more dynamic than the earlier phase, which was limited mostly to commerce. The emergence of early Islamic capitals such as Lakhnawti, Gaur, Pandua, Ekdala and Tanda in the north, and later on Sonārgāʼon and Dhaka in the east and Sātgāʼon in the southwest, played an important role in the further consolidation of Muslim settlements in the region. Unlike Delhi, the Indian Muslim capital, Bengali Muslim capitals gradually turned into Muslim majority areas. Because of Bengal's distance from Delhi, this easternmost region proved from the very beginning to be difficult for the central government at Delhi to control and administer. The governors in this remote province, appointed from Delhi at the earlier stages, often tended to exercise their authority like sovereign rulers, a phenomenon that led to the creation of independent political structures in the region from the very beginning.

While this new wave of contacts through land routes overshadowed the age-old sea link that was once instrumental in the diffusion of Arab-Islamic culture in the coastal areas in the south, the northern overland contact introduced a fresh element in the cultural dimension that came from Central Asia with certain blends of the old Sasanid-Persian legacy. But at the same time, Central Asian 'Ulamā', *mashāyikh* and sufis, particularly from Khurasan (e.g. Muẓāffar Shams Balkhī) played an important role in introducing Islamic literature and disseminating Islamic education in the region. Many Persian words started appearing in the daily vocabulary of the Bengali language.[40] A number of the earliest Islamic inscriptions in Bengal (including the first Islamic inscription in the reign of Sultan 'Alā' Dīn Khaljī [1210–1213] and the third Islamic inscription in the reign of Balkā Khān Khaljī [1229–1231]) were inscribed in Persian. The highly Persianized ruling elite obviously favoured Persian as the court language. Though Arabic maintained its superiority in religious discourse, as we find in a khānqāh inscription dated 1221 (ins. no. 2), sufis such as Nūr Quṭb al-'Ālam (d. 1459?) freely used Persian for their writing, such as *malfuẓāt* (mystical tracts) and *maktūbāt* (letters). One also notices the spread of a few *rawḍa*s (shrines associated with the veneration of saints) in this early period.[41]

The emergence of the independent Sultanate and the spread of Islamic culture

Sultan 'Alā' Dīn Khaljī, the second Muslim ruler of Bengal, proclaimed himself sultan (see ins. no. 1, pl. 1) as early as 607/1210, only six years after the Muslim conquest of Bengal, as did some of the other early rulers who were offshoots of the Delhi-based Balbani Dynasty. During the reign of Muḥammad ibn Tughluq of Delhi, Bengal came to be ruled by Fakhr al-Dīn Mubārak Shāh at Sonārgā'on, 'Alā' al-Dīn 'Alī at Lakhnawti in the northwest, and Qadr Khān probably in Sātgā'on. In this power struggle, it was Ḥājjī Ilyās Shāh (740–59/1339–1358) who finally emerged as victorious in Sātgā'on and then in Lakhnawti. Under his able leadership, all three mini-states were merged into an independent Bengal Sultanate whose territories were gradually expanded. Thus it was Ilyās Shāhī rulers who successfully established a real independent Sultanate around the middle of the fourteenth century. Under this dynasty, Islamic art and architecture flourished, and commerce in Bengal's textiles and agriculture rapidly increased. In the beginning of the fifteenth century, Ghiyāth al-Dīn A'ẓam Shāh strengthened cultural links with China, Persia and the Arab world. The port of Chittagong served as an important centre of trade with the outside world, particularly with the lands farther east, and a point of embarkation for the Muslim pilgrims to Arabia for the *ḥajj* (see Figure I.2).[42] Many Arab voyagers, travellers, traders and religious personalities visited Bengal during this period. Among the 'ulamā' from Makkah, who visited Bengal during this period was Aḥmad ibn Sulaymān ibn Aḥamd al-Tarūjī (a scholar and traveller from Alexandria, Egypt; d. 812/1410) who found this country very prosperous.[43]

As with most of the other parts of the Islamic world, the relationship between the ruling class and the 'ulamā' as well as sufi and shaykhs in Bengal during this period, could at best be called a love–hate relationship and was often mired in hidden tension, an uncomfortable state of mutual acceptance that prevails in the region to this day. 'Ulamā' and sufi shaykhs were particularly concerned about the growing influence of the Hindu elite and bureaucracy who held high positions in state affairs. Among the sufi shaykhs, Nūr Quṭb al-'Ālam, who resisted the growing political influence of Raja Kānsa (probably a misspelling of Sanskrit Ganeśa), was the most vocal. A powerful Bengali Hindu landlord of Bhaturia in Barindra, Raja Kānsa seized power around 1414 and again during 1416–1417, but finally lost his bid to impose high caste Hindu Sanskrit culture in the land, as his son Jadu embraced Islam through Nūr Quṭb al-'Ālam. After the enthronement of Jadu, who took the name of Sulṭān Jalāl al-Dīn Muḥammad Shāh (r. 1414–1433), Bengal looked to Makkah, Madinah, Damascus, Cairo and the other cultural and intellectual centres of the Arab world for its religious and cultural frame of reference, rather than depending solely on the Persian sphere of influence in north India and Central Asia. Conversion of an influential local Hindu elite to Islam had a far-reaching effect as it set another important precedent for the further Islamization of upper-class Hindus in Bengal.

Thus, a third phase of the consolidation of Islam began in the region in the form of Bengali Islamic culture. In his successful pursuit of formal recognition and nomination as amīr by the Abbasid caliph in Cairo, Sultan Jalāl al-Dīn sent his envoys to Sulṭān Bārsbāy in Egypt with royal gifts. He also sent generous endowments to Makkah and Madinah to build two madrasas there which became famous as Bengali madrasas. This renewed age-old Arab–Bengal connection helped Bengali Islamic culture draw closer to the important religious centres in Arabia. Though this Bengali Muslim Dynasty did not last long (as the former Ilyās Shāhi Dynasty was restored in 841/1437), the religious trend could not be averted.

Bengal enjoyed great prosperity under some of these independent sultans, and its cross-cultural ties were broadened. While Chinese emissaries were received at the royal courts in Bengal, ambassadors of the Bengali sultans travelled as far as Cairo and Herat on their diplomatic missions. Bengal maintained ties with both East and West. The restored Ilyās Shāhī dynasty ruled Bengal until 893/1487, when the leader of the Ḥabashīs or the black palace guards (originally slaves from Africa), the eunuch Sulṭān Shāhzāda, murdered the last Ilyās Shāhī Sulṭān Fatḥ Shāh and seized power. After a brief period of anarchy, order was eventually restored. But the power gradually passed over to Sayyid 'Alā' al-Dīn Ḥusayn Shāh in 898/1493, who claimed to be a descendant of a Sayyid family of Arab ancestry. This new dynasty further strengthened Islamic traditions by building a series of mosques and other religious edifices. So far, nearly 100 mosque inscriptions have been discovered from the Ḥusayn Shāhī period alone, which lasted only about forty-six years (from 1493 to 1538). The enlightened rulers of this dynasty patronized the arts, culture and, particularly, Bengali literature. Some of the great epics, such as the *Mahābhārata*, were translated into Bengali at this time. The public projects of many of the sultans (such as digging wells, construction of water-fountains, roads, dams, causeways and bridges as recorded in a large number of inscriptions) improved the lives of a vast number of non-Muslim subjects and contributed to the rapid spread of Islam in the region.

Inscriptions from this period provide us with much information about various aspects of life and society of the time. For example, three inscriptions of Baba Ṣāliḥ during the rule of Ḥusayn Shāh, now preserved in Bangladesh National Museum, Dhaka, depict what would have been perhaps considered a traditionally successful and exemplary life of a wealthy rural Muslim landowner of medieval Bengal. On the basis of what appears in the inscriptions, one can conjecture that towards the end of his life in 910 (1504), he built a mosque as an act of piety in the village of Azimnagar, in the present district of Dhaka (see the masjid inscription of Azimnagar dated 910/1504). In the following year in 911 (1505), he set out on a pilgrimage to Makkah. On his successful return, he assumed the title of Khādim al-Nabī Ḥājjī al-Ḥaramayn wa Zā'ir al-Qadamayn Ḥājjī (the servant of the Prophet – the one who made a pilgrimage to Ḥaramayn [the two most sacred places] and visited the two [holy] footprints – Ḥājjī Bābā Sāliḥ) as recorded in an inscription (see the masjid inscription of Bandar dated 911/1505). An inscription in the following year (the tombstone of Ḥājjī Bābā Sālih from Sonārgā'on dated 912/1506), with a Qur'ānic verse at the beginning, records the death of Ḥājji Ṣāliḥ, the pious. Apparently, the inscription was set on his tomb intended to be a shrine (rawḍa) for the locality.

The Ḥusayn Shāhī dynasty finally came to an end when the Afghan chief Shēr Shāh Sūrī took over Bengal and used it as a base from which to eject the Mughal emperor Humāyūn from India. From then on, Bengal's independence was thwarted. Once the Mughals were firmly re-established in Lahore and Delhi and the Afghans defeated, Mughal influence began to be felt in Bengal. Sulaymān Karrānī (r. 971–980/1564–1572), the former governor of southern Bihar and later on the ruler of Bengal, acknowledged the suzerainty of Emperor Akbar.

From syncretistic tradition to Islamic reassertion: the mighty Mughals and the British Raj

After a long campaign, Bengal was finally subdued by Akbar towards the end of the sixteenth century, and soon after was incorporated into the Mughal Empire. Henceforth, it became one of its *ṣūba*s or provinces.[44] Though its status was now reduced to a mere remote province of the mighty Mughal Empire, it was still considered one of the richest regions of South Asia. Its ports were used by many pilgrims in the East to travel to Makkah and Madinah. The Mughals were able to establish a very effective administrative and revenue system in the country. Under their firm administration, the region continued to show economic growth.

Many new settlements took place during this period in less populated or uninhabited parts of the Bengal delta, particularly in the south, which, in a way, contributed to the consolidation of Islam in the region. There is a popular expression in Bengali about the old landscape of these marshy lowlands which says: *Jāle Kumīr Dangai Bāgh* (which means: Crocodile in the water and tiger in the land). The semi-nomadic people at the edge of the Sundarban forest region in the south, locally known as *Buno* (forest people), depended solely on forest resources (such as hunting and honey collection). Many of them started identifying themselves with Islam as they came in touch with Muslims. Place names in the extreme south such as Bular Ati in Satkhira (literally: seven cucumbers, a symbolic reference to seven agricultural settlements) district, refers to the process of clearing the land from a kind of dense bamboo shoots (*bula* in the local dialect) for settlement.

New settlements in Bengal were quite often named after the pioneers who founded those settlements, such as Maḥmūdpūr (a *pūr* or settlement founded by Maḥmūd) in Satkhira, Mulla Tero Gharia (a settlement of thirteen families under a mulla) near Kushtia city and Baro Gharia (a settlement of twelve families) near the town of Chapai Nawabganj. The settlement process played such an important role in the region that during the colonial period, the English word 'settlement' itself became an important official term in the land and revenue administration. Thus, during the time of the British Raj, settlement surveys were conducted periodically and settlement records were prepared with every meticulous detail of the area on elaborate maps. For example, one of the surveys that took place on both sides of the upper Padma river in Chapai Nawabganj, Murshidabad and Malda districts (in the vicinity of Gaur and Pandua) was known as Diyār (meaning habitation in Arabic and Persian; Diyāṟa in local dialect) settlement, where the settled population claimed to be the descendants of the Afghan soldiers during Muslim rule.[45]

Overall, the Mughal rulers were liberal in their attitude towards their subjects regardless of their religion. Not only did they promote Muslim institutions such as madrasas and masjids through endowments and land grants such as *madad-i-ma'āsh*, but they also occasionally supported Hindu institutions such as mandirs and temples.[46] During this period, the Indo-Persianized syncretic tradition found a new impetus in the region. A class division in Muslim society existed in Bengal from the very beginning, as depicted in the first Islamic inscription from the reign of Sultan 'Alā' Dīn Khaljī, which refers to *khāṣ* (elite) and *'ām* (commoners). The division became more apparent during Mughal rule as a dividing line could easily be seen now between the noble class, the Brahmin class of the Muslim elite known as *ashraf* (nobles), consisting mainly of immigrant Muslims, and the non-Brahmin class of Muslim masses, known as *aṭraf* (sometimes also known as *ajlaf* or *arzal*, meaning people in the periphery, comparable to the term *mlechcha* in Hindu social classification) who formed the bulk of the indigenous Muslim population in the rural areas. With the gradual passing of power into the hands of the East India Company after the decline of Mughal rule in the second half of the eighteenth century, a Hindu version of *ashraf*, known as *bhadrolok* (elite people), replaced the Muslim *ashraf* who had, until then, held most of the administrative and other official and semi-official posts and formed a majority of the rich and middle-class of the Muslim population.

Ironically, it was during the time of the British colonial period that popular Islamic movements created a greater awareness among Muslims of their Islamic identity, and the 'ulamā' started asserting social leadership more vigorously than before. While Bengali 'ulamā' often looked towards north Indian Islamic institutions and 'ulamā' for their intellectual and scholarly direction, they were more successful than their counterparts elsewhere in conveying their religious message to the grass-roots level in rural areas of Bengal. The nineteenth and twentieth centuries witnessed many social, intellectual, religious and political movements in the region. For Muslims, it was an era of self-assertion, reformation, regeneration and, perhaps, reorientation also.

The nineteenth century Muslim struggle against colonial power, particularly the Jihād movement, drew substantial support from the rural masses. However, it antagonized many *ashraf*s as well as a large portion of the traditional *mulla*s, whose vested interests were hurt by the movement, since it rejected the age-old syncretistic tradition. Led by the 'ulamā' of the madrasas, this movement found its frame of reference in Arabia. The egalitarian nature of the movement necessarily resulted in class conflict between the Bengal Muslim peasantry and the elite class of both Muslim *ashraf* and Hindu *bhadrolok*. But at the same time, it strengthened the Islamic identity of the Muslim masses in vast rural areas of Bengal, many of whom were still Muslims by name only.

The Jihād movement (sometimes branded as the Mawlawī Movement) had a profound impact as a large number of the Bengali followers of Sayyid Aḥmad Shahīd (1786–1831) and his disciple Sayyid Ismā'īl Shahīd (1779–1831) travelled to many remote regions of Kashmir and the North West Frontier Province to participate in jihād. Some of these *mujāhidūn* (freedom fighters) went as far as Yaghistan and Chamarqand in Afghanistan, for training and safe refuge.[47] Mawlānā 'Ināyat 'Alī (1792–1858), the brother of Mawlānā Wilāyat Alī (1790–1852) and one of the deputies of Sayyid Aḥmad Shahīd, spent almost twelve of the last years of his life as an Islamic activist deeply engaged in *da'wa* (Islamic propagation) in various parts of Bengal. The village of Hakimpur in Jessore served as his headquarters at one point. The movement, referred to sometimes as Ṭarīqa Muḥammadiya, gained popular support particularly in the western and northern districts of Bengal. Many of its followers became known later on as Ahl al-Ḥadīth because of their strict adherence to the Qur'ān and Sunna. They are still numerous in certain parts of those areas.

The institution of the ḥajj provides an ideal occasion for Muslims all over the world to interact with each other. It played a key role in re-centring the Muslim world after the onslaught of the Mongols and the demise of the Baghdad Caliphate. The pilgrims in the Holy Lands imbibed the original teachings of the Prophet and his companions, and then returned to their homeland to serve as beacons of the 'true Islam' to peoples at the edge whose Islam, in strict interpretation of *sunnah*, in their opinion, was dangerously encrusted with local custom and syncretic belief. For many, it was also a rare opportunity for exposure to different pan-Islamic and revolutionary movements such as the Wahhabi (more accurately Salafī) movement in the Arabian peninsula. Muslim activists such as Ḥājjī Sharī'at Allah, a pioneer of the Farā'iḍī movement (a symbolic reference to *farḍ* or fundamental religious duties and obligations), and, later on, his son Dudu Miah were profoundly influenced by the movement of Shaykh Muḥammad ibn 'Abd al-Wahhāb in the Arabian peninsula as well as the Jihād movement. Tītūmīr (Sayyid Mīr Nithār 'Alī, 1782–1831), an anti-colonial Islamic activist and leader of peasant uprisings in Bengal, was another forerunner of these movements. Influenced by Sayyid Aḥmad Bareilliwī in Makkah while on the ḥajj, Tītūmīr called for a revival of the original teaching of Islam stripped of the influence of syncretic culture and tradition. A pioneer of the Bengali egalitarian 'ulamā', Tītūmīr called for a kind of class struggle (misunderstood by Karl Marx, who regarded it as merely a sort of religious fanaticism)[48] firmly based on Islamic ideology which has continued in different forms and under various names to our own times, such as the political movement led by the peasant leader Mawlānā Bhasani (d. 1976).[49] While analysing the social and religious history of this period, we also have to note a new development in society, that is, the spread of religious debates known as *baḥth* or *munāẓira* between the traditionalists (Sābiqī) and the reformists (known by various names linked to different movements such as the Ta'yyunī school[50] of Mawlānā Kirāmat 'Alī [1800–1873]) which contributed indirectly to a greater religious awareness in society, for in the remote rural areas many Muslims had still not been exposed to formal Islamic teaching and were Muslims in name only. All of these different elements played almost the same role as a relatively modern Islamic movement, the Tablīghī Jamā'a, is playing today.

Until the end of the eighteenth century, lower Bengal, and more particularly, its southern areas, were sparsely populated. In 1793 for instance, only 60 per cent of Bengal was cultivated. But in 1900, Bengal became one of the most densely populated cultivated areas in South Asia with a rapid increase in its Muslim population. Until the mid-nineteenth century, Bengal was, somehow considered to be inhabited largely by low-caste Hindus, described as 'semi-amphibious aborigines of Bengal', by H. Beverly, author of the very first census report of Bengal. They were, according to him, 'merely the hewers of wood and drawers of water for a set of masters in whose eyes they were unclean beasts and altogether abominable'.[51] However, the census of 1872, the first of its kind in the region, produced an unexpected result. Surprising as it was to the colonial power, it was found that Muslims constituted more than one-third of the total population of Bengal, most of them farmers. This census, however, was not a perfect one, since the Muslim population did not participate in it wholeheartedly, as they were suspicious about the intentions of the British colonials in conducting it. Many of them thought that listing their names in the census report as Muslims was not free from danger since it could be used to identify them as potential participants in anti-colonial struggles such as the Jihād movement. However, the census process itself contributed indirectly to making the Muslim rural population aware of its Islamic identity. Faced with new challenges and growing pressure both from colonial rule and local Hindu landlords, a sense of solidarity grew among the Muslims which made them realize that they were part of the *ummah* (a traditional concept about the Muslims as a single united nation) that stretched beyond any geographic boundaries. The next few censuses, especially those held in 1881, 1891 and 1901, produced more accurate results, as the Muslims began to understand that the census process was not a plot against them. The growing cooperation of the Muslims in the census made the later census reports more accurate and reliable, and they reported a rapid growth in the Muslim population. Of these, the 1901 census produced the startling statistical development that Muslims had become the overwhelming majority of the rural population, particularly in eastern, southern and northern Bengal, an unexpected demographic change even noticed by Bengali literary laureates of the time such as Tagore and Sharat Chandra Chattapadhdhay in their extremely popular novels and short stories.[52]

At different times, Bengal played an important role in shaping the political destiny of the Muslims in South Asia. It was in Dhaka – the capital of the province of East Bengal and Assam in British India – that the Muslim League was founded towards the end of 1906. Its leaders as well as the masses took part in the struggle for Pakistan. Its role as the most populous Pakistani province, and later on its liberation from Pakistan to become a fully independent country, is a long and interesting story, but one beyond the scope of this study.

Royalty and ruling establishment

The history of Muslim rule in Bengal is full of events and developments. Bengal witnessed major changes during this period in almost every sphere of life as Islam started spreading in different corners of this region. Some of the early sources such as *Riyāḍ al-Salāṭīn* offer a few accounts of the royal palaces, the public and private lives of the rulers, their interests and day to day activities, ethnic background, legal and actual positions, patronage of art and culture, religious leanings, contact with the outside world and many other facets of the ruling class. The foundation as well as the continuity of Muslim rule was not an easy process, for some of the rulers were actually born outside the region and thus could be viewed as foreigners in the land that they ruled. Even if they were born in the region, they inherited an ancestry that originated outside, most probably in Khurasan (particularly in the present region of Afghanistan) or Central Asia. The problem of legitimacy, henceforth, could sometimes undermine their claims as rulers. Moreover, very few of them had royal ancestry in a strict sense. In fact, the very foundation of the Muslim ruling establishment of Bengal was laid by those who rose to higher ranks in the army from ordinary and humble backgrounds (such as slaves). The difficulties that many of them faced were enormous; the challenges in front of them were quite often countless. Yet the Bengali Sultanate prospered from time to time, and lasted for two centuries (740–944/1339–1538). The civilization and culture that grew up under the patronage of these sultans were not only fabulous, but were also all-embracing. They stimulated not only Muslims of different ethnic origins and backgrounds from various regions of the Islamic world and more particularly from the Persian world of Central Asia, but they also encouraged the participation of the local population, many of whom were Hindus. A very interesting aspect of Muslim rule in Bengal is the Hindu–Muslim relation itself. Non-Muslims in general lived in harmony with the Muslims to which the ruling class belonged. Their rights were normally well-protected. Seldom was there any destruction of their temples in peace time.

The deeply rooted Persian culture of the Muslim capitals influenced almost every aspect of the elite's lives, from titles to court language, as can be conclusively inferred from the first and third inscriptions of Bengal rendered in Persian. The rulers and administrators were sometimes eager to create new urban centres and cities as symbols of their authority and power. They over-guarded their interests, typical of the ruling class. A few of them were absorbed in pastimes or were obsessed with sensual pleasures. Some of them kept large harems. Many were inspired by philanthropic ideas as they carried out numerous welfare projects for the general public as well as the elite (*khayr kardah dar ḥaqq-i-khāṣ 'ām*, as expressed in Persian in the very first Islamic inscription [ins. no. 1] of Bengal). During their reign, many important educational institutions (e.g. madrasa) and hospitals (*bīmāristān*) were established. These welfare activities played a crucial role in the diffusion of Islam.

In spite of many glories and successes, these rulers in general failed to achieve some basic developments at the national and state levels. Their reign witnessed very little progress in science, engineering, advanced scholarship, higher education and, most importantly, mass education. In spite of Islam's encouragement of education for everyone, the idea of mass education was never given any serious consideration during the Muslim rule in Bengal. Hence this new civilization making process failed to earn popular participation in some of the very basic areas of a civil society, namely education.

From the point of a long-term defence policy, very few Bengali rulers were able to create a strong naval force in this riverine deltaic region that could protect them from potential naval attacks coming from the Bay of Bengal in the south. Thus during Mughal rule, the southern part of the region became an easy target for the Magh pirates of Arakan, Portuguese and other European naval powers. Lack of advancement in military technology was one of the prime reasons for their loss of power finally to the East India Company.

Commerce and maritime activities

Commerce and trade played important roles in the formation of an international system in the Old World. In spite of occasional setbacks, these traditional methods of trade continued in the Muslim world for centuries. In his remarkable travelogue *Deshe-Bideshe* (Bengali text), Sayyid Mujtaba Ali, a famous Bengali writer, provides a lucid eye-witness description of the thriving caravan routes in

Afghanistan in the early part of the twentieth century which once connected Central Asia with many neighbouring countries including Bengal. These commercial links were the natural outcome of traditional societies based on need and supply, rather than aggressive marketing policies through highly organized professional networks, which were yet to be introduced by Europeans at a later time. In spite of having little or sometimes no state support from the ruling establishment, these traditional trade-links and commercial activities flourished for centuries. They declined only after losing ground to their aggressive European rivals, who did not hesitate to use their far superior naval power to monopolize Asian commerce and maritime trade routes.

There are a few important sources in Arabic, Persian and Turkish as well as South Asian languages that provide us with details about Muslim maritime activities. For example, both the remarkable works of the early sixteenth century Omani captain Sulaymān ibn Aḥmad ibn Sulaymān – *al-'Umda al-Mahriyyah fī Ḍabt al-'Ulūm al-Baḥriyyah* and *al-Minhāj al-Fākhir fī 'Ilm al-Baḥr al-Zākhir* discuss in detail maritime routes, tides, waves, currents and the directions of winds in the Bay of Bengal and also effective ways of using these elements in sailing. These were the secrets to success for Muslim sailing activities in the Indian Ocean, which had yet to be passed to European sailors enabling them to set out on their own Asian maritime adventures.

Mosques: the nucleus of Islamic society

In his famous *Muqaddima*, Ibn Khaldūn observed that architecture is the most powerful visual expression of *al-'umrān* (civilization). Islamic civilization attached great importance to architecture. Rulers are often tempted to treat architecture as a symbolic act for legitimacy, power and grandiosity. The mosque, the key to Islamic architecture, is a natural expression of Islamic society and the nucleus of the religious, spiritual and social life of the community. As its root *sjd* (meaning prostration) indicates, *masjid* (mosque) is a visual embodiment of the spiritual realm of Islam, where the relation between architecture and Islamic belief is clearly visible. It is the very form of the mosque, its minaret, minbar and different other architectural vocabularies that communicate a powerful visual language of Islamic culture. The long arcade on the both sides of the *saḥn* (courtyard) leading finally towards the vast space of the *qibla* (hall) reminds visitors of the transition from earthly life to eternal life. The direction of every miḥrāb towards *qibla* (i.e. Ka'ba) symbolizes the unity of *ummah* (Muslim people) and conveys the powerful message of *tawḥīd* (Divine unity). The mosque has a strong appeal to its community members for it attracts a large gathering many times a day, not to mention the Friday congregation of *Jum'a* prayer. Thus it integrates the overall life of Muslims.

One may be surprised to note that the number of mosques in Bengal as well as in many other Muslim countries, still remains higher than the number of primary schools. One of the underlying reasons for this is that among the multifaceted functions of mosques in Islamic societies, until very recently, they often

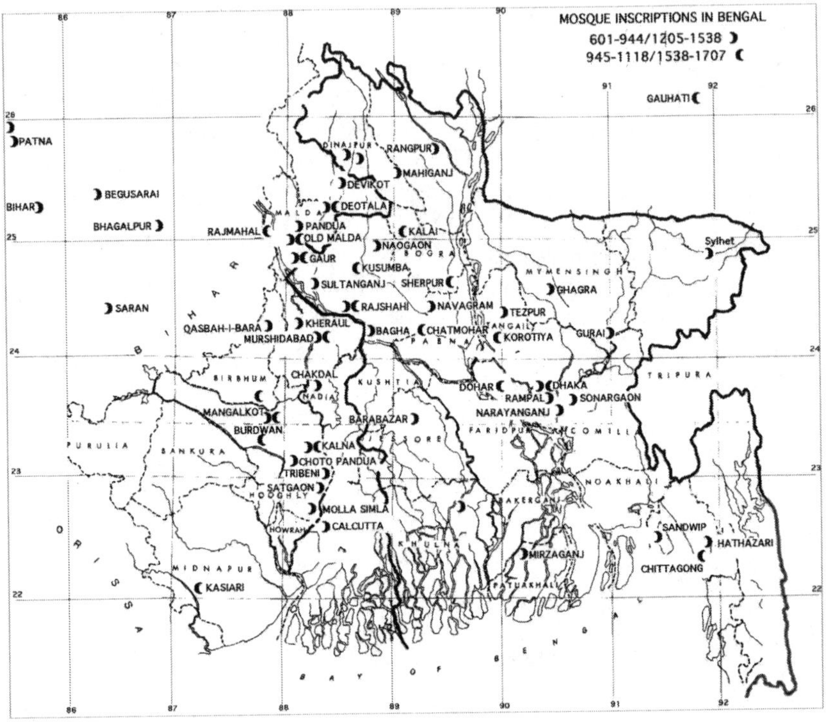

Figure 2.1 Diffusion of mosques in medieval Bengal (source: copyright by author).

served as *maktab* or primary schools for their communities. In urban settings, sometimes we find a shopping arcade or market place added to the mosque complex, which is again symbolic of the fact that the activities of daily life are not divorced from the practice of religion. Thus, mosques are built for the continuous flow of the surrounding population towards them like some other religious traditions.

In a way, every new Islamic settlement in Bengal evolved around a congregational mosque. Construction of public places such as markets, inns, caravansaries, hospitals, fountains, wells and ponds around the central mosque in the city centre not only created a bridge between the religious domain and public sphere, but also helped spread welfare activities on a popular level, which ultimately helped spread Islam in the region. This is particularly true in Bengal, where the construction of mosques and the welfare activities of the Bengali sultans played an important role in introducing Islam to the local population. Quite a few early Islamic inscriptions refer to these public works.[53]

Among the Islamic inscriptions of Bengal dating from 1204 to 1707, mosque inscriptions constitute the most numerous (approximately 300), a phenomenon that points to the important role mosques played in overall religious, social and cultural life.[54] Like elsewhere, mosques evolved as powerful social institutions and symbols of new settlements in Bengal. At times, they served as meeting places for Muslims and the local population, both intellectually and socially, and contributed to the diffusion of Islam. In the earliest surviving Islamic literary work in Bengal, *Ḥawḍ al-Ḥayāt*, it is mentioned that non-Muslims were welcomed to visit mosques, inquire about Islam and even debate religious issues. Opening the gates of masjids and *jāmi*'s to non-Muslims must have had a positive effect on the popular sentiment in a land where entrance to mandirs and temples was often restricted to upper castes in Aryan Vedic culture. In some rare cases, even wealthy and influential Hindus supported mosque construction as a part of public works.

One fascinating aspect of natural harmony can be found in the traditional architecture of the Bengali mosque, which is seen as fitting within a natural setting rather than forcing itself on its surroundings. The monumental mosque architecture of the fabulous capitals, such as Gaur, Pandua, Dhaka, Murshidabad and Rajmahal, gives us a different message, as this architecture represents royal patronage and majestic taste. Both the Adina mosque of Pandua (founding inscription dated 776/1374) and Shāit-Gumbuj masjid of Bagerhat (see the tombstone of the founder of this congregational mosque dated 863/1459) are still considered among the largest mosques ever built in South Asia, perhaps, in all of the old world of Islam.

Despite its stature, the overall nature of Islamic art and architecture in Bengal is not imposing; rather, it belongs to the natural background in its basic character. While royal patronage helped construct hundreds of mosques in and around the capitals and other big cities and occasionally in small towns in the vast rural areas of the Bengal, simple forms of vernacular mosques are used for daily prayers that draw their architectural vocabularies from local traditions and natural settings. Typical examples are the Bengali village mosques that have thatched roofs and mud walls, somewhat similar to the original Masjid al-Nabawi (the Prophet's mosque), one of the earliest mosques in Madinah. Often, natural ponds are attached to these Bengali mosques. These serve as a place of *wuḍū* (ablution), which at the same time helps create an aesthetic effect on the landscape of the surroundings. Interestingly, the simple vernacular mosque architecture in the vast rural areas of Bengal bore, until very recently, a striking similarity with the hypostyle rectangular planning of the original Prophet's mosque in Madinah. In some remote rural areas where palm-groves are abundant such as in the Arabian desert or the villages of northern Bengal, even palm-grove pillars can be seen supporting the roof of the prayer hall. The *Saḥn* (courtyard) is another legacy of the Prophet's mosque that can be seen in many village mosques in a great part of the rural area in Bengal. It is interesting to note that many of these architectural traditions of mosque design have been followed across the ages without conscious effort to associate them with the design of the original Prophet's mosque. Thus in its basic characteristics, there is a continuity in mosque architecture from the time of the Prophet to this day, even in the far-flung region of Bengal. These simple praying structures spread all over the rural areas of Bengal, often serving as the nuclei of Bengali Muslim villages across the region. Most of the mosques in Bengali villages are still built in this traditional way, often with the collective resources of the poor rural folk (and in most cases with the active support of religious laymen in the area). The vernacular architecture of Muslim villages reminds us that the focus of Islamic architecture should not be solely on building; rather, it should be on the people and their environment and nature.

This simple form of prayer place also contributed to the easy acceptance of Islam by rural folk. While most urban mosques were constructed under the patronage of sultans, members of the royal family, viziers, officials and wealthy men and women of the cities (e.g. the generous lady Boa Maloti of Purulia in Gaur [see Jahānniyan Jāmi‘ Masjid Inscription dated 941/1534–1535]), rural mosques came into existence either due to the common efforts of community members, or through the individual initiatives of religious personalities such as sufi shaykhs, 'ulamā' and even petty religious laymen. These rural mosques helped in the formation of new settlements through clearing forests, particularly in the southern part of the Bengal delta and eventually the consolidation of Islam in the region.[55] Quite often, these mosques received tax-free land grants. The revenue generated through the cultivation of these lands supported the maintenance of the mosque as well as of the people attached to it, particularly its caretakers. The institution of endowment, known as *madad-i-ma'āsh*, provided financial support to religious institutions, such as mosques, madrasas and khānqāhs, as well as to those who were attached to them, such as imāms, sufis, 'ulamā' and even to poor and destitute commoners attending those institutions (see inscription at Bahrām Saqqā' Shrine, dated 1015/1606–1607; and Brarakatra inscription, dated 1055/1645).[56] Sometimes these land grants were awarded directly to pioneers who founded mosques in distant remote areas which were inaccessible and previously uninhabited, such as in forests and the newly emerged lands in the delta caused by the changing patterns of the river channels in Bengal. The District Collectorate Record Rooms of Bengal, particularly in Noakhali, Sylhet and Chittagong still preserve a number of Mughal land deeds (*Sanad*), mostly in Persian, that refer to the establishment of such mosques with endowment lands granted by local administrative authorities.[57]

During the late Sultanate and Mughal periods, the institution of *madad-i-ma'āsh* played a key role in the massive growth of mosques everywhere in Bengal (see Nayabari ins., dated 1003/1595). Mosques thus played a very important role in new human settlements and the formation of agrarian societies in the sparsely populated lower delta and the forest areas in eastern and southern Bengal as new villages started emerging around the newly founded mosques supported by *madad-i-ma'āsh*.

The role of 'ulamā' and madrasas in the transmission of knowledge

Madrasas, as recorded by a number of inscriptions, played a pivotal role in diffusing education and in creating a class of 'ulamā' who spread Islamic education throughout the region together with sufis, most of whom were also great Islamic scholars. Madrasas were necessary for providing a large pool of educated professionals to fill various social, administrative, official and government ranks. Consequently they had a positive influence on the social, economic and cultural growth of the region. In the past, these institutions played the same role that modern educational institutions such as universities and colleges play in our modern period. Educated elite from madrasas assumed various roles and responsibilities in society. Thus, *qāḍīs* would act as teachers and imāms, while 'ulamā' would also be engaged in trade and commerce or in medical practice. Minhāj al-Dīn Sirāj gives us some information about the establishment of madrasas in Bengal by the early Muslim rulers.[58] Inscriptions offer information on the locations, dates of construction, names of patrons and so on, and help us identify centres of learning. In some cases, this information sheds light on links between the institutions, the transmission of ideas, student–teacher connections and intellectual genealogies.

There were many famous madrasas, *madrasa-bāris* and *dars-bāris* (i.e. school; *dars* means lesson, *bāri* in Bengali means house or building) throughout the country where learning flourished. Congregational mosques often served as

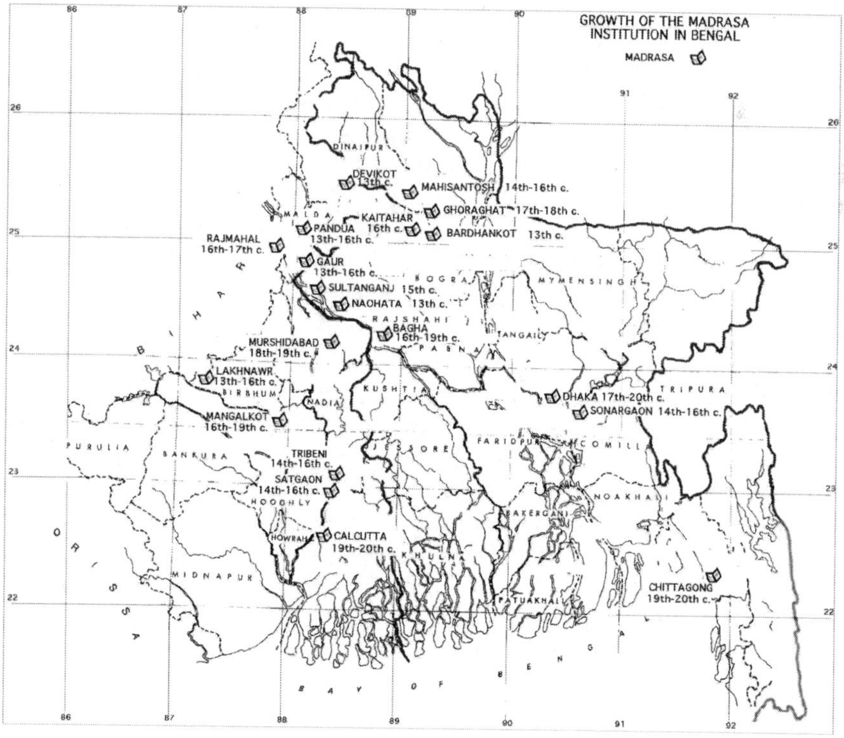

Figure 2.2 Growth of the madrasa institution in medieval Bengal (source: copyright by author).

centres of higher learning and masjids often functioned as *maktab*s, as they still do in many cases. An early inscription from Naohata from the reign of Balkā Khān (626–28/1229–1231) records such a mosque that also served as an academy for the area where scholarly subjects were discussed. Epigraphic texts suggest that the capital Gaur evolved as one of the earliest intellectual and cultural centres in the north. It had numerous mosques (more than fifty mosque inscriptions have been discovered in the area), madrasas and khānqāhs as early as in the thirteenth century. Another early capital of the north, Ḥaḍrat Pandua (similarly rich in inscriptions), also became a prosperous cultural centre where many mosques and madrasas flourished. In eastern Bengal, Sonārgā'on (near Dhaka) became a famous educational centre after the arrival of the famous Ḥanbalī scholar Shaykh Sharaf al-Dīn Abū Tawwāma in the middle of the fourteenth century. Abū Tawwāma's fame attracted many students to Sonārgā'on madrasa from different corners of the Islamic world. Shaykh Sharaf al-Dīn Yaḥyā Manerī, who became a well-known sufi figure of the Subcontinent, also attended this madrasa. Tandah, Rajmahal, Murshidabad and Jahangirnagar (today's Dhaka) became noted centres of learning in the sixteenth and seventeenth centuries. In northern Bengal, Ghoraghat, in the present district of Dinajpur, attracted many 'ulamā' and students during the Mughal period. In southwest Bengal, Tribeni and Chota Pandua (in the present district of Hooghly) had a number of madrasas (the earliest one, Dār al-Khayrāt, was established around 713/1313 according to an early inscription), during the Sultanate period. The town of Mangalkot (in the present district of Burdwan), not far from Tribeni, also earned fame as a great seat of learning, a reputation it maintained until the nineteenth century. In the southeast corner of Bengal, Chittagong evolved as the main educational centre where the Madrasa Muḥsiniyyah in the nineteenth century and the Hathazari madrasa in the twentieth century played a crucial role in spreading Islamic education.

The cultural interactions of the Bengal Sultanate often surpassed the political and geographical boundaries of South Asia. Many 'ulamā' and sufis came to and settled in Bengal from Central Asia, Asia Minor and the Arab world. Some of the madrasas and khānqāhs that they established attracted students from other regions. Sultan A'ẓam Shāh had two madrasas built during 813–814 (1410–1411), one near Umm al-Hānī gate (situated on al-Rukn al-Yamani or Yamani corner) of al-Ḥaram al-Makkī (the Grand Mosque) at Makkhah,[59] and the other near Bāb al-Salām (the Gate of Peace) of the Prophet's mosque at Madinah. He also endowed a large property to support these two institutions which were considered among the best seminaries in the region during that period. Renowned scholars, such as Shaykh Taqī al-Dīn al-Fāsī (775–832/1374–1428), a pioneer in the field of epigraphy, taught Maliḳi school of *fiqh* (jurisprudence) at the al-Madrasa al-Sulṭāniyyah al-Ghiyāthiyyah al-Bangāliyyah (named after its Bengali patron al-Sulṭān Ghiyāth al-Dīn A'ẓam Shāh) in Makkah. Construction of this madrasa began in the month of Ramaḍān in 813 (1411) and was finally completed in 814 (1412). A number of scholars from the family of Shībī (who became famous through their educational and scholarly activities in Makkah during the fifteenth century) taught at this madrasa. A few prominent Makkan scholars attached to this madrasa, as mentioned by al-Fāsī, were, Qāḍī Jamāl al-Dīn Muḥammad ibn ʻAbd Allāh al-Qarshī (d. 817/1414), Shihāb al-Dīn Abū 'l-Khayr Aḥmad ibn Muḥammad al-Sāghānī (d. 825/1422), Qāḍī Muḥy al-Dīn ʻAbd al-Qādir al-Ḥusaynī al-Fāsī (d. 827/1424) and Shaykh Abu 'l-Ḥasan ʻAlī ibn Aḥmad al-Mārdīnī al-Ḥaṣkafī (d. 825/1422).[60] The syllabus of this madrasa covered *fiqh* of the four famous schools of Islamic sharīʻa, which, in a way, indicates the liberal policy and religious tolerance that prevailed in Bengal. Sultan Jalāl al-Dīn (r. 1414–1433) also sent generous endowments to Makkah and Madinah to establish two madrasas there which came to be known as al-Madrasah al-Bangāliyyah too over time.

Bengali students often travelled for their religious training to famous centres of learning in Jaunpur and Delhi, and sometimes as far away as Khurasan, Central Asia and Arabia. The Dār al-ʻUlūm in Deoband, Maẓāhir al-ʻUlūm in Saharanpur, Madrasa Raḥmāniya in Delhi and Nadwat al-ʻUlamā' in Lucknow attracted many students from Bengal during the colonial period and afterwards. Many of the ʻulamā' who graduated from these madrasas returned to establish their own madrasas in Bengal, a tradition that still continues.

Most of these madrasas followed a model known as al-Madrasa al-Niẓāmiyya that started appearing first in Baghdad, Nishapur and many other important cities in Khurasan under the patronage of Niẓām al-Mulk, the famous intellectual Abbasside vizier, in the eleventh century. Soon afterward, these institutions spread to the central and the eastern parts of the Islamic world, from Anatolia in the west to Bengal in the east. In South Asia, the curriculum was known as *Dars-i-Niẓāmi* (after Mulla Niẓām al-Dīn of Aurangzeb's time), in which a special emphasis was given to the Ḥanafī *fiqh*. At times, these institutions contributed significantly to promoting *al-ʻulūm al-naqliyyah*, namely, transmitted (classical/religious scholarship) as well as *al-ʻulūm al-ʻaqliyyah* (rational knowledge or sciences).

After the first war of independence in 1857, the vast majority of ʻulamā' turned their attention to Islamic education, which they considered an alternative to armed struggle against colonial rule or *jihād*. This process of arming the younger generation with educational power was itself a sort of lesser *jihād*, albeit a passive one, for it neglected the modern sciences (*al-ʻulūm al-ḥadīthah*) and concentrated solely on classical religious scholarship (*al-ʻulūm al-naqliyyah*). In doing so, the institution of madrasa, which once contributed greatly to the growth of intellectual and scientific advancement in the Islamic world, adopted a closed door policy, reducing its sphere of academic interest to the preservation of a selection of classical Islamic scholarship. Undoubtedly, the changing political environment led these ʻulamā' to follow this passive path as participation of many of them in the Jihād movement had made the colonial powers suspicious about their activities, and madrasa institutions came under special scrutiny.

Most of the pre-colonial madrasas during Muslim rule were supported by endowments, until the East India Company passed orders in 1828 to acquire all *awqāf* (endowments) of madrasa, depriving these institutions completely from their main source of income. The final blow came during the time of Lord Harding when he passed a law in 1844 forbidding graduates of Persian and Arabic (non-governmental Islamic) madrasas to be given employment in government. Even the official jobs of *qāḍī* with the government, previously exclusively reserved for madrasa graduates, were now offered only to those formally trained in British law.

Still, the colonial power could not completely override local custom, law and culture since they needed to understand them in order to run their administration smoothly. To find a solution, they embarked on introducing new curriculum and institutions which would accommodate both classical and modern education, effectively serving the needs of the British administration without abruptly upsetting the traditional values of local communities. Thus, towards the end of the eighteenth century, a new curriculum was introduced under government patronage at Calcutta madrasa which was established in 1781 during the time of Governor-General Warren Hastings (1773–1784). With the passage of time, it became famous as Calcutta 'Ālia madrasa, which is still in operation today (with a recent change in its name to 'Ālia University). In this institution, secular subjects such as Bengali and English language and literature were added, to the traditional theology curriculum. Later on, all government-sponsored madrasas which taught this new curriculum became known as 'āliya madrasas (literally: higher institutes). Though they initially were not popular with the mainstream rural Muslim population as they received support from the British raj, slowly and gradually, 'āliya madrasas spread throughout Bengal. Since independence, 'āliya madrasas have spread further in the region; thousands of students graduate from 'āliya madrasas every year.

Notes

1 *Ṭabaqāt-i-Nāṣirī*, ed. 'Abd al-Ḥay Ḥabībī (Kabul, AH 1342): 425–467.
2 Chakrabarti Dilip K., *Ancient Bangladesh: A Study of the Archaeological Sources* (Dhaka: University Press Ltd, 2001): 25.
3 Niharranjan Ray, *History of the Bengali People* (*Ancient Period*), trans. with an introduction by John W. Hood (Calcutta: Orient Longman Ltd, 1994): 84.
4 For details on Sundarban, see *Encyclopaedia of Islam*, 2nd edn, s.v. 'Sundarban'.
5 For details on Ruhmī, see *Encyclopaedia of Islam*, 2nd edn, s.v. 'Ruhmī'.
6 Aḥmad ibn Abī Ya'qūb, *Tā'rīkh Ya'qūbī*, ed. M. Th. Houtsma (Leiden: E. J. Brill, 1960): 106.
7 Al-Hamadānī, *Kitāb al-Boldān*, ed. M. J. De Goeje (Leiden: E. J. Brill, 1967): 15.
8 *Sharaf al-Zamān Ṭāhir Marvazī on China, the Turks and India*, ed. and trans. V. Minorsky (London: Royal Asiatic Society, 1942): text 35.
9 Sulaymān al-Tājir and Ābū Zayd al-Sīrāfī, *Akhbār al-Ṣīn wa 'l-Hind* (237/851), ed. and trans. J. Sauvaget, *Relation de la China et l'Inde* (Paris: Sociētē 'ēdition, 1948): text 13–14.
10 *Kitāb al Masālik wa 'l-Mamālik*, ed. M. J. De Goeje (Leiden: E. J. Brill, 1967): 63–67.
11 Trans. V. Minorsky (London: Oxford University Press, 1937): 87.
12 Shahnaj Husne Jahan, *Excavating Waves and Winds of (Ex)change: A Study of Maritime Trade in Early Bengal* (Oxford: British Archaeological Reports (BAR), John and Erica Hedges Ltd, 2006): 43–50.

13 M. Mohar Ali, *History of the Muslims of Bengal*, vol. 1A (Riyadh: Imām Muḥammad ibn Sa'ūd Islamic University, 1985): 33–35.
14 *Encyclopaedia of Islam*, 2nd edn, s.v. 'Ruhmī'.
15 For details, see Dinesh Chandra Sarkar, 'Mainamatir Chandra Bangshiyo Tamra Shasantroy', in *Abdul Karim Sahitya Visharad Commemorative Volume*, ed. Mohammad Enamul Hoque (Dacca: Asiatic Society of Pakistan, 1972).
16 A place by the name of Sakanat appears in a map in an early European work, *His Pilgrims*, by Samuel Purcha.
17 Minhāj al-Dīn, *Ṭabaqāt-e-Naṣirī*, ed. W. N. Lees (Calcutta, 1863–1864): 148–153.
18 It is a compound Persian name meaning new village (*naw* means new, and *deh* or *diyah* means village or villages [particularly in the low and marshy land]). The name itself bears a great sociological implication as it symbolizes the new settlements that started appearing in this hinterland right after Bakhtiyār's campaign. The more accepted form of spelling in Bengal – *Nawdiya* (*Navadipa* in Sanskrit) – can also be interpreted as new lamp which is quite interesting since it symbolizes the advent of light (Islam) in the Bengal frontier with its conquest by Muslim forces. There were a number of villages that once bore the name of Nawdah in the districts of Malda, Chapai Nawabganj and Murshidabad, such as the present *mauja* (village) of Uttar 'Umarpur, on the southeast of Gaur (or more precisely the present village of Mahdipur), about one kilometre west of Kotwali Darwaza. But it is the archaeological site of Nawdapara, near Rohanpur railway station in Chapai Nawabganj district which was most likely the capital of Lakhshman Sen conquered by Bakhtiyār. The site consists of a huge mound of old baked bricks of the type used in the ancient monuments in Gaur and the surrounding area. Local traditions still identify the ruins as Lakhkhan Sener Bari (Lakhshman Sen Palace) which had a back door (for emergency escape, known in Bengali as *Khirki*) opening to a jetty on Mahanada river. Another set of nearby ruins of a monument is locally known as Nawda Burj (sometimes also as Shāṛ Burj), apparently a victory tower built by Bakhtiyār after his sudden conquest of the capital.
19 From it, the land on both sides of the river Padma (Ganges) in Chapai Nawabganj, Mushidabad and Malda districts became gradually known as Diyaṟ, and the Muslim population of the area as Diyaṟa, and occasionally as Shērshabadiya (author's own clan) referring to their ancestral link to Afghan soldiers of Shēr Shāh Sūrī in the region. Shērshabadiya may possibly have also been a reference to the Muslim inhabitants of the area, known previously as Shēr Shāh Ābād Parganah. Their Bengali dialect is heavily influenced by Persian (e.g. the Persian adjective *khasta* [tired] in Bengali is a verb form meaning getting tired).
20 Sulaymān ibn Aḥmad ibn Sulaymān al-Mahrī, *al-Minhāj al-Fākhir fi 'Ilm 'l-Baḥr al-Zākhir*, ed. Ibrahim Khuri (Damascus, 1970): 16–27; idem., *'Umda al-Mahriyya fī Ḍabṭ al-'Ulūm al-Baḥriyya* (Damascus, 1970), 113–120.
21 The most brilliant discussion about these theories can be found in Richard M. Eaton, *The Rise of Islam and the Bengal Frontier, 1204–1760* (Berkeley, CA: University of California Press, 1993): 113.
22 See also, Eaton, *The Rise of Islam*, 268–303.
23 Some of the royal titles in the early Islamic inscriptions, such as *malādh al-warā* (shelter of mankind) *Rukn al-Danā* (support of the commoners) in the madrasa inscription at Ẓafar Khān Masjid in Tribeni dated 698/1298 (ins. no. 12), indicate this trend.
24 Minhāj al-Dīn, *Ṭabaqāt-e-Nāṣirī*, ed. W. N. Lees (Calcutta, 1863–1864): 149–153.
25 *JASB*, 47 (1898):116.
26 Mohar Ali, *History of the Muslims of Bengal*, vol. 1: 36.
27 Mohammad Yusuf Siddiq, 'An Epigraphical Journey to an Islamic Land', *Muqarnas*, 7 (1990): 83–108.
28 *JASB*, 13 (1844): 36.

29 Muhammad Enamul Haq, *Purbo Pakistane Islam* (Dhaka, 1948): 17; M. A. Rahim points out, 'Reading of term *Thu-ra-tan* as *Sulṭān* cannot be dismissed as fantastic.' He thinks that it is reasonable to suggest that the term *surtan* is an Arakanese corruption of *sulṭān* since such a word did not exist in Arakanese or Buddhist tradition. The *sulṭān* was the 'chief of the influential community of Arab merchants in the Chittagong locality, not the ruler of a kingdom covering the Chittagong and Noakhali districts, as it is supposed'; see Muhammad Abdur Rahim, *Social and Cultural History of Bengal*, vol. 1, CE 1201–1576 (Karachi, 1963): 44.

30 Cortesão, *The Suma Oriental of Tomé Pires* (London: Hakluyt Society, 2010): 142.

31 Abū 'Abd Allah Yāqūt al-Ḥamawī, *Mu'jam al-Buldān*, vol. 4 (Cairo: Matba' al-Sa'āda, 1906): 213; Gabriel Ferrand, *Relations de Voyages et Textes Gēographiques Arabes*, Persans et Turks (Paris, 1913): 180–181.

32 Mohar Ali, *History of the Muslims of Bengal*, vol. 1: 225.

33 Eaton, *The Rise of Islam*, 308.

34 This date can be confirmed based on numerous beautiful gold and silver coins that were intricately struck in the mints of Gaur and Delhi in the consecutive years of Bakhtiyār's victory, some of which are now preserved in Delhi Museum, the British Museum and the Smithsonian Institution. Almost all of these coins depict a horseman charging at full gallop holding a mace in his hand, symbolizing the powerful cavalry of the Muslims that helped them conquer this land. See Parameshwari Lal Gupta, 'The Date of Bakhtiyār Khiljī's Occupation of Gauḍa', *Journal of the Varendra Research Museum*, 4 (1975–76): 29–34; G. S. Farid, 'Hitherto Unknown Silver Tankah of Sultan Alauddin Ali Mardan Khilji, 607–610 A.H', *Journal of the Asiatic Society*, 18, 1–4 (1976): 104–106; John Deyell, *Living without Silver: The Monetary History of Early Medieval North India* (Delhi: Oxford University Press, 1990), 364–367, coin no. 298.

35 Nicholas W. Lowick, 'The Horseman Type of Bengal and the Question of Commemorative Issues', *Journal of the Numismatic Society of India*, 35 (1973): 196–208; idem, *Coinage and History of the Islamic World*, vol. XVII (Aldershot: Variorum, 1990): 195–208; Parameshwari Lal Gupta, 'Nagri Legend on Horseman Tankah of Muhammad bin Sam', *Journal of the Numismatic Society of India* 35 (1973): 209–212; Parameshwari Lal Gupta, 'On the Date of the Horseman Type Coin of Muhammad bin Sam', *Journal of the Numismatic Society of India*, 38 (1976): 81–87; *Delhi Museum Catalogue* 6, Coin 3a.

36 Niharanjan Roy, *Bangalir Itihas* (Calcutta, 1359 Bengali year): 501.

37 It was known as Tishu Lamba (the seat of Luma) situated roughly between 20.7° latitude (north) and 89.2° longitude (east), about eighty miles from Rangpur.

38 Minhāj al-Dīn, *Ṭabaqāt-e-Nāṣirī*, ed. W. N. Lees (Calcutta, 1863–1864): 149–153. Mech and various other tribal people still inhabit the northern area of Kochbihar (about twenty-five miles from Alipur), West Bengal and occasionally support local insurgent groups aiming to regain old political entities, such as Kamrup and Kamta lands, that survived contemporaneoulsy with the Bengal Sultanate.

39 See also Eaton, *The Rise of Islam*, 195–227.

40 This influence can be felt more strongly in certain local Bengali dialects used by the rural Muslims of North Bengal, particularly in and around early Muslim capitals such as Gaur and Pandua, and in the dialect of the Shērshabadi clan (to which the author himself belongs) on the both sides of the river Ganges in Malda, Murshidabad and Chapai Nawabganj districts. On the other hand, an Arabic linguistic influence can be observed more in the Bengali dialects of southern Bengal, particularly in Chittagong division.

41 For instance, see Rawḍa Inscription in Barahdari dated 663/1268 (ins. no. 7) and Rawḍa Inscription in Mahasthangarh dated 700/1300 (ins. no. 13).

42 Muẓaffar Shams Balkhī (d. 1400), for instance, used this port with the permission of Sulṭān Ghiyāth al-Dīn A'ẓam Shāh (r. 1389–1410) to embark on a trip from

Chittagong to Makkah; see Muẓaffar Shams Balkhī, *Maktūbāt-i-Muẓaffar Shams Balkī*, Khuda Bakhsh Oriental Public Library, Patna, Persian MS Acc. no. 1859, Letter 148. See also S. H. Askari, *Maktub and Malfuz Literature as a Source of Socio-Political History* (Patna: Khuda Bakhsh Oriental Public Library, 1981): 16.

43 Taqī al-Dīn al-Fāsī, *al-'Aqd al-Thamīn*, vol. 3 (Beirut: Dār al-Kutub al-'Ilmiyyah, 1998): 26.

44 C. E. Bosworth, *The Islamic Dynasties* (Edinburgh: Edinburgh University Press, 1967): 194–195.

45 Descendants of Afghans and other immigrants from Khurasan and Central Asia gradually assimilated with the local population (e.g. through marriages) and have barely maintained their separate identities in the long run. However, there are still some traditional families which have retained their ancestral family names (i.e. surnames such as Khān, Paththān, Yūsufzai, Lohānī, Afrīdī and Pannī) or have been able to preserve their family trees to some extent indicating their Afghan or Central Asian origin. To cite a typical example, we may mention here a family line (the author's own ancestors) in the village of Gopalganj near Sujnipara railway station in Murshidabad district which claims its ancestry from the Khurasān region. This family originally bore the surname of Khān, though the surname was dropped at some point. The family tree runs as follows: Usama (Shahraaz) Yūsuf > (i.e. son of) ibn Yūsuf Ṣiddiq > ibn Mujīb al-Raḥmān > ibn 'Abd al-Ghanī > ibn Ayyūb Ḥusayn > ibn Ḥājī Shahādat Mondol > ibn Bulāqī Mondol > ibn Nizām al-Dīn Mondol > ibn 'Abd al-Karīm Mondol > ibn Ḥaydar 'Alī Khān. Another branch of this family living in the village of Ambhua near Rajgram railway station in the district of Birbhum records its family tree as following: Kulthūm Bibi (author's grandmother) > bint Mawlānā 'Abd al-Raḥīm > ibn Ḥājjī Qalandar Ḥusayn > ibn Shihāb al-Dīn Khān > ibn La'al Muḥammad Khān > ibn Shēr Khān Peshāwarī. A family line of a female from the same clan in the village of Ambhua is: Mājida Khātūn (mother of Kulthūm Bibi) > bint Taplū Khān > ibn Samīr al-Dīn Khān > ibn Ḍamīr al-Dīn Khān > ibn Nakbīr Khān Paththān. All these three families pioneered a religious movement, known as Ahl al-Ḥadīth, in their respective localities, and supported the Jihād movement against colonial rule in one way or other.

46 'Register of sanads', Sylhet District Collectorate Record Room, nos 17:75, 243, 18; nos 94, 154, 158, 279, 19; nos 334, 618, 619, 20; nos 851, 853, 959; nos 397, 400.

47 The name *Yāghistān* (lit. 'the land of the rebels' *yāghīī* 'rebel', *istān* 'region']) referred to different sanctuaries used by Mujāhid, for Muslim freedom fighters against the British authorities in the nineteenth and early twentieth centuries, in the various independent tribal areas, mainly inhabited by the Pakhtūns, in the hinterland of what became the North West Frontier Province (currently Khyber Pakhtunkhwa province of Pakistan) of British India such as Mohmand Agency, Bajur Agency, Dīr, Swat (particularly Bunair), Kohistan (particularly what is known as district of Hazara these days) and Chamarqand (extended both in the Kunār province of Afghanistan and Bajor agency in Khayber Pakhtunkhaw). A popular term rather than a formally recognized one, the name was in use long before the British colonial period, historically referred to as Yāghistān-i-Qadīm, and sometimes as Riyāsat-hā'i-Yāghistān.

Though Yāghistān comprised mainly mountainous terrain, the Mujāhidūn carefully selected their centres around fertile valleys, lakes and rivers in order to be self-reliant with respect to agricultural products and to find hideouts to support their guerilla warfare. With the rise of Muslim resistance, first to Sikh rule in Punjab and Kashmir, and then to the gradual British colonial expansion in South Asia at the cost of Muslim rule there, the Mujāhidūn from different regions started gathering in Yāghistān. In spite of their initial success under the charismatic leadership of Sayyid Aḥmad Barailiwī, the movement had a tremendous setback in Balakot on 6 May 1831, in which Aḥmad Barailiwī and most of his companions were killed by the Sikhs. During the first Afghan–British war (1839–1842), the Mujāhidūn leader Mawlawī Naṣīr al-Dīn sided with Dost Muḥammad by sending a contingent of fighters from Yāghistān to Kabul and Gaznah. After him, the leadership of the Mujāhidūn gradually passed over, first, to Mawlānā Wilāyat ‘Alī (d. 1852) and, then, to his younger brother Mawlānā ‘Ināyat ‘Alī (1858). Through an effective network which extended as far as Bengal, the Mujāhidūn regularly received fresh recruits, money and moral support in their frequently changing centres in Yāghistān such as Sitāna, Mulka and Ambila. The Yāghistāni Mujāhidūn always kept close contact with their supporters, and, at times, they used secret messages in code. Though most of the jihād centres in Yāghistān were attacked and destroyed by the colonial army during the second half of the nineteenth century, the resistance of the Mujāhidūn continued under such leadership as Najm al-Dīn Hadda Mulla (d. 1902) and Sa‘d-Allah Khān Mulla Mastān (branded as a ‘mad mulla’ by his opponents; d. 1916).

In 1902, the Mujāhidūn leader ‘Abd al-Karīm ibn Wilāyat ‘Alī chose Asmast in Bunair near Swat valley as his headquarters. During the First World War, a rival centre slowly grew up and prospered in the Afghan part of Chamarqand, where leaders such as Mawlāna Muḥammad ‘Alī Qaṣūrī (see his book *Mushāhdāt-i-Kabul wa Yāgistān* [Lahore: Idāra Ma‘ārif-i-Islāmī, 1986]), Mawlawī ‘Abd al-Karīm Qannuji (d. 1922), Mawlawī Muḥammad Bashīr (d. 1934), Ḥājjī Tarangza’ī (d. 1937) and Mawlawī Faḍl ’Ilāhī Wazirābādī (d. 1951; see his book *Kawā’if-i-Yāghistān* [Gujranwala, 1981]) led a number of skirmishes against the colonial army in Shabqadar, Chakdarah, Mohmand Agency and many other places in NWFP. At times, the Yāghistāni Mujāhidūn also developed alliances with a number of other anti-colonial movements such as Ḥizb-Allah, Junūd Rabbāniyyah, Ḥukūmat-i-Muwaqqata-i-Hind and Jam‘iyyat al-Anṣār. In order to curtail the revolutionary influences of the Mujāhidūn in the other regions, entry into Yāghistān was regulated by permits during the British period, a system abolished only in 1959.

With the independence of Pakistan in 1947, Yāghistān gradually became part of the historical past. The original Jihād movement also lost its impetus, although the independent character of certain Pakhtūn tribes (e.g. the Afrīdīs) and their systems (i.e. *Jirgah*) in these areas are still recognized by Pakistan. Many tribal Mujāhidūn and the activists of the Jihād movement took part in the war of independence of the Kashmiri Muslims against India in 1948 and thereafter, and subsequently in the popular Afghan uprising against the Soviet Russian supported communist regime in Kabul in the 1980s. The same region also served lately as sanctuaries for the Afghan Ṭālibān and the Arab al-Qā‘ida movements (led by Mulla ‘Umar and ’Usāmah ibn Lādin). For details, see *Encyclopaedia of Islam*, 2nd edn, s.v. ‘*Yāgistān*’; Mawlanā ‘Ubayd Allah Sindhī, *Sarguzasht-i-Kabul* (Islamabad: Qawmī Idara Barā’i Taḥqīq wa Thaqāfat, 1980); Muḥammad Khawāṣ Khān, *Ru’īdād-i-Mujāhidīn-i-Hind* (Lahore, 1983); Muin-ud-Din Ahmad Khan, *Selections from Bengal Government Records on Wahhabi Trials* (Dacca, 1961); Sayyid Muḥammad ‘Alī, *Makhzan-i-Aḥmadī* (Agrah, 1881); Qeyamuddin Ahmad, *The Wahhabi Movement in India* (New Delhi: Firma K. L. Mukhopadhay, 1966); Colonel John Adye, *Sitana: A Mountain Campaign on the Borders of Afghanistan* (London: Richard Bentley, 1867); M. Asadullah Al-Ghalib, *Ahl al-Ḥadīth Andolon* (Bengali text) (Rajshahi, 1996).

48 Karl Marx, *Notes on Indian History* (Moscow, n.d.): 152.

49 *Encyclopaedia of Islam*, 2nd edn, s.v. ‘Tītūmīr’.

50 Ironically religious movements, such as Ta‘ayyunī of Mawlānā Karāmat ‘Alī, (and more particularly the Qādiyānī [popularly known as Mirzā’ī] sect of the Punjab in the early twentieth century) that did not advocate *jihād*, were not only tolerated by colonial power, but were often encouraged as well as favoured.

51 H. Beverly, *Report of the Census of Bengal* (Calcutta: Bengal Secretariat Press, 1872): para. 525.

52 See, for instance, Sharat Chandra Chattapadhdhay, *Polli Somaj* (Dhaka: Salma Book Depot, 1999): 131.

53 For example, Jāmi' Masjid (ins. no. 9) from Lakhisarai dated 697 (1297) refers to these activities by the phrase *zāda khayruhu* (May his benevolence increase).

54 The influence of mosques is referred to in the phrase *a'lā āthār al-masjid* (lit. who has exalted the influence of the masjid) in 'Alā al-Ḥaq Masjid inscription dated 743/1342 (ins. no. 19).

55 Eaton, *The Rise of Islam*, 229–267.

56 The institution of *madad-i-ma'ash* still exists in Afghanistan, Iran and Central Asia.

57 See, for instance, 'Kanun Daimer Nathi', Chittagong District Collectorate Record Room, bundle 62, case no. 4005 for a thatched mosque established in 1735 in Sundarpur, Fatikchhari Thana; bundle 29, case no. 1808 for a thatched mosque in Lohagara, Satkania Thana; and bundle 51, case no. 3329 for another thatched mosque in Dabra, Hathazari Thana. For plans and other details of these mosques, see Eaton, *The Rise of Islam*, pp. 241–243.

58 Minhāj al-Dīn, *Ṭabaqāt-e-Nāṣirī*, ed. W. N. Lees, 151.

59 Ever since, the Umm al-Hānī gate of the Grand Mosque at Makkhah has been the gathering place of Bengali pilgrims during daily prayers.

60 For details, see Taqī al-Dīn al-Fāsī, *al-'Aqd al-Thamīn fī Tārīkh al-Balad al-Amīn* (Beirut: Dār al-Kutub al-'Ilmiyyah, 1998).

3 Nature, aesthetic perception and mysticism

Spiritual dimensions of the Islamic inscriptions of Bengal

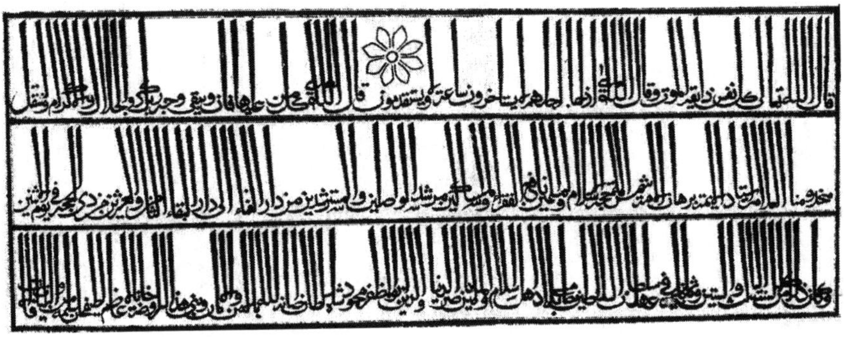

Figure 3.1 **(Ins. 51)**: The funerary inscription of Nūr Quṭb al-ʿĀlam at his khānqāh in Ḥaḍrat Pandua dated 863/1459, with seven spiritual titles used for the Shaykh (source: photo courtesy by ASI).

Original epigraphic text (in Arabic):

L-1 قال الله تعالى كل نفس ذائقة الموت وقال الله تعالى [فـ] إذا جا[ء] أجلهم لا يستأخرون ساعة ولا يستقدمون قال الله تعالى كل من عليها فان ويبقى وجه ربك ذو الجلال والإكرام وانتقل

L-2 مخدومنا العلامة استاد<أستاذ>الأيمة برهان الأمة شمس الملة حجة الإسلام والمسلمين نافع الفقراء والمساكين مرشد الواصلين والمسترشدين من دار الفناء إلى دار البقاء الثامن والعشرين من ذي الحجة في يوم الإثنين

L-3 وكان ذلك من السنة الثالث<<الثالثة> والستين وثمانماية في عهد {ال} سلطان السلاطين حامي بلاد أهل الإسلام والمسلمين ناصر الدنيا والدين أبو <أبي> المظفر محمود شاه سلطان صانه الله بالأمن والأمان وبنى هذا <هذه> الروضة خانا لاعظم لطيفخان سلمه من البليات والآفات

Translation:

L-1 Allah the Exalted said: ‘Every soul will taste death.’
Allah, the Exalted, also said: ‘When their time comes, neither can they delay an hour nor can they advance it.’ Allah the Great said: ‘All that is on the earth shall perish, and the only thing that will remain will be the appearance of your Creator, full of majesty and magnanimity’ [55:26–27] .

L-2 Our lord – the greatest scholar, the teacher of the

> imāms, the demonstrator of the umma, the sun of the nation, the authority for Islam and the Muslims, beneficent to the faqīrs and beggars, the guide of the communicants and the seekers of the right path – has departed from the house of extinction to the house of sustenance, on the twenty-eighth of Dhū 'l-Ḥijja on Monday.
>
> L-3 And it took place in the year eight hundred and sixty three [25 October 1459] in the reign of the sultan of the sultans, Hāmī Bilād Ahl al-Islām wa 'l-Muslimīn (the protector of the lands of Islam and the Muslims), Nāṣir al-Dunyā wa 'l-Dīn Abū <Abī> 'l-Muẓaffar Mahmūd Shāh Sulṭān, may Allah uphold him with peace and protection. The great Khān Laṭīf Khān built this mausoleum; may He (Allah) protect him from calamity and mishap.

The extra-ordinary titles in this epigraphic text are deeply imbued in spiritual connotation indicating a profound attachment and respect that the common Bengali masses of rural Bengal always expressed for Nūr Quṭb al-'Ālam, one of the most celebrated sufi-saints of Bengal. The inscription is simple and spontaneous, yet rhythmic artistic expression in it, is fascinating. The calligraphy is rendered in Bihārī style on a plain background. It is devoid of any overwhelming decoration or any superficial embellishment. The elongated vertical shafts, arrayed in a symmetrical order, start at the bottom with a thin line that grows thicker as it ascends. The unusual elevation of the verticals upward and their arrangement in a row can be interpreted as representing departed souls on their journey upward or descending angels with blessings for the participants in the funerary prayers, as well as for the deceased soul. The clustered letters at the bottom may be interpreted as symbols of a congregation lined up for the funeral prayer. An eight-lobed flower in the middle of the upper part of the first line symbolizes the eight heavens, an appropriate motif in this setting, since it coincides with the position of the deceased in the arrangement for prayer when the body is placed in front of the funeral congregation. The spiritual dimension finds an expression in various spheres of life in Islamic culture. It is not surprising then to discover the influence of nature and mysticism in the artistic manifestation displayed in architectural calligraphy in Bengal.

The sufi message of simple living, profoundly attached to the nature and deeply infused in the spiritual quest for human salvation, harmonized well with the agrarian lifestyle in the vast rural areas of Bengal. Defined by the Prophet Muḥammad as *dīn al-fiṭra* or the religion of nature, Islam spread in the region forming a close relation between the human spiritual realm and nature. From an Islamic point of view, the whole environment – the universe – is a living organism in its own way, every element of which is deeply engaged in worshipping the Creator.[1] There exists a strong relationship between the Creator and the creation, which achieves perfection only when developed properly in harmony. The Creator is manifested everywhere through His creation, a concept popular among the sufis of Bengal, often known in Islamic mystical literature as *waḥdat al-shuhūd* (lit. universal evidence of Divine Unity). A true believer, then, constantly finds testimony of divine presence everywhere in the universe. For a believer, every element of time and space recalls the greatness of Allah, evoking a tremendous sense of awe and excitement deep within the heart leading the believer to a peak spiritual experience and to communion with the Creator. At that point, the believer spontaneously exclaims with great wonder and surprise the glory of God, a message found abundantly in the Qur'ānic verses as well as sayings of the Prophet in the inscriptions of Bengal.

The basic sufi message in Bengal focuses on the unity of Allah who is the ultimate universe (existence), being the All-Encompassing (in the Qur'ān, *al-Muḥīṭ*) in a deeper sense.[2] He surrounds everything and is present everywhere (in the Qur'ān, *al-Mawjūd*, meaning ever-present, a divine attribute). The ultimate reality (*al-ḥaqq*,[3] another divine attribute) of existence (*al-wujūd*) lies in the essence of divine unity, or *tawḥīd* (lit. the oneness of God) – the pivotal message of Islam – best explained in the sufi concept of *waḥdat al-wujūd* (lit. the unity of existence). Thus, in sufi teaching, all is unity, and *al-dīn* (lit. the religion), in essence, is the return to primordial unity, a message, symbolically expressed in the funerary inscription of Nūr Quṭb al-'Ālam.

The role of natural phenomena in the Qur'ān and their place in Qur'ānic spiritual message is very prominent, although this has seldom been explored as a topic in its own right.[4] According to the Qur'ānic view, all the elements of the universe follow natural laws which are divine and henceforth Islamic. According to the Qur'ān, everything that exists glorifies Allah (17:44). Qur'ānic verses referring to nature can be found in a number of inscriptions in Bengal.[5] Pious acts and worship (*'ibāda*) help human beings come closer to nature and nurture a human understanding of the delicate ecological balance and their intimate relationship with it.

The Earth thus has a sacred aspect in the Islamic mystical idea. The Prophet declared the whole of the Earth as sacred and as clean as a mosque.[6] Therefore, the whole universe is uniquely created as a place of worship; and Muslims, wherever they may happen to be, in the jungle, on a mountain, in the desert or at sea, are bound by their religious duty to remember their Creator at least five times daily in the form of *ṣalāt* (prayer). While mosques play an important role in different spheres of life in Islam, they have never been the only place of worship or prayer, nor does the mosque constitute a liturgical centre in a true sense.[7] Indeed, this simple approach to religious practice suited the Bengali rural peasant folk, making their religious practice easier and more natural. Like sufis elsewhere, in Bengal too they emphasized the need for *sharī'a* (the Islamic code of life) in Islamic societies. To them, it ensures felicity for both the individual and the community in a healthy environment and natural setting in this world, and a spiritual reward in the hereafter in the form of an eternal peak experience of happiness, symbolically expressed as *janna* (lit. garden), that is full of life, plants, flowers, rivers and waters in a most harmonious setting.

Beauty is a cherished quality in Islamic mystical teaching because of its relationship with truth. The concept 'beauty is truth and truth is beauty'[8] thus finds an important place in the Islamic tradition. Perceiving the splendour of nature is considered an essential quality for a *mu'mīn* (believer) in order to understand divine beauty. The Prophet Muḥammad's saying, 'Allah, being beautiful Himself, loves beauty',[9] signifies the importance that Islam attaches to aesthetic perception. The origin of beauty thus has its reality in the existence of Allah, which is so magnificent that a naked human eye cannot bear it. When manifested in a simpler form in divine creation, this beauty can be perceived by those who are pious, who have deep spiritual vision. Exploring this divine beauty in the universe is an integral part of religious piety, which finally leads a believer to form a close relationship with nature.

The Islamic spiritual message is wonderfully expressed in Islamic art in Bengal, which draws its motivation from the endless beauty in the divine creation scattered in nature. Imagining the process of creation, the rhythmic yet contrasting patterns in nature, and the uniqueness of elements in the cosmic system is an essential duty for a believer. Lack of interest in the splendour of existence is compared to mental blindness (Qur'ān 22:46). According to the Qur'ān, it is the foremost duty of every human being to contemplate the uniqueness of the cosmic order (Qur'ān 3:190). In Islamic culture, an artist's perception is considered a divine gift. It enables a person to look minutely at nature and to see its beauty in a more comprehensive way.[10] During the course of his artistic efforts, he expands his vision of truth and soon realizes the limitations of his imaginative power and creativeness. In this process, he discovers that the origin of every form has its reference in the creation of Allah. Every creation in its original form carries the essence of pure beauty (Qur'ān 32:7), which loses its original character when being copied. As the artist's perception grows, he realizes that the origins of every colour, motif, form and design have their realities only in the divine creation.[11] Therefore, no matter the degree of perfection the artist achieves in his art, he cannot create anything new, or of his own in a true sense. Thus, a true work of art helps a believer come closer to the cosmic truth. In the course of his artistic endeavour, he perceives his Creator with greater intimacy.

While a Muslim enjoys considerable freedom in his creative work, his Islamic perspective means he has a positive and useful goal in his creativeness, so that it serves humanity. Islamic art ideally should express truth, supreme beauty, true human values and virtuous life. In a way, it means the rejection of anything that does not lead towards positive creativity. Henceforth, Islamic life cannot be divided into profane and sacred domains. As a Muslim artist strives to reach his Islamic goal, his work of art turns into an act of devotion (expressed as *'ibāda* in the Qur'ān). In his pursuit of artistic creativity, a Muslim is not supposed to cross the boundaries of natural law (*dīn al-fiṭra*). Furthermore, he is not allowed to cause any disturbance (*fasād*)[12] to the divine setting of nature (*al-fiṭra*) through excessive or unwise exploitation of natural resources or by harming the delicate natural balance.

Deeply imbued with these spiritual messages, Islam reached the riverine deltaic region of Bengal – the gateway to rice culture – at the beginning of the thirteenth century. This was a time when Bengal was still sparsely populated, with natural forests and wilderness covering a large part of its fertile soil.[13]

Although the penetration of the Aryan race and Vedic culture had begun almost 1,500 years earlier, a majority of the population of Bengal was still non-Aryan (called *mleccha*, or unclean barbarians, by the Aryan conquerors) and many of the indigenous people had not yet adopted a settled agrarian life. In addition to the Vedic religious tradition and local animistic cults, Buddhism also spread in the region prior to Islam and survived for a long time, in spite of the disapproval of some Hindu ruling dynasties from time to time particularly from the Sena rulers.

Much of the consolidation of Islam in the region was possible due to the fact that the Islamic message was conveyed in a popular language often using indigenous religious imageries, but not necessarily in a syncretic form. Bengal's ecological balance and harmony with nature left a strong imprint in its popular literature, folklore, art, architecture and culture. Unlike the Vedic religion, Islam did not impose itself in Bengal as a foreign agent. Resembling very much the earlier diffusion of Buddhism in the region, it penetrated the deep Bengali psychic and social life in a smooth, slow transformational way without creating much upheaval or social unrest. In a way, it harmonized well with the natural lifestyles of the native population, some of whom were still nomadic, while others were in the process of adopting a settled agrarian life. It appealed, as the religion of nature (*dīn al-fiṭra*), to the heart of the indigenous people, whose traditional lifestyle had remained very close to nature for centuries. Thus the spread of Islam in Bengal was very much evolutionary, rather than revolutionary. Slowly and gradually, it became a rural way of life as agrarian settlement expanded in the delta.[14] Some early Sultanate inscriptions, such as the Madrasa-Masjid Inscription Navagram dated 858/1454 during the restored Ilyās Shāhī ruler Maḥmūd Shāh, clearly indicate the consolidation of sharī'a (*sha'ā'ir al-shar'*) or Islamic way of life with the support of the ruling establishment and the efforts of the 'ulamā' in the Bengali villages (*khiṭṭa rifiyya*).

Islam rapidly became the popular religion of the growing Bengali villages as human settlement expanded along the delta bringing with it rice cultivation, often clearing the forest of its otherwise low marsh land. Bengal experienced great prosperity during the rule of some of the independent Muslim sultans, whose far-reaching welfare works, such as public roads and *siqāya* (water tanks, wells), helped spread Islam to the farthest corners of the region. In a number of Islamic inscriptions of Bengal (e.g. a few inscriptions from the period of Mughal emperor Akbar), we find reference to institutions such as *waqf* and *madad-i-ma'āsh* (special endowment in support of living expenses) that benefited all commoners regardless of their religion.[15] During the subsequent Mughal period (seventeenth and eighteenth centuries), Bengal also witnessed sustained growth in the utilization of its natural resources, without losing its ecological balance, and came to be considered the granary of the empire. Calligraphic features of Bengali *ṭughrā'* style found abundantly in Sultanate inscriptions beautifully depict the harmony between Islam and the agrarian way of life in rural Bengal expressed often through the elongated and symmetrically arranged verticals of letters symbolizing ploughs ready for cultivation, or perhaps representing reeds of the marshlands as well as the forested landscape of Bengal.

Islam finally emerged as the popular and primary faith, as well as the dominant culture, of Bengal during the eighteenth century. Although there has been much speculation about the factors that led to the spread of Islam in this region, it seems that Islam entered the region as a religion close to nature (*dīn al-fiṭra*).[16] The religion appealed profoundly to rural Bengalis, whose traditional lifestyle had remained very close to nature for centuries and left a strong imprint on its popular literature, art, architecture, culture and folklore during the Sultanate and Mughal periods.

During the first 100 years of Muslim rule in Bengal, approximately thirteen Arabic and Persian inscriptions have been discovered, so far, that date from between 1205 and 1304. Six of these inscriptions commemorate the establishment of khānqāhs, a vital religious institution that played an important role in disseminating Islamic spiritual values in the life and society of Bengal through the ages (see Figure 3.2). Khānqāhs also served as centres of learning on a par with madrasas. During the medieval period in the Islamic world, the intellectual and educational role of the khānqāhs was considered so important that the famous historian and philosopher of the time, Ibn Khaldūn (d. 1406), was appointed by the Mamluk ruler of Egypt as the head of the Khānqāh of Baybars

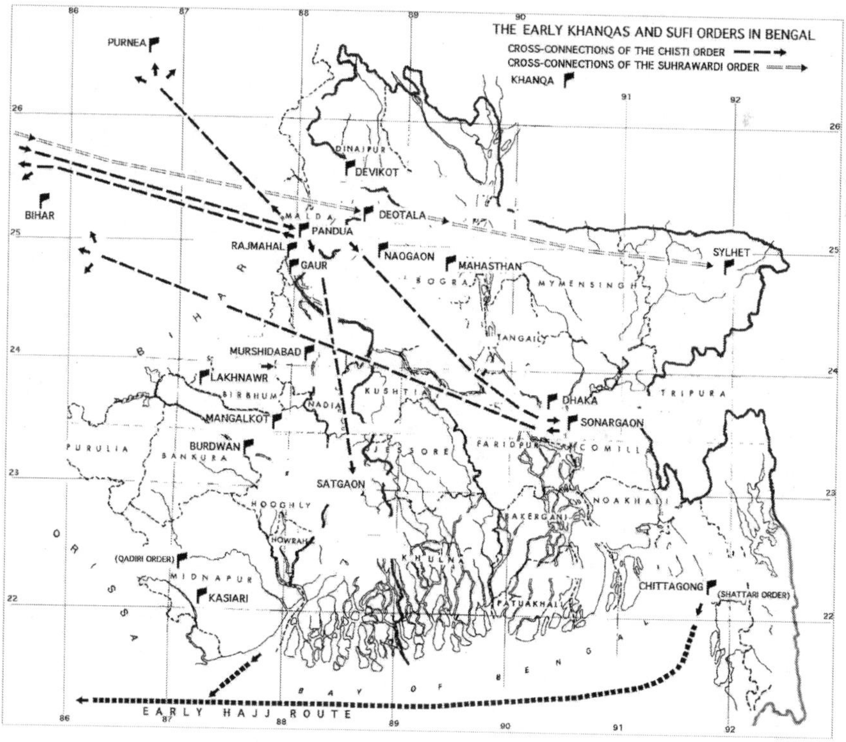

Figure 3.2 Early khānqāhs, appearance of sufi orders and ḥajj routes, in medieval Bengal (source: copyright by author).

in Cairo, a key spiritual centre of the Islamic world at that time.[17] Numerous bits of historical evidence suggest that Islamic mystic movements started in Bengal as early as at the beginning of the thirteenth century and that they appealed deeply to the indigenous population. The Sian inscription dated 618/1221 (the second oldest Islamic inscription in Bengal) is the first record of a khānqāh dedicated exclusively for sufis. It was not far from Lakhnōr, an early Muslim administrative centre, in the northwest Rā̱r region (in the present Birbhum district of West Bengal). Rather than *sufi* or *Shaykh*, the founder (ibn Muḥammad al-Marāghī) preferred to be referred to as *faqīr* in the inscription, a popular term in South Asia, that harmonized more with the idea of a mendicant (the popular Sanskrit term: *bhikshu* भिक्षु) in the local Buddhist and Hindu mystical traditions. While the site of the khānqāh at Sian itself might have been a demolished Buddhist monastery or a Hindu temple, the stone slab (which also has a Sanskrit inscription on the reverse side) containing this Arabic inscription was found in a temple there. The community of these Muslim mystics has been referred as *ahl al-ṣuffa*,[18] reminding us of the earliest spiritual community of Madinah during the time of the Prophet, who spent most of their time worshipping in the Prophet's mosque at the cost of poverty. The edifice, described in the inscription, also served the community as a mosque, a common practice in the region to this day. That the inscription contains Qur'ānic verse as well *ḥadīth*, is an indication that these early sufis were faithful adherent of *sharī'a*, a trend that started weakening over time.

The *nisba* of the founder of the Sian Khānqāh, al-Murāghī, suggests that he had migrated to Bengal from the town of al-Muragha on the Caspian Sea. This also indicates mass-migration prevalent in those days in certain parts of the Islamic world. Though it is possible that the sufis arrived through sea routes in the southern coastal areas of Bengal even before Bakhtiyār Khiljī's successful military incursion in the region in 1205, their flow from Central Asia to this remote hinterland started in earnest in the thirteenth century when a significant part of Central Asia, Khurasan, Persia and adjacent regions faced constant Mongol invasion. Thus, socio-economic factors, in addition to spiritual fervour, definitely played a significant role in their migration to this far-flung land.[19] In line with their Turko-Mongol predecessors in Central Asia, it is likely that they also brought with them their nomadic nature.[20] A number of early sources and local traditions indicate that they were sent to this region by their spiritual mentors from north India, Central Asia or West Asia. It is not surprising then that Bengal sufis, like their brethren elsewhere, were always keen to maintain their spiritual connection with their mentors in the lands of their origins. Whenever some of them moved to the region as an extension of a mystical fraternity, they formed a brotherhood organization after settling in the area in which spiritual bondage between *murshid* (spiritual master) and *murīd* (disciple) played a vital role.

To make their way to the Bengal frontier for embarking on Islamic activities was not easy for the sufis. They often had to struggle in this remote hinterland. Although there are stories of them waging holy war (*jihād*) against the local non-Muslim rulers, these are more likely popular legend than fact. While examining the hagiographic and biographic literature written after their death, it is important to remember that they may exaggerate a life of piousness and over-inflate achievements according to the intentions of their authors. In order to bestow on the sufis a larger than life image and to make them into charismatic figures, local traditions also depict them as *mujāhid* or religious fighters who fought their way into the region in order to uphold the banner of Islam, though we seldom find any historical evidence for such accounts. The main focus of the sufis was always the greater *jihād* (inner struggle) against lower-self (worldly temptations/desires). Thus, we find very few sufis of Bengal using the title *ghāzī* (victorious) or *mujāhid* (religious warrior), though some of them occasionally engaged in lesser *jihād* (holy war) in some unavoidable circumstances to dislodge adversary local non-Muslim or feudal authorities (such as kings or zamindars) from power.[21] On a popular level, however, the title of *ghāzī* has been attributed occasionally to some local *pīr*s (saints) such as Shāh Ismā'īl Ghāzī, buried, according to local tradition, in the village of Mandaran, Hoogly district, West Bengal. As the sufis moved into the region, they allowed (and in many cases, encouraged) their disciples to settle down, adopting household lives (close to the idea of *kad-khuda* or family life in the old Turkish tradition).[22]

In Bengal, the influence of the sufis can be felt not only in the spiritual domain, but also in different aspects of political and social life. Many of the sufis were, indeed, active participants in historical events. They greatly influenced public life, society and state affairs. After all, they were the moral governors of the universe.[23] As some early sources indicate, the blessings of sufis, in some cases, provided a sort of religious legitimacy to a number of rulers who were to become future leaders of a certain region as a reward for a particular good deed.[24] Indeed, a number of early Muslim rulers started their political career after being blessed by sufis.[25] Ibn Baṭṭūṭā in his *Riḥla* mentions meeting a number of celebrated Muslim saints even in remote places such as Sonārgā'on and Sylhet. He also mentions a faqīr named Shaydā who revolted against Fakhr al-Dīn Mubārak Shāh (r. 739–750/1338–1349), the ruler of Sonārgā'on, and was killed in an ensuing struggle. Sufis, such as Nūr Quṭb al-'Ālam (d. 1459 according to his tomb inscription), played an important role in the politics of their time. Also interesting is the fact that many of the early conquerors with charismatic personalities, such as Khān Jahān in Bagerhat in the south, were gradually elevated to the position of *pīr*s after their death in the folk tradition and their graves were turned into shrines. Similarly, the tomb of Bakhtiyār Khalji, supposedly located atop a mound (that may contain unexplored ruins of earliest Muslim capital there) in a little known village near Devikot in Dakhshin Dinajpur, is revered as the shrine of a Muslim saint by Muslim and non-Muslim local indigenous residents alike.

Sufis were influential in both politics and society, and the ruling class often patronized them. Nevertheless, their authority and popularity sometimes led towards negative relations with the ruling class. Sultan Sikandar Shah was so suspicious of Shaykh 'Alā' al-Ḥaq's growing influence in the capital that he banished the saint to Sonārgā'on in eastern Bengal. In general, however, Muslim rulers of Bengal respected the sufis as spiritual mentors and listened to their advice (at least publicly, to maintain their popularity with the masses). Some rulers sent their sons to the sufis for religious education. Muẓaffar Shams Balkhī, for instance, tutored A'ẓam Shāh (*circa* 792–813/1390–1410). There was always a strong presence of sufis in urban centres and capitals, such as Gaur, Pandua and Sonārgā'on, which provided the sufis with ample opportunities to exert influence on the political environment and royal household. Many sufis contributed significantly to Islamic literature, established madrasas and hospitals and actively participated in the overall welfare of the common people.

Early sufis of Bengal were spiritual mentors on the one hand, and 'ulamā' and *muḥaddithūn* (recognized scholars of the Prophet's traditions) on the other hand. Some of them played a leading role in popularizing the teaching of *ḥadīth* in the region. Many took an interest in various branches of learning. In general, they used Persian particularly for their intellectual communication. Consequently, many of their written works, such as *malfūẓāt* and *maktūbāt*, can be found in Persian. Since most sufis had strong backgrounds in religious education, they usually had a good command of the Arabic language as well. In fact, some of them compiled their scholarly works in Arabic too.

One of the earliest Islamic literary works in Bengal, *Mir'āt al-Ma'ānī li-Idrāk al-'Insānī* (popularly known as *Ḥawḍ al-Ḥayāt* [The Spring of Life], originally an Arabic translation of a *yoga* manual entitled *Amrit-Kunda* [The Eternal Lake]),[26] describes such interactions quite vividly. The central theme of this great work is a spiritual life journey that passes through different stages, yet it remains, in effect, a dream-like experience, the true nature of a life (*al-wajūd al-ẓillī*) according to the sufis. The manuscript begins with a historical background as it introduces Bhojar Brahmin, a famous Hindu Yogi from Kamrup and a Hindu scholar of considerable fame at that time, who went to the Bengali capital of Lakhnawti during the reign of 'Alī Mardān (1210–1213) to inquire about the faith of this newly conquering force. It was in the jāmi' masjid at Friday prayer that he met Qāḍī Rukn al-Dīn, a leading Ḥanafī jurist, philosopher and logician of his time in the Islamic East. Known also as al-'Amīdī, Qāḍī Rukn al-Dīn Abū Ḥamīd Muḥammad ibn Muḥammad Samarqandī (d. 615/1218?) he had a special interest in the field of *'ilm al-jadal* (the art of dialectics) in which he wrote a few books such as *al-Irshād* and *al-Ṭarīq al-'Amīdī yya fī 'l-Khilāf wa 'l-Jadal*. Bhojar Brahmin debated religious issues with Qāḍī Rukn al-Dīn and finally accepted Islam. After going through formal training in religious curricula, he eventually reached the stage of a *muftī* (deliverer of formal legal opinions). In this early Hindu–Muslim encounter, Hindu holy scriptures are described as sacred literature coming from the Abrahamic tradition, which were, according to the language of *Ḥawḍ al-Ḥayāt*, 'the *maṣḥaf* of the two Brahmas, namely, Abraham and Moses'.[27] Thus, the Hindu scripture of Veda as well as the Aryan Vedic religion were comfortably fit by the early Muslim scholars of Bengal into the wider context of the Islamic world view (more precisely, the concept of *risāla* or divine revelation). This assimilating approach had a profound effect, for it granted the non-Muslim majority (Hindus and Buddhists) in this newly conquered land the status of *mushābih bi-ahl al-kitāb* (similar to the status awarded to Christians and Jews in an Islamic state) who would enjoy clearly defined legal rights as *dhimmī* (free non-Muslim subjects in an Islamic state). This little noticed but important act, however, was not new in South Asian Islamic history. Occasionally referred to as *ṣulḥ-e-kull*, or peace for all (lit. truce with all) in sufi literature, Muḥammad ibn al-Qāsim adopted very much the same policy exactly 500 years earlier after his conquest of Sind, which eventually turned the region into a Muslim-majority area. Identifying Brahmas as the symbol of the Prophet Ibrāhīm (Abraham) and Mūsā (Moses) by the Muslim 'ulamā' of Bengal was the first step in creating a bridge of understanding between the two most populous religious communities in the region, Hindu and Muslim. On a religious level, this interaction symbolizes the beginning of an interfaith dialogue between Hindu and Muslim scholars at a very early stage. It seems that Muslim sufis took great scholarly interest in yoga and various tantric practices, including those which were practised in the remote forest regions in the east and northeast of Bengal, particularly Kamrup and Assam.

The use of indigenous religious imagery and metaphors in order to simplify the message of Islam to the local population was, however, not limited to Bengal, as Gujarat and several other regions went through the same historical experience. This interesting feature continued finding an expression in medieval Muslim Bengali poetry (*pūthī*).[28] Conversion of a Brahmin Yogi to Islam at an early stage of Muslim rule in Bengal was symbolically quite important as it implied that the conversion process started immediately after the advent of the Muslims in the region and affected all strata of the population, from the Brahmins to the Mlechchhas. It is also important to note that most of the early 'ulamā' in Bengal, such as Qāḍī Rukn al-Dīn Samarqandī, came from Central Asia. Since they were followers of the Ḥanafī *fiqh*, their influence led to the wide acceptance of the Ḥanafī *fiqh* among the Bengali Muslim masses. Interestingly, it was only certain Ḥanafī jurists in the Subcontinent who considered Hindus as *mushābih bi-ahl al-kitāb* (akin to the people of book) while the Shāfi'ī and other *madhāhib* (different Islamic legal schools) in general considered them as *mushrikūn* (polytheists). The liberal attitude of Ḥanafī jurisprudence, which soon prevailed in the region, treated Hindu, Buddhist and other religious communities on an equal plane with Muslims, and hence demanded equality for everyone before the law under Muslim rule. Many Muslim jurists such as Ibrāhīm al-Nakha'ī (a famous student of Ibn Mas'ūd who served as a *qāḍī* in Iraq, d. AH 95) promoted this view from the early days of Islam, particularly in Iraq and other newly conquered regions in the East. Some of the early jurists went as far as recommending repentance as sufficient punishment for apostasy, or no punishment at all. Historically speaking, Bengali Muslims always looked towards Iraq and Khurasan, the original seats of the Ḥanafī school of jurisprudence, with great reverence as well as a source of spiritual and intellectual inspiration.

Both the 'ulamā' and the sufis were successful in communicating with the common folk and conveying the Islamic message in a simple language understandable to the rural masses. In general, sufis played various important roles in shaping Islamic society, sometimes silently, at other times quite articulately and expressively. Quite naturally, the degree of their influence and the intensity of their activity have not been the same in every time and location. A great majority of the sufis actually lived in mainstream Islamic societies strictly adhering to *sharī'a* and maintained a harmonious relationship with the 'ulamā'.

It is the regional diversity of cultural expression within the larger framework of unity that makes Islam a rich, vital and great civilization. It is its infinitely complex and creative processes of interaction between basic religious principles and the necessity of time and space, the ideal and the actual, between innovation and stability that have kept this civilization living, vibrant and dynamic to this day. As its message started spreading in the remote corners of the old world, Islam faced two challenging issues: syncretion and indigenization. Though quite often mistakenly used as synonyms, both of these words have somewhat different semantic backgrounds. While in the indigenization process, foreign elements find local and native characteristics in their expression, the term 'syncretism' historically speaking, stems from a more Christian usage connoting essentially the fusion and reconciliation of conflicting beliefs in creolized forms and their uncritical acceptances by the people in question.

Indigenization is one of the characteristics of the regional expressions of the Islamic proselytization process that is to be found everywhere in the Islamic world and Bengal is not an exception. Bengal, as a matter of fact, provides an excellent paradigm of a regional formation of an Islamic community while maintaining its strong ties with the rest of the *ummah*. 'Ulamā' and sufi shaykhs in general encouraged indigenization as it helped popularize Islamic propagation (*da'wa*) among the masses. In their efforts to present Islam to the local communities in a living and popular language, they practised, sometimes, a certain degree of flexibility in adapting to the local system as long as it was in harmony with the basic Islamic spirit.

Syncretism, on the other hand, was never accepted by the 'ulamā' and sufi shaykhs, on the grounds that it did not conform to the *sharī'a*. But, occasionally, it did find tacit support among the ruling Muslim elite, many of whom themselves were bearers of the syncretistic tradition of the old Sassanian imperial legacy of Central Asia. But what made the syncretistic traditions popular from time to time was the proselytizing of a particular class of cultural mediators, namely, the *pīr*s and the mullas (known by various names such as *sābiqī*s or the traditionalists, *bi-shara'* or non-conformists to *sharī'a*, *ibāḥī*s or unrestrained ones). Because of their vested social and economic interests, they were always eager to defend the status quo. It may be worthwhile to point out here that there is no significant difference in meaning in the popular or idiomatic usage between the words sufi, shaykh and *pīr*, or for instance between *'ālim* and mulla, and, quite often, they are used interchangeably or as synonyms for each other. But at the same time, one indeed finds two separate social undercurrents that left a strong impact in the religious transformation of Bengal's common people. While one group of sufis, the shaykhs, *awliyā'* and *'ālim* always adhered to *sharī'a* and advocated strongly for it, another group popularly known as *pīr*, *faqīr*, dervish and mulla, served as the bearers of syncretic culture. It is not surprising then to find a deep-rooted tension between *sharīʻa*-oriented sufi, shaykhs and ʻulamāʼ, and the defenders of the syncretistic traditions among the *pīr*s and mullas of the region. The sufi shaykhs of different *silsilah*s (spiritual orders) provided spiritual leadership side by side with the intellectual leadership of ʻulamāʼ (also known as *munshī*, *mawlawī* or *mawlānā*) and were normally selected on the basis of merits and religious piety. The traditionalist *pīr*s, on the other hand, formed a sort of priest class (similar to Brahmin) based on family lineage where succession used to be hereditary. Conservative *pīr*s and mullas resisted the reform movements of the later days led by the progressive sufis and ʻulamāʼ. They stood, for instance, against the peasant uprising under Tītūmīr and the egalitarian movements of ʻulamāʼ (occasionally described as Mawlawī movements by the early colonial writers).

As the Muslims gradually grew in the region as a community, the prime goals and priorities of many of the successive generations of sufis slowly started moving away from their basic spiritual goal of living a simple life and attaining spiritual salvation. A growing number of shrines, popularly known as *dargāh*, *rawḍa* and *mazār* (shrines) started emerging in Bengal, while the original mission of the sufis and khānqāhs, namely *daʻwah* or the preaching of Islamic messages, gradually began to fade. In the course of time, these shrines became popular places for syncretistic traditions which attracted common people for the veneration of saints. Members of the ruling class often tended to build grandiose mausoleums on the graves of the popular saints to turn them into popular shrines in order to gain mass popularity. These shrines, over time, would become lucrative sources of income for those attached to their management and maintenance. An inscription fixed on the eastern wall of the mausoleum of Shāh Nafā near the southern gateway of the Monghyr Fort in Bihar indicates that Sultan Ḥusayn Shāh built a monumental dome on the grave of the saint in 903/1497–1498.

In this process, most of the sufi traditions lost their emphasis on moral virtues and spiritual training of self-denial as well as control of lower self and sensual desires (*ḍabṭ al-nafs*). Eventually, a new class of Muslim saints (i.e. *pīr*s) gradually started to appear. They sought devotion from the uneducated rural folks whose approach towards Islam was more of a pantheistic nature. Many *dargāh*s actually turned into a profitable means of financial support for the *pīr*s. It did not take a long time for this new class to pass through the stage of khānqāh into the stage of *ṭarīqah* (various spiritual brotherhoods) and finally to the stage of *ṭāʼifah* (sectarian denominations). Many of these changes occurred due to the close relationship of the *pīr*s with the ruling establishment because the *pīr*s accepted various economic favours from the state, such as *inʻām*s or *madad-i-maʻāsh* (land-grants) at the cost of their own independent status.

Thus we do find an ongoing historical discord between the reformist sufis/ʻulamāʼ and the traditionalist dervishes or *pīr*s which grew more and more over time. While the early sufis left a great impact on the common people and, to a lesser extent, on the ruling class, the *pīr*s of the later periods were themselves influenced by local traditions, namely religious trends and cults, such as the

Bhakti movements, *math* (Hindu monastery) and the guru–disciple relationship of Hindu tradition. Under the justification of *ṣulḥ-e-kull* (peace with all, harmony with everything), a principle occasionally endorsed by some minor *ṭarīqā*s, some of the later *pīr*s absorbed local non-Muslim practices that eventually turned into mere cults. In a way, the later tradition of saint veneration defeated the very purpose of the original sufi movement, which emphasized the spiritual dimensions of religion such as *taqwa* (religious piety, God fearing) rather than ritual obsession and *riyā'* (eye-service of rituals).

Interestingly enough, syncretistic traditions did not necessarily bring the Hindu and Muslim communities any closer together. One of the famous early Bengali novel writers Sharat Chandra Chattapadhdhay, in his widely read novels and short stories, depicts the true ethos of Bengali villages of the early twentieth century, where Hindus and Muslims shared the same space for centuries, yet retained a clear dividing line that distinguished their religious and cultural life, although interactions did take place on various planes.[29]

Khānqāhs had a strong influence in rural Bengal at the grass-roots level. The people attached to the khānqāhs, including the poor commoners living in the vicinity of the khānqāh, were often supported by endowment, particularly *madad-i-ma'āsh* (see, for instance, Bahrām Saqqā' inscription, dated 1015/1606–1607). Some of the khānqāhs had public facilities attached to them, such as kitchens and free hospitals. Thus khānqāhs also played important roles in the formation of new Muslim villages in many sparsely populated areas, particularly in the lower delta in eastern and southern Bengal.

Notes

1 As the Qur'ān says, in a profound and meaningful way, in the chapter *al-Isrā'* (17:44): *wa 'in min shay'in illā yusabbiḥu bi-ḥamdihi* [Everything that exists glorifies Allah].
2 One of the 100 most beautiful Divine Names that appear in the Qur'ān in the chapter *al-Nisā'* (4:126).
3 The Qur'ān, the chapter *Yūnus* (10:32).
4 William A. Graham, 'The Winds to Herald His Mercy' in *Faithful Imagining Essays in Honor of Richard R. Niebuhr*, eds Sang Hyun Lee and Wayne Proudfoot (Atlanta, GA: Scholars Press, 1995): 22.
5 The sound of thunder in nature is a common phenomenon in Bengal during monsoon season. The Qur'ānic verse 'thunder glorifies Allah repeatedly, and so do the angels, with awe' (13:13) can be seen in the Sultanganj inscription dated 789 (1474) as well as in a few other inscriptions.
6 Al-Qurtubi, *al-Jāmi' li Aḥkām al-Qur'ān*, vol. 3, chapter al-Baqara, verse 253. The Arabic text of the *ḥadīth* is as follows: *ju'ilat li 'l-'arḍ masjid wa ṭuhūr*.
7 Titus Burckhardt, *Mirror of the Intellect* (Albany, NY: State University of New York Press, 1987): 224.
8 Burckhardt, *Mirror of the Intellect*, 216. This concept can be found in the work of Plato, the English poet John Keats and many others.
9 *Al-Saḥīḥ al-Muslim*, 'Kitāb al-'Imān' [The Book of Faith], chapter *taḥrim al-kibr* [the prohibition of pride].
10 Titus Burckhardt, *Sacred Art in the East and West* (Albany, NY: State University of New York Press, 1987): 101–119.
11 Ibid.

12 A verse in the Qur'ān says: 'When he turns away from divine message, he attempts to terrorize the earth through destroying agriculture and human civilization; and Allah does not like terrorism' (*al-Baqara*, 2:205).

13 The wilderness, swamps and the natural setting of the region have found an expression in a popular Bengali proverb: *Jale Kumir-Dangay Bagh*, which means 'The lands are full of tigers while the marshes are full of crocodiles.'

14 See also Eaton, *The Rise of Islam*, 308–313.

15 See, for instance, *waqf* inscription of a religious edifice in Sylhet dated 996 (1588), *waqf* inscription for a jāmi' masjid in Dohar, dated 1000 (1591), *madad-i-ma'āsh* inscription for Bhāgal Khān Masjid in Nayabari dated 1003 (1595) and *madad-i-Ma'āsh* inscription for the Bahrām Saqqā' Astāna in Burdwan dated 1015 (1606–1607).

16 The Qur'ān, the Chapter *al-Rūm* (30:30); *Al-Saḥīḥ al-Muslim*, 'Kitāb al-Tahāra' [The Book of Cleanliness], chapter 16 *khiṣal al-fiṭra* [Natural Disposition].

17 M. Talibi, s.v. Ibn Khaldūn, in *The Encyclopaedia of Islam*, 2nd edn, vol. 3 (Leiden: E. J. Brill, 1987): 827.

18 Eaton, *The Rise of Islam*, 72.

19 Ibid., 71–73.

20 Ibid., 75.

21 Ibid., 74.

22 Ibid., 75.

23 Ibid., 83.

24 Ibid., 83–84.

25 Ibid., 85.

26 'Ḥauḍ al-Ḥayāt', ed. Yusuf Hussain, *Journal Asiatique*, 213 (October–December, 1928): 291–344. The original Sanskrit manual was probably compiled by Kanamah, a Hindu Tantrik Yogi. This work was based on a Yogic Tantric concept of mystic physiology with esoteric significance attached to nerve-plexuses, veins, limbs, breath control and retention of semen which seemed to arouse scholarly interest among a number of sufi scholars of South Asia.

27 In South India, a renowned sufi shaykh Mirza Maẓhar Jān-i-Jānān also declared the Veda as a revealed book.

28 Ḥajji Muḥammad, *Nūr Jamāl* (Dhaka University Library MS no. 374, sl. 260), fol. 6 mc.; Saiyid Murtaza, *Yoga-Qalandar* (Dhaka University Library MS no. 547, sl. 394), fol. 1a.; 'Ali Raja, *Ināna-sāgara* (Dhaka University Library MS no. 146b, sl. 9), fols 109, 215, 216.

29 See, for instance, Sharat Chandra Chattapadhdhay, *Polli Somaj* (Dhaka: Salma Book Depot, 1999): 130–132 (an early twentieth century popular Bengali novel).

4 Worldly authority and paradisiacal ambition

Diversity of titles in the Islamic inscriptions of Bengal

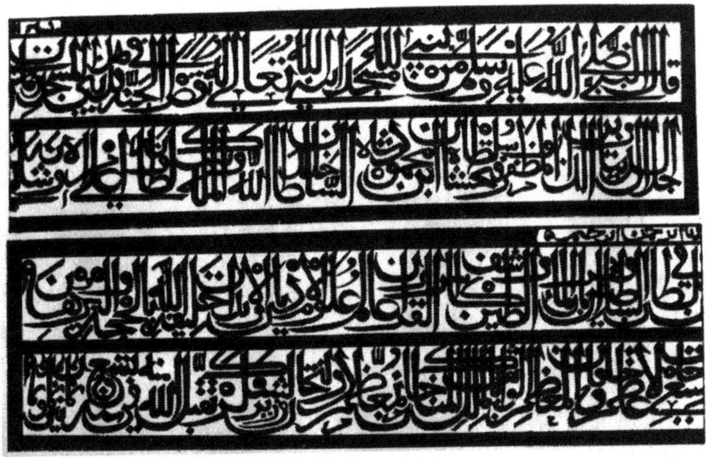

Figure 4.1 Exuberant titles for Fatḥ Shāh in an inscription in Gaur dated 889/1484 (source: Archaeological Survey of India).

Original epigraphic text (in Arabic):

Middle of the Upper Rim بسم الله الرحمن الرحيم

L-1 قال النبي صلى الله عليه وسلم من بنى مسجدا لله بنى الله تعالى له قصرا في الجنة قد بنى هذا المسجد في زمان سلطان السلاطين قهرمان الماء والطين كاشف أسرار القرآن عالم علوم الأديان والأبدان خليفة الله بالحجة والبرهان

L-2 جلال الدنيا والدين أبو<أبي> المظفر فتحشاه سلطان ابن محمود شاه السلطان خلد الله ملكه وسلطانه وأعلى أمره وشأنه بسعي خان الأعظم وخاقان المعظم الواثق بالملك المنان خانمعظم دولتخان وزير لشكر تقبل الله منه في سنة تسع وثمانين وثمانماية

Translation:

Top: In the name of Allah, the Compassionate, the Merciful.

L-1 The Prophet, peace and the blessings of Allah be upon him, said, 'Whoever builds a mosque for the sake of Allah, Allah the Exalted will build for him a palace in Paradise.' This mosque was built in the era of Sulṭān al-Salāṭīn, Qahramān al-Mā' wa 'l-Ṭīn, Kāshif Asrār al-Qur'ān, 'Ālim 'Ulūm al-'Adyān wa 'l-'Abdān, Khalīfat Allah bi 'l-Ḥujja wa 'l-Burhān.

L-2 Jalāl al-Dunyā wa 'l-Dīn Abū 'l-Muẓaffar Fatḥ Shāh Sulṭān ibn Maḥmūd Shāh al-Sulṭān, may Allah perpetuate his kingdom and authority and make his position and prestige high; [it took place] through the effort of the exalted khan and the sublime khāqān, al-Wāthiq bi 'l-Malik al-Mannān, Khān al-Mu'aẓẓam Dawlat Khān, the chief of the army, may [Allah] accept from him [this deed]; in the year eight hundred and eighty nine.

Titles in Islamic culture and their historical importance

The above epigraphic text from the Gunmant mosque in Gaur exemplifies the exuberance of titles in royal inscriptions in Bengal.[1] In the limited space of the two lines on this stone slab, we find seven royal titles for Sultan Fatḥ Shāh from the Ilyās Shāhī dynasty. Interestingly, some of these titles sound more academic and scholarly rather than political. Indeed, many of the Ilyās Shāhī rulers were great patrons of learning and some of them (e.g. Sultan Ghiyāth al-Dīn A'ẓam Shāh who studied under al-Shaykh al-Qāḍī Ḥamīd al-Dīn Nagori Kunjshikan) were sent to educational institutions (madrasas) for formal education. The royal titles in this particular inscription, such as *kāshif asrār al-Qur'ān* (the opener of the secrets of the Qur'ān), *'ālim 'ulūm al-'adyān wa 'l-'abdān* (scholar of the science of religions and physiology), tell us something about Fatḥ Shāh's educational and scholarly background. These titles suggest that not only did he know *'ulūm al-tafsīr* (exegesis of the Qur'ān) and *'ulūm al-'adyān* (science of religion), but he was also interested in anatomy and physiology. The title *kāshif asrār al-Qur'ān* has a Sufi connotation too, for it implies that the title bearer attained a high level of spiritual enlightenment which revealed to him the secret meanings of the Qur'ān.

The large number of honorific titles used by the ruling class in many parts of the Islamic world can be sometimes confusing, as searching for the original name of the person in the fully fledged line of *ism* or *'alam* (name), *laqab* (title), *khiṭāb* (a honorary title in Urdu and Persian), *kunya* (agnomen), *nisba* (an attribution to the place of origin), *nasab* (lineage) and *takhalluṣ* (a penname by which a poet identifies himself in the last line of his poem in Indo-Persian culture) can be a challenging task at times.

Titles are an interesting aspect of human social, political and religious vocabulary expressing various individual and cultural trends, state policy, religious moods, prevailing sectarian thoughts, traditions and norms. While they have great historical significance linked with specific offices and administrative institutions, they also reflect the religious and cultural ethos of the period. The nature, substance and idiomatic expression in titles vary according to person, time and space. Certain titles were used on some extraordinary occasions to express a special message or to imply some particular meaning. Political titles are particularly intriguing as they often portray the worldly ambition of power and glory of the ruling class. To earn popular support, some historical titles can be designated in modern political language as 'euphemism'. Black Abyssinian slaves promoted to high official positions in Bengal as well as in the other Islamic regions were sometimes not only given grandiose titles such as *malik* (lord), but also special names such as Kāfūr (camphor-like white and pure) and Abū 'l-Misk (father of musk). The bestowing of such titles can be seen as an act that can perhaps be termed in today's vocabulary as politically correct. Cover up political expressions were not unusual in those days. In the early 1980s, the king of Saudi Arabia assumed the title *khādim al-ḥaramayn* [Custodian of the Two Holy Mosques], an act calculated to neutralize an undeclared and tacit Iranian campaign to shift the jurisdiction of the holy cities of Makkah and Madinah to a pan-Islamic council, a modern example of the political message that a title can convey.

In the politics of titles, it is not surprising to find politicians sometimes using words to try to play with public sentiment to the extent of deception, though unsuccessfully at times. When there was an attempt by the Buyids to seek Caliphal endorsement of an ancient Persian imperial title 'Shāhanshāh' for them through its formal pronouncement in the Friday *khutba* (congregational sermon) in Baghdad in AH 429 (CE 1038), there was an unwelcome reaction among the public to the point of near riot. In a way, this reaction recalls the public discontent with the late Iranian monarch Reza Shah Pahlawi's claim to use the title 'Shāhanshāh', which resulted in the Islamic revolution in the country. On the other hand, there are titles which honestly represent popular sentiment, such as the title 'Sher-i-Bangla' (the Lion of Bengal) given to Fazlul Haque, a popular Muslim leader of undivided Bengal during the last days of British raj, or the title of 'Mahatma' (Great Soul) given to Mohandas Gandhi.

Titles can give hints about territorial expansion, sectarian policy, political allegiance and so forth. They can indicate the aspirations and ambitions of the title bearer. In some cases, the smaller the kingdom or fiefdom, the longer the title of its ruler, perhaps in compensation for the unimportant role the bearer likely played in the larger scheme of things. As the court scribes, eulogists and panegyrists exaggerated regnal titles to win rulers' favour, they silently competed among themselves in their expression of humility and loyalty to the authority and the ruling class, a natural human weakness that can be found perhaps everywhere in varying degrees. Even to this day, in Punjab subordinates often pay tribute to their superior by calling themselves *nawkar* or *khādim* (servant of their immediate boss), or in Egypt, by using submissive expression such as *'anā taḥta amrika yā sayyidī* (I am at your disposal, O my lord).

On the other hand, the grandiosity of titles and their possible political use (or misuse) can also be noticed from time to time in human history. The political use of titles caught the attention of early Muslim scholars and historians. Ibn Khaldūn, for instance, quotes some sarcastic verses by Ibn Abī Sharf mocking the prevailing trend of petty rulers in Andalusia of using pompous royal titles that hardly matched the power and influence of the rulers. The Andalusian poet ibn Rashīq at one point sighs and says: 'Royal epithets not in their proper place – Like a cat puffing itself up imitates the lion.'[2] Similarly, al-Bayrūnī criticised the Būyīds for their nonsensical use of extravagant titles and pompous epithets such *kāfī 'l-kufāt* (most capable among the qualified ones), saying that this was 'nothing but one great lie and clumsy to the highest degree'. However, he complimented the relatively modest titles of the Samanids.[3] Likewise, Saljūq vizier, Niẓām al-Mulk commented that overinflated titles naturally started losing their meaning.[4] Rulers and fief-holders in the frontier regions of the Islamic world competed with each other to get endorsement of titles from the Abbasid caliphs in Baghdad, and later on from the nominal caliphs in Cairo, seeking to stand out above the rest. Placing allegiance to the ruling caliph of the time gave their rule and authority a sort of religious and moral legality. Titles could also contribute in their own way to glorifying the title-bearers' status in society and the state. *Tashrīfiyyah* (honorific) titles with strong religious claims and divine support often expressing dependence on God provided a strong foundation of legitimacy that rulers often sought for. On the other hand, pretentious titles were eagerly sought after by power hungry rulers to show off their grandiosity. The post-Awrangzib period of the Mughals serves as a good example of the extensive conferring of embellished titles by emperors and provincial rulers when political and military power starts shrinking rapidly. As a result of this overstatement of power, the social importance of the titles also declines. Thus once much valued titles, such as Beg, Khān and Mirzā (a Persian title meaning a 'prince' or 'son of an Emir') in Bengal and other South Asian regions became nothing more than equivalent of what is known in modern days as family names (or surnames).

It is also interesting to note that some classical titles (considered very rewarding ones in the past) have turned into popular proper names, such as Shams al-Dīn and 'Alā' al-Dīn, to name a few. In general, titles of the Islamic East (sometimes known as *al-alqāb al-mashriqiyyah* or the eastern titles) seem to be more lavish and exaggerated than their counterparts in the Islamic West such as al-Andalus or North Africa. It was also a common practice to give honorific titles to high-profile non-Muslims while carefully avoiding religious references, keeping in mind religious sensitivity. In the historical evolution of Islamic titles, we find a few titles especially assigned to women. However, the number of titles assigned to women is almost negligible, indicating the marginal role women had in public life in the past, particularly in politics.

In Islamic titles, we find influences coming from the diverse historical experiences of different nations, regions and from various directions. Thus a title as such Ḥātim al-Milla (حاتم الملة) appearing in an inscription dated 1020/1612 at the tomb of Shaykh Nūr Quṭb al-'Ālam in Ḥaḍrat Pandua, West Bengal, draws its inspiration from Ḥātim al-Ṭā'ī, a proverbial icon in benevolence, generosity and goodness in pre-Islamic Arab history. On the other hand, the title 'Sulṭān al-Zamān alladhi Mulkuhu Mulku Sulaymān (سلطان الزمان الذي ملكه ملك سليمان, the sultan of the age, whose kingdom matches the kingdom of King Solomon' (ins. no. 19) present the Bengali Sultan as a role model and an ideal ruler on par with King Solomon (*ca.* tenth century BCE). The figure of King Solomon symbolized in the Jewish tradition a successful world ruler with a legendary vast, powerful and prosperous kingdom. Pre-Islamic Persian (namely, Sassanid) influence can be seen in titles such as 'Khusrow-i-Zaman (خسرو زمان) Khusrow of the age)' as Khusrow Anoshirvan (*ca.* 531–597 BCE), the Just, was believed to be an exemplary great

Persian monarch. The title appeared in an inscription (no. 10) fixed on the Mausoleum of Mawlanā Shāh 'Aṭā in Dakhshin Dinajpur, West Bengal. The title Sikandar al-Thānī (سكند الثاني the second Alexander) appearing for Ẓafar Khān Bahram Aytgīn Sulṭānī in a masjid inscription (no. 10) in Southern Dinajpur, West Bengal is also interesting. It compares the title bearer with the famous Macedonian conqueror Alexander the Great, whose conquest in the northwest of South Asia left far-reaching impacts on culture and civilization of the region. Symbolically, the title refers to the Muslim conquerors coming from the West to the East as the torch bearers of high culture and advanced civilization, on the footsteps of the monarch Sikandar or Alexander (seemingly mentioned in the Qur'ān as Dhū 'l-Qarnayn). Khān (خان nobleman/lord) is also a popular title in Bengal that appeared in a number of inscriptions in Bengal, quite often in a compound form with other adjectives such as Khān Mu'aẓẓam or al-Khān al-Mu'aẓẓam. Originally a title for the kings and rulers of certain Turk tribes (mainly Khatai and Tatar tribes of Central Asia), the title 'khān' found its way to Bengal through Turko-Afghan tribes (such as Khaljī) who came to Bengal as conquerors in the thirteenth century. Similarly khāqān (خاقان overlord), a synonym for khān, used for those in the imperial ranks and kings in the eastern parts of Central Asia, particularly by Tatars and Mongols also appeared, often in a compound form with different adjectives, in a number of inscriptions of Bengal. Khāqān appeared, for instance, for Abū 'l-Fatḥ Ṭughril al-Sulṭānī, the ruler of Bengal and Bihar, in an inscription of a religious edifice (no. 4) dated Muḥarram 640 (July 1242) in Bari Dargah, Bihar Sharif, Bihar (see also ins. nos 9 and 16).

With the formation of Islamic civilization, the Muslim ruling elite gradually started taking an interest in the protocols and royal styles of the neighbouring centres of civilizations. Titles played a significant role in the official recognition of important personalities in the Byzantine and Persian traditions. This was a crucial time period in the Islamic world when various innovative and new institutions came into existence as a result of cultural continuity and interaction with the neighbouring Persian and Byzantine civilizations, or, in other words, through their direct or indirect influences. Many early state officials and bureaucrats of these institutions, particularly in the newly conquered regions, were non-Muslims. Their professional cooperation contributed significantly to the growth and advancement of these newly established institutions, in spite of the initial apprehension of some Muslim rulers about employing non-Muslims in these sensitive state positions. Caliph 'Umar was particularly unhappy with employing non-Muslims, though he had to employ a number of them. Thus we find that many chiefs of the state secretariat (namely, Dīwān al-Inshā') responsible for official correspondence during the early period of the Fatimid rule in Egypt happened to be from the Christian minority; they were given various honorary titles in recognition of their professional competency. Among the early bureaucrats to lead this institution during the Fatimid era were Ya'qūb ibn Kals, Fahd ibn Ibrāhīm al-Naṣrānī (honoured with the title al-Ra'īs in 388/998),[5] Abū 'l-Naṣr ibn 'Abdūn al-Naṣrānī (honoured with the title al-Kāfī in 400/1008),[6] Waz'a ibn 'Īsā ibn

Nasṭūras al-Naṣrānī (honoured with the title al-Shāfī in 401/1010)[7] and his brother Sā'id ibn 'Īsā ibn Nasṭūras al-Naṣrānī (honoured with the title al-Amīn), all of whom were Christians. Similar trends could be found in other Islamic regions during this era.[8]

It is important to note that not everyone was encouraged or allowed to coin a royal title for the sultan on his own initiative. The process needed some sort of formal, official and institutional endorsement. Hence we see the inception of a special office, namely Dīwān al-Inshā', in the leading Islamic capitals. This office contributed extensively towards innovating new titles that were deemed proper for the ruling authority, and issued formal titles, in addition to conducting a variety of other tasks related to official correspondence and protocols. While the institution worked for creating suitable phrases for titles, it also scrutinized the appropriateness of titles conferred on rulers in other regions of the caliphate or in the titular states in the hinterlands. This important state institution was so professional in its work that every detail of its tasks, including the technical aspects, were minutely codified. Such details included the quality of ink and stationary, special pens for different calligraphic styles, varieties of (Arabic/Islamic) scripts, calligraphic innovations and their suitability for a particular thematic expression, and manuals of writing styles. While writing to the caliph, for instance, Ḥajjāj ibn Yūsuf would inscribe the name of the caliph in a bold calligraphic style at the top, whereas he would write his own name at the end thinly to express his humility. The choice of proper wording was extremely important for maintaining official protocol and formal communication since an unwise choice of phrases would convey unclear messages and send the wrong signals, as pointed out by Abū 'l-Hilāl al-'Askarī.[9] Titles were sometimes given so much importance as a medium of carrying messages that any breach of protocol in the use of title could be considered a great offence.[10]

The formal name of this office varied from time to time and from one region to another. While the original name of Dīwān al-Inshā' remained popular in general during most of the period, particularly in the early Abbasid era, sometimes it was also known as Dīwān al-Kitāba, Dīwān al-Dast al-Sharīf, Dīwān al-Ṭughrā' etc. During the Tulunid era in Egypt, it was known as Dīwān al-Mukātibāt. Responsible for imperial writing protocol and chancellery script, this particular office issued formal titles for the ruling class and their family and other dignitaries of the government, in addition to endorsing formal texts for official inscriptions for state-sponsored architecture. The title of the chief office-holder/office-bearer varied from region to region. In North Africa (particularly in Morocco), the chief of this office was called Ṣāḥib al-Qalam al-A'lā. During the Fatimid era in Egypt, the office was sometimes called Diwān-i-Dast-Sharīf (a compound Persian phrase meaning Office of the Blessed Hand). In spite of its geographic distance, Bengal continued to be influenced culturally by the Arab world. While Persian remained the court language during Muslim rule in the region, Arabic was, in general, the medium of intellectual and academic activities (e.g. education in madrasas) until the advent of the Mughals. Though it may not be hard to presume that some sort of institution such as Dīwān al-Inshā' may have existed in the Bengal frontier too, there is hardly any mention of it in the limited historical sources about the Bengal Sultanate. In all probability, the 'ulamā' in the capitals of Bengal had some kind of involvement in suggesting and coining correct forms of Arabic expression for official and royal titles.

Historical sources for Islamic titles are various. Classical sources (particularly medieval Arabic and Persian history books) provide us with rich information about various Islamic titles during different periods. Official decrees, *farmans*, chronicles and royal correspondence and archives also offer rich clues about the diversity of titles used in Islamic culture. Coins are also a good source, though their spatial limits hardly allow any scope for exaggeration in the number of titles. Over time, a special genre of literature (under various names such as *al-rasā'il*, *al-mukātibāt* and *al-inshā'*), started evolving in the Islamic world. Not surprisingly, many of the great works in this field were compiled under the supervision of Dīwān al-Inshā' in order to codify official protocols for titles and for state correspondence.

Because of the important symbols and meanings that many of these titles convey, many medieval Muslim historians and scholars took an interest in them and left an enormous and rich body of literature dealing with the subject. Fortunately, a few of those interesting works have survived to this day which provide us glimpses of the diverse titles used at various places during different periods. Ibn Qutayba (Abū Muḥammad 'Abd-Allah ibn Muslim al-Dīnūrī, d. AH 270/CE 882–883) touched on the subject in his book *Adab al-Kātib*[11] as early as the middle of the third century Hijra (CE 9), so did Abū 'Abd-Allah Muḥammad ibn 'Abdus al-Jahshiyārī (d. AH 331/CE 941–942) in *Kitāb al-Wuzarā' wa 'l-Kuttāb*,[12] just to name a few among the earliest works. With the passage of time, more focused works started appearing such as *Ma'ālim al-Kitāba wa Magānim al-'Isāba* by Jamāl al-Dīn 'Abd al-Raḥīm ibn 'Alī ibn al-Shīth (d. AH 625),[13] *al-Ta'rīf bi 'l-Muṣṭaliḥ al-Sharīf* by Shihāb al-Dīn ibn Faḍl-Allah al-'Umarī (d. AH 748)[14] and the famous early ninth century Hijra work *Ṣubḥ al-A'shā fī Ṣanā'at al-Inshā'* by the renowned Egyptian scholar Shihāb al-Dīn Aḥmad ibn 'Alī al-Qalqashandi.[15] These books, which can be considered as the *magna opera* of the time, are distinctive due to their rich, creative and interpretive approaches. A number of notable Muslim historians, including ibn Khaldūn and al-Bīrūnī,[16] found the topic of titles so intriguing that they devoted special chapters to titles in some of their illustrious works.

There have been quite a few studies of Islamic titles during modern period, the most important of which is the ground-breaking work of Ḥasan al-Bashā (d. 2001) in the Arabic language, *al-Alqāb al-Islāmiyyah fī 'l-Tārīkh wa 'l-Wathā'iq wa 'l-Āthār*.[17] This book surveys the diverse titles used by different Islamic dynasties during various periods. Bashā's work is especially characterized by its great depth and remarkable interpretive style, though focusing more on the Fatimid, Ayyubid and Mamluk periods in Egypt (which has somewhat limited its approach). Western scholarship on the subject is also considerably rich. C. E. Bosworth's extensive article *lakab* in the *Encyclopaedia of Islam*[18] represents a remarkably thorough study in the field in the English language. Annemarie

Schimmel's interesting book *Islamic Names* is another excellent treatise on the topic.[19] The recent publication of an Arabic work on Islamic epigraphy *al-Nuqūsh al-Kitābiyya al-Islāmiyya fī Bilād al-Bangāl* is an important addition to this field since it contains an elaborate discussion of Islamic titles found in the inscriptions of Bengal.[20]

Though mostly honorific in nature, Islamic titles in general are largely shaped by the place, time and status of the title bearer. This led Hasan al-Basha to coin a special phrase, *al-alqāb al-makāniyya* (positional titles). As in modern times, in the past *laqab* used to be categorized on the basis of profession, ranking, responsibility and power. The great diversity of Islamic titles can be loosely grouped into various categories such as religious, spiritual, royal, secular, chancery, ceremonial, administrative, professional, military, honorary and honorific etc. There are family titles as well referring to family trade or profession such as *al-mi'mār* (architect or mason). In addition, as described earlier, there are titles which are a mere exhibition of cosmetic power and glory, while others are coined in a thoughtful process with a deeper message, or perhaps with a visionary sense of history.

The Arab-Islamic tradition of titles has a long history which goes back to the era before Islam. The very term *laqab* (title) started with a negative connotation in pre-Islamic Arab tradition, as indicated also in the Qur'ān.[21] In spite of its initial use in the negative sense of *nabaz* (nasty nicknames particularly for enemies) in which the ancient Arabs apparently excelled, the word *laqab* was used in the later Islamic period in a positive sense in general like the term *na'at* (plural: *nu'ūt* meaning adjectives, praise, epithets or appellations). *Laqab* invariably required *ism* (proper noun), and in many cases *kunya* (somewhat akin to agnomen of a person with which he is popularly known, usually *abū* or *umm* followed by the name of the son or daughter), *nisba* (attribution), *nasab* (patronymic name based on lineage), in addition to some other expressive words such as prayer formulas.

Titles started appearing from the time of the Prophet who himself conferred *alqāb* (plural of *laqab*) to some of his companions, albeit informally and quite often congenially. The titles of the early era of Islam were spontaneous, simple as well as limited to necessity and devoid of any extravagance and flowery expression. Early titles, such as Khalīfa and Amīr al-Mu'minīn represented popular sentiment as well as the nature of the job. These two titles in particular embedded in them the spirit of democracy (albeit in the Islamic sense of *shūrā*), political loyalty to the leader of the ummah and a spiritual dimension. Essentially connoting successor, the title *khalīfa* used for the early Muslim rulers, encompasses multidimensional implications including carrying out the political and religious responsibilities of the ummah. Historically, it has been used in various forms and for various purposes in different parts of the Islamic world, such as Yamīn Khalīfat-Allah (يمين خليفة الله the right hand of the vicegerent of Allah), a title assumed by Kaykā'us Shāh of Bengal that appeared in a jāmi' masjid inscription dated 697/1297 (in Lakhisarai in Monghyr district, Bihar) in addition to four other inscriptions during his rule. By assuming the title Yamīn

Khalīfat-Allah, the ruler could express his symbolic allegiance, at least in a spiritual sense, to caliphal authority of the Islamic world. Titles such as Amīr and Khalīfat-Allah 'Alā 'l-Mukawwanīn (خليفة الله على المكونين vicegerent of Allah over all created things) in two different inscriptions from the time of Sultan Jalāl al-Dīn Muḥammad dated 835/1432 and 836/1433, an indigenous Bengali ruler, clarify the standing of the Muslim rulers of Bengal vis-à-vis other rulers such as the sultans of Delhi and the Abbasid caliphs of Egypt. Strangely enough, the word *khalīfa* is used for a tailor-master in present day popular Bengali bazaar culture, a crude departure from its original meaning. Two early Muslim rulers of Bengal, Giyāth al-Dīn 'Iwaḍ and Abū 'l-Fatḥ Tughril, assumed the title Burhān-i-Amīr al-Mu'minīn (برهان أمير المؤمنين) in a bid to express their religious allegiance to Abbasid caliphs in Baghdad. In spite of the frequent power struggle among the throne contenders of the Bengal Sultanate, none of the aspirants of the throne or the rulers ever proclaimed himself caliph or Amīr al-Mu'minīn. Such proclamations would have been interpreted by the Muslim masses as an act of betrayal to the spirit of universal Muslim unity well embedded in the idea of ummah.

On the other hand, the majority of the Umayyad kings used the title 'Malik' (king), indicating their lust for power, glamour and political influence. Shāh (شاه), a roughly equivalent Persian title, has a widespread use in a number of South Asian languages used by the Muslims, sometimes in different compound forms, such as Bādshāh or Pādshāh (باد شاه containing two words: *pād* meaning throne, and *shāh* meaning the lord), a popular Persian imperial title. Shāh thus stands for monarch, which has become part of the popular vocabulary over years in a number of major South Asian languages including Bengali, Urdu and Hindi, in addition to the languages of neighbouring regions. The last Afghan king Zāhir Shāh, for instance, used to be called 'Bādshāh' until his dethronement in 1973. Used by all the Mughal emperors in India, the title appeared in a few Sultanate inscriptions as well as in the majority of Mughal inscriptions in Bengal.

With the passing of power to the Abbasids, there was a sudden surge of formal titles as if it became an important medium of expressing glory and the power of the ruling class. Persian influence can also be seen in the formation of titles during this period. In this newly emerging cultural setting, the term *laqab* became popular for connoting titles, albeit in a positive sense, in spite of the fact that some other vocabularies (such as, *na'at*) continued to be used for denoting more or less the same meaning of title.

Whether they are Islamic titles of Bengal or any other region, we may find some sort of historical clues of their direct or indirect origin in the titles that appeared in the early period of Islam in the central Islamic world, particularly in the Abbasid capitals, namely Baghdad. Likewise, close geographic proximity as well as political and cultural links always played an important role in setting trends in coining titles in the newly conquered regions. While the early titles in Bengal bore resemblance with their counterparts in Delhi, titles of the early rulers in Delhi were greatly influenced by the pattern set in the capitals in Khurasan (and more particularly Afghanistan), such as Ghaznah. Interestingly, the honorific title 'Ḥāfiz Bilād-Allah' (حافظ بلاد الله the custodian of God's lands), which was given by the Abbasid caliph al-Qādir (القادر بأمر الله) to Sulṭān Mas'ūd ibn Maḥmūd Ghaznavi around the year AH 421/CE 1030 in recognition of Mas'ūd's rule in the Islamic East, travelled further east in Bengal. Consequently it appeared a few centuries later for a contender of Bengal Sultanate, Abū 'l-Muẓaffar Maḥmud Shāh in 934/1528 apparently in his bid to have an edge over the throne, during the reign of his elder brother Sulṭān Nuṣrat Shāh.

Since religion plays a strong role in Muslims' lives as well as in Islamic societies, Islamic titles are historically full of religious fervour. The symbolic appearance of the word *Islam* as a suffix in a large number of titles and proper names in Bengal is a good example of this trend. In a way, this trend helps us understand the religious undercurrent prevailing in the region during that period. A title containing, for instance, the Shī'ī phrase *ithnā 'ashariyya* (followers of twelve *imāms*) helps us identify a prevailing sectarian setting in a given time and place. To cite an example, the title '*murawwiju maḍhab a'immat ithnā 'ashara*' (مروج مذهب أئمة اثنا عشر the patron of the faith of twelve *imāms*) mentioned in an inscription at Shāh Makhdūm Dargāh in Rajshahi dated 1045/1634 clearly bears a reference to the largest Shī'a sect that followed the twelve *imāms* from the house of the Prophet. Its inscriber, 'Alī Qulī Bayg (an Iranian origin Shī'ī elite), did not hesitate to express his allegiance to Shāh 'Abbās Ṣafawī al-Ḥusaynī[22] rather than to the ruling authority of Shāh Jahān, even though he was living and thriving in a Mughal administered territory far away from Iran. The word *imām* (إمام leader) appears in several sayings of the Prophet connoting the leader of a Muslim community. In the Shī'a tradition, the term connotes a central religious position, and thus carries much deeper spiritual and political dimensions since the Imām of the age is also given divine providence, custodianship and guardianship (ولاية الفقيه) over those in need of it. An interesting example would be Imām Khomeini who led the Islamic revolution in Iran. On the popular level, however, the imām of a mosque is the person who is assigned by the community to lead daily prayers. While the Shī'ī communities have special titles for their religious personalities (e.g. Ayat-Allāh), Sunnis also have various titles for their religious scholars such as Mawlānā, widely used in South Asia. In contrast, in North Africa, Mawlānā was used mostly for rulers or the dignitaries in the ruling class.

The title *ḥājjī* (which appeared, for example, in an inscription from Burarchar as well as in another inscription from Dohar in Bengal, both of them dated 1000/1591) helps us trace the extent of religious and cross-cultural links of Bengali Muslims with the Arabian Peninsula. While most modest epithets and phrases expressing humility were aimed to please title-bearers' masters in power hierarchy, some appear to be purely spiritual in nature, depicting an unassuming character in the vastness of divine creation. An example is the *laqab* 'aḥqar al-khalā'iq', used for Ḥajjī Bahrām Eytgin in a masjid inscription (no. 17) from Ḥāṭim Khān's Palace in Bihar Sharif dated 715/1315. Religious figures had, for instance, their own titles indicating their scholarly and spiritual status, as evident in a funerary inscription of Nūr Quṭb al-'Ālam in Bengal (dated 863/1459).

Titles specially coined on the occasion of coronation, usually known as *julūs* (لقب الجلوس على العرش) titles (more in a Persian sense than Arabic), offer us important clues about the trend of the new ruler. In South Asia, these titles often had two parts. Often, they would start with an official regnal title that would usually contain at the end two words '*al-dunyā wa 'l-dīn*' (the world and the religion) in genitive construction, preceded by an adjective (usually as a subjective genitive, such as *'Alā'*, *Ghiyāth*, *Jalāl*, *Nāṣir*, *Sayf*, *Shams*, *Shihāb* etc.). These two words in pair at the end, connected by a conjunction, were likely to produce the effect of *saja'* (سجع) or a rhythmic expression, making the title more poetic and graceful. Combination of both the words *dīn* and *dunyā'* in a single title fitted well with the ambition and power play of the Muslim rulers or the aspirants to the throne in those days. Using composed pairs often aimed to include both the dimensions of the opposite ends, such as *al-Mā' wa 'l-Ṭīn* (الماء والطين water and soil), *al-'Arab wa 'l-'Ajm* (العرب والعجم the Arabs and non-Arabs) and *Barr wa Baḥr* (بر وبحر the earth and the sea). Indeed, *dīn wa dunyā* pattern titles became quite popular in Sultanate Bengal. We also find them in various other Islamic regions during different periods (e.g. Ayyubid as well as Mamluk eras in Egypt) to the extent that more than 200 different varieties of this type of title can be traced in the history of Islam, at times quite ingeniously constructed. Normally each ruler would coin his own special regnal title that reflected the need of the time, place, state policy and, most importantly, the particular message that he wanted to convey through his title. Regnal titles would usually be followed by an official single *kunya* starting with Abū and then a qualitative word such as al-Fatḥ, al-Naṣr or al-Mujāhid etc. The most popular *kunya* in Bengal, however, happened to be Abū 'l-Muẓaffar (victorious) as it symbolized victory and success in worldly life as well as in spiritual life. Traditionally, a ruler would assume only one regnal title containing *al-dunyā wa 'l-dīn* and a single *kunya* which would not change during his lifetime. These regnal titles were meant to convey the power, stature, influence and ability of the ruler.

Because of their religious implications, titles containing the word *dīn* were reserved for Muslims only, while titles containing the word *dawla* could be awarded to non-Muslims as well. Though somewhat rare, we do find a few titles in Bengal containing the word *dawla* (i.e. state) such as Mu'aẓẓam al-Dawla. During the period of the later Abbasid rulers, *dawla* titles were commonly reserved for military commanders and the Turks, a practice criticized by Niẓam al-Mulk because of the pointlessness of conferring such titles to undeserving persons. With a radically politicized religious outlook, Shī'i ruling establishments at times found *dawla* honorifics quite appealing, whereas *dīn* (albeit, in compound form often with the word *dunyā* or *dawla*) gained more popularity in the Sunni world. This sentiment reverberates in some titles of Quṭb al-Dīn Aybak (later on followed by his successors such as Shams al-Dīn Iltutmish) appearing in Quwwat (more correctly Qubbat) al-Islām mosque. With a Turko-Afghan background in addition to having connection with their original masters (namely, the sultans of Delhi) in one way or other, the early Bengal rulers were greatly influenced by their counterparts in North India in every sphere of life including coining titles. This resonates in the titles on the very first inscription of Bengal belonging to the reign of Sulṭān ʻAlī Mardān (607–610/1210–1213), the third Khalji ruler of Bengal where he is pronounced as ʻAlā' Dīn wa Dunyā (علاء دين ودنيا the greatness of the religion and the world). Interestingly, the word *dīn* exceptionally precedes the word *dunyā* in this earliest Islamic inscription of Bengal, to underscore the historic change in the region with the advent of Islam. Indeed, we find in a few early Islamic titles the word *dīn* placed before the word *dunyā* symbolically indicating the priority of religion over worldly affairs. This arrangement is noticeable in some titles appearing in Baghdad and the regions that were highly influenced by the early Abbasid caliphate. In Bengal, however, we notice in almost all the later inscriptions that the word *dunyā* is placed before the word *dīn*, perhaps keeping in mind the natural chronological order of things in the real world as *dunyā* (the present world/worldly life) is considered as an opening ground (المزرعة or farm land, according to a pious saying in Arabic) for *dīn* whose final goal is hereafter. But overall, these two strands of human existence (namely, *din* and *dunyā*) were regarded as interdependent in this temporal life and their fortunes inextricably interwoven.[23] We also notice a traditional appearance of the word *dīn* in religious titles, namely titles of ʻulamā', sufi-saints and various other religious personalities.

Interestingly, none of the titles of Sultan Sikandar Shāh (758–795/1357–1393, the second ruler of the Ilyās Shāhi dynasty in Bengal) contains the popular term ʻ*al-dunyā wa 'l-dīn*'. Rather his *kunya* Abū 'l-Mujāhid (أبو المجاهد the father of the [holy] warrior), which appears in an inscription dated 765/1363 in Adinah Masjid, Pandua seems to be more expressive. It also appears for Maḥmūd Shāh as well as for Bārbak Shāh. With a reference of *jihād* in the title, Sikandar Shāh was perhaps trying to convey the message that the gradual formation of this Muslim kingdom in the Bengal hinterland became possible only as a result of a long process of *jihād*. In the light of the traditions (i.e. *ḥadīth*) of the Prophet, *jihād* perhaps can be interpreted as a pious struggle against evil as well as fight in the path of Allah. Henceforth, its inclusion in a title served as a mission statement for a Muslim ruler that boosted his legitimacy. There are many references to *jihād* in the Qur'ān such as the verse in the *ṣūra* (chapter) 'Repentance' (9:20–22) that signifies the importance of this institution. We find several other titles with reference to *jihād*, such as al-Mujāhid (المجاهد the warrior in the cause of religion) appeared for Bahādur Shāh in a treasury inscription dated 722/1322, al-Mujāhid fi Sabīl Allah al-Mannān (المجاهد في سبيل الله المنان the warrior in the path of Allah, the All-Giver) appeared in a madrasa inscription dated 907/1502 and al-Mujāhid fī Sabīl al-Raḥmān (المجاهد في سبيل الرحمن The fighter in the path of the most merciful) appeared in a masjid inscription in Bara dated 854/1450.

Like the word *dīn* in a title (e.g. Nāṣīr al-Dunyā wa 'l-Dīn [ناصر الدنيا والدين the helper of the world and the religion]), titles containing religious zeal (e.g. al-Mujāhid fi Sabīl Allah al-Mannān [المجاهد في سبيل الله المنان The warrior in the path of Allah; the All-Giver], Muḥy 'l-Sunna [محي السنة revivalist of the Prophet's traditions]) carried a messianic appeal in them which helped boost the legitimacy of the rulers on the frontier. Quite often, such titles were adopted by presumptuous and rebellious *amīr*s and governors,[24] examples of which can be seen in an inscription from the reign of Bahādur Shāh who ruled Bengal intermittently during 722–733/1322–1333. Most of the fourteen titles (such as, al-Mujāhid [the holy warrior], al-Murābiṭ [the advance guard in the frontier] and al-Ghāzī [the conqueror]) in the inscription portray him as the defender of the faith in an Islamic frontier region. Interestingly, similar titles were used by the Saljūqs in Anatolia, the Mamlūks in Egypt, Rasūlīd rulers in Yemen and a few defiant *amīr*s in Syria. Many of these rulers seem to have been influenced by the court-culture of Ayyūbīds and Mamlūks.

One of the most sought after titles for aspirants of rule and power was the title 'sultan' (سلطان the king). Originating from the root *sulṭa*, it literally means authority, power and dominion.[25] One of the most common titles of the rulers and kings in the history of Islam throughout the Islamic world, it became the most popular royal title in Bengal during the Sultanate period, appearing in more than 200 pre-Mughal inscriptions. An interesting example would be the third Muslim ruler of Bengal, 'Alā' Dīn 'Alī Mardān, who declared himself sultan (as evident in the first Islamic inscription of Bengal). Thus, 'Alā' Dīn 'Alī Mardān was the first in Bengal to use the title Sultan, strike coins in his own name and behave like an independent ruler. Yet he successfully avoided any conflict with the newly established central government in Delhi. Starting from the reign of Rukn al-Dunyā wa 'l-Dīn Kaykā'ūs Shāh in 690/1290 (see, for example, a citadel inscription dated 692/1293 from Maheshwara near Begusarai, Bihar), the title started appearing in most Bengal inscriptions until the arrival of the Mughals in the Subcontinent, who opted for the title Pādshāh (بادشاه Emperor). Traditionally, sons inheriting the throne from their father would assume also the additional title al-Sulṭān ibn al-Sulṭān (the king, son of the king) and sometimes al-Sulṭān ibn al-Sulṭān ibn al-Sulṭān (in case his grandfather also was king) and so on in order to boost the legitimacy of his kingship.

It is interesting to find sometimes innovative titles on particular occasions that carry a special message or meaning. A good example is the title 'fātiḥ Kāmrū wa Kāmtah bi 'awn Allah al-Ḥannān al-Mannān' (فاتح كامرو وكامته بعون الله الحنان والمنان the conqueror of Kamru[p] and Kamta with the help of Allah the Compassionate and Benefactor), which appeared for Sultan Ḥusayn Shāh in an inscription that originally belonged to an unknown Sultanate mosque near a ruined fort at the village of Kantaduar in Pirganj police station, Rangpur district, Bangladesh. Because of the close geographic proximity of the discovery location of this inscription to Kamrup and Kamta, the title which announces the victory over Kamrup and Kamta must have been inscribed after Ḥusayn Shāh's return from his war campaign against those two feudal kingdoms. Only two inscriptions with this title (with this particular message and phrase) can be found in the long list of various titles (numbering close to fifty) in nearly 100 inscriptions of Ḥusayn Shāh discovered so far.

In most inscriptions mentioning Ḥusayn Shāh, we find family titles of a sort, namely, Sayyid (سيد) as well as al-Ḥusaynī (الحسيني), seemingly to earn sympathy from the Muslim masses. A popular word in Arabic used as an adjective to connote various meanings such as a lord or a person of noble origin, the title *sayyid* often expresses spiritual connection with the family of the Prophet. In a stricter sense, however, the title is used in the Islamic world to refer one's lineage to Fāṭima, the daughter of the Prophet. Ḥusaynī, on the other hand, was used by Ḥusayn Shāh to assert his ancestry to Imām Ḥusayn (the grandson of the Prophet) and his descendants.

While eulogy and prayers were a regular feature of day to day usage in the Arabic language even before Islam, they started appearing more frequently after names during the Abbasid period, a tradition that spread over times to other parts of the Islamic world as well. With the passage of time, aspects of these formulas were also well codified by Dīwān al-Inshā' such as their size and length, varying in accordance to time, place and person.[26] Quite often, they appear to be pious invocations, a tradition, that might have been influenced by *taṣliya* and *taslīm* (a pious wish for the Prophet). In Bengali inscriptions too, we find an exuberance of various prayer formulas such as *khallada Allah mulkahu wa sulṭānahu* (may Allah make his kingdom and sovereignty everlasting), which appear usually towards the end of epigraphic texts and contain pious wishes for the long life of the sultan, and the prosperity and longevity of his rule.

Titles are indeed a fascinating source for understanding the history and culture of the world of Islam. They are found abundantly in Islamic inscriptions in various regions. Their dissemination in various Islamic regions in diverse ways point to a natural (albeit silent) process of globalization that resonated throughout the historical experience of the Islamic world during its early and medieval periods until the advent of European colonial power in these lands. One is truly amazed to find the remarkable cultural continuity in these vast regions, as if ideas travelled from one corner of the world of Islam to the other, in a literary manner as well as spiritually. But at the same time, a great diversity also existed in the regional cultural expressions of the Islamic world throughout history. The intriguingly long list of titles on the Bengal frontier serves as an interesting example of the enormously rich historical and cultural content that Islamic titles offer to us.

Notes

1 These are still much humbler and more modest in number when compared with the twenty-three titles that appeared in one of the inscriptions of a Mamlūk sultan of Egypt, Qala'ūn (*ca.* 1279–1290), that runs along the east façade of a funerary complex at mid-height overlooking the Qasaba, the main street of medieval Cairo.

2 Ibn Khaldūn ('Abd al-Raḥman ibn Muḥammad al-Maghribī), *Kitāb al-'Ibr wa Dīwān al-Mubtadā' wa 'l-Khabr* (popularly known as *Muqaddima*), vol. 1 (Cairo, AH 1348): 281; see also its Urdu translation by Mawlānā Sa'ad Ḥasan Yūsufi (Arambagh, Karachi: Mīr Muḥammad Kutub Khana, Markaz 'Ilm wa Adab, n.d.): 231–233.

3 Abū Rayḥān al-Bīrūnī, *al-Āthār al-Bāqiya*, trans. Edward C. Sachau, *Chronology of Ancient Nations* (London: Oriental Translation Fund of Great Britain and Ireland, 1879): 131; for further details, see also C. E. Bosworth, *Encyclopaedia of Islam*, 2nd edn, vol. V (Leiden: E. J. Brill, 1986), s.v. 'Lakab', 622.

4 *Siyāsat Nāma* (Tehran, 1340/1962): 189–200, tr. Herbert Darke, *The Book of Government or Rules for Kings* (London, 1960): 152–163.

5 For details, see Ibn al-Ṣīrafī (Amīn al-Dīn Abū 'l-Qāsim 'Alī ibn Munjib, d. 1147), *al-Ishāra ilā' Man Nāla al-Wazāra* (Cairo: Dār al-Fikr al-'Arabī, 2000): 26.

6 al-Maqrīzī (Taqī al-Dīn Aḥmad ibn 'Alī) *al-Khiṭaṭ wa 'l-Āthār*, vol. 2 (Cairo, AH 1370): 15.

7 al-Maqrīzī, *al-Khiṭaṭ wa 'l-Āthār*, vol. 2: 287.

8 Hasan al-Bāshā, *al-Alqāb al-Islāmiyyah fī 'l-Tārīkh wa 'l-Wathā'iq wa 'l-Āthār* (Alexandria: Dār al-Nahḍa, 1978): 18–19.

9 *Kitāb al-Ṣana'atayn wa 'l-Kitāba* (Istanbul, AH 1319): 118–119; see also Ibn Qutayba, *'Uyun al-Akhbār* (Cairo, 1925): 70–71, al-Bāshā, *al-Alqāb al-Islāmiyyah*, 16.

10 al-Bāshā, *al-Alqāb al-Islāmiyyah*, 10; for further details, see also Abū Bakr Muḥammad ibn Yaḥyā al-Ṣūlī, *Adab al-Kuttāb* (Cairo, 1341).

11 Leiden, 1901.

12 Cairo, 1938.

13 Beirut, 1913.

14 Cairo, AH 1312.

15 14 vols, Cairo, 1913–1919.

16 *Kitāb al-Hind*, trans. Edward C. Sachau as *Alberuni's India* (London: Kegan Paul, Trench, Trübner & Company Ltd, 1910).

17 Alexandria, Dār al-Nahḍa, 1978.

18 Vol. V, 2nd (new) edn, 618–631.

19 Lahore, Sang-e-Meel Publications, 2005.

20 Mohammad Yusuf Siddiq, *Riḥla ma'a al-Nuqūsh al-Kitābiyya fī Bilād al-Bangāl: Darasa Tārīkhiyya Haḍāriyya* (Damascus: Dar al-Fikr, 2004); see also its Persian translation by Layla Musazadeh, *Katī bah hā* (Tehran: Kelk Simin, 2014); Mohammad Yusuf Siddiq, *Mashriq men Islāmī Tahzīb ke Athār: Bangāl ke 'Arbī wa Fārsī Katbāt* (Urdu text) (Islamabad: National University of Science and Technology University, 2013).

21 Al-Qur'ān (49:11).

22 Shāh 'Abbās himself bore nearly a similar title: *murawwiju maḍhab al-a'immat al-ma'ṣumīn* (مروج مذهب الأئمة المعصومين; the patron of the faith of the infallible *imāms*).

23 Bosworth, *Encyclopaedia of Islam*, 2nd edn, s.v. 'Lakab', 623.

24 Ibid., s.v. 'Lakab', 628.

25 For further details, see al-Jawharī (Ismā'īl ibn Ḥammād), *al-Siḥāḥ Tāj al-Lugha wa Siḥāḥ al-'Arabiyya*, vols 3 and 5 (Beirut: Dar al-Kitab al-'Arabi, AH 1402).

26 al-Bāshā, *al-Alqāb al-Islāmiyyah*, 20; al-Qalqashandi, *Ḍaw al-Ṣubḥ al-Musfar wa Jana al-Dawḥ al-Muthmar* (ضوء الصبح المسفر، وجنى الدوح المثمر), vol. 1 (Cairo, 1906): 50; Ibn al-Ṣīrafī, *Qānūn Dīwān al-Rasā'il* (Cairo, 1905): 138–139.

5 Early Islamic inscriptions

Inscriptions of the Khaljī chiefs

(1) A bridge inscription from Sultanganj from the reign of ʻAlā' Dīn ʻAlī Mardān, the first Sultan of Bengal

ORIGINAL SITE: Though originally belonging to an unnamed Sultanate bridge near Sultanganj, this inscription was found on a tomb in the village of Jahanabad near Sultanganj, four miles west of Godagari in Chapai Nawabganj district, Bangladesh. **CURRENT LOCATION:** Varendra Research Museum, Rajshahi, inventory no. 266. **MATERIAL, SIZE:** Black basalt, 42 × 8 inches. **STYLE, NO. OF LINES:** A non-traditional style somewhat resembling *tawqī*ʻ; three lines. **REIGN:** Sulṭān ʻAlā' al-Dīn (607–610/1210–1213), the third Khaljī ruler after the Muslim conquest of Bengal. **LANGUAGE, METER:** Classical Persian; *Baḥr Muḍāriʻ Muthamman Akhrab Makfuf Maḥdhūf* (مفعول فاعلات مفاعيل فاعلن). **TYPE:** Commemorative inscription of a bridge written in Persian couplets. **PUBLICATION:** Ahmad Hasan Dani, *Bibliography of the Muslim Inscriptions of Bengal*, published as an appendix to the *Journal of Asiatic Society of Pakistan* 2 (Dhaka: Asiatic Society of Pakistan, 1957): 65–66 and 124; Abdul Karim, *Corpus of the Arabic and Persian Inscriptions of Bengal* (Dhaka: Asiatic Society of Pakistan, 1992): 319–320; Mohammad Yusuf Siddiq, *Riḥla maʻa 'l-Nuqūsh al-Kitābiyya al-Islāmiyya fī'l-Bangāl: Darāsa Tārīkhīyya Ḥadariyya* (Damascus: Dār al-Fikr, 2004): 94–96; Siddiq, *Mashriq men Islāmī Tahzīb ke Athār: Bangāl men ʻArbī wa Fārsī Katbāt* (Islamabad: NUST, 2013): 125.

On the top edge of the stone slab

Text:

بسم الله الرحمن الرحيم الله خير حافظا وهو أرحم الراحمين من بنى{ال}مسجد[اً] في الدنيا بنى الله[له]أربعين قصرا في الجنة

Translation:

In the name of Allah, the Most Kind, the Most Merciful. Allah is the best protector; and He is the most kind among kindest ones. Whoever builds a mosque in the world, Allah will build forty palaces (for him) in the Paradise.

Figure, Text and Translation of the main inscription: For the photograph, its complete text and translation, please see the beginning of the Introduction: Epigraphy of Muslim Bengal.

Discussion:

In this inscription, the calligrapher followed no conventional style; he uses a peculiar script that combines characteristics of *tawqīʿ*, *thulth* and *nastaʿlīq*. The script style is closest to *tawqīʿ*, which was otherwise almost never used for architectural calligraphy. There are only one or two other examples in all of Bengal (one of them is the Wazirpur-Beldanga inscription dated 722/1322). Among the peculiarities of its calligraphic features is the *shākila*, or horizontal stroke, at the upper end of the letter *kāf*, which has a sword-like curve. Particularly distinct is the *shākila* in the word *baḥikmate* in the middle of the first line, which at first appears to be missing, but is placed for calligraphic convenience with the preceding word *kārāst* on the top of the letter *sīn*.

The stone slab has been used more than once. On its top edge, we find *basmala*, a Qur'ānic verse and a saying of the Prophet on the virtue of building mosques. Written by an inexpert person, the *ḥadīth* is full of grammatical mistakes. On the reverse side is another inscription in Arabic from the time of a later ruler, Sulṭān Jalāl al-Dunyā' wa 'l-Dīn Muḥammad Shāh in 835/1431, in an elegant Bihārī style suggesting that the slab was produced at an early era of Muslim rule in the area. The scarcity of stone in the area sometimes led to this practice of multiple inscriptions. The undated inscription records only the royal titles *sulṭān 'alā' dīn wa dunyā shah-e-jahān* without referring to the actual given name of the ruler. The phrase *Shāh Jahān* (the king of the world) started appearing in the inscriptions of Bengal from quite an early period. It appears, for example, in two monumental gate inscriptions of Bārbak Shāh dated 871/1466, namely Chand Darwazah and Nim Darwaza, in Mianeh Dar located in the Sultanate palace complex in Gaur. *Shāh Jahān* was also the title of the fifth great Mughal emperor, Khurram. As was customary, he was known by that title rather than by his name. This inscription has nothing to do, however, with the Mughal Shāh Jahān, for none of the Mughal emperors of South Asia ever used the title *sulṭān* or *'alā' dīn*. Moreover, in this inscription, *shah-e-jahān* (with a noticeable variation in the spelling of the word *shah* [شه] rather than shāh [شاه]) is used as a eulogistic exaggeration rather than a title. There were several rulers in Bengal who used the title *sulṭān 'alā' al-dunyā' wa 'l-dīn*, for example, Dawlāt Shāh (Balkā Khaljī), 'Izz al-Mulk Malik 'Alā' al-Dunyā' wa 'l-Dīn Jānī 628–29/1231–1232, 'Alā' al-Dunyā' wa 'l-Dīn 'Alī Shāh 742–43/1341–1342, 'Alā' al-Dunyā' wa 'l-Dīn Ḥusayn Shāh 899–925/1494–1519 and 'Alā' al-Dunyā' wa 'l-Dīn Fīrūz Shāh 939–940/1532–1533). Of them, only Ḥusayn Shāh became famous with this title.

This inscription, however, pertains to none of these figures. Rather, it seems to belong to 'Alī Mardān, one of the earliest Khaljī rulers, who appeared on the political scene of Bengal immediately after its first Muslim conquest in 601/1205. Another variation in this inscription can be noticed in not using the Arabic definite article *al* before the Arabic words *dīn* and *dunyā* as was customary in the titles of the later sultans of Bengal. The inscription also records the benefactor's title as *'alā' dīn wa dunyā* instead of the more common *'alā' al-dunyā wa 'l-dīn* found in the inscriptions of the later sultans. After proclaiming himself sultan, 'Alī Mardān became known as Sulṭān 'Alā' Dīn, as is recorded in this inscription and other historical sources (such as *Ṭabaqāt-e-Nāṣirī*). Most of his coins, however, record his title as Rukn al-Dunya wa 'l-Dīn. Nevertheless, a gold fraction of a tankah from his era, minted probably in Lakhnawti (Gaur) and now in the British Museum, records his name on the reverse side of the coin as:

السطان المعظم الا الدين [والدنيا] ابو المظفر على مرد ان

The engraving, as on most early issues of Muslim Bengal, is inexpert. We notice, for instance, a spelling mistake where the Arabic character *alif* (أ) has been substituted for *'ayn* (ع), thus raising the possibility that the engraver was a local Muslim who had converted recently. The obverse of the coin depicts a galloping horseman armed with a mace, symbolizing the powerful cavalry that the Muslims maintained in this newly conquered land to ensure their military superiority. Quite surprisingly, his name also finds a place on the reverse of a later silver coin dated 20 Rabī' al-Ākhir AH 620 minted by 'Alā-Dīn 'Alī Mardān's successor Ghiyāth al-Dīn 'Iwaḍ in Lakhnawti, now in the British Museum, which can be read as follows:

غياث الدنيا والدين ابو الفتح عوض بن الحسين قسيم امير المومنين سلطان السلاطين معز الدنيا والدين على مردان امير المومنين
خلد الله ملكه

The phrase (or title) *qasīm amīr al-mu'minīn* (associate of the commander of the faithful) indicates Ghiyāth al-Dīn 'Iwaḍ's showy allegiance to the rule of the Abbasid caliphs in Baghdad in the capacity of a partner in an imagined pan-Islamic caliphate of the Muslim *ummah*. At the same time, he maintained a policy of distancing from the grip of the central government in Delhi, a trend set forth for the first time in the region that was to be followed by many successive rulers of Bengal in the coming days.[1]

'Alī Mardān was indeed one of the most important early rulers in the history of Bengal, being the first ever to proclaim himself as sultan, as the inscription under discussion clearly indicates. Remarkably, this important event in Bengal's history has never been fully assessed before. Originally, 'Alī Mardān was a soldier of fortune who accompanied Bakhtiyār Khaljī on his Bengal campaign in 1205 and was rewarded with a fiefdom in Narankot (i.e. Narayankot). It is said that after Bakhtiyār's unsuccessful campaign to Tibet, 'Alī Mardān conspired against him and eventually assassinated him through treachery.[2] Consequently 'Alī Mardān was imprisoned by one of Bakhtiyār's generals, Muḥammad Shirān, but escaped with the help of a *kotwāl* (jailor) and went to Delhi to start his ambitious political life anew. There he was able to obtain a royal decree of governorship for Bengal from Sulṭān Quṭb al-Dīn Aybak. Sometime around March 1210, he returned to Bengal, this time as a ruler, until he was removed from power by other Khaljī chieftains, who assassinated him in 1213.

'Alī Mardān assumed the title of *sulṭān* immediately after the death of Sulṭān Quṭb al-Dīn Aybak in 1210.[3] In all of the coins from his rule discovered so far, we find him using the title *al-sulṭān al-mu'aẓẓam* (the august king). This phrase refers to him merely as *sulṭān* without giving any royal descent, for he obviously had none. He not only proved to be a tyrant, but also suffered from vanity, claiming to be 'emperor of the world' (*shah-e-jahān*), the expression used in this inscription. Earlier sources, such as *Ṭabaqāt-e-Nāṣirī* and *Ḥawḍ al-Ḥayāt* also indicate that he assumed these titles. Sometimes 'Alī Mardān would even issue writs of investiture for places over which he had no control, such as Ghaznah, Khurasan and Isfahan.[4] No one dared to criticize him; the present inscription says that even a wolf does not dare to attack a lamb in his domain. He regarded his tyrannical policy as justice. According to *Ṭabaqāt-e-Nāṣirī*, Sulṭān 'Alā' Dīn 'Alī Mardān's seat of power at the beginning was in Devikot, which is located at present in Dakshin (South) Dinajpur district in West Bengal, India, not far from Bangarh, one of the ancient capitals of the Buddhist Pala dynasty. Traces of his tomb can still be found in the ruins of some Islamic architectural remains in a nearby village there. Interestingly, Devikot is not very far from the place where the inscription was found, in Sultanganj in Bangladesh. The capitals of the earlier dynasties, the Senas and the Palas, such as Gaur, Pandua and Nadia (probably the present village of Nawdah near Mahdipur in Gaur, Malda district, or the village of Nawdapara, near Rohonpur Railway Station in Chapai Nawabganj district in Bangladesh) were all located in nearby areas. According to *Ḥawḍ al- Ḥayāt*, 'Alī Mardān's kingdom was known as Salṭanat-i-Lakhnawti (probably a synonym for Gaur region) with Lakhnot (misspelled sometimes by the early Muslim historians as Lakhnor) as its capital. It was in the jāmi' masjid of Lakhnot that a famous Hindu Yogi from Kamrup, Bhojar Brahmin, embraced Islam during his reign, setting an early tradition of religious conversion of the upper class Hindu population. 'Alī Mardān was the first ruler to move his capital to Lakhnot which later on became famous as Gaur, after the name of the region.

In spite of all his weaknesses and the wrongdoings that were recorded in many early sources, 'Alī Mardān carried out a number of welfare works and built bridges and mosques in and around his capitals. Hence, the construction of the bridge in the region referred to in the present inscription above was surely not an isolated event in this region of rivers. Architectural and constructional projects had indeed become important after the Muslim rule was established in the area.

A number of early Islamic inscriptions made under the patronage of the rulers in this particular area were rendered in Persian or in a combination of Arabic and Persian. However, inscriptions made in areas remote from the Bengali capital in the same period, such as the inscription of Makhdum Shāh at Sian in the Birbhum district dated 618/1221 and Bari Dargāh inscription dated 640/1342, were rendered entirely in Arabic. A very interesting aspect of this epigraphic record is its elegant poetic expression in Persian, which is not otherwise typical of the period. Though Persian inscriptions appeared as early as in the mid-eleventh century (1055–1060) in a tomb of Safid Buland in the northern part of Farghana valley in Uzbekistan, and then during the Ghaznavid period at the beginning of twelfth century,[5] Persian did not begin to gain popularity in Indian epigraphs until the middle of the thirteenth century. One of the earliest Persian inscriptions in north India, is a funerary inscription dated 616/1219 discovered in the Mehrauli near Delhi.[6] The inscription from Sitalmat (in the district of Naogan, not far from Gaur) dated 652/1254, though rendered in Arabic, contains a few Persian sentences.[7] The third among the earliest inscriptions so far discovered in Bengal, which can surely be ascribed to the period of Balkā Khaljī (627–628/1229–1230), is inscribed completely in Persian. The Khān Jahān 'Alī Mausoleum Complex at Khalifatabad (present Bagerhat) dated 863/1459 contains perhaps the largest number of Persian inscriptions in any single monument which can rarely be found elsewhere. Thus assigning this unique Persian inscription to the earliest period of Muslim rule in Bengal is quite plausible. If this inscription refers to 'Alī Mardān is correct, then this must be the earliest Islamic inscription known in Bengal. This epigraphic evidence at the same time will imply that the use of Persian in Bengal began immediately after the Muslim conquest of that region.

(2) Khānqāh inscription from Sian dated 618 (1221)

ORIGINAL SITE: An unnamed khānqāh in Sian, Birbhum district, West Bengal. **CURRENT LOCATION:** Found lying near the mausoleum of Makhdum Shāh at Sian, Police Station Bolpur, Suri (Sadar) Subdivision, Birbhum district in West Bengal. **MATERIAL, SIZE:** Black basalt, 33 × 20.6 inches. **STYLE, NO. OF LINES:** *naskh* closely resembling *riqā*' style; six lines. **REIGN:** *Ca.* 618/1221 during the reign of Sulṭān Giyāth al-Dīn 'Iwaḍ, the third Khaljī ruler, who ruled during the early period of the consolidation of Muslim power in Bengal. **LANGUAGE:** Arabic. **TYPE:** Dedicatory inscription for a khānqāh. **PUBLICATION:** *Annual Report in Indian Epigraphy*, 1 (1972–1973): 20; *Indian Archaeology 1972–73:* A *Review* (New Delhi, 1978): 52; Ziauddin Ahmad Desai, 'An Early Thirteenth-Century Inscription from West Bengal', *EIAPS* (1975 [published in 1983]): 6–12, pl. 1 (b); Sukhamay Mukhopadhaya, *Banglāi Muslim Adhikārer Adiparva* (Calcutta, 1988): 40–44, pls 2–3; A. Karim, *Corpus of Inscriptions*, 17–24.

Text:

L-1 بسم الله الرحمن الرحيم [في بيوت أذن الله أن ترفع ويذ] كر فيها اسمه يسبح له فيها بالغدو والاصال

L-2 رجال لا تلهيهم تجارة ولا بيع عن ذكر [الله وإقام الصلاة] و[إ]يتاء الزكاة يخافون يوما تتقلب فيه

L-3 القلوب والابصار عن رسول الله صلى الله [عليه وسلم في] الصحيح الناس في مساجدهم والله في حوايجهم

L-4 وقف هذه الخانقاه الفقير الخاطي الذي يرجو [إلى رحمة ربه . . .] بن محمد المراغي لاهل الصفة الذين يلزمون لحضرة

L-5 الله تعالي ويشغلون بذكر الله تعالي في أ[يام . . الدولت غياث الإ] سلام والمسلمين صدر الملوك والسلاطين المخصوص

L-6 بولاية العهد في العالمين على شير بن عوض برهان أمير المؤ [منين في يوم السا] بع من جماد الآخر سنة ثمان عشر وستماية

Translation:

L-1 In the name of Allah the Most Compassionate and Merciful [in houses which Allah has permitted to be raised and] where His name is remembered and glorified in the mornings and evenings.

L-2 People whom neither merchandise nor selling activities divert from the remembrance [of Allah and the establishment of prayers] and the practice of obligatory charity; they fear a day when

L-3 'Hearts and eyes will be transformed' (24:37–38). It is quoted from the messenger of Allah, peace and blessings of Allah [be on him, in] the Ṣaḥīḥ [authentic collections of *ḥadīth*]: 'When the people are in their mosques, Allah looks after their need.'

L-4 A faqīr (poverty-stricken dervish), al-khāṭi' (a sinful one) who hopes [for the mercy of his Lord] … ibn Muḥammad al-Marāghī endowed this khānqāh for the 'ahl al-ṣuffā (sufis) who are fully dedicated to the Exalted

L-5 Almighty Allah, and are engaged in the remembrance of the Exalted Allah; in the days and [the government of Ghiyāth] al-Islām wa 'l-Muslimīn (shelter of Islam and the Muslims), Ṣadr al-Mulūk wa 'l-Salāṭīn (chief among the kings and the sulṭāns); the one designated

L-6 as the governor of the period in the two areas (territories) 'Alī Sher ibn 'Iwaḍ Burhān-i-Amīr al-Mu'[minīn] (a symbolic evidence [testimony] of the commander of the believers) in the seventh day of Jumād al-Akhir of the year six hundred and eighteen.

Discussion:

This is the earliest dated Arabic inscription discovered so far in Bengal. The stone slab most likely originally belonged to a Hindu building, for its reverse side has a Sanskrit inscription from the Pala period. The slab is broken into two pieces and the parts are damaged, resulting in the loss of some text. Unlike other Islamic inscriptions from Bengal, the writing is not in relief, but incised, as in the Sanskrit inscriptions in the region. It is also free of any decorative features. The calligraphy bears characteristics of the *riqā'* style, which was rare in Bengal, but more common in contemporary inscriptions in the west and northwest of India, particularly in Gujarat. The Qur'ānic verses in the first three lines are also rare in the epigraphic tradition of Bengal, though sometimes used in mosque inscriptions elsewhere in the Islamic world. Similarly, the *ḥadīth* in the third line is also not seen in any other inscription from Bengal. The selections of both the Qur'ānic verses and *ḥadīth* reflect the pious intention and philosophy attached to the structure, identified as a khānqāh in the inscription.

This is one of the very few inscriptions from Bengal which clearly records the establishment of a Sufi centre. Since it is also one of the earliest Islamic inscriptions so far discovered in Bengal, this epigraphic record is important, suggesting as it does that the institution of the khānqāh took root in the social and religious life of Muslim Bengal from the very beginning. The institution of khānqāh also played an important role in disseminating the teachings of Islam among the masses and consolidating Islam on a popular level. We can also surmise that the *mashāyikh* (sufi saints) started arriving in Bengal at a very early stage and enjoyed harmonious relations with both the elite and the common people. The inscription was discovered not far from Lakhnor, or Nagor, an early Muslim settlement at the extreme west of Bengal, which became an important sufi centre. Sufis such as Shaykh Ḥamīd al-Dīn Nagorī also lived in this area.

As the text indicates, the tablet was inscribed by the order of Ibn Muḥammad al-Murāghī, who endowed the khānqāh for those sufis who had dedicated their lives to the path of Allah. He appears to have been a person of means, as he was also able to endow property for the khānqāh. This is the first time that the term *waqf* (charitable and public welfare endowments) was used in the Islamic inscriptions of Bengal. This usage of *waqf* indicates that the institution of *waqf* started spreading at the very outset of Muslim rule in the region. This text was inscribed for a number of purposes, including commemorating the ruler/endower and to invoke *baraka* (blessings) by recording divine messages and sayings of the Prophet. Inscribed on stone to ensure its longevity, the inscription would serve as a permanent record of the endowment. Ibn Muḥammad al-Murāghī's complete name could not be deciphered, as a number of words are damaged. However, Ibn Muḥammad al-Murāghī or his ancestors must have migrated to Bengal from the town of Marāghā in Azerbaijan. The *nisba*, al-Murāghī, suggests that migration of Muslims to Bengal from Central Asia had started at a very early stage.

'Alī Sher, during whose tenure this record was inscribed, was the governor of the northwestern part of Bengal, comprising the present district of Birbhum and the adjacent areas. As indicated in the text, he was the son and heir-apparent of the ruler of Bengal Sulṭān Giyāth al-Dīn 'Iwaḍ Khaljī.

(3) Masjid-Madrasa inscription from Naohata from the reign of Balkā Khān Khaljī

ORIGINAL SITE: An unnamed masjid and madrasa from the village of Naohata in Rajshahi district, Bangladesh. **CURRENT LOCATION:** Varendra Research Museum, Rajshahi, inv. no. 2855. **MATERIAL, SIZE:** Black basalt; 32 × 8.50 inches. **STYLE, NO. OF LINES:** A peculiar variety of *thulth*, somewhat resembling *tawqī'*; three lines. **REIGN:** *Ca.* 626–628/1229–1230 in the brief rule of the rebel Khaljī chief Balkā Khān in Bengal. **LANGUAGE:** Persian. **METER:** *Baḥr Hazaj Musaddas Maqṣūr* (مفاعيل مفاعيلن فعولن) **TYPE:** Eulogy to Balkā Khān for constructing a mosque/madrasa. **PUBLICATION:** Siddiq, *Riḥla ma'a 'l-Nuqūsh al-Islāmiyya fī 'l-Bangāl*, 94–96.

Text:

L-1 [سلا] مت باد شاه أهل إيمان سپاس خان بلكاخان سرايم كه از اخلاص بركت كرد بنيان
L-2 كه[هست او] ذات لطف واحسان بگاه حل مشكلهاء علمي ز طبع پاك باشد موشگا فان
L-3 <سلا>مت مسجد از الطاف پنهان بود تا در جهان نام مساجد بقاء ذات خان بادا بليهان

Translation:

L-1 Hail, emperor of the believers! I sing the praise of Khān Balkā Khān, the one who erected this edifice with blessed sincerity,
L-2 Being a man of benevolence and kindness. A place where scholarly problems and minute questions find answers in a natural way.
L-3 May this mosque remain safe due to its hidden graces. May the [noble] name of Khān be truly sustained so long as mosques remain on the earth.

Discussion:

This is the only inscription discovered so far that records the name of Khān Balkā Khān, a rebel chieftain and the last Khaljī ruler to dominate the political arena of Bengal in the history. It is the third oldest Islamic inscription from Bengal. The historical sources provide very little information about him. Some scholars, such as Desai, believe that he was one of the sons of a previous Khaljī ruler of Bengal, Ghiyāth al-Dīn Husām al-Dīn 'Iwaḍ, who was killed when the imperial forces from Delhi under Prince Naṣīr al-Dīn Maḥmūd attacked and seized Lakhnawati (March to April 1227).[8] After a brief rule of two years, Prince Naṣīr al-Dīn suddenly died in May 1229, and Balkā Khān, known as Malik Ikhtiyār al-Dīn Balkā Khān Khaljī, seized power and ruled Bengal for nearly eighteen months. However, Balkā Khān soon followed the fate of his predecessor Sulṭān Giyāth al-Dīn 'Iwaḍ. This time Sulṭān Iltutmish himself led his imperial army from Delhi on a campaign against Bengal in November 1230. The Khaljī chief fought bravely, but was finally killed. One coin from this period refers to 'Dawlat Shāh ibn Mawdūd', which led some historians to believe that the name refers to Balkā Khān and that Balkā Khān was the son of Mawdūd Shāh, not of Husām al-Dīn ʻIwaḍ.[9]

Unfortunately, the first part of the inscription is broken off, so some important information has been lost. The title *badshāh-e-ahle īmān* (monarch of the believers) does not clearly refer to the title-bearer. It may be a reference to the Abbasid caliph or to the sultan in Delhi, though most likely it refers to Balkā Khān. The previous Khaljī ruler Ḥusām al-Dīn ʻIwaḍ formally gave his allegiance to the Abbasid caliph in defiance of the sultan of Delhi.

It seems that Balkā Khān, like his predecessors, was a great patron of masjids and madrasas. The masjid mentioned in this text was probably a great seat of learning at that time. The institution of masjid/madrasa played an important role in the emerging Muslim Bengal culture. Even the first Muslim ruler Bakhtiyār Khaljī paid significant attention to the construction of masjid and madrasas.[10]

What remains of the text displays a high standard of Persian poetic composition. The Semi-Turkish-speaking Khaljīs, though they opted for Persian as a court language, favoured Arabic for the purpose of inscribing on religious edifices. In general, Arabic had the upper hand in architectural calligraphy until the advent of the Mughals in Bengal. However, this inscription and a bridge inscription from the reign of ʻAlī Mardān (the first Islamic inscription of Bengal), suggest that Persian was introduced as a formal official language in Bengal as early as the establishment of Muslim rule itself, that is, at the beginning of the thirteenth century. The *thulth* style of this inscription is somewhat peculiar as it resembles closely *tawqīʻ* style. The *shākila* of the letter *kāf* is twisted and extended horizontally to form a shape known as *al-kāf al-thuʻbānī*, or the python shape *kāf.*

Inscriptions of the early rulers appointed by the Delhi Sultans

(4) Inscription of an edifice in Bari Dargah dated Muḥarram 640 (July 1242)

ORIGINAL SITE: An unnamed monument from in or around Bihar Sharif city in the state of Bihar. **CURRENT LOCATION:** Bari Dargah mausoleum in Bihar Sharif. **MATERIAL, SIZE:** Black basalt, 50 × 26 inches. **STYLE, NO. OF LINES:** Monumental *thulth* against foliated background; three lines. **REIGN:** Ṭughril, a semi-independent ruler of the eastern Indian region of Bihar and Bengal (*ca.* 632–642/1235–1244). **LANGUAGE, TYPE:** Arabic; foundation inscription of a building. **PUBLICATION:** H. Blochmann, *JASB*, XL(part 1) (1871): pl. VII; H. Blochmann, *JASB*, XLII (1873): 245–246, pl. 1; G. Yazdani, *EIM* (1913–1914): 16–17, pl. V; S. Ahmed, *Inscriptions of Bengal*, 1–3; Qeyamuddin Ahmad, *Corpus of the Arabic and Persian Inscriptions of Bihar* (Patna: K. P. Jayaswal Research Institute, 1973): 2–6; P. I. S. M. Rahman, *Monumental Islamic Calligraphy* (Dhaka: Dhaka University Press, 1979): 33; M. Y. Siddiq, 'Calligraphy in the Early Islamic Inscriptions of Bengal', *Muslim Educational Quarterly*, 2(3) (1985): 77–88; A. Karim, *Corpus of Inscriptions*, 24–30.

Text:

L-1 أمر ببنا[ء] هذه العمارة في أيام مملكة المجلس العالي خان الأعظم خاقان [المعظم]
L-2 عز الحق والدين غياث الاسلام والمسلمين مغيث الملوك والسلاطين أبي الفتح طغرل
L-3 السلطاني خلد الله ملكه العبد مبارك الخازن تقبل الله منه في المحرم سنة أربعين وستماية

Translation:

The humble creature Mubārak, al-Khāzin (the treasurer), may Allah accept from him (this noble work), ordered the construction of this building during the reign of His Highness, the great Khān, [the glorious] Khāqān, 'Izz al-Ḥaq wa 'l-Dīn (the glory of truth and religion), Ghiyāth al-Islām wa 'l-Muslimīn, Mughīth al-Mulūk wa 'l-Salāṭīn, Abū 'l-Fatḥ Ṭughril al-Sulṭānī, may Allah sustain his kingdom. (It was built) in Muḥarram of the year six hundred and forty.

Discussion:

The text of this inscription begins with the phrase *amara bi binā'i* (أمر ببناء) which starts appearing in Islamic inscriptions in Iran and Central Asia as early as the mid-tenth century.[11] The inscription records two names with titles. The first name, Ṭughril, a well-known figure in contemporary historical accounts (see, for example, *Tabaqāt-e-Nāṣiri*), was originally a Qarah Khitai Turkish (or more correctly a Tatar) slave purchased by the Mamlūk Sultan Iltutmish of Delhi and trained in the royal household. He held different offices such as *sāqi-i-khās* (cup-bearer), *sar-i-dawāt-dār* (keeper of the imperial seal), *chāshnigīr* (taster of royal food) and *amīr-i-akhūr* (superintendent of the royal stable) before he was sent to Badaon as feudal chief. Soon afterward he was made governor of Bihar. After the demise of Malik Sayf al-Dīn Aybak, the ruler of the neighbouring Lakhnawati region in Bengal who was allegedly killed by conspirators, another Turkish slave by the name of Awr Khān Aybak seized power in Lakhnawati. Ṭughril took advantage of this confusing situation and attacked Awr Khān, who was killed in a battle near Lakhnawati. Shortly after that, Ṭughril moved his capital to Lakhnawati, a safer place because of its distance from Delhi. From that time, he was the unchallenged ruler of a large territory comprising Bihar and Bengal. Ṭughril Khān was a shrewd politician as he tried to pacify the Delhi sulṭāns by regularly sending gifts to them, although in practice he often behaved as if he was an independent ruler. His long, grandiose and stately titles in this inscription are sufficient to indicate his ambitious character, though at the end of his titles he does not forget to declare himself *al-sulṭānī* (royal servant). The title, mughīth al-mulūk wa 'l-salāṭin (helper of kings and monarchs), is especially interesting for its patronizing tone towards the sulṭāns. However, it may refer as well to his willingness to help the imperial authority at Delhi during the period of crisis resulting from continuous power struggles in the capital, though he purposely avoids naming any of the short-lived sulṭāns of this era. This inscription was produced shortly before the historian Minhāj al-Dīn Sirāj came from Delhi to Oudh to join Ṭughril. The appearance of a ruler from a different branch of Turk from Central Asia, in place of Kahljīs from Khurasan, in Bengal indicates the fluidity of the political situation during this chequered period of history.

The treasurer Mubārak in the inscription is a less well-known personality. A similar name along with titles (e.g. mu'ayyid al-dīn mehtar mubārak al-khāzin al-sulṭānī) briefly appears in *Tabaqāt-e-Nāṣirī*. According to *Tabaqāt*, this person also started his career as a royal slave of Sulṭān Iltutmish in Delhi. The inscription above presents a highly stylized form of calligraphy in a thickly decorated background that contains an arabesque pattern of interlaced floral and foliated ornamentation resembling grape vines. The verticals of the upright letters are unusually elongated upward; they start from a thin point at the bottom and then get bolder as they go up. The calligraphy of this inscription certainly reminds us the monumental calligraphy of the Qutb Minar in Delhi, some of the earlier inscriptions in Ghaznah, and the *thulth* style of the Mamluk period in Egypt with which it has great resemblance.

(5) Inscription of a religious edifice in Gangarampur dated 647 (1249)

ORIGINAL SITE: An unnamed religious edifice somewhere near the village Pichhli Ghatal, half a mile to the east of Gangarampur in Dakhkhin Dinajpur district, West Bengal. **CURRENT LOCATION:** Not known. **MATERIAL:** Not known. **SIZE:** 91.50 × 14.50 inches. **STYLE, NO. OF LINES:** *ruq'a* in bold character; two lines. **REIGN:** During the reign of Sulṭān Maḥmūd Shāh (*ca.* 644–664/1246–1266) of Delhi. **LANGUAGE:** Arabic. **TYPE:** Commemorative inscription referring to the construction of a religious edifice. **PUBLICATION:** Cunningham, *ASR*, XV: 45 & 171, pl. XXI; *List of Ancient Monuments in Rajshahi Division* (Calcutta: Government of Bengal Public Works Department, 1896): 14 (no. 8); Abid Ali Khan, *Memoirs of Gaur* (Calcutta: 1931): 163–164; G. Yazdani, *EIM* (1913–14): 19–22, pl. VIII(a); Dani, *Bibliography of Muslim Inscriptions*, 2; S. Ahmed, *Inscriptions of Bengal*, 4–8; W. E. Begley, *Monumental Islamic Calligraphy* (Villa Park, IL: Islamic Foundation, 1985): 34–35; A. Karim, *Corpus of Inscriptions*, 30–32.

Text:

L-1 أمر ببنا[ء] هذه البقعة المباركة السلطان المعظم شمس الدنيا والدين أبي <أبو> المظفر ايلتتمش السلطان يمين خليفة الله ناصر أمير المؤمنين أنار الله برهانه وثقل بالحسنى جزاءه و جُدّدَ < جُدّدَت > العمارة في أيام دولت السلطان الأعظم

L-2 ناصر الدنيا والدين أبو المظفر محمود شاه بن السلطان ناصر أمير المؤمنين خلد الله ملكه وسلطانه في نوبة ايالت الملك المعظم جلال الحق والدين ملك ملوك الشرق مسعود شاه جاني برهان أمير المؤمنين خلد الله دولته في غرة محرم سنة سبع و اربعين وستماية

Translation:

L-1 The magnificent Sulṭān Shams al-Dunyā' wa 'l-Dīn (the sun of the state and religion) Abū 'l-Muẓaffar Iltutmish, al-Sulṭān, Yamīn Khalīfat-Allah (the right hand of the caliph of Allah) Nāṣir Amīr al-Mu'minīn (the helper of the commander of the faithful), may Allah illuminate his argument and may his balance be weighed with good deeds, ordered the construction of this sacred edifice. The building was renovated during the reign of the great sulṭān,

L-2 Nāṣir al-Dunyā' wa 'l-Dīn (the helper of the state and the religion) Abū 'l-Muẓaffar Maḥmūd Shāh ibn al-Sulṭān Nāṣir Amīr al-Mu'minīn, may Allah perpetuate his kingdom and majesty, and during the governorship of the great malik (lord), Jalāl al-Ḥaq wa 'l-Dīn (the glory of truth and religion) Malik Mulūk al-Sharq (the lord of the lords of the East) Mas'ūd Shāh Jānī, Burhān Amīr al-Mu'minīn, may Allah perpetuate his government, on the first of Muḥarram, the year six hundred forty-seven.

Discussion:

This inscription was found in the ruins of an old structure known as the *chilla-khana* of Shāh Jalāl in a place called Pichhli Ghatal or Pichhli Ghat (lit. the landing platform of a river) near the old village of Gangarampur, which was known in ancient times as Damdama (cantonment).

The inscription records the construction of a sacred edifice, possibly a reference to a khānqāh that was built for the famous sufi Shāh Jalāl al-Dīn Tabrīzī (d. 1244–1245) by an imperial order towards the end of the reign of Sulṭān Iltutmish (d. 29 April 1236). After the demise of the shaykh, the building was renovated by order of the governor of the province, Mas'ūd Shāh Jānī, in the year 1249. The date on the inscription carries a very important historical clue as it implies that in 1249, Mas'ūd Shāh Jānī ruled the region where the inscription was found.

Calligraphically, the writing is close to *ruq'a* rendered in an intricate pattern. Towards the end of the inscription, at the far left of the second line, the writing is congested due to lack of space. We find this practice common in many early Islamic inscriptions of Bengal, probably due to lack of appropriate outlining of the calligraphic layout beforehand. We also find a minor grammatical error towards the end of the first line, where *juddidat* (renovated) is written as *juddida.*

(6) Waqf *inscription of a khānqāh in Sitalmat dated 652 (1254)*

ORIGINAL SITE: Sitalmat village, Naogaon district, Rajshahi, Bangladesh. **CURRENT LOCATION:** Bangladesh National Museum, inv. no. 68.89. **MATERIAL, SIZE:** Black basalt; 45.50 × 11.50 inches. **STYLE, NO. OF LINES:** *thulth* of a local variety; four lines. **REIGN:** *Ca.* 652/1254 in the governorship of Abū 'l-Fatḥ Yuzbak al-Sulṭānī. **LANGUAGE:** Arabic, except the fourth line, which contains many Persian words. **TYPE**: Foundation inscription.

PUBLICATION: A. B. M. Habibullah, 'An Unpublished Inscription from Sitalmat', *Bangladesh Lalit Kala*, 1(2) (1975): 89–94; Enamul Haque, *Islamic Art in Bangladesh* (Dhaka: Dacca Museum, 1978): 24; A. Karim, *Corpus of Inscriptions*, 32–36.

Text:

L-1 [بسم الله الرحمن] الرحيم أمر ببناء هذه العمارة المباركة للمتقين المحبين القرآن . . والصالحين والأبرار
والذاكرين بالليل والنهار . و[المتطهرين] . .
L-2 خان العادل [جليل القدر] الباذل الكامل في [سبيل الله] مغيث الإسلام والمسلمين أبي الفتح يوذبك السلطاني ناصر
أمير المؤمنين خلد الله سلطانه
L-3 و قام ببنائه . المخير أحمد بن مسعود المراغي الحسين صدرالملة و وصى عنه و عن والديه و شرط النظر فيها لنفسه .
مدة كيلا . و لمن رضي عليه فمن بدّله بعدما سمعه فإنما إثمه
L-4 على الذين يبدّلونه إن الله سميع عليم اين نصيحت . . نقشه [كنده] بادر نصب شده اند لعنت برانكس باد كه اين
قاعده را متغير گرداند و خلل كند تاريخ شهر رمضان سنة اثنتين و خمسين و ستماية

Translation:

L-1 and L-2 In the name of Allah, the Compassionate and Merciful. The just, exalted and benevolent *khān*, the perfect one in the path of Allah, helper of Islam and the Muslims, Abū 'l-Fatḥ Yūzbak al-Sulṭāni, Nāṣir Amīr al-Mu'minīn (helper of the Commander of the believers), ordered the construction of this blessed building for the pious, and those devoted to the Qur'ān,… upright, virtuous people and those who are engaged in the remembrance of Allah day and night, and the pure ones, may Allah perpetuate his Sultanate.

L-3 The person in charge, Aḥmad ibn Mas'ūd al-Marāghī al-Ḥusayn Ṣadr al-Milla (the leader of the nation), built it for the sake of Allah and left a bequest on his behalf and on behalf of his parents, and he himself subjected it to an office of trustees for a fixed period. Whoever accepts [this responsibility of trusteeship], must follow the teaching of the verse: 'Whoever changes it (the will) after he has heard (known) it, the sin of this (act)

L-4 will be on those who make such changes; indeed Allah is all-hearing and all-knowing (2:181).' These engraved admonitions are fixed on the door. Cursed be those who bring any change to its statutes or disrupt them; dated in the month of Ramaḍān, the year six hundred and fifty-two.

Discussion:

Like the khānqāh inscription in Sian dated 818/1221 (ins. no. 2), and the inscription in Gangarampur dated 647/1249 (ins. no. 5), this inscription records the construction of a sacred building, most likely a khānqāh in 652/1254–1255, that played an important role in introducing Islam to the masses in this early stage of Muslim rule in Bengal. The text contains a Qur'ānic verse that warns of severe punishment for anyone who would deliberately try to make any changes in the *waqf.* The same verse appears in another mosque inscription in Gaur dated 793/1487, now in the British Museum, and a number of other endowment inscriptions elsewhere. The existence of this text suggests that endowments for religious edifices, such as khānqāhs, masjids and madrasas were instituted quite early in the Islamic period in the region.

Abū 'l-Fatḥ Yuzbak, whose name is recorded in the inscription as the ruler, was an adventurer and military leader who led an army expedition to Kamrup. Like the Tibet expedition of Bakhtiyār, this turned into a disaster in which Yuzbak and his army eventually perished. While inscriptions no. 1 and 3 are completely rendered in Persian, only a part of this inscription (namely, most of L-4) is written in Persian.

(7) Mausoleum inscription in Baradari dated 663 (1265)

ORIGINAL SITE: The tomb of Faḍl-Allah Gosain at Baradari in Bihar-Sharif, the state of Bihar in India. **CURRENT LOCATION:** In situ. **MATERIAL, SIZE:** Not known; 59 × 10 inches. **STYLE, NO. OF LINES:** A local variety of *naskh* resembling somewhat the style of *riqā'*; four lines. **REIGN:** The Rule of Tātār Khān in Bengal (*ca.* 663–666/1265–1268). **LANGUAGE:** Arabic. **TYPE:** Funerary inscription. **PUBLICATION:** H. Blochmann, *JASB*, XLII (1873): 247; G. Yazdani, *EIM* (1913–14): 23–25; A. H. Dani, *Bibliography of Muslim Inscriptions*, 3; S. Ahmed, *Inscriptions of Bengal*, 9–10; Q. Ahmad, *Inscriptions of Bihar*, 6–9; A. Karim, *Corpus of Inscriptions*, 36–38.

Text:

L-1 . . .ملك العالمين . . معظم الخلافة صاحب العدل والرأفة المخصوص بعناية الرحمن أبي المكارم تاتار خان خليفة المسلمين [خلّد الله] ملكه وإمارته وأبقى في ديار الممالك عمارته [أمر] ببناء هذه المقبرة المتبركة في شهور سنة خمس وستين وستماية

L-2 سلطانشاه اللهم نوّر تربته و بيض غرته و اجعل قبره [روضة] من رياض الجنان ولا [تجعله حفرة] من حفر النيران في ليلة الأحد الثامن عشر من جمادى الأولى سنة ثلاث وستين وتسعماية والمعمار عبدهما الممنون بإنعامهما مجد الكابلي

Translation:

L-1 Lord of the worlds ... the respected one of the caliphate, the just and gracious, the one who is distinguished with special favour by the Merciful, Abū 'l-Makārim Tātār Khān the caliph of the Muslims, may Allah perpetuate his kingdom and his emirate and may He sustain his structures in the localities of the kingdom, ordered to build this blessed mausoleum in the months of the year of six hundred and sixty-five.

L-2 Sulṭān Shāh, O Allah fill his grave with light and brighten his forehead and make his grave a garden among the gardens of the paradise and do not make it a pit from the pits of hellfire. [He died] on the night of Sunday, eighteenth of Jumād al-'Ūlā, the year six hundred and sixty-three; the architect is Majd Kābulī, a servant of both persons, grateful to both of them for their favours.

Discussion:

This inscription records the name of the architect as Majd Kābulī. The *nisba* (Kābulī) indicates that the architect came from Kabul to work in the region. Thus, it suggests that Muslim artisans and architects started coming to this region from different parts of Khurasan and Central Asia immediately after the establishment of the Muslim rule in the region.

The inscription does not record a khānqāh, but, rather, a Sufi shrine built on the grave of Sulṭān Shāh. The phrase *al-maqbarah al-mutabarrakah* (المقبرة المتبركة) and the overall tone of the text indicate the possibility that saint and shrine veneration were introduced at this early stage in the region by the ruling class, most of whom came from Central Asia and Iran and favoured a syncretic tradition.

The titles recorded in the inscription for Tatār Khān imply that he had high political ambitions and aspired for more political authority, though he formally refrained from declaring independence from Delhi. During his governorship of Bihar and Bengal, Tatār Khān regularly sent valuable presents to the Delhi sulṭān as an appeasing gesture.

Inscriptions of the Balbanī rulers

(8) Citadel inscription from Maheshwara dated 692 (1293)

ORIGINAL SITE: An unnamed fort on the bank of the Gandak river near Maheshwara village in the north of Begusarai, Monghyr district, State of Bihar, India. **CURRENT LOCATION:** Patna Museum, inv. no. 10886. **MATERIAL, SIZE:** Black basalt; 75 × 16 inches. **STYLE, NO. OF LINES:** *Riqā'* of a local variety; two lines. **REIGN:** Sulṭān Rukn al-Dunyā wa 'l-Dīn Kaykā'ūs Shāh (690–701/1290–1301). **LANGUAGE:** Arabic. **TYPE:** Commemorative inscription of a fort. **PUBLICATION:** Radhakrishna Chowdhury, *Annals of the Bhandarkar Oriental Research Institute*, XXXVI (1955): 163–166; A. H. Dani, *Bibliography of Muslim Inscriptions*, 4; S. Ahmed, *Inscriptions of Bengal*, 11–12; A. A. Kadiri, *EIAPS* (1961): 35–36, pl. XI (a); Q. Ahmad, *Inscriptions of Bihar*, 9–10; A. Karim, *Corpus of Inscriptions*, 43–45.

Text:

L-1 أمر بناء هذا الحصن الحصين في عهد {ال} سلطان السلاطين ركن الدنيا والدين أبو <أبي> المظفركيكاؤس شاه السلطان بن السلطان بن السلطان يمين خليفة الله ناصر أمير المؤمنين

L-2 الخان الكبير العالم العادل اختيار الحق والدين المخاطب بخان خانان أبو المعالي فيروز ايتگين السلطاني ضاعف الله قدره في السلخ من المحرم سنة اثنى <إثنتين> وتسعين وستماية

Translation:

L-1 During the reign of the sulṭān of the sulṭāns, Rukn al-Dunyā wa 'l-Dīn (supporter of the state and the religion), Abū 'l-Muẓaffar Kaykā'ūs Shāh the sulṭān, son of the sulṭān, (who was also) son of the sulṭān, the right hand of the caliph of Allah and the succour of Amīr al-Mu'minīn,

L-2 the great *khān*, the scholar and the just Ikhtiyār al-Ḥaq wa 'l-Dīn (the choice of truth and religion), titled Khān-i-Khānān (khan of the khans), Abū 'l-Ma'ālī (highly exalted) Fīrūz Eytgīn al-Sulṭānī ordered the construction of this invincible fort, may Allah double his dignity, dated in the last day of (the month of) al-Muḥarram, the year six hundred and ninety-two.

Discussion:

Tirhut, where this inscription was found,[12] often referred to as Mithila in Indian epics, is the historic name of the northern tract of the Indian state of Bihar bordering Nepal, comprising Darbhanga (Persian *Dār-i-Bang* meaning gateway to Bengal), Muẓaffarpur and the adjoining districts, sometimes extending as far as the river Mahananda (and Purnabvaba) in northwest Bengal.[13] Located in the present district of Champaran, Simarāon is one of the oldest capitals of the region. The Pala empire (*ca.* 750–1161) of Bengal periodically dominated the area. Several Hindu dynasties ruled the kingdom of Mithila, such as the Karnāta between 1087 and 1325, the Oinwāra between 1325 and 1532 and Khanḍawāla (founded by Maheśa Thākura in 1556) who took Bhoura as their capital.

Because of its strategic location on the central route between north India and Bengal, the green, fertile land of Tirhut (known as the granary of Bihar) was one of the earliest regions in eastern India to be known to the Muslims. Its south-eastern part came under the sway of Muslim rule when Bengal was conquered by Bakhtiyār Khaljī in 1205. Narasimhadeva (*ca.* 1188–1227), the third king of the Karnāta dynasty, agreed to pay tribute to this new power, but it did not save Tirhut from further military pressure from Muslim rulers of Bengal, Bihar, Oudh and Delhi. Islamic inscriptions in Tirhut such as this one suggest that Muslim settlement began in this region as early as the thirteenth century.[14]

This inscription (as well as a number of other inscriptions) suggests that quite a few forts were built over time at various strategic locations on the Bengal frontier by the Muslim rulers. The text of the inscription is rendered elegantly in *riqā'* style. The raised borderlines on all four sides as well as in the middle of the two lines of text were originally richly decorated with floral and foliated motifs, but most of the decorations have faded away with the passage of time.

(9) Jāmi' Masjid inscription from Lakhisarai dated 697 (1297)

ORIGINAL SITE: An unnamed jāmi' masjid near the village of Lakhisarai in Monghyr district of the state of Bihar in India. **CURRENT LOCATION:** Found lying at the head of a grave of an unknown saint in Lakhisarai village. **MATERIAL, SIZE:** Black basalt; 75 × 9 inches. **STYLE, NO. OF LINES:** *riqā'*; two lines. **REIGN:** Sulṭān Rukn al-Dunyā wa 'l-Dīn Kaykā'ūs Shāh (690–701/1290–1301). **LANGUAGE:** Arabic. **TYPE:** Commemorative inscription of a mosque. **PUBLICATION:** Blochmann, *JASB*, XLII (1873): 247–248, pl. V; Yazdani, *EIM* (1917–18): 10–11, pl. XV(a); Dani, *Bibliography of Muslim Inscriptions*, 4–5; S. Ahmed, *Inscriptions of Bengal*, 12–15; Q. Ahmad, *Inscriptions of Bihar*, 11–13; A. Karim, *Corpus of Inscriptions*, 45–48.

Text:

L-1 وفق لبناء هذا المسجد الجامع في عهد الدولت <دولة> السلطان المعظم مالك رقاب الأمم مولى ملوك الترك والعجم صاحب التاج والخاتم ركن الدنيا [والدين أبي المظفركيكاؤ] س شاه السلطان بن السلطان بن السلطان يمين خليفة الله ناصر أمير المؤمنين

L-2 في نوبة الخان الأعظم خاقان المعظم اختيار الحق والدين خان خانان الشرق والصين سكندر الثاني فيروز ايتگين السلطاني خلد الله دولته وملكه . . . المظفر المنصور الغازي ضياء الدولة والدين الغ خان ادام الله دولته وزاد خيره في الغرة من المحرم سنة سبع وتسعين وستماية

Translation:

L-1 Construction of this congregational mosque was granted during the reign of the great sulṭān, Mālik Riqāb al-'Umam (master of the destinations [necks] of nations), Mawlā Mulūk al-Turk wa 'l-'Ajam (lord of the kings of the Turks and Persians), Ṣāhib al-Tāj wa 'l-Khātim (master of the crown and the seal), Rukn al-Dunyā wa 'l-Dīn Kaykā'ūs Shāh, al-Sulṭān ibn al-Sulṭān ibn al-Sulṭān, Yamīn Khalīfat Allah, Nāsir Amīr al-Mu'minīn.

L-2 During the governorship of the great khān, the exalted khāqān, Ikhtiyār al-Ḥaq wa 'l-Dīn, Khān Khānān al-Sharq wa 'l-Ṣīn (Khān of the Khāns of the East and China), Sikandar al-Thānī (the second Alexander) Fīruz Aytgīn al-Sulṭāni; may Allah sustain his government and state ... al-Muẓaffar (victorious) al-Manṣūr (the triumphant), al-Ghāzī (the warrior in the path of Allah), Ḍiyā' al-Dawla wa 'l-Dīn (the glow of the state and the religion) Ulugh Khān, may Allah perpetuate his state and increase his benevolence; the first of Muḥarram of the year six hundred and ninety-seven.

Discussion:

In inscription no. 1, we find that 'Alā' Dīn Khaljī, an early ruler of Bengal, used the title sulṭān in 607–610/1210–1213. After almost a century, we find that Kaykā'ūs Shāh, himself a grandson of a sulṭān of Delhi (Sulṭān Ghiyāth al-Dīn Balban), used the same title in all of his inscriptions. Strangely enough, none of his inscriptions ever mentions the name of his grandfather, Sulṭān Ghiyāth al-Dīn Balban. His father, Nāṣir al-Dīn Maḥmūd Bughrā Khān, also assumed the title sulṭān. Of the other titles of Kaykā'ūs Shāh, mawlā mulūk al-turk wa 'l-'ajam, emphasizes his authority over al-Turk (the Turks) and al-'Ajm (the Persian world), while the title of his governor (Fīrūz Aytgīn) khān khānān al-Sharq wa 'l-Ṣīn emphasized his authority in the east. Most of the inscriptions of Kaykā'ūs Shāh record the construction of mosques in western and northwest Bengal.

(10) Masjid inscription in Devikote dated 697 (1297)

ORIGINAL SITE: An unnamed masjid somewhere near Devikot, Southern Dinajpur district (about eighteen miles southwest of Dinajpur city in Bangladesh), West Bengal. **CURRENT LOCATION:** Mausoleum of Mawlānā Shāh 'Aṭā near the old fort on the eastern bank of the river Purnavaba at Devikot. **MATERIAL, SIZE:** Black basalt; 41 × 13 inches. **STYLE, NO. OF LINES:** *riqā'*; three lines. **REIGN:** Sulṭān Rukn al-Dunyā wa 'l-Dīn Kaykā'ūs Shāh (690–701/1290–1301). **LANGUAGE:** Arabic. **TYPE:** Commemorative inscription of a mosque. **PUBLICATION:** D. Money, *JASB*, VIX (1847): 349, 394; E. Thomas, *Chronicle of the Pathan Kings of Delhi* (London, 1871): 149; Blochmann, *JASB*, XLI (1872): 102–104; Yazdani, *EIM* (1917–18): 11–13; Buchanan, *Geographical, Statistical and Historical Description of the District or Zilla of Dinajpur*, 51; E. Thomas, *List of Ancient Monuments in Rajshahi Division* (Calcutta: Government of Bengal Public Works Department, 1896): 14, no. 9; Dani, *Bibliography of Muslim Inscriptions*, 5; S. Ahmed, *Inscriptions of Bengal*, 15–18; A. Karim, *Corpus of Inscriptions*, 48–53.

Text:

L-1 بنى هذا العمارة < عمارة هذا > المسجد في عهد {ال} سلطان السلاطين ركن الدنيا والدين ظل الله في الأرضين
كيكاؤس شاه بن محمود *شاه* السلطان يمين

L-2 خليفة الله ناصر أمير المؤمنين خلد الله ملكه وسلطانه بفرمان خسرو زمان شهاب الحق والدين سكندر ثاني الغ أعظم
همايون ظفر خان

L-3 بهرا م ايتگين سلطاني خلد الله ملكه وسلطانه ومد الله عمره بتوليت صلاح جيوند ملتاني في الغرة من المحرم شهور سنة
سبع وتسعين وستماية

Translation:

L-1 The edifice of this mosque was built during the reign of Sulṭān al-Salāṭīn (the king of the kings), Rukn al-Dunyā wa 'l-Dīn, Ẓill-Allah fī 'l-Arḍayn (Allah's shadow on the lands), Kaykā'ūs Shāh ibn Maḥmūd al-Sulṭān,

L-2 Yamīn Khalīfat-Allah, Nāṣir Amīr al-Mu'minīn, may Allah perpetuate his kingdom and authority; by the order of the Khusrow-i-Zamān (Khusrow [an exemplary great Persian king] of the age), Shihāb al-Ḥaq wa 'l-Dīn (the flame of truth and religion), Sikandar thānī, the great exalted, auspicious, Ẓafar Khān

L-3 Bahrām Aytgīn Sulṭānī; may Allah sustain his dominion and power and may Allah prolong his life. [It was done] under the supervision of Salāh Jīwand Multānī on the first of Muḥarram in the months of the year six hundred and ninety-seven.

Discussion:

The history of Devikote, where the inscription was found, goes back to the early Gupta period when it was known as Kotivarsa. Later, it was also known as

Bāngarh. Because of its strategic importance, the first Muslim ruler of Bengal, Muḥammad Bakhtiyār Khaljī, conquered the area and made it his capital after renaming it Damdama (lit. cantonment).

Ẓafar Khān Bahrām Aytgīn, whose name is recorded in this inscription as well as in the inscriptions no. 12 (dated 698/1298) and no. 16 (dated 713/1313) was the administrator of the area. Shortly after this tablet was inscribed in 698/1298, he moved to Tribeni in the south where he lived during 698–713(1298–1313). Whether he was related to Fīruz Aytgīn, the administrator in eastern Bihar whose name appears in the previous two inscription, cannot be ascertained.

Ẓafar Khān Aytgīn played an important role in the consolidation of Islam in the southwestern part of Bengal, which he conquered during the reign of Sulṭān Kaykā'us Shāh. According to local sources (such as the Kursī Nāma found in the tomb of Ẓafar Khān at Tribeni and consulted by D. Money), he was accompanied by the famous sufi saint Shāh Safi al-Dīn on his campaign to this region. Ẓafar Khān established a number of mosques and madrasas in the area.

The *nisba* of the mason of the mosque, Salāḥ Jīwand, 'Multānī' suggests that he originally came from the city of Multan in Punjab, which is historically associated with many skilled masons who participated in different architectural activities in many parts of South Asia.

(11) Monumental inscription of an unknown edifice in Kagol dated 697 (1297)

ORIGINAL SITE: An early Sultanate masjid in Kagol, Bihar, India. **CURRENT LOCATION:** Most likely in situ. **MATERIAL, SIZE:** Probably black basalt; not known. **STYLE, NO. OF LINES:** *riqā'*; two lines. **REIGN:** Sulṭān Rukn al-Dunyā wa 'l-Dīn Kaykā'ūs Shāh (690–701/1290–1301). **LANGUAGE:** Arabic. **TYPE:** Commemorative inscription. **PUBLICATION:** None.

Text:

L-1 [في عهد كيكاؤ]س شاه السلطان بن السلطان بن السلطان يمين خليفة الله ناصر أمير المؤمنين

L-2 [ابو] لمظفر المنصور الغازي ضيا[ء] الدولة والدين الغ خان ادام الله دولته وزاد خيره في الغرة من المحرم سنة سبع وتسعين وستماية

Translation:

L-1 [During the reign of the great Sulṭān Rukn al-Dunyā wa 'l-Dīn] Kaykā'ūs Shāh, al-Sulṭān ibn al-Sulṭān ibn al-Sulṭān Yamīn Khalīfat Allah, Nāṣir Amīr al-Mu'minīn.

L-2 Abū 'l-Muẓaffar (victorious) al-Manṣūr (the triumphant), al-Ghāzī (the warrior in the path of Allah), Ḍiyā' al-Dawla wa 'l-Dīn (the glow of the state and the religion) Ulugh Khān, may Allah perpetuate his state and increase his benevolence; the first of Muḥarram of the year six hundred and ninety-seven.

Discussion:

A photograph of this inscription was accidentally found by the author in his personal archive with no reference to it whatsoever. Probably it reached him through some sources from the Archaeological Survey of India. A significant part of the right side of the inscription is broken, resulting in the loss of the initial part of the text. Judging from the contents of the remaining text, it seems that the inscription belonged to a masjid built under the patronage of Ulugh Khān, an active officer in the eastern part of Bihar. His name also appeared in Jāmiʿ Masjid inscription in Lakhisarai dated 697/1297 (no. 9).

(12) Madrasa inscriptions at Ẓafar Khān Masjid in Tribeni dated 698 (1298)

ORIGINAL SITE: An early Sultanate madrasa known later on as Ẓafar Khān Masjid, Tribeni, Hoogly district in West Bengal. **CURRENT LOCATION:** An inscriptional band of a miḥrāb at the second bay from the south inside Ẓafar Khān Masjid at Tribeni. **MATERIAL:** Probably black basalt. **SIZE:** (A) The religious text above the lintel of the niche: 13.5 × 7.5 inches. (B) First twelve verses on the lintel of the southern niche below inscription A: 80 × 13 inches. (C) Verses 13–14 on the right jamb of the niche: 65.5 × 5.5 inches. (D) The last two verses (15–16) on the left jamb of the niche: 65.5 × 5.5 inches. **STYLE, NO. OF LINES:** Inscription A is in *jalī* (bold) *thulth*, the rest is in *riqāʿ*. **REIGN:** Sulṭān Rukn al-Dunyā wa 'l-Dīn Kaykā'ūs Shāh (690–701/1290–1301). **LANGUAGE:** Arabic. **TYPE:** Inscription A records a *ḥadīth* of the Prophet. The rest of the text commemorates in verse the establishment of a madrasa in the edifice and its academic activities. **PUBLICATION:** Blochmann, *JASB*, XXXIX (1870): 285–286; Yazdani, *EIM* (1917–18): 13–15, pl. II; Dani, *Bibliography of Muslim Inscriptions*, 6; S. Ahmed, *Inscriptions of Bengal*, 18–21; A. Karim, *Corpus of Inscriptions*, 53–56.

Text: (A) Below the lintel of the southern niche:

L-1 قال عليه السلام تعلموا العلم فإن تعلمه لله طاعة وطلبه عبادة
L-2 ومذاكرته تسبيح والبحث عنه جهاد وتعليمه خشية وتحسينه لله مسرة

Text: (B) On the lintel of the southern niche, just above inscription A:

First line (on the top):

[لقد شيدت هذه العمارة الفخمة]	لنصب دروس واتخاذ مدارس
سليل القضاة النصير محمد	يلقب بالبرهان قاضي الحمارس
وقد أنفق الأموال في الدرس حسبة	ليرضى به الرحمن عن كل دارس
فيرزق أهل الفضل من عرض ماله	لتدريس علم الشرع فوق الطنافس

Second line (at the middle):

. . . . . .   لإظهار دين الله بين الغطارس
. . . من الدارس يتقى   به الشر ما لا يتقى بالتارس
بنوبة سلطان السلاطين عهده   حكى عن عهود الجم كل المجالس
ملاذ الورى ركن الدنى كيكاؤس   تدوم له الدنيا دوام الهواجس

Third line (the last one at the bottom):

. . . . . .   تبدى ظفر خان هزبر العنابس
بفتح بلاد الهند كل ركضة   وشيد بناء الخير بعد الدوارس
وقلع علوج الكفر بالسيف والقنا   بذل كنوز المال في كل بائس
وأحيى بقاع الشرع من بعد ميتة   بتلخيص برهان العلوم الفرانس

Text: (C) Inscription on the right jamb of the niche:

فيرجو من الفقهاء بانيه دعوة   لتثبيت إيمان أوان الحنادس
جزاه الله خيرا إنه محض رحمة   و بر و إحسان لأهل القلانس

Text: (D) Inscription on the left jamb of the niche:

تعظيم علماء الشريعة جملة   و لإعلاء أعلام العمالس
بتاريخ جاء من حاء وصادها   خاء و حروف الوفق حسبان قائس

Text: (E) Right of mihrāb, second bay from the south (viewed from the eastern side):

L-1 الله لا إله إلا هو الحي القيوم لا تأخذه سنة ولا نوم له ما في السموات وما في الأرض من ذا
L-2 الذي يشفع عنده إلا بإذنه يعلم ما بين أيديهم وما خلفهم ولا يحيطون بشيء
L-3 من علمه إلا بما شاء وسع كرسيه السموات والأرض ولا يؤده حفظهما وهو العلي العظيم

Translation:

(A) He [the Prophet], peace be on him, said: 'Acquire knowledge, for acquiring it for the sake of Allah is indeed [true] submission [to Him], its search is adoration, its discussion is glorification and its embellishment for the sake of Allah is pleasure.'

(B) [This magnificent building complex was established?] to institute lectures and to establish madrasas (seats of learning) by the offspring of *qāḍī*s al-Naṣīr Muḥammad, who is duly styled Qāḍī al-Ḥummāris [lit. the lion]. He has spent a large sum of money on education from a pure motive (*ḥisba*, lit. accountability, arithmetical problem), so that the Merciful One [Allah] may be pleased with every student. Many noble ones (namely, 'ulamā') are supported from the generosity of his wealth, to teach the knowledge of sharī'a on the carpets (of the madrasa/masjid) … to manifest the religion of Allah on the arrogant. Through the students, he protects himself more than he could through his shield. During the reign of Sulṭān al-Salāṭīn, whose age copied of every age all their best qualified. Malādh al-Warā (the shelter of mankind), Rukn al-Danā (the support of the commoners) Kaykā'ūs, may the earth continue to exist for him as long as the idea of existence continues.... Where Ẓafar Khān, the fierce lion, appeared in every battle, in conquering the country of India in every expedition and established benevolent institutions that rose from their ashes. He destroyed the uncouth among the infidels with his sword and spears and spent the wealth of [his] treasure for every wretched person. He revived the institutions of sharī'a after its death, by outlining the powerful arguments of intuitive knowledge.

(C) Its builder requests the *fuqahā'* (jurists) to pray for the sustenance of [his] *īmān* (faith) at the time of intense darkness [of the grave]. May Allah reward him with the best, for He is all Merciful, Benevolent and Beneficent for the wearer of caps [pious people]

(D) And [he wishes to express] respect for all the scholars of the *sharī'a* so that the characteristics of [pious people like] *'amālas* (scholars) can be illuminated. [The date [of the construction] can be obtained from *hā'*, *ṣād* and *khā'*, if their chronogrammic value is calculated and taken into account.]

(E) L-1 'Allah; there is no God but He, the Living, the Everlasting. No slumber can seize Him, nor sleep. To Him belongs all that is in the heavens and the earth. Who is there

L-2 that shall intercede with Him without His permission? He knows what lies before them and what is after them, and they cannot comprehend anything

L-3 of His knowledge except what He wishes. His throne extends over the heavens and the earth and He feels no fatigue in guarding them for He is the All-high and the All-glorious.

Discussion:

These inscriptions were traced by H. Blochmann around 1870 in the centuries old city of Tribeni.[15] The Sanskrit form of this city name is Tri-venī or 'Three Braids' referring to the convergence of the Bhagirathi, Jamuna and Saraswati rivers, in the district of Hooghly, West Bengal. Tribeni is an ancient place of Hindu pilgrimage and Sanskrit learning, mentioned in classical Greek (e.g. Pliny's *Natural History*), Sanskrit (e.g. Dhoyī's *Pavanaduta*) and Bengali sources (e.g. Chandimangala) and early European travelogues.[16]

Ẓafar Khān Ghāzī, whose name appears in this inscription, conquered this city towards the end of the thirteenth century. Tribenī was also known by the Muslims as Fīruzābād after Sulṭān Fīruz Shāh (r. 1301–1322) and its environs (e.g. Satgaon and Chota Pandua) prospered under Muslim rule as evidenced by the impressive architecture of the period, which was influenced by Islamic and local traditions. The present inscription and the inscription of Madrasa Dār al-Khayrāt suggest that in addition to holding an important commercial and political position in southwest Bengal, the area was a notable Islamic educational and cultural centre. With the emergence of the new port city of Hooghly in the sixteenth century after the advent of European traders, and later Kolkata farther south, Tribeni and its surrounding cities lost their importance and urban character and declined to villages.[17]

The *ḥadīth* quoted in this inscription also appeared in a Sultanate mosque in Yusufganj (Goaldi) village near Sonārgā'on, Dhaka (see Moghrapara inscription dated 899/1493). The calligraphic style of this inscription closely resembles the style appearing in another inscription dated 697/1297 in Lakhisarai of Monghyr district, Bihar. The royal titles in this inscription, such as malādh al-warā (the shelter of mankind) and Rukn al-Danā (the support of the commoners), suggest that Islam had started spreading during this period in this region as a religion of commoners, a social wave with which the ruling power wanted to be associated and credited. The welfare institutions and benevolent works, such as madrasas, inns, wells and ponds initiated under the patronage of the ruling class in the region, referred to in this inscription as *binā al-khayr* (بناء الخير i.e. establishing munificent projects) – disseminated the egalitarian message of Islam to the commoners very effectively.

This epigraphic text indicates that a thriving madrasa with a huge endowment was established on the site by the offspring of Qāḍī al-Nuṣayr Muḥammad where *sharī'a*, *ḥisba*, *fiqh* and other important disciplines were imparted to students from different regions. Though the term *ḥisba* may not have been used here to imply in a strict sense the institution of accountability which existed in the world of Islam as an independent watchdog office to implement moral and ethical standards in day-to-day affairs of state, it does indicate that the concept of *ḥisba* indeed existed in the country. The inscription also suggests that *qāḍī*s (court judges) had a very important role in social and intellectual life in Bengal, and they also played an important role in disseminating Islamic messages to the common public. This is the first Arabic epigraphic text in Bengal written in poetic form. Though not very common, inscriptions appeared in poetic form in different Islamic regions from time to time. A number of examples of inscriptions in poetic form can be found in Khurasan (e.g. an inscription in the Timurid citadel in Herat dated AH 818).

(13) Mausoleum inscription in Mahasthangarh dated 700 (1300)

ORIGINAL SITE: Man Kali Bhita in Mahasthangarh, Bogra district, Bangladesh. **LOCATION:** Probably in the Indian Museum, Calcutta. **MATERIAL, SIZE:** Black flint kind of stone, 17 × 6.25 inches. **STYLE, NO. OF LINES:** A crude type of *naskh*. The inscribed surface is divided into four panels, three of which contain three lines, the fourth five lines. **REIGN:** Sulṭān Rukn al-Dunyā wa 'l-Dīn Kaykā'us Shāh (690–701/1290–1301). **LANGUAGE:** Arabic. **TYPE:** Commemorative inscription containing a *ḥadīth* and a Throne verse from Qur'ān. **PUBLICATION:** R. D. Banerjee, *Journal of the Bihar and Orissa Research Society*, IV (1918): 178–179; Dani, *Bibliography of Muslim Inscriptions*, 6; S. Ahmed, *Inscriptions of Bengal*, 21–23; A. Karim, *Corpus of Inscriptions*, 56–58.

Text:

First panel:

L-1 {لـ}بسم الله الرحمن الرحيم
L-2 قال النبي صلى الله عليه وسلم
L-3 من قرأ آية الكرسي لم يمنعه

Second panel:

L-4 من دخول الجنة إلا الموت
L-5 الله لا إله إلا هو الحي القيوم
L-6 لا تأخذه سنة ولا نوم له ما في

Third panel:

L-7 السموات وما في الأرض من ذا
L-8 الذي يشفع عنده إلا بإذنه يعلم
L-9 ما بين أيديهم وما خلفهم ولا يحيطون

Fourth panel:

L-10 بشيء من علمه إلا بما شاء وسع كرسيه
L-11 السموات والأرض ولا يؤوده حفظهما
L-12 وهو العلي العظيم- بنى<بنيت> هذا<هذه> الروضة
L-13 لخان معظم ومكرم ميرنامور خان
L-14 شهر شوال سنة سبعماية

Translation:

First panel:
L-1 In the name of Allah, the Merciful, the Compassionate.
L-2 The Prophet, peace be on him, said,
L-3 ‘Whomsoever reads the Throne verse, none prevents him

Second panel:
L-4 from entering paradise except death.’
L-5 ‘Allah; there is no God but He, the Living, the Everlasting.
L-6 No slumber can seize Him, nor sleep. To Him belongs all

Third panel:
L-7 that is in the heavens and the earth. Who is there
L-8 that shall intercede with Him without His permission? He knows
L-9 what lies before them and what is after them, and they cannot comprehend

Fourth panel:
L-10 anything of His knowledge except what He wishes. His throne extends
L-11 over the heavens and the earth and He feels no fatigue in guarding them
L-12 for He is the All-high and the All-glorious.’ This mausoleum was built
L-13 for the exalted and respected Khan, Mir Nāmwar Khan,
L-14 (in) the month of Shawwal, the year seven hundred.

Discussion:

The inscription was probably found during 1911–1912 either near Man Kali Bhita or near the ruins of an old tomb near fifteen-domed mosque in Mahasthangarh, Bogra district, Bangladesh. The name of the reigning sulṭān, Kaykā'ūs Shāh, is not mentioned in this inscription. It is quite interesting to note the appearance of a *ḥadīth* in such early inscriptions, though the *matn* (متن, i.e. text) of this particular *ḥadīth* does not appear in the six most authentic books of the sayings of the Prophet (known as *al-Ṣīḥaḥ al-Sitta*). The term *rawḍa* connoting shrine (lit. garden) appears for the first time in an inscription in Bengal; later on it became a popular Bengali word used for the same meaning. Worshipping at a *rawḍa* shrine gradually became institutionalized on a popular level in the Hindu–Muslim syncretistic tradition of Bengal.

(14) Commemorative inscription from the Mausoleum of Shāh Jalāl in Sylhet dated 703 (1302–1303)

ORIGINAL SITE: Sylhet in Bangladesh (most likely at the mausoleum of Shāykh Shāh Jalāl). **CURRENT LOCATION:** Bangladesh National Museum, Dhaka. **MATERIAL:** Granite. **SIZE:** Not known. **STYLE, NO. OF LINES:** Crude form of *muḥaqqaq*; nine lines equally divided into three rectangular panels in addition to a single line on the top border in very small letters. **REIGN:** Actual date of inscription is 918/1512–1513 during the reign of Ḥusayn Shāh, though the inscription also records another year 703/1302–1303 corresponding with the reign of Sulṭān Shams al-Dīn Fīrūz Shāh 701–716 (1301–1316). **LANGUAGE:** Persian except the date, which is written in Arabic. **TYPE:** Commemorative inscription. **PUBLICATION:** Stapleton, *Dacca Review* (August 1913): 154; Stapleton, *JASB*, (n. s.) XVIII (1922): 413–414, pl. IX; A. H. Dani, *Bibliography of Muslim Inscriptions*, 7, no. 9 and 58, no. 108; S. Ahmed, *Inscriptions of Bengal*, 24–26, pl. IX; Sayyid Murtaḍā 'Alī, *Haḍrat Shāh Djalāl O Sileter Itihās* (Dhaka, 1988); Abdul Karim, *Corpus of Inscriptions*, 296–98, pl. 52(a).

Text:

Above the main panels of writing in a single line:

بعظمت شيخ المشايخ مخدوم شيخ جلال مجرد بن محمد

First panel:

L-1 أول فتح اسلام شهر عرصه
L-2 سريهت بدست سكندر خان غازي
L-3 در عهد سلطان فيروز شاه

Second panel:

L-4 د لوي<دهلوي> سنة ثلاث وسبعماية اين
L-5 عمارت ركنخان كه فتح كننده
L-6 هشت كامهاريان وزير {و} لشكر بوده

Third panel:

L-7 شهرها وقت فتح كامرو وكامتا
L-8 وجازنگر واريشا لشكري كرده باشند جابجا
L-9 بدنبال بادشاه سنة ثمان وعشر وتسعماية

Translation:

Top: In honour of the exalted Shaykh al-Mashāyikh (spiritual master), Shaykh Jalāl ibn Muḥammad

First panel:
L-1 The first Islamic conquest of the city in the *'arṣah* (عرصه an administrative unit)
L-2 of Sylhet was accomplished at the hand of Sikandar Khān Ghāzī
L-3 during the reign of Sulṭān Fīruz Shāh

Second panel:
L-4 Dalwi (Dahlawi), the year seven hundred three. This
L-5 edifice (has been erected) by Rukn Khān who conquered
L-6 Hasht Kāmhāriyān (the eight tribes), being the vizier and the chief of the army;

Third panel:
L-7 for months at the time of the conquest of Kamrup and Kamta
L-8 and Jaznagar and Orissa as he served the army at different places
L-9 following the king in the year nine hundred and eighteen.

Discussion:

Sylhet, also known as Jalālābād, is the name of a district and the district headquarters in the easternmost part of Bangladesh.[18] Before the arrival of Islam, Sylhet formed part of Samatata region[19] and was divided into small kingdoms (Laor, Jayantia, Gauḍa) ruled by Hindu dynasties. Some parts of Sylhet were also ruled by the neighbouring kingdom of Kamrup. An economically prosperous land where cowrie-shells were used for currency, Arab traders sometimes visited Sylhet on their overland route to China. The celebrated Suhrawardī Shāykh, Shāh Jalāl Mujarrad kunyā'ī, whose name is inscribed at the beginning of this inscription, and his disciples played an important role in the consolidation of Islam in this region. Around 1345, the famous Moroccan traveller Ibn Baṭṭūṭa visited the saint in Sylhet. Mughal rule was extended to Sylhet in the early seventeenth century.[20]

This inscription suggests that the Muslim conquest of the area began as early as the fourteenth century during the reign of Sulṭān Fīrūz Shāh (d. 1322) of Lakhnawati. The inscription also mentions another name, Danbāl Bādshāh, in the last line, which is probably a reference to Prince Dānyāl, who was killed in a military expedition during the reign of Ḥusayn Shāh. As is clear from the text, this epigraphic record was inscribed in 918/1512–1513. Interestingly, on the reverse side of the same stone slab, there is another inscription from the early period of Mughal expansion in Bengal in 996/1588 during Akbar's reign (963–1014/1556–1605).

The word *Dalwi* in the fourth line seems to be erroneous transcription for *Dahlawi*, a *nisba* to Delhi, suggesting that Fīrūz Shāh, the reigning sulṭān of Bengal (*ca.* 1301–1316) during that period came from Delhi. The region of Kāmta mentioned in the inscription was a buffer state between the Bengal Sultanate and Kamrup in northern Rangpur, Kuch Bihar and the neighbouring regions. Jājnagar, which also appears in this inscription, was a Hindu feudatory kingdom of Orissa on the river Vaitarani, in southwest Bengal. All these names appear in a number of other inscriptions and on coins. Rukn Khān appears in two other inscriptions from the time of Ḥusayn Shāh.

Hasht Kāmhāriyān probably refers to the eight most influential tribal chiefs in the region. The entire area was populated by tribes, many of whom started coming under the sway of Islam in early sixteenth century during the Ḥusayn Shāhī period. At least one major tribe, the Mech, embraced Islam at the very beginning of the Muslim conquest by Bakhtiyār Khaljī, as reported in *Ṭabaqāt-i-Nāṣirī*.

While the inscription records an earlier date, 708/1302–1303, it was actually inscribed at a much later date in the year 918/1512. Thus it contains more than one date referring to the early establishment of Islamic rule in the area. On the reverse side of the same stone slab, there is another inscription from the early period of Mughal expansion in Bengal in 996/1588 during Akbar's reign (963–1014/1556–1605).

(15) Ḥatim Khān Palace inscription in Bihar Sharif dated 707 (1307)

ORIGINAL SITE: Ḥātim Khān Palace in Bihar Sharif in the state of Bihar, India. **CURRENT LOCATION:** In the tomb of the Ṣūfī Badr-i-ʻĀlam in Choti Dargah of Bihar Sharif in the state of Bihar, India. **MATERIAL, SIZE:** Black basalt; 75 × 21 inches. **STYLE, NO. OF LINES:** *riqāʻ al-musalsal*; two lines. **REIGN:** Sulṭān Shams al-Dīn Fīrūz Shāh 701–16/1301–1316. **LANGUAGE, TYPE:** Arabic; commemorative inscription of an annex to a previously constructed building. **PUBLICATION:** Blochmann, *JASB*, XLII (1873): 249; Yazdani, *EIM* (1917–18): 22, pl. VI(b); Dani, *Bibliography of Muslim Inscriptions*, 7–8; S. Ahmed, *Inscriptions of Bengal*, 26–27; Q. Ahmad, *Inscriptions of Bihar*, 13–15; A. Karim, *Corpus of Inscriptions*, 59–62.

Text:

L-1 بنی <بنیت> هذه العمارة المزيدة في عهد السلطان الاعظم شمس الدنيا والدين أبي المظفر فيروز شاه السلطان خلد الله ملكه و سلطانه

L-2 و نوبة ايالة الخان العادل الباذل الغازي تاج الحق والدين حاتم خان ابن السلطان خلّد ملكه العبد الضعيف محمد حسن بكمبروری في شهور سنة سبع وسبعماية

Translation:

L-1 This additional building was constructed during the reign of the great Sulṭān Shams al-Dunyā wa 'l-Dīn Abū 'l-Muẓaffar Fīrūz Shāh al-Sulṭān – may Allah perpetuate his kingdom and his sovereignty.

L-2 During the succession of the regency of the khān, the just, the benevolent, the conqueror, Tāj al-Ḥaq wa 'l-Dīn (the crown of the truth and the religion) – Ḥātim Khān ibn al-Sulṭān – may Allah perpetuate his kingdom. The humble servant Muḥammad Bikampruri; in the months of the year seven hundred and seven.

Discussion:

Henry Blochmann originally found this inscription in a dilapidated building, known as Ḥātim Khān's palace, near Choti Dargah of Bihar Sharif in the state of Bihar, India. According to Blochmann, the inscription was attached to a lofty gateway which, together with an arched hall fast falling to decay, and a roofless mosque (to which the Masjid Inscription dated 715/1315, no. 17, pl. 17, refers), formed the ruins of what local tradition called Ḥātim Khān's palace.

This Arabic inscription is inscribed in a very elegant *al-riqā' al-musalsal* style, in which the tails of each of the letters are connected to the next letter. No vocalization has been used in the writing. In some letters, even diacritical points are purposefully not used, due to calligraphic considerations. The text records construction of an *'imāra al-mazīda* (lit. an annex to a building, synonymous with the popular architectural term of *zā'ida*). Another inscription on the other side of the slab records the name of the Delhi Sulṭān Fīrūz Shāh Tughluq.

Tāj al-Ḥaq wa 'l-Dīn Ḥātim Khān ibn al-Sulṭān was the son of the Bengal Sulṭān Shams al-Dīn Fīrūz Shāh, who served as governor of the Tirhut region of Bihar, which formed the northwestern part of the Bengal Sultanate at that time.

(16) Madrasa Dār al-Khayrāt inscription in Tribeni dated 713 (1313)

ORIGINAL SITE: Madrasa Dār al-Khayrāt in Tribeni, Hoogly district, West Bengal, India. **CURRENT LOCATION:** Found fixed to the northern wall of Ẓafar Khān's tomb at Tribeni in Hoogly district, West Bengal, India. **MATERIAL, SIZE:** Carved on two separate long slabs of black basalt each measuring 75 × 10 inches. **STYLE, NO. OF LINES:** *ruq'a*; two lines. **REIGN:** Sulṭān Shams al-Dīn Fīrūz Shāh 701–722/1301–1322. **LANGUAGE:** Arabic. **TYPE:** Commemorative inscription of Madrasa Dār al-Khayrāt. **PUBLICATION:** Blochmann, *JASB*, XXXIX (1870): 287–288; R. D. Banerjee, *Sahitya Parishad Patrica*, XV: 24–25; Yazdani, *EIM* (1917–18): 33–34, pl. XII; Dani, *Bibliography of Muslim Inscriptions*, 8–9; S. Ahmed, *Inscriptions of Bengal*, 28–29; A. Karim, *Corpus of Inscriptions*, 62–69.

Text:

Vertical writing to the right of the first line

الحمد لولي الحمد

Main text of the first line (the upper part)

بنيت هذه المدرسة المسماة دار الخيرات في عهد سلطنة والي المبرّات صاحب التاج والخاتم ظل الله في العالم المكرم الأكرم
الأعظم مالك رقاب الأمم شمس الدنيا والدين المخصوص بعناية رب العالمين وارث ملك سليمان أبي المظفر فيروزشاه السلطان

Vertical writing to the left of the first line

خلد الله سلطانه

Text:

بأمر الخان الاجل الكريم المبجل الجزيل العطا الجميل الثنا نصير الإسلام ظهير الأنام شهاب الحق والدين معين الملوك
والسلاطين مربى أرباب اليقين خانجهان ظفر خان أظفره الله على أعدائه وعطفه بأوليائه في غرة محرم المضاف إلى سنة ثلاث
وعشرة وسبعماية

Translation:

Vertical writing to the right of the first line:
Praise be to Him to Whom all praises belong.

First line:
This madrasa, named Dār al-Khayrāt, was built during the tenure of the governor Wālī al-Mabarrāt (the lord of beneficence), Ṣāḥib al-Tāj wa 'l-Khātim, Ẓill-Allah fī 'l-'Ālam (divine shadow in the world), the honoured, the generous, the great, Mālik Riqāb al-'Umam, Shams al-Dunyā wa 'l-Dīn, al-Makhṣūṣ bi-'Ināyat Rabb al-'Ālamīn (the chosen one for the attention of the Lord of the universe), Wārith Mulk Sulaymān (the heir of the kingdom of Solomon), Abū 'l-Muẓaffar Fīrūz Shāh, al-Sulṭān,

Vertical writing to the left of the first line:
may Allah perpetuate his authority;

Second line:
By the order of the great *khān*, the noble, the munificent, the benevolent in [bestowing] gifts, the man of good praise, the helper of Islam, the supporter of mankind, Shihāb al-Ḥaq wa 'l-Dīn (luminous star of the truth and religion), Mu'īn al-Mulūk wa 'l-Salāṭīn (the supporter of the kings and sulṭāns), Murabbī Arbāb al-Yaqīn (the patron of the sufi gnostics), Khān-i-Jahān (the *khān* of the world) Ẓafar Khān; may Allah make him victorious over his enemies and make him kind to his friends; on the first of Muḥarram of the year seven hundred and thirteen.

Discussion:

The patron of this madrasa is Ẓafar Khān, who was mentioned above in another madrasa inscription in Tribeni, dated 698/1298 (ins. no. 12). The institution of the madrasa started growing in Bengal from the very beginning of the Muslim rule as reported in *Ṭabaqāt-i-Nāṣirī*. The masjid–madrasa inscription from Naohata from the reign of Balkā Khān Khaljī (ins. no. 3) and the madrasa inscriptions at Ẓafar Khān masjid in Tribeni dated 698/1298 (no. 12, pl. 12) shed some light upon the academic and educational activities as well as the growth of the madrasa institution in the region. However, it is in this inscription that the word madrasa appears for the first time.

The *shākila* (the top horizontal bar resembling the character ك) of the letter *kāf* occasionally appears in a very small size at the top of the cluster of symmetrically arranged verticals.

(17) Masjid inscription from Ḥātim Khān's Palace in Bihar Sharif dated 715 (1315)

ORIGINAL SITE: A ruined Sultanate masjid attached to Ḥatim Khān's Palace (no longer – extant) near Chhoti Dargah of Bihar Sharīf in the state of Bihar. **CURRENT LOCATION:** Indian Museum, Calcutta, inv. no. 4448/4444. **MATERIAL, SIZE:** Black basalt; 42 × 12 inches. **STYLE, NO. OF LINES:** *riqā'*; two lines. **REIGN:** Sulṭān Shams al-Dīn Fīrūz Shāh 701–722/1301–1322. **LANGUAGE, TYPE:** Arabic; commemorative inscription of a mosque. **PUBLICATION:** Chinmoy Dutt, *Catalogue of Arabic and Persian Inscriptions in the Indian Museum* (Calcutta: Indian Museum, 1967): 5; S. Ahmed, *Inscriptions of Bengal*, 29–30; Dani, *Bibliography of Muslim Inscriptions*, 9; Yazdani, *EIM* (1917–18): 34–35, pl. XII; Blochmann, *JASB*, XLII (1883): 249–250, pl. 1; P. Horn, *Epigraphia Indica*, II (1892): 291; Q. Ahmad, *Inscriptions of Bihar*, 15–19; A. Karim, *Corpus of Inscriptions*, 69–71; Desai, *EIAPS* (1961): 27.

Text:

L-1 بنى هذا المسجد في نوبة السلطان الأعظم شمس الدنيا والدين أبي المظفر فيروز شاه السلطان وأيام إمارة خاقان الزمان المخاطب بحاتمخان

L-2 أدام الله ظلالهما العبد الواثق بالله ولكرمه الراجي أحقر الخلائق بهرام بن حاجي تاب الله عليه وغفر لوالديه في الغرة من رجب سنة خمس عشر وسبعماية

Translation:

L-1 This mosque was built during the time of the great Sulṭān Shams al-Dunyā wa 'l-Dīn, Abū 'l-Muẓaffar Fīrūz Shāh al-Sulṭān, and in the administration of the Khāqān al-Zamān (overlord of the age) known as Ḥāṭim Khān.

L-2 May Allah perpetuate their shadows. [By] the servant [who is] trusting in Allah and soliciting his magnanimity, [being] the humblest of creatures,

Bahrām ibn Ḥājjī, may Allah accept his repentance and forgive his parents; on the first of Rajab in the year seven hundred and fifteen (1 October 1315).

Discussion:

According to Qeyamuddin Ahmad, this inscription, and not the one dated 707/1307 (no. 15), originally belonged to Ḥāṭim Khān's palace in Bihar Sharif. This is the last inscription from the reign of Fīrūz Shāh. Its intricate pattern of writing in *riqā'* style is calligraphically fascinating as the endings of all the words are joined to others to create the effect of a *musalsal*, or chain of continuity. Some horizontal strokes are deliberately elongated and thickly arranged so as to create the impression of the waves in the flow of the writing. One of the calligraphic innovations in this text is the word *al-khalā'iq* in the middle of the second line, where the middle form of the letter *khā'* is stretched out and joined to a rather peculiar looking *lām-alif*. The upper horizontal strokes of the letter *kāf*, known as *shākila* in Arabic, appear rather distinctively in a crown-like form which is mounted on the verticals of the letters *kāf*, thus distinguishing them from the rest of the verticals.

(18) Treasury inscription from Wazir-Beldanga dated 722 (1322)

ORIGINAL SITE: Wazir-Beldanga village, Mullikpur post office in Nachol police station, Chapai Nawabganj district, Bangladesh. **CURRENT LOCATION:** Varendra Research Museum, Rajshahi, inv. no. 3471. **MATERIAL, SIZE**: Black basalt; 10 × 40.5 inches. **STYLE, NO. OF LINES:** *tawqī'*; two main lines, each divided into two sub-lines of writing. **REIGN:** Sulṭān Bahādur Shāh (722–733/1322–1333). **LANGUAGE, TYPE:** Arabic; commemorative inscription. **PUBLICATION:** Abdul Karim, 'The First and Only Unpublished Inscription of Ghiyath-al-Din Bahadur Shah', *Journal of the Varendra Research Museum* 6 (180–181): 5–9; A. Karim, *Corpus of Inscriptions*, 71–76.

Text:

Upper panel:

L-1 بسم الله الرحمن الرحيم لا إله إلا الله محمد رسول الله
هذا مال الملك الكبير الكريم المؤيد المظفر المنصور المجاهد المرابط الغازي
L-2 مصرف الدولة والدين أسد الإسلام والمسلمين أبو الملوك والسلاطين المعروف

Lower panel:

L-1 بإيثار حب السلطاني أدام الله إقباله في عهد نوبت السلطان الأعظم غياث الدنيا والدين أبو المظفر بهادر شاه السلطان
[بن] السلطان صمد الله قوانين مملكته ومهد براهين
L-2 سلطنته شهور سنة اثني عشرين وسبعماية بناء صحيحا لوجه الله تعالى تقبل الله منه بخط العبد الضعيف محمد بن محمد
بن أحمد غفر الله أجمعين

Translation:

Upper panel:
In the name of Allah, the most merciful and compassionate. There is no God but God alone, and Muḥammad is His messenger.

L-1 This is the treasury of al-Malik (the king), al-Kabir (the great), al-Karīm (the benevolent), al-Mu'ayyad (the supported one), al-Muẓaffar (the victorious), al-Manṣūr (the aided one), al-Mujāhid (the holy warrior), al-Murābiṭ (the advance guard), al-Ghāzī (the conqueror),

L-2 Maṣrif al-Dawla wa 'l-Dīn (the treasurer of the state and the faith), Asad al-Islām wa 'l-Muslimīn (the lion of Islam and the Muslims), Abū 'l-Mulūk wa 'l-Salāṭīn (the father of the kings and sulṭāns), known

Lower panel:

L-1 for [his] sacrifice for the imperial cause. May Allah perpetuate his prosperity. At the time of the succession of the great sulṭān, Ghiyāth al-Dunyā wa 'l-Dīn (the succor of Islam and the faith), Abū 'l-Muẓaffar (the father of the victorious), Bahādur Shāh al-Sulṭān ibn al-Sulṭān, may Allah preserve the laws of his kingdom and establish the legitimacy of

L-2 his dominion. In the months of the year seven hundred and twenty-two, a rightful construction for the sake of Allah, the exalted. May Allah accept [it] from him. In the handwriting of the humble servant Muḥammad ibn Muḥammad ibn Aḥmad, may Allah forgive all.

Discussion:

This is an interesting inscription both calligraphically and historically. Inscribed in *al-tawqī' al-musalsal* style, which is rather unusual in monumental calligraphy, the text has no vocalization or diacritical marks.

This is the only inscription from the reign of Sulṭān Bahadur Shah. It belonged to a building that functioned as a government treasury. It was found in an area not far from the early Muslim capitals Guar, Pandua and Devikot.

Notes

1 G. S. Farid, 'Hitherto Unknown Silver Tankah of Sultan Alauddin Ali Mardan Khilji, 607–610 A.H', *Journal of the Asiatic Society* 18(1–4) (1976): 104–106; John Deyell, *Living without Silver: The Monetary History of Early Medieval North India* (Delhi: Oxford University Press, 1990): 364–367, coin no. 298; Nicholas W. Lowick, 'The Horseman Type of Bengal and the Question of Commemorative Issues', *Journal of the Numismatic Society of India* 35 (1973): 196–208; idem, *Coinage and History of the Islamic World*, vol. XVII (Aldershot: Variorum, 1990): 195–208.

2 Minhāj Sirāj, *Ṭabaqāt-e-Naṣiri*, ed. W. N. Lees (Calcutta: 1863–1864): 150.

3 Jadunath Sarkar, *The History of Bengal 1200–1757* (Patna: Academica Asiatica, 1973): 19.

4 Ibid.

5 The date of Safid Buland Gulistan (tomb) inscription of the Farghāna Valley seems to be some time during 447–351/1055–1060; see Sheila S. Blair, *The Monumental Inscriptions from early Islamic Iran and Transoxiana* (Leiden: E. J. Brill, 1992): 128–129.

6 Z. A. Desai, 'An Early Thirteenth Century Epitaph from Delhi', *EIAPS* (1975): 1–5.

7 A. B. M. Habibullah, 'An Unpublished Inscription from Sitalmat', *Bangladesh Lalit Kala*, 1(2) (July 1975): 89–94.

8 Ziauddin Ahmad Desai, 'An Early Thirteenth Century Inscription from West Bengal', *EIAPS* (1975 [published in 1983]): 6–12.

9 Jadunath Sarkar, *History of Bengal 1200–1757*, 28 and 44.

10 Minhāj Sirāj, *Ṭabaqāt-e-Nāṣiri*, ed. by W. N. Lees, 148.

11 Blair, *Monumental Inscriptions from Early Islamic Iran and Transoxiana*, 30 and 51.

12 *Encyclopaedia of Islam*, 2nd edn, s.v. 'Tirhut'.

13 For details on the history of Tirhut, see the following sources: Bihārī Lāl, *Ain-i-Tirhut* (Persian MS); Muḥammad Ṣadr A'lā Aḥmad Dabīr, *Basātīn al-Uns* (MS in British Museum), fols 9–12; Darbārī Moalla, *Akhbārāt-i-Darbārī Mo'alla* (unpublished Persian MS); D. N. Singh, *History of Tirhut*, Rādhākrishna Choudhary, *History of Muslim Rule in Tirhut*, Chowkhamba Sanskrit Studies Series, vol. 72 (Varnasi, 1970); Mullā Taqia, Bayāz (Persian MS).

14 *Encyclopaedia of Islam*, 2nd edn, s.v. 'Tirhut'.

15 Ibid., s.v. 'Tribenī'.

16 For details on Tribeni, see: Bipradās, *Manasā Mangala* (sixteenth century Bengali MS [Ga 3530] in the Asiatic Society of Bengal, Calcutta); *Bhakti Ratnākara*, ed. Rama Nārāyana Vidyāratna (Berhampore, 1887): 538–539.

17 For details, see *Encyclopaedia of Islam*, 2nd edn, s.v. 'Tribenī'.

18 Ibid., s.v. 'Sylhet'.

19 Minhāj al-Dīn Sirāj mentions it as Suknāt; see *Ṭabaqāt-i-Nāṣirī*, ed. W. N. Lees (Calcutta, 1863–1864): 150.

20 For details, see *Encyclopaedia of Islam*, 2nd edn, s.v. 'Sylhet'.

6 Inscriptions of the Sultanate period

Inscriptions of the early Ilyās Shāhī rulers

(19) Shaykh 'Alā' al-Ḥaqq Masjid inscription, now in Bania Pukur dated 743 (1342)

ORIGINAL SITE: Shaykh 'Alā' al-Ḥaqq Masjid (no longer extant, somewhere in West Bengal). **CURRENT LOCATION**: Affixed to a masjid built in the late nineteenth century in Bania Pukur, Kolkata, West Bengal. **MATERIAL, SIZE:** Black basalt; 51 × 9 inches. **STYLE, NO. OF LINES:** *ijāza*; two lines. **REIGN:** *Ca*. 743/1342 at the beginning of the consolidation of power of Sulṭān Ilyās Shāh (740–759/1339–1358). **LANGUAGE:** Arabic **TYPE:** Commemorative inscription of a mosque built for a famous saint, 'Alā' al-Ḥaqq. **PUBLICATION:** S. Ahmad, *EIM* (1939–40): 7–9, pl. IV (a); Dani, *Bibliography of Muslim Inscriptions*, 10; S. Ahmad, *Inscriptions of Bengal*, 31–33; A. Karim, *Corpus of Inscriptions*, 77–82.

Text:

L-1 الحمد لمن أعلى آثار المسجد والشكر لمن أولى بالمحامد وأعطى التوفيق ببناء هذا المسجد المبارك في عهد {ال}سلطان الزمان الذي ملكه ملك سليمان ظل الله في العالمين شمس الدنيا والدين المنصور بعناية الرحمن ناصرأهل الإيمان

L-2 أبو<أبي> المظفر الياس شاه السلطان خلد الله ملكه فاولى انصرام الأزمان للشيخ المنعم المكرم الذي أعماله بالتقوى جليلة عالية أنار الله قلبه بنور المعرفة والإيمان وهو الهادي إلى دين السبحان علاء الحق والدين دامت تقواه الثاني من شهر النبي شعبان سنة ثلاث وأربعين وسبعماية

Translation:

L-1 Praise be to Him who has exalted the influence of mosques, and all thanks are due to Him Who is the most worthy of all excellences and Who has bestowed the opportunity of the construction of this blessed mosque during the reign of Sulṭān al-Zamān alladhi Mulkuhu Mulku Sulaymān (the sulṭān of the age whose kingdom matches the kingdom of King Solomon), Ẓill-Allah fī 'l-'Ālamayn (Allah's shadow both the worlds), Shams al-Dunyā wa 'l-Dīn, al-Manṣūr bi-'Ināyat al-Raḥmān (the supported one by the grace of Allah), Nāṣir Ahl al-'Īmān (the supporter of the faithful)

L-2 Abū 'l-Muẓaffar Ilyās Shāh the Sulṭān, may Allah perpetuate his kingdom. (This was done) to pay homage to the bygone era of the (spiritually) rewarded and revered shaykh, 'Alā' al-Ḥaqq wa 'l-Dīn, whose deeds are exalted and sublime; Allah illuminated his heart with the light of *ma'rifa* (divine perception) and *'imān* and who is the guide to the religion of al-Subḥān (Divine attribute meaning the Glorious), may his piety last long; second of the month of the Prophet – Sha'bān – the year seven hundred and forty-three.

Discussion:

This epigraphic text begins with a statement that underscores the important and influential role masjids were playing in the social transformation of Bengalis' lives during the period. This inscription from the reign of Ilyās Shah, found in Bania Pukur near Kolkata, refers to a famous sufi, 'Alā' al-Ḥaqq, who lived in Pandua and spent a great deal of his life preaching Islam. He was the son of Shaykh 'Umar ibn Asad, a treasurer of the sulṭān. The family supposedly descended from the famous companion of the Prophet and army commander, Khālid ibn al-Walīd of the Quraysh tribe of Makkah. According to a number of sources, 'Alā' al-Ḥaqq had two sons, Nūr Quṭb al-'Ālam (recorded in an inscription dated 1493, during the reign of Shams al-Dīn Muẓaffar Shāh) and A'ẓam Khān. Nūr Quṭb al-'Ālam had two sons, Anwār al-Ḥaq Shahīd and Rif'at al-Dīn (Rafqat al-Dīn or Rafīq according to some sources). Shaykh Rif'at al-Dīn's son's name was Shaykh Zāhid (d. 863/1459). Several descendants of Shaykh Zāhid became renowned Sufis over time namely, Muḥammad al-Khālidī (recorded in an inscription dated 1572 on 'Alā' al Ḥaq's tomb); Makhdūm Shaykh (recorded in an inscription dated 1582 at Quṭb Shāhī Masjid); and Shaykh al-Islām Shaykh Mas'ūd (Mirza Nathan, the author of *Bahāristān-e-Ghaybī*, met him in 1612).[1]

'Ala' al-Ḥaqq's family arrived in Bengal probably during the early part of Ilyās Shāh's rule. Even though one of his sons (according to some sources, his brother), A'ẓam Khān, was a vizier at the Pandua court, the Shaykh never sought any official position for himself. He established a seminary at Pandua, besides running a khānqāh left by his spiritual mentor Akhī Sirāj al-Dīn. Another of his spiritual mentors was Shaykh Jalāl al-Dīn Tabrīzī.

Shaykh 'Alā' al-Ḥaqq wielded a strong influence over the populace because of his vast learning, unblemished character and charity. Even the ruler of Jaunpur listened to him. Over time, Sulṭān Sikandar Shāh grew jealous of his virtue and popularity, and banished him to Sonārgā'on. After only two years of exile, Shaykh 'Ala' al-Ḥaqq returned to Pandua, and devoted himself completely to the seminary, expanding it to include a hospital, and later on a large residence for scholars.

The madrasa of Pandua, established by Shaykh 'Alā' al-Ḥaqq, persisted long after his death, sustained by an unbroken stream of royal patronage. Shaykh Anwar served as the superintendent of the institution during the reign of Shams al-Dīn Muẓaffar Shāh (896–898/1491–1493). Sulṭān ‘Alā’ al-Dīn Ḥusayn Shāh endowed it with forty-two villages. The Mughal prince Shāh Shujā‘ supported the madrasa with a grant.

Among the famous students of Shaykh ‘Alā’ al-Ḥaqq were his own son Shaykh Nūr Quṭb al-‘Alam, Mīr Sayyid Ashraf Jahāngīr Simnānī (originally from Central Asia), Shaykh Nāṣir al-Dīn Mānikpūrī (from Manikpur, North India), Mawlānā Imām Muẓaffar Balkhī, Ḥusayn Nawsha-i-Tawḥīd, Makhdūm Shāh Sulṭān Ḥusayn (killed by Shiv-Singh, the son of Diva-Sing, the ruler of Tirhut in Bihar) and Shaykh Ḥusayn Dhukkarpūsh of Purnia. Mīr Simnānī subsequently went to Jaunpur to organize a madrasa there. ‘Alā’ al-Ḥaqq died on the first of Rajab, AH 800 (20 March 1398). His son Nūr Quṭb al-‘Ālam continued his mission, eventually becoming more famous than his father. It is quite probable that the original site of this inscription in southwest Bengal (in the present city of Kolkata) came under the sway of Ilyās Shāh at some point and the place might have been visited by the shaykh. At the same time, we cannot rule out the possible transfer of this inscriptional slab from Pandua to Calcutta at a later stage during the colonial period when a large amount of building materials was transported down the Ganges to Kolkata from the ruins of Gaur and Pandua.

(20) Dome inscription of ‘Aṭā Shāh Mausoleum in Devikot dated 765 (1363)

ORIGINAL SITE: Affixed to the wall of the mausoleum of ‘Aṭā Shāh at Devikot in Southern Dinajpur district, West Bengal. **CURRENT LOCATION:** In situ. **MATERIAL:** Not known. **SIZE:** 23 × 12 inches. **STYLE, NO. OF LINES:** *Rayḥāni*; 4 lines. **REIGN:** Sulṭān Sikandar Shāh (758–795/1357–1393), the second ruler of the Ilyās Shāhi dynasty in Bengal. **LANGUAGE:** Persian with a few phrases in Arabic. **TYPE:** Commemorative inscription for a shrine. **PUBLICATION:** Blochmann, *JASB* XLI (1872): 102–107; Cunningham, *ASR*, vol. 15, p. 98; Yazdani, *EIM* (1929–30): 9–11, pl. VI (a); Dani, *Bibliography of Muslim Inscriptions*, p. 11; S. Ahmad, *Inscriptions of Bengal*, pp. 34–35; A. Karim, *Corpus of Inscriptions*, pp. 82–84.

Text:

L-1

درین گنبد که بنیاد عطایست   عمارت خانه کونین بادا
ملائك برثباتش خوانده تا محشر   بنينا فوقكم سبعا شدادا (12:78)
بعنايت هفت ايوان بديع كه   الذي خلق سبع سموات طباقا (3:67)
تقدست أسماؤه بإتمام رسيد عمارت

L-2

گنبد رفيع كه نسخه ايست ازتخمه سقف جلال – ولقد زينا السماء الدنيا بمصابيح (5:67) در روضه متبرك قطب الوليا
<الأولياء> وحيد المحققين سراج الحق والشرع والدين مولانا عطا أعطاه الله تعالى

L-3

فضيلة الامرفي الدارين صاحب العهد وزمان باعث العدل والإحسان حامي البلاد راعي العباد السلطان العادل العالم الأعظم ظل
الله في العالمين المخصوص بعنايت الرحمن

L-4

أبو المجاهد سكندر شاه بن الياس شاه السلطان خلد الله ملكه
بادشاه جهان سكندر شاه كه بنا مش درّ دعا سفتند
نوّر الله شأنه خواندند خلد الله ملكه گفتند
في تاريخ سنة خمس وستين وسبعماية عمل بنده درگاه غياث زرين دست

Translation:

L-1 In this *gunbad* (i.e. *qubba* or a dome) whose foundation has been laid by 'Aṭā', may it become the sanctuary of both worlds.

May the angels recite for its durability, till the day of resurrection, 'We have built over you seven firmaments' (Qur'ān, 12:78).

By the grace of the (architect of) seven unique *iwān*s (Royal Chamber/hall), 'Who has created the seven heavens one above another' (Qur'ān, 3:67), may His names be glorified. The building of

L-2 this lofty dome, which is a copy of the exalted heavenly ceiling, was completed. 'And indeed we have embellished the lowest heaven with lamps' (Qur'ān, 5:67) in the blessed garden [shrine] of Quṭb al-Awliyā' (pole of the saints) Waḥīd al-Muḥaqqiqīn (singled out among those who conceived reality or الحقيقة) Sirāj al-Ḥaqq wa 'l-Shar' wa 'l-Dīn (Candle of the reality, *sharī'a* and religion) Mawlānā 'Aṭā', may Allah the exalted bless him,

L-3 with favour in both worlds. [It was done] by the order of Ṣāhib al-'Ahd wa 'l-Zamān (lord of the age and the time), Bā'ith al-'Adl wa'l-'Iḥsān (instrumental to establishing justice and benevolence), Ḥāmī al-Bilād (defender of the country), Rā'i al-'Ibād (protector of the people), al-Sulṭān, al-'Ādil, al-'Ālim, al-A'ẓam, Ẓill Allah fī 'l-'Alamīn, al-Makhṣūṣ bi-'Ināyat al-Raḥmān (the chosen one for the attention of the Most Merciful)

L-4 Abū 'l-Mujāhid Sikandar Shāh ibn Ilyās Shāh the sulṭān, may Allah perpetuate his kingdom. The monarch of the world Sikandar Shāh, in whose name the pearls of the prayer have been shaped; and they have prayed [for him] 'May Allah brighten his status'; and they have said [for him], 'May Allah perpetuate his kingdom.' In the date of the year seven hundred and sixty-five, slave of the shrine Ghiyāth – Zarrīn Dast – (the golden handed) rendered [it].

Discussion:

This inscription belongs to the mausoleum of the famous Muslim scholar and sufi-saint Mawlānā Shaykh 'Aṭā' Waḥīd al-Dīn, known as Quṭb al-Awliyā' (pole of the friends [of Allah]). As the inscription records, Sulṭān Sikandar Shāh erected this mausoleum. Even today, we can see the tomb and ruins of an old mosque near a large water tank, known as Dhaldighi. Several other inscriptions can still be seen there. Shaykh 'Aṭā' Wahīd al-Dīn established a seminary at Devikot near Gangarampur, a cultural and educational centre at that time, after settling there with his followers. Many antiquities and archaeological relics have been found in Devikot. Over time, the seminary received the patronage of a number of different rulers. Mawlānā Shaykh 'Aṭā' Waḥīd al-Dīn was very popular and highly respected because of his vast learning and exemplary piety. During his lifetime, he worked mainly in the Dinajpur region.

The custodian of the shrine has been mentioned as Ghiyāth, who must have earned the prestigious title of 'zirin-dast' after demonstrating a high order of mastery in Islamic calligraphy. The title can be well compared to the title 'shīrīn-qalam' bestowed by the Mughal emperor Jahāngīr to his court calligrapher 'Abd al-Ṣamad Shīrāzī.

(21) Masjid inscription in Champanagar dated 769 (1367)

ORIGINAL SITE: An unnamed Sultanate masjid in Amarpur police station, Champanagar, state of Bihar. **CURRENT LOCATION:** In the private collection of R. N. Ghose in Champanagar. **MATERIAL, SIZE:** Black basalt; 30 × 15.6 inches. **STYLE, NO. OF LINES:** Upper panel of the inscription resembles *riqā'*, the other two lines in the lower panel are rendered in *tawqī'* of a local variety; three lines in total, one in the upper panel and two in the lower panel. **REIGN:** Sulṭān Sikandar Shāh (758–795/1357–1393). **LANGUAGE, TYPE:** Arabic; foundation inscription. **PUBLICATION:** Qeyamuddin Ahmad, 'A New Inscription of Sikandar Shāh of Bengal from Bihar', *EIAPS* (1963): 1–4; Q. Ahmad, *Inscriptions of Bihar*, 52–56; P. C. Singh, *Journal of Bihar Research Society*, XVII (1961): pl. I–IV; Annual Report, *Epigraphia Indica* (1962–63): D 17; A. Karim, *Corpus of Inscriptions*, 84–87.

Text:

Upper panel: L1

بسم الله خير . الاسما [ء] بنا<بني> هذا المسجد فـ[ـي] عهد السلطان المجاهد سكندر شاه ابن الياس شاه السلطان صاحب

Lower panel:

L2 البناء خانكبير وتهمتن بينظير الغ طغيخان بن بغراخان ادام الله معاليه اصرف ماله في رضاء

L3 الله تعالى قال النبي عليه السلام من بنى مسجدا في دار الدنيا بنى الله له قصرا في الجنة في الغرة من المحرم سنه تسع وستين وسبعماية

Translation:

L-1 In the name of Allah, the best of names. This mosque was built during the reign of al-Sulṭān, al-Mujāhid (the warrior in the cause of religion), Sikandar Shāh, son of Ilyās Shāh, the sulṭān. The master of

L-2 [this gracious] construction (i.e. the patron) is the great Khān and incomparable brave warrior Ulugh Taghī Khān ibn Bughrā Khān, may Allah perpetuate his glories. He spent his money seeking the pleasure of

L-3 Allah most high. The Prophet, peace be on him, said, 'Whoever builds a mosque in the abode of this world, Allah will build a palace for him in paradise.' On the first of Muḥarram of the year seven hundred and sixty-nine.

Discussion:

This interesting inscription, although discovered in Bihar, records the name of the sulṭān of Bengal, Sikandar Shāh. Contemporary historical sources indicate that the Delhi sulṭān, Fīruz Tughluq, after his expedition to Bengal in 1357–1358, brought almost the entire region of Bihar under his control. However, the discovery of this inscription in the northern part of Bihar suggests that there were still pockets of territory in Bihar near the Bengal border where the Bengali sulṭān had enough influence to assert his sovereignty. Thus, Ulugh Taghī Khān, a local feudal lord, expresses his allegiance to the Bengali sulṭān instead of the sulṭān of Delhi. It is also possible that the inscription was made in the territory ruled by Sikandar Shāh, but later carried to the place where it was found. The calligraphy is mediocre and devoid of any ornamental motifs.

(22) A Commemorative inscription at the west façade of Adina Masjid in Ḥaḍrat Pandua dated 776 (1374)

ORIGINAL SITE: West façade, lower tier, central chamber projection of the *qibla* wall of Adina mosque facing outside, Ḥaḍrat Pandua. **CURRENT LOCATION:** In situ. **MATERIAL, SIZE:** Black basalt; 57 × 10 inches. **STYLE, NO. OF LINES:** Monumental *thulth*; single line. **REIGN:** Sulṭān Sikandar Shāh (758–795/1357–1393). **LANGUAGE, TYPE:** Arabic; commemorative inscription of a mosque. **PUBLICATION:** W. Franklin, *Journal of a Route from Rajmahal to Gaur* (MS in India Office Library): 14; Shayam Prasad, *Ahwal-i-Gaur wa Pandua*, 27; A. A. Khan, *Memoirs of Gaur and Pandua*, 139–140; Paul Horn, 'Muhammadan inscriptions from Bengal (with facsimiles)', *Epigraphia Indica*, II (1892): 282–283; Cunningham, *Archaeological Survey Report*, XV: 282–283; Ravenshaw, *Gaur, its Ruins and Inscriptions*, 62–64, pl. 46, no. 4; Blochmann, *JASB*, XLII (1873): 256–257 and (1895): 212; S. Ahmad, *Inscriptions of Bengal*, 35–38; Dani, *Bibliography of Muslim Inscriptions*, 12 (no. 15); Syed Mahmudul Hasan, *Mosque Architecture of Pre-Mughal Bengal* (Dhaka: University Press Limited, 1979): 87–90; M. Hasan, *Gaud and Pandua* (Dhaka: Islamic Foundation, 1987): 210–218; A. Karim, *Corpus of Inscriptions*, 87–92.

Text:

أمر ببنا[ء] {ال}عمارة هذا المسجد الجا[مع] في أيا[م] {ال}دولة السلطان الأعظم الأعلم أعدل أكرم أكمل {ال}سلاطين
العرب والعجم الواثق بتأييد الرحمن أبو المجاهد سكندر شاه سلطان بن الياس شاه السلطان خلد خلافته إلى يوم الموعود كتبه في
التاريخ رجب سنة ست وسبعين وسبعماية

Translation:

The construction of this congregational mosque was ordered during the time of the reign of the great sulṭān, the most learned, A'dal Akram Akmal al-Salāṭīn al-'Arb wa 'l-'Ajm (the most just, benevolent and complete among the sulṭāns of both the Arabs and non-Arabs), al-Wāthiq bi Ta'yīd al-Raḥman (who trusts in the support of the most Merciful) Abū 'l-Mujāhid Sulṭān Sikandar Shāh ibn al-Sulṭān Ilyās Shāh, may his reign be perpetuated to the promised day. [The scribe] wrote it in Rajab of the year seven hundred seventy-six.

Discussion:

The Adina mosque was one of the largest and loftiest mosques ever built in South Asia, or in the entire Islamic world. Its overly imposing grandiosity itself constituted an expression of the glory of the establishment of a Muslim Sultanate in the East. In spite of all the elegance of the inscriptions of this exquisitely impressive and magnificent religious monument, errors can be found in the epigraphic texts, as is the case with some other inscriptions in the region. In this particular inscription (dated 776/1374), for instance, the calligrapher or perhaps the craftsman (namely, the inscriber) forgot to inscribe the letters *mi'* [مع] while writing the word *al-jāmi'* and similarly the letter *mīm* [م] in the word *ayyām*.

(23) Adina Masjid inscription above the Central Miḥrāb

ORIGINAL SITE: Above the central miḥrāb at the middle of the *qibla* wall (west façade) in the main prayer hall, lower tier of the interior chamber projection inside the Adina Masjid. **CURRENT LOCATION:** In situ. **MATERIAL, SIZE:** Black basalt; not known. **STYLE, NO. OF LINES:** Monumental *thulth* with a thin band of Kufī interwoven with the upper part of the elongated verticals of the main body of *thulth* writing; single line of writing in addition to a medallion on the top of the inscription containing a verse in *thulth* style in the decorative form of *ṭughrā'*. **REIGN:** During the reign of Sulṭān Sikandar Shāh probably around 776 (1374–1375) when the other inscriptions in the mosque were inscribed. **LANGUAGE:** Arabic. **TYPE:** Religious invocation. **PUBLICATION:** Same as the previous inscription (no. 22).

Discussion:

There are a number of interesting texts inscribed above the miḥrāb in the middle of the *qibla* wall inside the Adina mosque. The medallion on the top contains the phrase:

قال الله تعالى

(Allah, the Exalted, said) followed by the Qur'ānic verse 22:77:

يأيها الذين آمنوا أركعوا و أسجدوا واعبدوا ربّكم

(O those who are believers, bow, prostrate and worship your Lord).

Below this inscription is a single panel of exquisitely executed text which accommodates two bands of writing in the same line. The upper band of the line in Kufī style contains the *basmala*, Sura al-Fātiḥa (the opening chapter). The lower band in monumental *thulth*, which dominates the overall calligraphic background, contains the following Qur'ānic verse 9:18–19 which appears in many mosque inscriptions all over the Islamic world. It is important to note that this is perhaps the only inscription in Bengal where Kufī style has been used. The raised borderline above the upper panel of Kufī writing is decorated with vegetal motifs. In these decorative motifs, we find a rhythmic pattern that moves symmetrically along with the flow of calligraphic movements below.

Kufī writing appearing on the upper rim of the inscription:

بسم الله الرحمن الرحيم الحمد لله رب العالمين الرحمن الرحيم مالك يوم الدين إياك نعبد وإياك نستعين إهدنا الصراة المستقيم صراة
الذين أنعمت عليهم غير المغضوب عليهم ولا الضالين آمين

Translation:

In the name of Allah, the Most Gracious, the Most Merciful. All the praises and thanks be to Allah, the Lord of the universe; Who is the Most Gracious and the Most Merciful. He is the Ruler of the day of resurrection. We worship You Alone, and we seek help from You Alone. Guide us to the straight path. The path, that has been bestowed with grace by you, not the path of those who earned your anger, nor of those who went astray; Amen.

Thulth writing appearing on the main body of the inscription at the bottom:

قال الله تعالى إنما يعمر مساجد الله من آمن بالله واليوم الآخر وأقام الصلاة وآتى الزكاة ولم يخش إلا الله فعسى
أولئك أن يكونوا من المهتدين أجعلتم سقاية الحاج وعمارة المسجدالحرام كمن آمن بالله واليوم الآخر وجاهد في سبيل الله لا
يستوون عند الله والله لا يهدي القوم الظالمين

Translation:

Thus says Allah, the Exalted: 'The mosques of Allah shall be visited and maintained only by those who believe in Allah and the last day, they establish prayers and practice regular charity, they fear none except Allah; it is they who are rightly guided. Do you consider the mere giving of drink to pilgrims, or the maintenance of the Sacred Mosque equal to (the faith of) those who believe in Allah and the Last Day, and strive in the path of Allah. Nay, they are never comparable in the sight of Allah, neither Allah guides the nations who are transgressors' [9:18–19].

(24) Adina Masjid inscription above the twenty-fourth Miḥrāb from the south in the north wing

ORIGINAL SITE: On the right, top and left of the twenty-fourth miḥrāb from the south at Adina masjid. **CURRENT LOCATION:** In situ. **MATERIAL, SIZE:** Black basalt, not known. **STYLE, NO. OF LINES:** Monumental *thulth*; single line on the right, top and left of the twenty-fourth miḥrāb from south. **REIGN:** Sulṭān Sikandar Shāh (758–795/1357–1393). **LANGUAGE:** Arabic. **TYPE:** A verse from the Qur'ān (9:20–22). **PUBLICATION:** A. A. Khan, *Memoirs of Gaur*, 136; S. M. Hasan, *Gaur and Hazrat Pandua*, 243; Proddato Ghose, *Gaoro Banger Sthapatya*, 50.

Text:

قال الله عز من قائل وجل من متكلم أعوذ بالله من الشيطان الرجيم إن الله هو السميع العليم بسم الله الرحمن الرحيم الذين
آمنوا وهاجروا وجاهدوا في سبيل الله بأموالهم وأنفسهم أعظم درجة عند الله وأولئك هم الفائزون يبشرهم ربهم برحمة منه ورضوان
وجنات لهم فيها نعيم مقيم خالدين فيها أبدا إن الله عنده أجر عظيم

Translation:

Allah, the Powerful and Exalted, and I seek refuge from Satan, the most cursed one, (and) I take refuge in Allah, the All Hearer, the Most Knowing; in the name of Allah, the Most Kind, the Most Compassionate. [It is He, Who said:] Those who believe and emigrate and strive in Allah's cause with their possessions and lives have the highest rank in the sight of Allah; and they are the real successful. Their Lord gives them the glad tidings of His mercy and pleasure. And they will dwell in the paradise wherein all the lasting blesses await them forever; indeed Allah has the greatest reward.

Discussion:

Verses in this inscription (9:20–22) are a continuation of the verses of the previous inscription (appearing on the main body of ins. no. 23 in *thulth* style). They are all from the *sura* (chapter) 'Repentance'. While the verses in the previous inscription signify the importance of the mosque in the community and the establishment of prayers there, the verse in the present inscription invites the attention of believers to the importance of *hijra* for the sake of Allah (perhaps to this new Islamic frontier state of Bengal) and calls for *jihād* (struggle in the path of Allah). By assuming the title Abū 'l-Mujāhid in the inscription no. 22, Sulṭān Sikandar Shāh was pointing out the same message, that the gradual formation of this Sultanate in this hinterland became possible as a result of a long process of *jihād*. It is also interesting to note the introduction of the phrase قال الله تعالى (God, the Exalted, said) for the first time before the Qur'ānic verses; this phrase did not appear in earlier inscriptions in the region.

(25) Adina Masjid inscription in the Royal Chamber (Badshāh Kā Takht) on the northern side, Ḥaḍrat Pandua

ORIGINAL SITE: On the right, top and left of the twenty-third miḥrāb from the south at the western wall (north wing), popularly known as Badshāh Kā Takht, an elevated chamber for royal dignitaries (also identified by some as Zenana Khanah or ladies gallery) inside the Adina mosque. **CURRENT LOCATION:** In situ. **MATERIAL, SIZE:** Black basalt; not known. **STYLE, NO. OF LINES:** *thulth*; single line on the right, top and left of the twenty-third miḥrāb from the south. **REIGN:** During the reign of Sulṭān Sikandar Shāh, probably around 776 (1374–1375), when the other inscriptions in the mosque were inscribed. **LANGUAGE:** Arabic. **TYPE:** Verses from the Qur'ān (48:27–29 and 33:56). **PUBLICATION:** Same as inscription no. 22.

Text and translation:

On the right of the miḥrāb from bottom to top:

لقد صدق الله الرّء يا بالحق لتدخلن المسجد الحرام إن شاء الله آمنين محلقين رؤوسكم ومقصرين لاتخافون

Translation:

Truly did Allah fulfil the vision for His messenger. You will indeed enter the sacred mosque, if Allah wills, secured, with heads shaved and hair trimmed, and without any fear [48:27].

Continuation of the same verse and the next on the lintel at the top:

فعلم ما لم تعلموا فجعل من دون ذلك فتحا قريبا هو الذي أرسل رسوله بالهدي ودين الحق ليظهره علي الدين كله وكفي بالله
شهيدا

Translation:

For he knew what you did not know, and he granted besides this, a speedy victory. It is He Who has sent His messenger with guidance and the religion of truth to make it prevail over all religion, and enough is Allah for a witness [48:27–28].

The beginning of the next verse (48:29) is inscribed on the left of the miḥrāb from top to bottom, the text of which is:

محمد رسول الله و الذين معه أشداء علي الكفار رحماء بينهم تراهم ركعا سجدا يبتغون فضلا من الله ورضوانا

Translation:

Muḥammad is the messenger of Allah, and those who are with him are strong against unbelievers, but compassionate among each other. You will see them bow and prostrate themselves seeking grace from Allah and His pleasure.

Below the lintel, just above the miḥrāb, from right to left is inscribed another verse (33:56), the text of which is:

إن الله وملائكته يصلون علي النبي يأيها الذين آمنوا صلوا عليه وسلموا تسليما

Translation:

Indeed Allah and His angels send blessings on the Prophet. O you believers, send your blessings on him; and salute him with all respect.

Discussion:

This inscription contains verses of the Qur'ān from two different *sura*s (chapters), running diagonally on all three sides (top, right and left) of the miḥrāb. It consists of verses 27–29 from the *sūra* al-Fatḥ (48). Verse 33:56 is inscribed centrally just above the arch of the miḥrāb slightly below the horizontal portion of the other inscription.

(26) Adīna Masjid inscriptions in the Royal Chamber (Badshah Kā Takht) on the southern side, Ḥaḍrat Pandua

ORIGINAL SITE: On top of another miḥrāb (probably the twenty-second from the south) in the northern part of the *qibla* wall, in the elevated portion specially reserved for the ruling class dignitaries (identified by some scholars as the *Zenana Khanah*, or ladies' gallery) inside Adina Masjid. **CURRENT LOCATION:** In situ. **MATERIAL, SIZE:** Black basalt; not known. **STYLE, NO. OF LINES:** *thulth*; single line on the right, top and left of the above-mentioned miḥrāb. **REIGN:** During the reign of Sulṭān Sikandar Shāh, probably around 776 (1374–1375) when another dated inscription in the mosque was inscribed. **LANGUAGE:** Arabic. **TYPE:** Throne verse from the Qur'ān (2:255–256). **PUBLICATION:** Same as inscription no. 22.

Text:

الله لا اله الا هو الحي القيوم لا تاخذه سنة و لا نوم له ما في السموات و ما في الارض من ذا الذي يشفع عنده الا باذنه يعلم ما بين ايديهم و ما خلفهم و لا يحيطون بشيء من علمه الا بما شاء وسع كرسيه السموات و الارض و لا يوده حفظهما و هو العلي العظيم لا اكراه في الدين قد تبين الرشد من الغي فمن يكفر بالطاغوت و يومن بالله فقد استمسك بالعروة الوثقي لانفصام لها و الله سميع العليم

Translation:

There is no God but Allah alone, [and] Muḥammad is His messenger. Allah; there is no God but He, the Living, the Everlasting. No slumber can seize Him, nor sleep. To Him belongs all that is in the heavens and the earth. Who is there that shall intercede with Him without His permission. He knows what lies before them and what is after them, and they cannot comprehend anything of His knowledge except what He wishes. His throne extends over the heavens and the earth and He feels no fatigue in guarding them for He is the All-high and the All-glorious. There is no compulsion in the religion; for the truth stands out clearly from misguidance. Whoever rejects evil and brings faith in Allah, he indeed grasps the most trustworthy handclasp that never breaks. Allah hears and knows everything.

Inscription (comprising *tahlīl*) at the centre of the upper jamb of the southernmost entrance of the *qibla* wall:

لا اله الاالله محمد رسول الله

Translation: 'There is no God but God Alone, and Muhammad is God's messenger.'

Discussion:

Inscription no. 26 consists of Qur'ānic verses 2:255–256 running on three sides (right, left and top) of the miḥrāb. The Qur'ānic verses in the inscriptions of Bengali mosques are carefully chosen. They convey a message that reflected the spirit of the *ummah* (Muslim community) in this newly conquered land which was still largely inhabited by non-Muslims.

(27) Masjid inscription in Mulla Simla dated 777 (1375)

ORIGINAL SITE: An unnamed Sultanate masjid in the village of Mullah Simla in Hoogly district, West Bengal. **CURRENT LOCATION:** Affixed to the entrance of the *dargāh* of Ḥaḍrat Muḥammad Kabīr Sāḥib in Mullah Simla village. **MATERIAL, SIZE:** Black basalt, not known. **STYLE, NO. OF LINES:** Bengali *ṭughrā'*; single line. **REIGN:** Sulṭān Sikandar Shāh (758–795/1357–1393). **LANGUAGE:** Arabic. **TYPE:** Commemorative inscription of a mosque. **PUBLICATION:** H. Blochmann, *JASB*, XXXIX (1870): 291–292; S. Ahmad, *Inscriptions of Bengal*, 38–40; Dani, *Bibliography of Muslim Inscriptions*, 12–13; A. Karim, *Corpus of Inscriptions*, 92–94.

Text:

قال الله تعالى و أن المساجد لله فلا تدعوا مع الله أحدا قال النبي عليه السلام من بنى مسجدا لله في الدنيا بنى الله له في الجنة
سبعين قصرا بنى المسجد الخان الأعظم الغ مخلص خان – في سنة سبعة<سبع> وسبعين وسبعماية

Translation:

Allah the Exalted has said, 'And verily the mosques belong to Allah only; so do not invoke anyone with Allah.' (72:18). The Prophet, peace be on him, said, 'Whoever builds a mosque in the world for Allah, Allah builds seventy palaces for him in paradise. al-Khān al-A'ẓam 'Ulugh Mukhliṣ Khān built the mosque in the year seven hundred and seventy-seven.

Discussion:

The text of this inscription suggests that it originally belonged to a mosque in the area which can no longer be identified. Like many other inscriptions with religious texts, this one was also removed from the ruins and placed at a *dargāh* (shrine) for preservation as well as for partaking in *baraka.*

The village of Mullah Simla, where the inscription was found, is located in the southwestern part of Bengal, quite far from the Sultanate capital. The inscription does not mention the name of the ruling sulṭān, Sikandar Shāh. It seems that the sulṭān had little or no influence in this remote area. Therefore, the builder of the mosque, Mukhliṣ Khān, did not think it important to mention the sulṭān's name, which was otherwise common especially in commemorative inscriptions.

(28) A Commemorative inscription from the reign of A'ẓam Shāh from Gauhati

ORIGINAL SITE: Reportedly discovered in Assam, though the exact site is not known. **CURRENT LOCATION:** Provincial museum, Gauhati in the state of Assam in India. **MATERIAL, STYLE, SIZE, NO. OF LINES:** Not known. **REIGN**: Sulṭān A'ẓam Shāh (792–813/1390–1410). **LANGUAGE:** Persian with a few Arabic phrases. **TYPE:** Commemorative inscription. **PUBLICATION:** S. Ahmad, *Inscriptions of Bengal*, 41–43; Dani, *Bibliography of Muslim Inscriptions*, 135; A. Karim, *Corpus of Inscriptions*, 95–97; Desai, *EIAPS* (1955–1956): 33–34.

Text:

L-1 در عهد همایون سلطان
L-2 سلاطین ظل الله في العالمین غیاث الدنیا
L-3 والدین أبو المظفر أعظم شاه
L-4 ابن سلطان المرحوم . أبو المجاهد
L-5 سکندر شاه سلطان ابن سلطان
L-6 المغفور شمس الدنیا والدین الیاس
L-7 شاه سلطان – جعل الجنة مثواه
L-8 وثقل بالحسنات(حسناته?)– میر اغما بحکم
L-9 فرمان کامکار همایون أعلی لا زال عالیا

Vertical line on the left [خدا] ئ وتعالی

Translation:

During the auspicious rule of the sulṭān of the sulṭāns, Ẓill Allah fī 'l-'Alamīn, Ghiyāth al-Dunyā wa 'l-Dīn Abū 'l-Muẓaffar A'ẓam Shāh, son of the late Sulṭān Abū 'l-Mujāhid Sikandar Shāh, Sulṭān ibn al-Sulṭān, al-Maghfūr (the deceased who has been forgiven by God) Shams al-Dunyā wa 'l-Dīn Ilyās Shāh Sulṭān; may Allah turn his abode into paradise and bestow on him His graces fully; Mīr Aghmā [carried out the job] in compliance with the lofty and exalted orders of Humāyūn (His Majesty), the highest Kāmkār (the chief executive/king); may he ever remain high and dignified.

Discussion:

This inscription was found in the Kamrup district of Assam, which lay on the northern frontier of the Bengal Sultanate. The region had been a target of a number of Muslim campaigns from the beginning of the conquest of Bengal. Its provenance suggests that Sulṭān A‘ẓam Shāh was successful in conquering the area and establishing his authority there.

(29) Inscriptions at the Khānqāh of Shaykh Jalāl al-Dīn Tabrīzī in Pandua

ORIGINAL SITE: A masjid somewhere near the Khānqāh of Shaykh Jalāl al-Dīn Tabrīzī (d. 1244–1245) in Pandua, Malda district, West Bengal, India. **CURRENT LOCATION:** Lying near the miḥrāb of the mosque in the Khānqāh of Shaykh Jalāl in Pandua. **MATERIAL, SIZE:** Greyish granite; 27 × 11 inches approximately. **STYLE, NO. OF LINES:** A local variety of *ijāzah*; two lines. **REIGN**: Sulṭān A‘ẓam Shāh (792–813/1390–1410). **LANGUAGE:** Arabic. **TYPE**: Commemorative inscription of a masjid. **PUBLICATION**: Probably none.

Figure 6.1 Commemorative inscription (Khānqāh in Pandua, Malda district, West Bengal) (source: copyright by author).

Text:

L-1 قال النبي صلى الله عليه وسلم من بنى مسجدا في الدنيا بنى الله له في الجنة [سبعين قصرا] . . . . . .

L-2 . . [غياث الدنيا والدين أبو المظفر] أعظم شاه سلطان خلّد الله ملكه وسلطانه باني لمباني الجنة حكمتيار . . .

Translation:

L-1 The Prophet, peace and blessings of Allah be upon him, said, ‘Whosoever builds a mosque in the world, Allah will build for him in Paradise [seventy palaces].’

L-2 [Ghiyāth al-Dunyā wa ’l-Dīn Abū ’l-Muẓaffar] Sulṭān A‘ẓam Shāh, may Allah perpetuate his kingdom and authority; builder of edifices in Paradise Ḥikmatyār…

Discussion:

Previously unknown, this is a rare inscription from the reign of A'ẓam Shāh discovered recently by the author near the miḥrab of a mosque located in the Khānqāh of Shaykh Jalāl al-Dīn Tabrīzī (d. 1244–1245) in Pandua, Malda district, West Bengal. There are several other previously undiscovered inscriptions, mostly in Persian, recording dates of the deaths of various spiritual mentors and sufi saints associated with the khānqāh. Most of these inscriptions are fixed under the extended ceiling at the eastern part of the monumental dome over the khānqāh.

Inscriptions of the indigenous Bengali sulṭāns (Sulṭān Jalāl al-Dīn Muḥammad Shāh and his son)

(30) An undated stone tablet of an unidentified Sultanate masjid in Pandua

ORIGINAL SITE: An unidentified Sultanate masjid in Pandua, Malda district, West Bengal, India. **CURRENT LOCATION:** Fixed on a grave adjacent to the northern wall of the mosque located in the Khānqāh of Shaykh Jalāl al-Dīn Tabrīzī (d. 1244–1245) in Pandua, Malda district, West Bengal. **MATERIAL, SIZE:** Black basalt; 20 × 9 inches. **STYLE, NO. OF LINES:** Monumental Bihārī; two lines. **REIGN:** Sulṭān Jalāl al-Dunyā wa 'l-Dīn Abū 'l-Muẓaffar Muḥammad Shāh (818–835/1415–1431). **LANGUAGE:** Arabic. **TYPE:** Commemorative inscription of a Masjid. **PUBLICATION:** M. Y. Siddiq, 'Calligraphy and Islamic Culture', *Bulletin of the School of Oriental and African Studies*, 68(1) (2005): 21–58.

Figure 6.2 Commemorative inscription (Pandua, Malda district, West Bengal) (source: copyright by author).

Text:

L-1 [قال الله تعالى وأن المساجد لله فلا تدعوا مع] الله أحدا قال النبي صلى الله عليه وسلم من بنى مسجدا [بنى الله له سبعين قصرا في الجنة]

L-2 [بنى المسجد في عهد السلطان جلال] الدنيا والدين أبو المظفر محمد شاه السلطان خلّد ملكه بناه معظم الدين والدولة الغ عزالدين سلمه الله. . . . . . .

Translation:

L-1 [Allah, the Exalted, has said, 'And verily the mosques belong to Allah only; so do not call anyone] with Allah (72:18).' The Prophet, peace and blessings of Allah be upon him, said, 'Whosoever builds a mosque, [Allah will build for him seventy palaces in Paradise.'

L-2 This masjid was built during the era of Sulṭān Jalāl al-Dunyā] wa 'l-Dīn abū 'l-Muẓaffar Muḥammad Shāh al-Sulṭān, may his kingdom perpetuate. Mu'aẓẓam al-Dīn wa 'l-Dawla (the honoured one in the religion and state) Ulugh 'Izz al-Dīn built it, may Allah protect him.

Discussion:

This stone tablet belongs to a very important transitional period of Sultanate rule in Muslim Bengal when an indigenous Bengali ruler, Sulṭān Jalāl al-Dīn Muḥammad, reigned in the region after converting to Islam. His rule was a significant departure from the previous traditions for a number of reasons, the most important being that he was a native Bengali Muslim rather than an immigrant. His father, Raja Ganesh, was an important Hindu vassal in the area who became quite influential and powerful towards the end of Ilyās Shāhī rule. As the power of Ilyas Shahi rulers started to wane, Raja Ganesh seized the opportunity to become the de facto ruler of the region. Raja Ganesh's son Jadu Sen, however, embraced Islam and finally became the sulṭān of Bengal after his father's death. This Bengali Muslim dynasty did not last long as the former Ilyās Shāhi dynasty was restored in 841/1437.

During the reign of this indigenous sulṭān, art, architecture and culture flourished in a distinctive regional style. Like this inscription, all of the other inscriptions of Sulṭān Jalāl al-Dīn Muḥammad were rendered in Bihārī, a regional calligraphic style that flourished in South Asia. The texts of most of the inscriptions of this period are written in pure Arabic with no Persian words, perhaps a reflection of the policy of Sulṭān Jalāl al-Dīn Muḥammad Shāh, who always preferred cultivating closer relations with the Arab world rather than depending solely on the cultural links with the Muslim Sultanates in Delhi and Central Asia.

(31) Masjid and Madrasa inscription from Sultanganj dated 835 (1432)

ORIGINAL SITE: Sultanganj village in Godagari, Rajshahi district, Bangladesh. **CURRENT LOCATION:** Varendra Research Museum, Rajshahi, inv. no. 2660. **MATERIAL, SIZE:** Black basalt, 42 × 8 inches. **STYLE, NO. OF LINES:** Bihārī; three lines. **REIGN:** Sulṭān Jalāl al-Dīn Muḥammad Shāh (818–835/1415–1431). **LANGUAGE:** Arabic. **TYPE:** Commemorative inscription of a mosque that also served as a madrasa. **PUBLICATION:** S. Ahmad, *Inscriptions of Bengal*, 46–48; Dani, *Bibliography of Muslim Inscriptions*, 14;

M. Abdul Ghafur, ‘Fresh Light on the Sultanganj inscription of Jalāl al-Dīn Muhammad Shāh’, *JASP*, VIII(1) (June 1963): 55–65; A. Karim, *Corpus of Inscriptions*, 100–105.

Text:

L-1 قال اللّه تعالى وأقيموا الصّلوة طرف النهار وزلفا من الليل إن الحسنات يذهبن السيّات ذلك ذكرى للذاكرين واصبر إن اللّه لا يضيع أجر المحسنين

L-2 قال النّبي صلى اللّه عليه وسلم خير البقاع مساجدها وشرّ البقاع أسواقها وقال عم(عليه الصلاة و السلام) من أنفق درهما على طالب العلم فكأنما أنفق جبلا من [ال]ذهب الأحمر في سبيل الله تعالى

L-3 بني هذا المسجد وتم في زمان أمير جلال الدنيا والدين أبو <أبي> المظفر محمد شاه سلطان خلد ملكه والباني لهذه الخيرة ملك صدر الملة والدين سلطاني أمير دهئه سوتية خاص طال عمره وابتدأ بها في يوم الأحد الخامس من جمادى الاولى سنة خمس وثلاثين وثمانماية

Translation:

L-1 Allah, the exalted, said: ‘And establish prayers at the both ends of the day and at the approaches of the night. Indeed those deeds that are good replace those that are bad. This is advice to those who are mindful. And be patient, for Allah will never let the good rewards of righteous people go to waste.’

L-2 The Prophet, the peace and blessings of Allah be upon him, said: ‘The best places [on the earth] are its mosques and the worst places are its market places.’ He *‘ayn-mīm* [an abbreviation for ‘alayhi al-salām meaning ‘Peace be on him’] also said, ‘Whoever spends a dirham on a student, it will be as if he spends a mountain of red [i.e. pure] gold in the path of Allah, the exalted.’

L-3 The mosque was built and completed in the time of the emir Jalāl al-Dunyā’ wa ’l-Dīn (the august of the world and the religion) Abū ’l-Muẓaffar Muḥammad Shāh Sulṭān; may Allah perpetuate his kingdom. And the builder of this beneficent work is Malik (Lord) Ṣadr al-Millat wa ’l-Dīn (heart of the nation and the religion), a royal servant and special emir of Daha-e-Sutiya (the town of Sutiya), may his life be long. He began it on Sunday, the fifth day of Jumād al-Awwal in the year eight hundred and thirty-five (12 January 1432).

Discussion:

The calligraphy in this inscription has been rendered in an elegant Bihārī style.

(32) Masjid inscription from Mandara dated 836 (1433)

ORIGINAL SITE: A no longer extant Sultanate mosque in the village of Mandara in the district of Dhaka, Bangladesh. **CURRENT LOCATION:** Bangladesh National Museum, Dhaka, inv. no. 143. **MATERIAL, SIZE:** Black basalt; 70 × 12 inches. **STYLE, NO. OF LINES:** Bihārī; four lines. **REIGN:**

Sulṭān Jalāl al-Dīn Muḥammad Shāh (818–835/1415–1431). **LANGUAGE:** Arabic. **TYPE:** Commemorative inscription recording construction of a mosque. **PUBLICATION:** Dani, *JASB*, XVIII(2) (1952): 165–166; S. Ahmad, *Inscriptions of Bengal*, 44–45; Dani, *Bibliography of Muslim Inscriptions*, 14; Enamul Hoque, *Islamic Art in Bangladesh: Catalogue of a Special Exhibition in Dacca Museum* (Dhaka: Dacca Museum, 1978): 24; A. Karim, *Corpus of Inscriptions*, 105–110.

Text:

L-1 قال الله تعالى وأن المساجد لله فلا تدعوا مع الله أحدا
L-2 حامدا وشاكرا لله ذي الحجّة الباهرة على نعمت<نعمة> العظام وكلفنا بالشرايع والأحكام مصلّيا ومسلّمالمحمد ذي
L-3 الشفاعة عليه السلام بنى المسجد باسم السلطان {ال} أعظم المعظمين خليفة الله على المكونين جلال
L-4 الدنيا والدين أبو المظفر محمد شاه السلطان خلد ملكه وسلطانه الغ خانمعظم دينارخان سلمه الله في الدارين شقدار معاملة نيك محمد. ونقل في عشر جمادى الأول من سنة ست وثلاثين وثمانماية

Translation:

L-1 Allah, the Exalted, has said, ‘And verily the mosques belong to God only; so do not call anyone with Allah’ [72:18].
L-2 Praises and thanks be to Allah, the One Who, with shining proof for his splendid gifts, has bestowed upon us the sharī‘a and the laws while blessing and wishing peace for Muḥammad,
L-3 the intercessor, peace be on him. The mosque was built in the name of the sulṭān, the greatest of all the greats, vicegerent of Allah over all created things, Jalāl
L-4 al-Dunyā wa ’l-Dīn Abū ’l-Muẓaffar Muḥammad Shāh al-Sulṭān; may Allah perpetuate his kingdom and sovereignty. [Built by] Ulugh Khān Mu‘aẓẓam Dīnār Khān; may Allah grant them peace in both worlds. Shiqdār of affairs Nayk Muḥammad and he copied [it] on 10 Jumād al-Awwal, eight hundred and thirty-six (3 January 1433).

Discussion:

This is the third inscription of Sulṭān Jalāl al-Dīn Muḥammad Shāh, who played a very important role in consolidating Islam in the early history of Muslim Bengal. The title *shiqdār* that we find in this inscription designates a land surveyor and is still used in the region.

(33) An unidentified Masjid inscription found at the Shrine of Ghazī Pīr in Shibganj dated 845 (1441)

ORIGINAL SITE: An unnamed masjid near the Shrine of Ghazī Pīr, Shibganj Police Station, Nawabganj district, Bangladesh. **CURRENT LOCATION:** Department of Archaeology, Dhaka, Bangladesh. **MATERIAL, SIZE:** Black basalt; not known. **STYLE, NO. OF LINES**: *thulth* in Bengali *ṭughrā'*; single line. **REIGN:** Shams al-Dunyā wa 'l-Dīn Aḥmad Shāh (834–845/1432–1441). **LANGUAGE:** Arabic. **TYPE:** Commemorative inscription of a mosque. **PUBLICATION:** M. Y. Siddiq, 'Inscriptions as an Important Means for Understanding History of the Muslims', *Journal of Islamic Studies*, 20(2) (May 2009): 231–232; Yaqub Ali, 'Two Epigraphs of Bengal Sultanate: A Study Historical and Aesthetic Aspects', *Journal of Bengal Art*, 11–12 (2006–2007): 49–55.

Figure 6.3 Commemorative inscription (the Shrine of Ghazī Pīr, Shibganj Police Station, Nawabganj district) (source: copyright by author).

Text:

قال الله تعالى إنما يعمر مساجد الله من آمن بالله واليوم الآخر وأقام الصلاة وآتى الزكاة ولم يخش إلا الله فعسى أولئك
أن يكونوا من المهتدين بنى هذا المسجد المظلل لله في عهد أبي المظفر السلطان الأعظم المعظم شمس الدنيا والدين أحمد شاه
خلّد اللّه ملكه وبناه خان معظم وخاقان المكرم ألغ خان في العشرين من شهر رجب سنة خمس وأربعين وثمانمأة

Translation:

Allah the Great, said, 'Mosques of Allah are inhabited only by those who believe in Allah and the last day; they establish prayer and practise regular charity, they fear none except Allah; it is they who are expected to be truly guided' [Qur'ān 9:18]. This shaded mosque was built for the sake of Allah during the reign of the great and honoured Sulṭān Abū 'l-Muẓaffar Shams al-Dunyā wa 'l-Dīn Aḥmad Shāh, may Allah perpetuate his kingdom. The great Khān and honoured Khāqān Ulugh Khān built it on twentieth of Rajab in the year eight hundred and forty-five.

Discussion:

This inscription was discovered in 2005 by Abdus Samad Mondal of the Varendra Research Museum in a private collection of one of the custodians of the Shrine of Ghāzī Pīr. The inscription is extremely interesting as it records Aḥmad

Shāh as the ruling sulṭān in the year AH 845/1441, previously thought to have ruled Bengal only until 840/1436.

(34) An undated commemorative inscription in Muazzampur

ORIGINAL SITE: Not known. **CURRENT LOCATION:** Affixed to a wall of a mosque at the dargah of Shāh Langar at Muazzampur village in Dhaka district. **MATERIAL, SIZE:** Not known. **STYLE, NO. OF LINES:** Not known. **REIGN:** Shams al-Dīn Aḥmad Shāh 835–840/1432–1436. **LANGUAGE:** Persian. **TYPE:** Foundation inscription. **PUBLICATION:** Dani, *JASB*, XV111 (1952): 162–167; Syed Aulad Hasan, *Notes on the Antiquities of Dacca* (Dhaka, 1904): 55; Dani, *Bibliography of Muslim Inscriptions*, 15; A. Karim, *Corpus of Inscriptions*, 110–111.

Text:

فيروزخان . . . . . كبير خلد اللّه ملكه إلي يوم الدين . . . . در وقت ايا لت مسند
شاهی أحمد شاه . . . على موسى سلطان راجى إلى . . . . . .

Translation:

Fīruz Khān … Kabīr, may Allah perpetuate his kingdom until the Day of Judgement … During the regency of the royal throne by Aḥmad Shāh … ‘Alī Musā Sulṭān who hopes to…

Discussion:

Very little is known about this inscription. When Aulad Hasan discovered it, it was already broken and damaged. The inscription records the name of Aḥmad Shāh who succeeded his father, Sulṭān Jalāl al-Dīn Muḥammad Shāh. The inscription records two more names, Fīruz Khān and ‘Alī Mūsā Sulṭān. Muazzampur, the place of provenance of this inscription, was a cultural centre in the area during this period. A number of other antiquities have been found here.

Inscriptions of the later Ilyās Shāhī rulers (the restored dynasty)

(35) Chilla Khāna inscription in Ḥaḍrat Pandua dated 847 (1443)

ORIGINAL SITE: A no longer extant Sultanate mosque in Ḥaḍrat Pandua, Malda. **CURRENT LOCATION:** Affixed to the lintel of the doorway on the right side of the eastern wall of Chilla Khāna of Nūr Quṭb al-‘Alam in Ḥaḍrat Pandua. **MATERIAL, SIZE:** Not Known. **STYLE, NO. OF LINES:** *ijāza* in Bengali *ṭughrā'*; two lines. **REIGN:** Sulṭān Maḥmūd Shāh (841–864/1437–1460). **LANGUAGE:** Arabic. **TYPE:** Commemorative inscription for a mosque.

PUBLICATION: Blochmann, *JASB*, XLII (1873): 288–289; Cunningham, *ASR*, 15: 83–84; Ravenshaw, *Gaur*, 76, pl. 49 (no. 8A); A. A. Khan, *Memoirs of Gaur*, 114; Dani, *Bibliography of Muslim Inscriptions*, 42; S. Ahmad, *Inscriptions of Bengal*, 141–142, pl. 33; Desai, *JASBD*, XXIII(1) (April 1979): 1–17; A. Karim, *JASP*, XIII(3) (December, 1968): 335–328; A. Karim, *Corpus of Inscriptions*, 113–116.

Text:

L-1 قال النبي صلى الله عليه وسلم من بنى مسجدا لله تعالى بنى الله له قصرا في الجنة في عهد سلطان الزمان بالعدل والإحسان غوث الإسلام والمسلمين ناصر الدنيا والدين أبو < أبي > المجاهد محمود شاه السلطان

L-2 خلد الله ملكه وسلطانه بنى مسجدا الخان الأعظم المعظم الغ مجلس خان. . أعلى الله تعالى بالخيرات وصانه عن الآفات والبليات في الثاني والعشرين من شهر ربيع الأول سنة سبع وأربعين وثمانماية

Translation:

L-1 The Prophet, peace and the blessing of Allah be on him, said, 'Whoever builds a mosque for the sake of Allah, the Exalted, Allah builds a palace for him in Paradise.' During the reign of Sulṭān al-Zamān bi 'l-'Adl wa 'l-Iḥsān (king of the age with the virtues of justice and beneficence) Ghawth al-Islām wa 'l-Muslimīn (succour of Islam and the Muslims) Nāṣir al-Dunyā wa 'l-Dīn (the helper of the world and the religion) Abū 'l-Mujāhīd Maḥmūd Shāh al-Sulṭān,

L-2 may Allah perpetuate his kingdom and his authority. The great and exalted khān Ulugh Majlis Khān built [this] mosque; may Allah make him exalted through [his] charitable activities and protect him from calamities and mishaps; on the twenty-second of the month of Rabī' al-Awwal in the year eight hundred and forty-seven [20 July 1443].

Discussion:

This inscription is currently fixed over the lintel of the doorway on the right side of the eastern wall of what is known as the Chilla Khāna of Nūr Quṭb al-'Ālam in Ḥaḍrat Pandua. While this may be the same structure which has been referred to in the inscription as a mosque, it is more likely that the inscription was brought from the ruins of the original mosque and affixed to the present building. The verticals of the upright letters of the text are arranged symmetrically in a typical Bengali *ṭughrā'* style; the other letters are given a somewhat round shape closely resembling *khaṭṭ al-ijāza*.

(36) Commemorative inscription of a religious edifice in Gaur from the reign of Sulṭān Maḥmūd Shāh, dated 847 (1443)

ORIGINAL SITE: An unidentified religious edifice near Gaur in Malda district, West Bengal. **CURRENT LOCATION:** Collected and preserved at Gaur Social Welfare Mission Museum (Registered with Department of Art and

Culture under Government Art and Antiquities Rule 10=973, Lalbazar, P.O.: Uttar Mahdipur, Registration no. S-85650) by its honorary curator Mr. Sadeq Shaykh. **MATERIAL, SIZE**: Black basalt; not known. **STYLE, NO. OF LINES:** *thulth*; single line. **REIGN:** Sulṭān Maḥmūd Shāh (841–64/1437–60). **LANGUAGE:** Arabic. **TYPE:** Commemorative inscription of a religious edifice. **PUBLICATION:** M. Y. Siddiq, 'Calligraphy and Islamic Culture' *Bulletin of the School of Oriental and African Studies* 68(1) (2005): 21–58; S. Pratip Kumar Mitra, 'Late Dr. Z. A. Desai and the Provisional Study of Some New Inscriptions of the Bengal Sultans', *Indo-Iranica, the Quarterly Organ of the Iran-Society* (Iran Society, Kolkata), 58(3 & 4) (September–December 2005): 26–29.

Figure 6.4 Commemorative inscription (Gaur in Malda district, West Bengal) (source: copyright by author).

Text:

ر . . [خلد الله] . . ملكه وأعلى أمره وشأ[نه] بني . . الله . . على يد شخص المخاطب بعالي الشان شرف
الزمان ابقاه [الله] وبني في التاريخ غرة شهر شعبان سنة سبع وأربعين ثمانماية

Translation:

...May Allah perpetuate his kingdom and elevate his affairs and position, it was built ... Allah ... at the hand of a person who is addressed as 'Ālī al-Shān (a person of high status) Sharf al-Zamān (honour of the age); May Allah protect him. It was built during the date, the first of the month of Sha'bān, in the year eight hundred and forty-seven.

Discussion:

This stone tablet is only a tiny fragment of what seems to be a fairly large stone inscription that once decorated an edifice (most likely a masjid) somewhere in Gaur. The edifice was erected under the patronage of a person who apparently enjoyed a respectable status in the area as indicated by his title, *'Ālī al-Shān Sharf al-Zamān*. Unfortunately, nothing more is known about this person. Calligraphically, the inscription represents a rather simple variety of *thulth* when compared with other monumental inscriptions of Gaur during this period.

(37) Masjid inscription in Baliaghata dated 847 (1443)

ORIGINAL SITE: A no longer extant Sultanate masjid, near Baliaghata village near Jangipur, district of Murshidabad, West Bengal, India. **CURRENT LOCATION:** Shrine of Shāh 'Uthmān in Sarkar Baliaghata village near Jangipur, Murshidabad district, West Bengal, India. **MATERIAL, SIZE:** Black basalt; 31 × 11 inches approximately. **STYLE, NO. OF LINES:** Bengali *ṭughrā'*; two lines. **REIGN:** Sulṭān Maḥmūd Shāh (841–864/1437–1460). **LANGUAGE:** Arabic. **TYPE:** Foundation inscription with the Throne verse in its first line. **PUBLICATION:** Babu Gurudas Sarkar, *JASB*, XIII (1917): 151, plates V and Vl; Abdul Wali, *JASB*, n.s. XX (1924): 502–503; S. Ahmad, *Inscriptions of Bengal*, 49–51; Dani, *Bibliography of Muslim Inscriptions*, 16; A. Karim, *Corpus of Inscriptions*, 116–119.

Text:

L-1 الله لا إله إلا هو الحي القيوم لا تأخذه سنة ولا نوم له ما في السموات و ما في الأرض من ذى <ذا> الذي يشفع عنده إلا بإذنه يعلم ما بين أيديهم وما خلفهم ولا يحيطون بشيء من علمه إلا بما شاء وسع كرسيه السموات والأرض ولا يؤوده حفظهما وهو العلي العظيم

L-2 باني هذا المسجد في {ال} عهد و {ال}زمان . . ناصر الدنيا والدين أبو<أبي> المظفر محمود شاه السلطان بانيه خانمعظم الغ سرافراز خان جامدار غير محلى في الثاني من شهر رمضان المبارك سنة سبع وأربعين وثمانماية

Translation:

L-1 Allah; there is no God but He, the Living, the Everlasting. No slumber can seize Him, nor sleep. To Him belongs all that is in the heavens and the earth. Who is there that shall intercede with Him without His permission? He knows what lies before them and what is after them, and they cannot comprehend anything of His knowledge except what He wishes. His throne extends over the heavens and the earth and He feels no fatigue in guarding them for He is the All-high and the All-glorious. (Throne verse [2:255].)

L-2 The builder of this mosque [happens to be] during the reign and time of… Nāṣir al-Dunyā wa 'l-Dīn Abū 'l-Muẓaffar Maḥmūd Shāh the Sulṭān. Its builder was Khān Mu'aẓẓam Ulugh Sarfrāz Khān Jāmdār Ghayr-Maḥallī, on the second of the blessed month of Ramaḍān [in] the year eight hundred and forty-seven [27 December 1443].

Discussion:

This inscription is almost identical to the next inscription (no. 38); both were found by Babu Gurudas Sarkar at the beginning of twentieth century at the Shrine of Shāh ‘Uthmān in Sarkar Baliaghata village near Jangipur. The only difference between the two is that the next inscription (no. 38) has the additional title, *wazīr dūn dar sharq* (a junior minister for eastern affairs?), for its builder. As Maulvi Abdul Wali suggested, the scribe may have forgotten to include this title in the first inscription. In order to correct such an error, it is possible that he had to produce a new inscription. Not much is known about the minister mentioned in the inscription. His title, jāmdār ghayr-Maḥallī, suggests that he was in charge of the royal robe outside of the palace (i.e. when the sulṭān travelled). His other title, wazīr dūn dar sharq, is rather confusing since the inscription was discovered in the southwest of the capital of Mahmūd Shāh, while the title suggests that Sarfrāz Khān was the deputy minister of the east, perhaps a reference to the then Bangalah itself, the easternmost part of Bengal Sultanate.

Stylistically, both this inscription as well as the next inscription are quite interesting. There is a rhythmic wave in the calligraphic flow in both of these inscriptions where one can easily imagine the symbolic representation of boat and oars in the overall layout of arrangement of their letters.

(38) Masjid inscription in Baliaghata dated 847 (1443)

ORIGINAL SITE: A no longer extant Sultanate masjid near Baliaghata village near Jangipur, district of Murshidabad, West Bengal, India. **CURRENT LOCATION:** Shrine of Shāh ‘Uthmān in Sarkar Baliaghata village near Jangipur, district of Murshidabad, West Bengal, India. **MATERIAL, SIZE:** Black basalt; 31 × 11 inches approximately. **STYLE, NO. OF LINES:** Bengali *ṭughrā’*; two lines. **REIGN:** Sulṭān Maḥmūd Shāh (841–864/1437–1460). **LANGUAGE:** Arabic. **TYPE:** Foundation inscription with the Throne verse in its first line. **PUBLICATION:** Babu Gurudas Sarkar, *JASB*, XIII (1917): 151, plates V and Vl; Abdul Wali, *JASB*, n.s. XX (1924): 502–503; S. Ahmad, *Inscriptions of Bengal*, 49–51; Dani, *Bibliography of Muslim Inscriptions*, 16; A. Karim, *Corpus of Inscriptions*, 116–119.

Text:

L-1 الله لا إله إلا هو الحي القيوم لا تأخذه سنة ولا نوم له ما في السموات و ما في الأرض من ذى <ذا> الذي يشفع عنده إلا بإذنه يعلم ما بين أيديهم وما خلفهم ولا يحيطون بشيء من علمه إلا بما شاء وسع كرسيه السموات والأرض ولا يؤوده حفظهما وهو العلي العظيم

L-2 بناء هذا المسجد في {ال}عهد و{ال}زمان ناصر الدنيا والدين أبو<أبي> المظفر محمود شاه السلطان بانيه خان أعظم وخاقان معظم الغ سرافراز خان جامدار غير محلى وزير دون در شرق في الثاني من شهر رمضان المبارك سنة سبعة وأربعين وثمانماية

Translation:

L-1 'Allah; there is no God but He – the Living, the Everlasting. No slumber can seize Him, nor sleep. To Him belongs all that is in the heavens and the earth. Who is there that shall intercede with Him without His permission? He knows what lies before them and what is after them, and they cannot comprehend anything of His knowledge except what He wishes. His throne extends over the heavens and the earth and He feels no fatigue in guarding them for He is the All-high and the All-glorious.'

L-2 The construction of this mosque [took place] in the reign and time of Nāṣir al-Dunyā wa 'l-Dīn Abū 'l-Muẓaffar Maḥmūd Shāh the sulṭān. Its builder was the great khān and sublime khāqān Ulugh Sarfrāz Khān Jāmdār Ghayr-Maḥalli, deputy minister (lit. a junior minister without portfolio) in the east, on the second of the blessed month of Ramaḍān [in] the year eight hundred and forty-seven [27 December 1443].

(39) Masjid inscription in Mandaroga dated 850 (1446)

ORIGINAL SITE: A no longer extant Sultanate masjid near Mahalla (the suburb of) Mandaroga in Bhagalpur City, Bihar. **CURRENT LOCATION:** Fixed to a tomb in a garden belonging to Rānī Bībī in Mahalla Mandaroga in Bhagalpur City, Bihar. **MATERIAL, SIZE:** Not known; 36 × 18 inches. **STYLE, NO. OF LINES:** *Jalī* (bold) Bihāri; single line. **REIGN:** Sulṭān Maḥmūd Shāh (841–864/1437–1460). **LANGUAGE:** Arabic with a few phrases in Persian. **TYPE:** Commemorative inscription of a mosque. **PUBLICATION:** Blochmann, *JASB*, XLI (1872): 106; P. Horn, *Epigraphia Indica*, II: 280, pl. 1; S. Ahmad, *Inscriptions of Bengal*, 51–52; Q. Ahmad, *Inscriptions of Bihar*, 93–96; A. Karim, *Corpus of Inscriptions*, 119–123.

Text:

قال النبي عليه السل[ا]م من بنى مسجدا فے الدنيا بنى الله له قصرا فے الجنة فے زمن [ال]ملك العادل محمود شاه السلطان بنا كرده اين مسجد خانمعظم خرشيد خان سر نوبت غير محليان فے العاشر من جماد الأول سنة خمسون <خمسين> وثمانماية

Translation:

The Prophet, peace be on him, said, 'Whoever builds a mosque in the world, Allah the Exalted, builds a palace for him in Paradise.' In the reign of the just king Maḥmūd Shāh al-Sulṭān, Khān Mu'aẓẓam Khurshīd Khān Sare-nawbat Ghayr-Maḥalliyān (head of the royal guards outside palace) built this mosque on the tenth of Jumād al-Awwal [in] the year eight hundred and fifty [3 August 1446].

Discussion:

This inscription is written in an elegant *Bihārī* style in bold characters. The verticals of the upright letters are elongated to the extreme at the top. As they move upward, they become bolder. They are arranged symmetrically to form a row. The Arabic preposition *fī* has been stylized to look like a pelican in three places. These pelican shaped *fī*s have been placed on the upper part of the symmetrically arranged verticals. There is a raised decorative borderline on all four sides of the inscription. As the text moves forward towards the end of the line, the letters are inscribed in a thickly crowded way to accommodate the rest of the text, a feature quite common in many inscriptions of Bengal. Khurshīd Khān, who is mentioned in this inscription, appears in a number of other inscriptions of this period.

(40) A bridge inscription in Kohin Kā Bāgh dated 854 (1450)

ORIGINAL SITE: An unnamed Sultanate bridge in Bhagalpur district in Bihar. **CURRENT LOCATION:** Affixed horizontally on two small brick pillars in the compound of T. N. B. College, Bhagalpur. **MATERIAL, SIZE:** Sandstone; 19 × 14 inches. **STYLE, NO. OF LINES:** Crude form of *naskh*; four lines. **REIGN:** Sulṭān Maḥmūd Shāh (841–864/1437–1460). **LANGUAGE:** Arabic. **TYPE:** Commemorative inscription of a bridge. **PUBLICATION:** Dani, *Bibliography of Muslim Inscriptions*, 135–36; S. Ahmad, *Inscriptions of Bengal*, 52–53; A. A. Qadiri, *EIAPS* (1961): 36–37, pl. XII (a); Q. Ahmad, *Inscriptions of Bihar*, 96–98; A. Karim, *Corpus of Inscriptions*, 123–124.

Text:

L-1 بنا[ء] هذا<هذه> القنطرة في زمن الملك العادل المؤيد
L-2 بتأييد الرحمن خليفة الله بالحجة والبرهان
L-3 ناصر الدنيا والدين أبو<أبي> المظفر محمود شاه السلطان
L-4 في الخامس من شهر {ال} صفر ختم الله بالخير والظفر
سنة أربع وخمسين وثمانماية

Translation:

L-1 The construction of this bridge [took place] during the reign of the just king, al-Mu'ayyad bi Ta'yīd al-Raḥmān (who was assisted
L-2 by the support of the all Merciful), Khalīfat-Allah bi 'l-Ḥujja wa 'l-Burhān
L-3 Nāṣir al-Dunyā wa 'l-Dīn Abū 'l-Muẓaffar Maḥmūd Shāh al-Sulṭān.
L-4 On the fifth of the month of Ṣafar, may Allah make it complete with grace and success; [in] the year eight hundred and fifty-four [1450].

Discussion:

This inscription was found in a place known as Kohin Kā Bāgh near the town of Bhagalpur in Bihar, India. It commemorates construction of a bridge. There are a number of inscriptions commemorating the construction of bridges in the riverine land of the Bengal Sultanate, including the first Islamic inscription of the region.That this inscription was found in Bhagalpur indicates that the eastern part of Bihar came under the sway of Sulṭān Maḥmūd Shāh. The calligraphy in this inscription is rather poor. The title of the sulṭān in this inscription, *khalīfat-Allah bi 'l-ḥujja wa 'l-burhān* (vicegerent of Allah with proof and evidence), which appears in the next two inscriptions as well, carries an important political message, as it implies the legitimacy of the rule of the sulṭān both dynastically and religiously.

(41) A Masjid inscription in Bara dated 854 (1450)

ORIGINAL SITE: An unnamed Sultanate mosque in Birbhum district. **CURRENT LOCATION:** Affixed to the wall of the mausoleum of Shāh Makhdūm Ḥusaynī at the village of Bara (Qasbah-i-Bara or Balnagar) near Lohapur railway station in the district of Birbhum, West Bengal. **MATERIAL, SIZE:** Basalt stone; not known. **STYLE, NO. OF LINES:** *naskh* with ornamental feature of Bengali *ṭughrā'*; two lines. **REIGN:** Sulṭān Maḥmūd Shāh (841–864/1437–1460). **LANGUAGE:** Arabic. **TYPE:** Commemorative inscription of a mosque. **PUBLICATION:** S. Ahmad, *Inscriptions of Bengal*, 53–54; *Birbhum Bibarani*, part II, series 2 (Birbhum Research Association: Birbhum): 63–67; Abdul Karim, *Corpus of Inscriptions*, 124–125.

Text:

L-1 فحوى كلام رباني من جاء بالحسنة فله عشر أمثالها وفي الخبر من بنى مسجدا في الدنيا بنى الله له سبعين قصرا في الجنة بنى هذا المسجد الجامع في عهد {الـ}زمان المؤيد بتأييد الديان المجاهد في سبيل الرحمن خليفة الله بالحجة والبرهان باسط العدل

L-2 والإحسان ضابط أطراف الأمم صاحب التاج والخاتم فخر سلاطين آدم الغازي في ظل الله المختص بعنايت الحنان المنان وارث ملك سليمان ناصر الدنيا والدين أبو < أبي > المظفر محمود شاه خلد الله ملكه وسلطانه بمنته وكرمه. . قالع الكفر وقامع الفجرة صفدر شهوار ميدان الغ أعظم أحمد خان سرور ووزير شهر سجلا . . العشرين من جمادى الآخر سنة أربع وخمسين وثمانماية

Translation:

L-1 The divine message thus contains: 'Whoever accomplishes a good thing, he will have ten times his reward.' According to the saying [of the Prophet], 'Whoever builds a mosque in the world, Allah builds for him seventy palaces in Paradise.' Destroyer of profanity and punisher of impudent, kingly brave commander in the [battle] field Ulugh A'ẓam Aḥmad Khān Sarwar, the vizier of the city of Sajla, built this congregational mosque in the reign of al-Mu'ayyad bi-Tā'yīd al-Dayyān (one who is assisted by the support of the ultimate judge), al-Mujāhid fī Sabīl al-Raḥmān (the fighter in the path of the most merciful), Khalīfat-Allah bi 'l-Ḥujja wa 'l-Burhān, Bāsiṭ al-'Adl

L-2 wa 'l-Iḥsān (administrator of justice and benevolence), Ḍābiṭ Aṭrāf al-Umam (administrator of the outermost points of nations), Ṣāḥib al-Tāj wa 'l-Khātim, Fakhr Salāṭīn Ādam (pride of the sulṭāns of mankind), al-Ghāzī fī Ẓill-Allah (the warrior in the divine shadow), al-Mukhtaṣṣ bi 'Inayat al-Ḥannān al-Mannān (the one singled out for the care of the Compassionate and the Benefactor), Wārith Mulk Sulaymān, Nāṣir al-Dunyā wa 'l-Dīn, Abū 'l-Muẓaffar Maḥmūd Shāh, may Allah perpetuate his kingdom and authority; on the twentieth of Jumād al-Ākhir [in] the year eight hundred and fifty-four [18 August 1450].

Discussion:

The district of Birbhum, where this inscription was found, was the western outpost of the Bengal Sultanate. Muslim settlements and the growth of Islamic cultural and spiritual institutions in this area (e.g. khānqāhs in places like Lakhnor) helped spread Islam.

Though the inscription belongs to a religious edifice, it records one of the longest titles ever used in any epigraphic text in Bengal, and surely the longest in all of the inscriptions of this sulṭān. The builder of the mosque, Aḥmad Sarwar, was a vizier and administrator of Shahr (originally a Persian word, literally meaning town or city) Sajla who played an important role in battles fought in the region, as implied by his titles. The pattern of writing in this inscription is quite intricate.

(42) Jāmi' Masjid inscription in Ghagra dated 856 (1452)

ORIGINAL SITE: A Sultanate jāmi' masjid in the village of Ghagra in Mymansingh district, Bangladesh. **CURRENT LOCATION:** In situ. **MATERIAL, SIZE:** Not known. **STYLE, NO. OF LINES:** Not known. **REIGN:** Sulṭān Maḥmūd Shāh (841–864/1437–1460). **LANGUAGE:** Arabic. **TYPE:** Commemorative inscription of a mosque. **PUBLICATION:** S. Ahmad, *Inscriptions of Bengal*, 54–55; Dani, *Bibliography of Muslim Inscriptions*, 136; A. Karim, *Corpus of Inscriptions*, 125–126.

Text:

قال الله تعالى وأن المساجد لله فلا تدعوا مع الله أحدا بنى هذا المسجد الجامع في عهد {الـ}سلطان العصر والزمان باسط الأمن
والأمان وارث ملك سليمان السلطان الأعظم المعظم – الأكرم والمكرم صاحب التاج والخاتم المؤ يد بتأييد الرحمن خليفة الله
بالحجة والبرهان ناصر أمير المؤمنين ناصر الدنيا والدين أبو <أبي> المظفر محمود شاه السلطان خلد الله ملكه وسلطانه وأعلى
أمره وشأنه {الـ}باني المسجد الجامع خان معظم الغ خان . . في التاريخ يوم الجمعة الثاني من شهر ذي القعدة سنة ست
وخمسين وثمانماية

Translation:

Allah, the Most High, said, 'And verily the mosques are for Allah, so do not invoke anyone with Allah' [Qur'ān 72:18]. This congregational mosque was built in the reign of the sulṭān of the age and period, Bāsiṭ al-'Amn wa 'l-'Amān,

Wārith Mulk Sulaymān, the great and exalted sulṭān, the generous and sublime, Ṣāḥib al-Tāj wa 'l-Khātim, al-Mu'ayyad bi Ta'yīd al-Raḥmān, Khalīfat Allah bi 'l-Ḥujja wa 'l-Burhān, Nāṣir Amīr al-Mu'minīn, Nāṣir al-Dunyā' wa 'l-Dīn abū 'l-Muẓaffar Maḥmūd Shāh al-Sulṭān, may Allah perpetuate his kingdom and authority and exalt his affairs and status. The builder of this congregational mosque is Khān Mu'aẓẓam Ulugh Khān…; on the date of Friday, the second of the month of Dhū 'l-Qa'da [in] the year eight hundred and fifty-six [19 November 1452].

Discussion:

Very little information is available about this inscription. The readings of Dani and Shamsuddin Ahmad of this epigraphic text vary, especially regarding the name of the sulṭān and his titles. Since a facsimile of this inscription could not be procured, the text could not be re-examined. Like the previous inscription, the lofty titles in this inscription translate the ambitions and aspirations of the sulṭān quite explicitly.

(43) A madrasa–masjid inscription in Navagram dated 858 (1454)

ORIGINAL SITE: A no longer extant Sultanate madrasa–masjid in the village of Navagram, Tarash police station in Pabna district, Bangladesh. **CURRENT LOCATION:** Varendra Research Museum, Rajshahi, inv. no. 3171. **MATERIAL, SIZE:** Black basalt; 37 × 9.7 inches. **STYLE, NO. OF LINES:** *naskh* with ornamental features of Bengali *ṭughrā'*; three lines. **REIGN:** Sulṭān Maḥmūd Shāh (841–864/1437–1460). **LANGUAGE:** Arabic. **TYPE:** Commemorative inscription of a madrasa–masjid. **PUBLICATION:** A. K. M. Yaqub Ali, 'Two Unpublished Arabic Inscriptions', *Journal of the Varendra Research Museum*, 6 (1980–1981): 101–108; A. K. M. Yaqub Ali, *Bangladesh Itihas Parisad Patrica*, 11(1) (Bayshakh-Ashar 1384 Bengali year): 39–46; A. K. M. Yaqub Ali, *Aspects of Society and Culture of the Barind, 1200–1576 A.D.*, PhD dissertation, Rajshahi University, 1981, 447–450, pl. VIII; A. Karim, *Corpus of Inscriptions*, 126–128.

Text:

L-1 أما بعد حمد الله على نعمائه والصلاة على النبي وأحبائه ولما أظهر شعائر الشرع و حرّكه وأمّنه سلطان العصر والزمان ناصر الدنيا والدين أبو المظفر محمود شاه خلد الله ملكه وسلطانه في خطة ريفية موسومة بسملا باد . . ولما اهتدى جناب الأعظم

L-2 صار أكرم العصر والإسلام الذي خوطب بخطاب مجلس منصور لا زال كاسمه منصورا ولما عزم الخير بنى مسجدا ليجعله ذخيرة في دار الجزاء إلى يوم الساعة جناب المعظم عضد الإسلام والمسلمين خان الأعظم وخاقان المعظم الغ رحيمخان يبقي الله ثراء ه وجعل الجنة مثواه ووفقه

L-3 الله قلع أعداء الله من الكفار والمشركين وأدار الإنعام على العلماء والمتعلمين مؤرخا في الثاني والعشرين من ذي القعدة في يوم الجمعة سنة ثمان وخمسين وثمانماية

Translation:

L-1 After that (thenceforth), praise be to Allah for His bounties and blessing be on the Prophet and his friends. When Sulṭān al-ʻAṣr wa ʼl-Zamān (lord of the time and age) Nāṣir al-Dunyā wa ʼl-Dīn Abū ʼl-Muẓaffar Maḥmūd Shāh the Sulṭān made the code of the sharīʻa known and activated it as well as made it secured in the rural region named as Simlabād.... And likewise when Junāb al-Aʻẓam (His excellency) was guided to the right path (i.e. was converted to Islam),

L-2 he became the most honoured one of the age and of Islam, the one who was addressed with the title Majlis Manṣūr (Council of the victorious); and he continues to be victorious as (reflected through) his name. And when he intended a good deed, he built this mosque so that he could make it a treasure [reward] for the abode of justice till the day of resurrection; Junāb al-Muʻaẓẓam (His honour), ʻAḍd al-Islām wa ʼl-Muslimīn (supporter of Islam and the Muslims), the great khān, the exalted khāqān, Ulugh Raḥīm Khān [carried it out]; may Allah preserve his fortune and make paradise his abode, and may Allah give him the opportunity

L-3 to uproot the enemies of Allah from among the unbelievers and polytheists and may he disseminate grants to scholars and learners; dated the twenty second of Dhū ʼl-Qaʻda, Friday in the year eight hundred fifty-eight [14 November 1454].

Discussion:

This inscription was found in the village of Navagram, Tarash police station in Pabna district, Bangladesh. The first two words, *amma baʻd* (thenceforth) indicate the possibility of some additional lines at the beginning which were lost at some point, though it may not affect much the meaning of the surviving text.

Like many other inscriptions of this sulṭān, this epigraphic text has a strong political message deeply imbued with a religious tone. According to most historians, Sulṭān Maḥmūd Shāh was a descendant of the Ilyās Shāhī dynasty that ruled Bengal until a local Bengali Hindu landlord, Raja Ganesh, rose to power. Ganesh's son Jadu (who took the name of Jalāl al-Dīn Muḥammad Shāh after his conversion to Islam) converted and became a devout Muslim after ascending the throne. His successor, Aḥmad Shāh, however, proved to be too weak a ruler to retain the throne. Subsequently, power was seized by Maḥmūd Shāh. The text of this inscription refers to the legitimacy of Maḥmūd Shāh's rule on the basis of his success in restoring the canons of the *sharīʻa.*

This is one of the rarest inscriptions that records conversion to Islam. The builder of the madrasa-cum-masjid, Ulugh Raḥīm Khān, was not only converted to Islam, but he became a great exponent of Islam. His titles suggest that he must have been a high-ranking officer who fought a number of wars successfully, especially against the non-Muslims in the area. He also seems to have been a patron of scholarship as he gave stipends to the scholars and students. The building to which this text refers served both as masjid and madrasa, a common feature during that period. Another important aspect of this inscription is that it refers to the consolidation of Islam in the rural areas of Bengal.

Inscribed by a local artisan in a place far from the capital, the calligraphy of this inscription is not of the highest standard.

(44) Masjid inscription in Mughaltoli dated 859 (1455)

ORIGINAL SITE: An unidentified Sultanate mosque in the district of Malda in West Bengal. **CURRENT LOCATION:** Affixed to the shrine of Shāh Gudā, over the gate of the enclosure at Mughaltoli, between the Katra and the Jami‘ Masjid in old Malda town in West Bengal. **MATERIAL, SIZE:** Not known. **STYLE, NO. OF LINES:** Not known. **REIGN:** Sulṭān Maḥmūd Shāh (841–864/1437–1460). **LANGUAGE:** Arabic. **TYPE:** Commemorative inscription of a mosque. **PUBLICATION:** Cunningham, *ASR*, XV: 77; Blochmann, *JASB* (1874): 294–295; Ravenshaw, *Gaur*, 72, pl. 46 (no. 3); A. A. Khān, *Memoirs of Gaur*, 149–150; S. Ahmad, *Inscriptions of Bengal*, 55–56; Dani, *Bibliography of Muslim Inscriptions*, 16; A. Karim, *Corpus of Inscriptions*, 128–129.

Text:

L-1 قال عليه السلام من بنى مسجدا بنى الله [له] قصرا في الجنة في {ال} عهد السلطان الأعظم المعظم ناصر الدنيا والدين أبو<أبي>

L-2 المظفر محمود شاه السلطان بنى هذا المسجد بنده درگاه هلال تحريرا في التاسع عشر من ماه شعبان عمت ميامنه سنة تسع وخمسين وثمانماية

Translation:

L-1 The Prophet, peace be upon him, said, ‘Whoever builds a mosque, Allah builds a palace in paradise.’ The servant of the shrine of Hilāl built this mosque in the reign of the great and exalted Sulṭān Nāṣir al-Dunyā wa ’l Dīn Abū ’l-

L-2 Muẓaffar Maḥmūd Shāh the Sulṭān; written on nineteen of the month of Sha‘bān, may the blessings of this [month] be all-embracing, [in] the year eight hundred and fifty-nine [4 August 1455].

Discussion:

This inscription, which originally belonged to a mosque, was discovered at the shrine of Shāh Gudā, over the gate of the enclosure at Mughaltoli, between the Katra and the Jami‘ Masjid in old Malda town in West Bengal.

(45) Masjid inscription in Tribeni dated 860 (1455)

ORIGINAL SITE: A Sultanate mosque at Tribeni (near Satgaon) in the district of Hoogly, West Bengal. **CURRENT LOCATION:** Lying loose near the grave of Ẓafar Khān near the compound of the mosque. **MATERIAL, SIZE:** Probably grey basalt; 26 × 18 inches. **STYLE, NO. OF LINES:** A local variety of Bengali *Ijāzah*; four lines. **REIGN:** Sulṭān Bārbak Shāh (864–878/1460–1474). **LANGUAGE:** Arabic. **TYPE:** Foundation inscription of a mosque. **PUBLICATION:** S. Ahmad, *Inscriptions of Bengal*, 68–70; Dani, *Bibliography of Muslim Inscriptions*, 21; Y. K. Bukhari, 'Four Unpublished Arabic Inscriptions of Sulṭān Barbak Shāh of Bengal', *EIAPS* (1953–1954): 20–21; R. D. Banerji, *Sahitya Parishad Patrica*, vol. X, 27; Blochmann, *JASB*, XXXIX (1870): 290; (1873): 273; A. Karim, *Corpus of Inscriptions*, 146–148.

Text:

L-1 قال الله تعالى [و] أن المساجد لله فلا تدعوا مع الله أحدا بني المسجد خاناالأعظم
L-2 و خاقاناالمعظم ألغ اجملخان سلمه الله تعالى في الدارين سرخيل خانمعظم اقرار خان جامدار غير محلي
L-3 و سر لشكر و وزير عرصئه ساجلا منكهباد شهر لابلا دامت معاليه في {ال}عهد الملك العادل الباذل
L-4 الفاضل الكامل باربك شاه بن محمود شاه السلطان في الحادى من المحرم [سنة] ستين و ثمانماية

Translation:

L-1 Allah the Most High said, 'Verily the mosques are for Allah, so do not invoke anyone with Allah' [Qur'ān 72:18]. The exalted khān and

L-2 the great khāqān Ulugh Ajmal Khān, may Allah, the Most High, protect him in both the worlds, built this mosque. [It was supervised by] the commander of the cavalry, the great khān Iqrār Khān Jāmdār Ghayr-Maḥallī (the guard of the royal robe outside the palace)

L-3 and commander of the army and vizier of the *'arṣa* [an administrative division] of Sajla Mankhabad and the city of Labela, may his greatness perpetuate. [It was] during the reign of the just, benevolent,

L-4 learned and perfect malik (lord) Bārbak Shāh ibn Maḥmūd Shāh the sulṭān on the date of the first of Muḥarram, [in the year] eight hundred and sixty [11 December 1455].

Discussion:

Like many other inscriptions, the last part of this inscription, the part containing the date, is not very clear as the text is abraded. As a result, it has led historians to some confusion since the conjectural reading of the epigraph suggests that the crown prince Bārbak Shāh bore the title *malik* as early as 860/1455 when his father Maḥmūd Shāh was still ruling. While the possibility of attributing this inscription to a later date always exists because of the hypothetical reading of the date, the relatively humble titles of Bārbak Shāh in this inscription may be taken as an indication that he was using the title *malik* to mean crown prince or lord, not in the proper sense of sulṭān. *Malik* was also a title of a high-ranking officer in the Sultanate army in Bengal, in charge of ten amirs. A third possibility is, that Bārbak Shāh was a military commander and governor in southwestern Bengal where the inscription was found.

(46) Masjid inscription in Satgaon dated 861 (1456)

ORIGINAL SITE: An unnamed Sultanate mosque at Satgaon in Hoogly district, West Bengal, India. **CURRENT LOCATION:** Tomb of Jamāl al-Dīn at Trishbigha in Hoogly district. **MATERIAL, SIZE:** Not known. **STYLE, NO. OF LINES:** Not known. **REIGN:** Sulṭān Maḥmūd Shāh (841–864/1437–1460). **LANGUAGE:** Arabic. **TYPE:** Commemorative inscription of a mosque. **PUBLICATION:** Blochmann, *JASB*, XXXIX, pt. 1 (1870): 290–293; *JASB*, XLII, pt. 1 (1873): 270–273; R. D. Banerjee, *Sahitya Parishad Patrica*, XV, 26–27; Dani, *Bibliography of Muslim Inscriptions*, 16–17; S. Ahmad, *Inscriptions of Bengal*, 56–57; Abdul Karim, *Corpus of Inscriptions*, 129–130.

Text:

قال الله تعالى إنما يعمر مساجد الله من آمن بالله واليوم الآخر وأقام الصلاة وآتى الزكاة ولم يخش إلا الله فعسى أولئك أن يكونوا من المهتدين وقال عز من قائل جل جلاله وعم نواله وأن المساجد لله فلا تدعوا مع الله أحدا وقال النبي صلى الله عليه وسلم وعلى آله وأصحابه من بنى مسجدا لله بنى الله له بيتا في الجنة . . المؤيد بتأييد [الرحمن] . [خليفة الله] بالحجة والبرهان غوث الإسلام والمسلمين ناصر الدنيا والدين أبو المظفر [محمو]د شاه السلطان خلد ملكه وسلطانه وأعلي أمره وشأنه بناه الخان الأعظم المعظم المكرم المخاطب بخطاب تربيت خان سلمه الله عن آفات الزمان بمنه وكمال كرمه في سنة الحادي <إحدى> وستين وثمانماية

Translation:

Allah the Great said, ‘The mosques of Allah are inhabited by those only who believe in Allah and the last day and establish prayer and offer prescribed charity and fear none but Allah; it is they who are expected to be truly guided’ [Qur’ān 9:18]. And the One Whose glory shines forth and Whose bounties prevail so commonly, and how Glorious a Sayer He is, said, ‘And verily the mosques are for Allah, so do not invoke anyone with Allah’ [72:18]. The Prophet, peace and the blessings of Allah be on him and on his family and his companions, said, ‘Whoever builds a mosque for Allah, Allah builds for him a house in Paradise.’ … al-Mu’ayyad bi-Tā’yīd al-Raḥmān (one who is assisted by the support of the most Merciful), Khalīfat-Allah bi ’l-Ḥujja wa ’l-Burhān, Gawth al-Islām wa ’l-Muslimīn (the succour of Islam and the Muslims), Nāṣir al-Dunyā wa ’l-Dīn, Abū ’l-Muẓaffar Maḥmūd Shāh the Sulṭān, may Allah perpetuate his kingdom and authority and may his affairs and status be exalted. The great exalted and sublime Khān, [who is] styled with the title Tarbiyyat Khān, built it, may Allah save him from the calamities of the ages by His grace and perfection of His mercy; in the year eight hundred and sixty-one.

Discussion:

This inscription was found in Satgaon[2] (Saptagrāma in Sanskrit), a famous medieval port city and administrative centre in southwestern Bengal at the juncture of the rivers Bhagirathi and Saraswati and adjacent to both Triveni, a holy place to the Hindus, and Chhota Pandua.[3] The city existed long before its conquest by the Muslim army commander Ẓafar Khān Ghāzī (see ins. no. 12, dated 698/1298) during the reign of Sulṭān Kaykā'us Shāh (*ca.* 1290–1301). It thrived during the Sultanate period both commercially and as a cultural and educational centre, with a large number of mosques and madrasas (such as Madrasa Dār al-Khayrāt recorded in ins. no. 16, dated 713/1313). Epigraphic sources provide us with a few names of its celebrated governors, such as Tarbiyat Khān (recorded in the present inscription), Malik Bārbak Shāh (later Sulṭān Bārbak Shāh) and Iqrār Khān in the previous inscription dated 860/1455.

Among its architectural remains is a mosque from the reign of Sulṭān Nuṣrat Shāh which has two inscriptions, both dated 936/1529 built by the sufi saint Sayyid Jamāl al-Dīn Ḥusayn ibn Sayyid Fakhr al-Dīn, an immigrant from the Caspian town of Amul. Satgaon had an important mint beginning in the fourteenth century; the earliest coin minted there during the Islamic period discovered so far is dated 729/1328; the most recent is 957/1550.[4]

(47) Masjid inscription in Narayandia dated 861(1457)

ORIGINAL SITE: Affixed above the door of an old mosque at Narayandia (Narinda), a northeastern suburb of Dhaka town. **CURRENT LOCATION:** Probably in situ. **MATERIALS, SIZE:** Not known; 15 × 8.25 inches. **STYLE, NO. OF LINES:** Crude form of *nasta'līq*; five lines. **REIGN:** Sulṭān Maḥmūd Shāh (841–864/1437–1460). **LANGUAGE:** First two lines in Arabic, the rest in Persian. **TYPE:** Foundation inscription of a mosque. **PUBLICATION:** Aulad Hosain, *Antiquities of Dacca*, 28; Stapleton, *JASB*, n.s., VI (1910): 144–145; S. Ahmad, *Inscriptions of Bengal*, 57–58; *Bibliography of Muslim Inscriptions*, 17; A. Karim, *JASP*, XII (August 1967): 289–292; A. Karim, *Corpus of Inscriptions*, 130–133.

Text:

L-1 بسم الله الرحمن الرحيم
L-2 لا إله إلا الله محمد رسول الله
L-3 شد مزين ببانگ وحي [علي الـ] فلاح
L-4 مسجد اين غريب ليل و صباح
L-5 مسماة بخت بينت دختر مرحمت
ستة ٨٦١

Translation:

L-1 In the name of Allah, the most kind, the most merciful.
L-2 There is no God but Allah, Muḥammad is His messenger.
L-3 Adorned by the call of *ḥayya 'ala al-falāḥ* [come towards salvation]
L-4 At night and morning in this mosque of a [humble] passer-by
L-5 [It was built by] Musammat Bakht Bīnat, the daughter of Marḥamat. Right margin: [in the] year 861.

Discussion:

Far from the capital under local patronage, this inscription records its date in Arabic numerals, which is rare for this period. Inscriptions under royal patronage were written in Arabic; this one is written in Persian in a very ordinary style. The use of Persian for the inscription suggests that Muslim immigrants commonly used Persian in daily life. The crude form of the text is devoid of any calligraphic ornamentation. It is also possible that the date was wrongly inscribed, since *nasta'līq* style, in which the text is inscribed, was introduced to Bengal much later, during the Mughal period. But if the date is correct, then this would be the earliest mosque inscription in Dhaka district. The inscription records that the patron of the mosque was a lady. Thus, it indicates that Muslim women also participated in social and religious activities at various levels.

(48) Bridge inscription near Kotwali Gate, Gaur dated 862 (1457)

ORIGINAL SITE: A bridge located between the Lattan mosque and the Kotwali mosque, not far from the Kotwali Gate, in Gaur. **CURRENT LOCATION:** In situ (Alexander Cunningham also found it at the same location in the 1870s). **MATERIAL, SIZE:** Sandstone; 18 × 13 inches. **STYLE, NO. OF LINES:** *thulth*; four lines. **REIGN:** Sulṭān Maḥmūd Shāh (841–864/1437–1460). **LANGUAGE:** Arabic. **TYPE:** Commemorative inscription of a bridge. **PUBLICATION:** Blochmann, *JASB*, XLIV (1875): 289; Dani, *Bibliography of Muslim Inscriptions*, 17; S. Ahmad, *Inscriptions of Bengal*, 59–60; A. Karim, *Corpus of Inscriptions*, 133–134.

Text:

L-1 بناء هذه القنطرة في زمن [ال] سلطان العادل
L-2 ناصر الدنيا والدين أبو<أبي> المظفر
L-3 محمود شاه السلطان في الخامس من {ال}صفر
L-4 ختمه الله بالخير والظفر سنة اثني <اثنتي > وستين وثمانماية

Translation:

This bridge was constructed in the time of the just king Nāṣir al-Dunyā wa 'l-Dīn Abū 'l-Muẓaffar Maḥmūd Shāh the sulṭān on the fifth of Ṣafar [23 December], may Allah complete it with blessing and success, [in] the year eight hundred and sixty-two [1457].

Discussion:

Like the Kohin Kā Bāgh inscription (dated 854/1450), this inscription also records the construction of a bridge during the reign of Sulṭān Maḥmūd Shāh. Though these inscriptions were executed in places distant from each other, they are dated the same day (i.e. fifth of Ṣafar) and have exactly the same religious invocation ختمه الله بالخير والظفر (may Allah complete it with blessing and success).

(49) Jāmi' Masjid Gate inscription in Naswa Gali dated 863(1459)

ORIGINAL SITE: A Sultanate mosque on the street known as 'Naswa Gali' in the Girdi-Qila quarter of old Dhaka. **CURRENT LOCATION:** Bangladesh National Museum, inventory no. 141. **MATERIAL, SIZE:** Black basalt stone; 54 × 11 inches. **STYLE, NO. OF LINES:** Bihārī rendered in the decorative feature of Bengali *ṭughrā'*; two lines. **REIGN:** Sulṭān Maḥmūd Shāh (841–864/1437–1460). **LANGUAGE:** Arabic. **TYPE:** Commemoration of renovation of a mosque entrance. **PUBLICATION:** Blochmann, *JASB*, XLI (1872): 107–108; Raḥmān 'Alī Taish, *Tawārikh-i-Dhaka* (Arrah, 1910): 259; Stapleton, *JASB*, n.s. VI (1910): 145–148; Aulad Hosain, *Antiquities of Dacca*, 34; Dani, *Bibliography of Muslim Inscriptions*, 18–19; S. Ahmad, *Inscriptions of Bengal*, 62–64; A. Karim, *JASP*, XII(11) (1967): 292–296; A. Karim, *Corpus of Islamic Inscriptions*, 134–137.

Text:

L-1 قال الله تعالى وأن المساجد لله فلا تدعوا مع الله أحدا استحكم هذا الباب
و بني [في] أيام خلافة الخليفة المستعان ناصر الدنيا والدين أبو<أبي>المظفر محمود شاه السلطان
L-2 خلد ملكه السبحان المخاطب بخطاب خواجه جهان صانه عن الآفات الرحمن
في الإقليم حد مباركاباد عصمها الله إلى يوم التناد
و ذالك <ذلك> كان في العشرين من شعبان سنة ثلاث وستين وثمانماية من سنن هجرة صلى الله عليه وآله أجمعين

Translation:

L-1 Allah the Most High said, 'And verily the mosques are for Allah, so do not invoke anyone with Allah' [Qur'ān 72:18]. This door was consolidated and built during the days of the caliphate of the caliph al-Musta'ān (lit. who is sought for help) Nāṣir al-Dunyā wa 'l-Dīn Abū 'l-Muẓaffar Maḥmūd Shāh al-Sulṭān;

L-2 may the ever Glorious perpetuate his kingdom; [it was done under the patronage of] the one styled by the title Khwāja Jahān, may the most Merciful protect him from calamities; within the territory of the district of Mubārakabād, may Allah save it to the last day. And this took place on the twentieth of Sha'bān, [in] the year eight hundred and sixty-three from the years of the hijra [13 June 1459] may the blessings and peace of Allah be on him [the Prophet] and on his entire family.

Discussion:

According to Khan Bahadur Aulad Husain, this inscription originally belonged to a dilapidated Sultanate mosque located on the street known as Naswa Gali in the Girdi-Qila quarter of Dhaka city. The mosque disappeared at the beginning of the twentieth century after it was damaged by an earthquake in 1897 and struck by lightning in 1902. The inscription was then removed to the record room of Dhaka District Collectorate from where it found its way to the Bangladesh National Museum, Dhaka. The text suggests that during the reign of Sulṭān Maḥmūd Shāh, Kwāja Jahān ordered the reinforcement of a gate of a mosque that already existed on the site.

(50) Khān Jahān Mausoleum complex inscriptions at Khalifatabad (present Bagerhat) dated 863 (1459)

ORIGINAL SITE: Mausoleum complex of Khān Jahān near Shāit-Gumbuj Masjid in Bagerhat, Bangladesh. **CURRENT LOCATION:** In situ. **MATERIAL, SIZE:** Not known. **STYLE, NO. OF LINES:** Varieties of calligraphic styles, namely Bihārī (e.g. inscriptions), *ijāzah*, *naskh* (e.g. *al-asmā' al-ḥusnā* on the top of the tomb of Khān Jahān in bold *naskh*), *Rayḥānī* (e.g. the Qur'ānic verses and *surā*s) and *thulth*; not known. **REIGN:** Sulṭān Maḥmūd Shāh (841–864/1437–1460). **LANGUAGE:** Arabic and Persian. **TYPE:** Tomb inscriptions. **PUBLICATION:** Babu Gaurdas Bysack, *JASB*, XXXVI, pt 1 (1867): 126–135; S. Ahmad, *Inscriptions of Bengal*, 64–67; Dani, *Bibliography of Muslim Inscriptions*, 19–20; A. F. M. Abdul Jalil, *Khān Jahān 'Alī* (Khulna, 1966): 91–99; idem, *Sundarbaner Itihas* (Dhaka: Ahmad Publication House, 1986); Enamul Haque, *Islamic Art Heritage of Bangladesh* (Dhaka: Bangladesh National Museum, 1983); *Islāmī Bishwakosh*, 9 (Dhaka: Islamic Foundation, 1990) s.v. 'Khān Jahān' by A. K. M. Ayub Ali, 503–506; A. Karim, *Corpus of Inscriptions*, 137–141.

Text of ins. 50.A:

انتقل العبد الضعيف
المحتاج إلى رحمة رب العالمين المحب لأولاد
سيد المرسلين المخلص للعلماء الراشدين
المبغض للكفار والمشركين والمعين للإسلام والمسلمين
الغ خان جهان عليه الرحمة والغفران من دار الدنيا
إلي دار البقاء ليلة الأربعاء في ستة وعشرين من ذي الحجة
ودفن يوم الخميس سبع وعشرين منه
سنة ثلاث وستين وثمانماية

Translation:

The feeble slave, who is in need of the mercy of the Lord of the universe, the lover of the offspring of the leader of the prophets, the sincere one for the righteous '*ulamā*', an opponent (lit. hater) of infidels and polytheists and the helper of Islam and the Muslims Ulugh Khān Jahān, mercy and forgiveness be upon him, passed away from the abode of this world to the abode of eternity on the night of Wednesday, twenty-six of Dhū ’l-Ḥijja [29 October] and was buried on Thursday, twenty-seventh of the same [30 October], [in the] year eight hundred and sixty-three [1459].

Text of ins. 50.B:

هذه
روضة مباركة
من رياض الجنة لخان الأعظم
خان جهان عليه الرحمة والرضوان تحريرا
في ست وعشرين من ذي الحجة سنة ثلاث وستين وثمانماية

Translation (ins. 50.B):

This is a blessed garden among the gardens of Paradise for the noble Khān Khān Jahān, the mercy and favour (of Allah) be on him; written on the twenty-sixth of Dhū ’l-Ḥijja, [in the] year eight hundred and sixty-three.

Text of ins. 50.C:

Panel containing supplication:

L-1 يا برهان يا بديع السموات
L-2 والأرض خَلّصْنا من النار

Translation:

O (Divine) Proof, O the Creator of Heavens and earth, save us from hell-fire.

Panel containing spiritual message:

L-1 الدنيا أوّلها بكاءٌ
L-2 وأوسطها عناءٌ
L-3 آخرها فناءٌ

Translation:

‘The worldly life starts with crying, its middle part is suffering, and the last part of it ends with obliteration of the self (in the mystical sense).’

Panel on the left containing Qur’ānic Verse (109:3–4):

L-1 [و] لا أنتم عابدون ما أعبد لكم
L-2 دينكم ولي دين

Translation:

[Verse 5] Nor will you worship that which I worship.
[Verse 6] To you be your Way, and to me, mine.

Several other prayers and supplications that start with the Arabic word يا (*yā* literally meaning: O), appear in Arabic on the southern side of the above mentioned inscriptions.

Discussion:

In addition to *Sūra* al-Kāfirūn, there are several other Qur'ānic verses and complete *sūra*s or chapters (particularly shorter ones from the end of Qur'ān), including the *Sūra* al-Takāthur, *Sūrā* al-Ikhlās, *Sūra* al-Falaq and *Sūra* al-Nās. We also find *al-ta'awwudh, al-basmalah, al-tahlīl, al-tashahhud* (the formula of faith) inscribed on different locations on the second level of raised platforms on the four sides of the grave, in addition to a number of other supplications and invocations in Arabic on all over the grave. These inscriptions also include a *ḥadīth* whose text runs as follows: من مات غريبا، فقد مات شهيدا 'Whoever dies as a stranger, dies as a martyr'. The names of the first four rightly guided caliphs are also inscribed, preceded by an epithet, إلهي بحرمت (My Lord, in the honour of), and after each name, there is a supplication, رضي الله عنه (May Allah be pleased with him).

Inscriptions on top of the grave consist of *al-asmā' al-ḥusnā* (ninety-nine beautiful Divine names), each written in a separate square panel that decorates almost the entire surface on the top of the sarcophagus. In addition, there are two lines of Qur'ānic inscriptions running parallel on the each end of the sarcophagus.

The two lines on the north side of the grave record the following two verses:

نصر من الله وفتح قريب وبشّر المؤمنين
هو الله الذي لا إله إلا هو عالم القدوّس المهيمن

The two lines on the south side of the grave record the following two verses:

وهو السميع العليم اللهم اغفر وارحم
السيد الصادق المصدق

The horizontal band of writing at the base of the sarcophagus records Chapter 102 (*Sūra* al-Takāthur) from the Qur'ān. Further below, there is another horizontal line that records Chapter 81 (*Sūra* al-Takwīr).

All of these inscriptions, which are, in essence, religious supplications and invocations reflecting deep love and attachment for the Prophet, start with the Arabic phrase اللهم صلّ على محمد سيّد (*Translation:* O Allah, bless Muḥammad, the leader of…) and end with different adjectives such as المحسنين (al-Muḥsinīn, meaning the gracious and benevolent). The text is rendered more or less in *ijāza* style. Overall, the inscriptions form a rectangular calligraphic band on the edge of the floor on all four sides of the second level of raised platforms.

These religious formulas are inscribed on all four sides of the second level of raised platforms and consist mainly of Qur'ānic verses, deeply imbued with spiritual supplications and other forms of invocations.

There are quite a few Persian mystical verses inscribed on the walls of the four sides of the first level of raised platforms. Some of them are the following:

Text of Persian ins. 50.D:

ياد اوريد أي دوستان الموت حق الموت حق
خارست اندر بوستان الموت حق الموت حق
مرگست خصمی محکمی پی جمله جانان ذو يقين
نئي همچو ديگر دشمنان الموت حق الموت حق

Translation:

Remember O friends, death is certain, death is (indeed) certain. There is a thorn in the garden; death is certain, death is certain. Death is a firm adversary for all souls, for sure. Not like other enemies, death is certain, indeed, death is certain.

Discussion:

These are mainly Persian mystical verses inscribed on the walls of the four sides of the first level of raised platforms.

Text:

هذه
روضة مباركة من
رياض الجنة روضة مجلس معظّم
مجلس طاهر . . . .

Translation:

This is a blessed garden among the gardens of Paradise and the resting place of the pure associate, Majlis Ṭāhir…

Text of ins. 50.E:

This is the second oval-shaped Arabic funerary inscription at the other side of the longitudinal end of the tomb of Muḥammad Ṭāhir.

هذه روضة مباركة من رياض الجنة وهذه صقبة لحبيبه إسمه محمد طاهر سنة ثلاث وستين وثمانماية

Translation:

This is a blessed garden among the gardens of Paradise and the adjacent is for his friend whose name is Muḥammad Tāhir, [in the] year eight hundred and sixty-three.

Discussion:

The architectural legacy and monuments of Khān Jahān in Bagerhat are perhaps the most important archaeological remains in southern Bangladesh. Named as Khalifatabad (meaning inhabited by the caliph or viceroy of the then sulṭān, namely Khān Jahān), the place started evolving as a significant administrative and religious centre of Muslim rule around the middle of the fifteenth century. Khalifatabad also prospered as an important mint-town alongside Muhammadabad, indicating the urbanization process of the region by Muslims during this period. In general, the whole area was named by Muslims as Fatehabad. Todar Mall's rent-rolls for Khalifatabad record that it was one of the nineteen sarkars (administrative divisions) of Bengal. The famous forest of Sundarban once extended deep into this region.

The most important historical personality associated with Khalifatabad during this period is Khān Jahān. In the folk traditions of southern Bengal, he is popularly known as Pīr Khanjālī. According to some legends, Khān Jahān immigrated with his parents from Delhi to Gaur when he was young and became a disciple of Nūr Quṭb al-'Alam. His most famous disciple was Pīr 'Alī Muḥammad Ṭāhir, an upper-caste Hindu (Brahmin) who became a Muslim. In all probability, Khān Jahān was entrusted by the then sulṭān of Bengal with the administration of southern Bengal adjoining the forest of Sundarban. He settled in the *qasba* (town) of Haveli (presently Bagerhat City).[5] His most impressive architectural work is Shāit-Gumbuj Masjid in Bagerhat, presently listed in the world heritage sites by UNESCO. It is one of the largest mosques in South Asia, possibly one of the largest in the fifteenth century Islamic world.[6] The pediment above its main entrance gate leading to the interior of the mosque is unique in the Islamic architecture of the region.

A charismatic saintly figure and a great commander, Khān Jahān consolidated Islam in southern Bengal mainly through massive public welfare works such as roads, ponds, wells, inns, etc. Islam spread rapidly during this period as people started clearing forest and settling in the region (as reflected in the names of the villages and towns with suffix *kātī* and *'ābād* meaning 'clearing' and 'inhabiting').[7] Islamic inscriptions in and around the tombs of Khān Jahān and his aid Pīr 'Alī Muḥammad Ṭāhir provide a number of clues to the historical development of consolidation of Islam during that period in the region. It seems that a group of 'ulamā', portrayed in one of the inscription as *al-'ulamā' al-rāshidūn* or the rightly guided religious scholars, actively participated in Khān Jahān's campaign of Islamization of the region. On the other hand, the proponents of syncretistic tradition (known as *sābiqī* or traditionalists) opposed him. Confrontation with non-Muslims in the region is expressed in his title *al-mubghiḍ li 'l-kuffār wa 'l-mushrikīn* (an opponent [lit. hater] of the infidels and polytheists).

The mausoleum complex is situated about three miles southwest of the Shāit-Gumbuj Masjid. There are two tombs at the site. The first and the more prominent one is the tomb of Khān Jahān, which is located inside an impressive mausoleum complex at the north of Khanjali pond covering an area of approximately 68×63 metres. The compound is surrounded by thick but low walls on four sides with several monumental entrances. Inside the funerary chamber, there are four tiers of raised stone platforms gradually leading towards the main sarcophagus of the tomb, which is richly decorated with varieties of inscriptions on all sides. The part of the structure with the richly inscribed sarcophagus is, however, an outer display of the tomb for general view, as the original grave, where the actual body of Khān Jahān is buried, is located in an underground chamber just beneath the tomb structure on the ground floor. Though somewhat rare, this architectural tradition can be found in a number of mausoleums in the Islamic world, such as the famous Tajmahal in Agra. Now completely closed, the original grave in the underground chamber also had a number of inscriptions on it which used to be accessible (until 1963) through a staircase.

The second tomb is located at the west of the funerary chamber of Khān Jahān. On both sides of the longitudinal ends of the sarcophagus one can see oval-shaped Arabic funerary inscriptions recording the name of Muḥammad Ṭāhir, the closest aid and the most renowned disciple of Khān Jahān. Like the tomb of Khān Jahān, the original grave where the body of Muḥammad Ṭāhir is buried, is also located in an underground chamber exactly below the external tomb structure at the ground floor. Though inaccessible now, this underground chamber used to contain a number of inscriptions. Written in Arabic and Persian, Islamic inscriptions in this mausoleum complex are extremely interesting in their content, decorative styles and calligraphic execution. Nevertheless, their discussion here cannot be considered complete or exhaustive, as a number of the inscriptions could not be deciphered satisfactorily.

(51) A funerary inscription at the Mausoleum of Nūr Quṭb al-'Ālam at Pandua dated 863 (1459)

ORIGINAL SITE: One of the tombs at the Mausoleum of the famous sufi saint Nūr Quṭb al-'Ālam in Ḥaḍrat Pandua. **CURRENT LOCATION:** Affixed to a passage in the kitchen at the mausoleum of Nūr Quṭb al-'Ālam at Ḥaḍrat Pandua in West Bengal. **MATERIAL, SIZE:** Black basalt; not known. **STYLE, NO. OF LINES:** Bihārī in Bengali, *ṭughrā'* style; three lines. **REIGN:** Sulṭān Abū 'l-Muẓaffar Maḥmūd Shāh (846–864/1442–1459). **LANGUAGE:** Arabic. **TYPE:** Funerary inscription. **PUBLICATION:** Blochmann, *JASB*, XLII (1873): 271–172 pl. V, no. 4; Cunningham, *ASR*, 15: 83–84; Ravenshaw, *Gaur*, 52, pl. 46; A. A. Khan, *Memoirs of Gaur*, 115–116, pl. 16 no. 2; Dani, *Bibliography of Muslim Inscriptions*, 17–18; S. Ahmad, *Inscriptions of Bengal*, 60–62; A. Karim, *Corpus of Inscriptions*, 141–145; Nūr Quṭb-i-'Ālam, *Maktūbāt-i-Shaykh Nūr Quṭb-i-'Ālam* (Persian MS in Aligarh Muslim University, Aligarh, Maulana Azad Library, Subḥān Allah no. 297671/18; Copy in the Indian National Archives, New Delhi, Or. MS no. 332); Nūr Quṭb-i-'Ālam, *Mu'nis al-Fuqarā'* (Persian MS no. 466, Asiatic Society of Bengal, Calcutta). Figure and text, translation of the inscription: For a detailed view of the inscription, its complete text and translation, please see the beginning of Chapter 3: *Nature, aesthetic perception and mysticism* (p. 58).

Discussion:

This funerary inscription originally belonged to one of the tombs at the mausoleum of Nūr Quṭb al-'Alam, one of the great sufi shaykhs of Bengal from the family of 'Alā' al-Ḥaqq. The name of the deceased person, however, is not mentioned in the text out of respect, as was customary in Bengal. H. E. Stapleton conjectured that it referred to Shaykh Zāhid, one of the sons of Nūr Quṭb al-'Ālam (a nephew of the Shaykh according to some other sources). Cunningham, however, thought that it referred to Nūr Quṭb al-'Ālam. Stapleton's hypothesis seems to be more likely if we take into consideration the date of the death of Shaykh 'Alā' al-Ḥaqq, the father of Nūr Quṭb al-'Ālam, which is 786/1384 (see also ins. no. 19 dated 743/1342). The impact of this saintly family on the religious and cultural life of Muslim Bengal deserves a detailed discussion.

Shaykh Nūr Quṭb al-'Ālam, ibn Shaykh 'Alā' al-Ḥaqq, ibn 'Umar ibn Asad Khālidī was born around 752/1350 in Pandua. Both of Nūr Quṭb al-'Ālam's sons, Shaykh Afqah al-Dīn (Shaykh Barkat al-Dīn, Rafqat al-Dīn, Rafīq al-Dīn or Rif'at al-Dīn according to different other sources) and Shaykh Anwar al-Ḥaq, were also spiritual mentors of the Chistiyyah Tarīqah.[8]

Nūr Quṭb al-'Ālam received *khilāfa* (spiritual succession) from his father, 'Alā' al-Ḥaqq, and in fact received most of his education from him. He carried on his father's educational and preaching activities with the support of Sulṭān Ghiyāth al-Dīn A'ẓam Shāh, a personal friend, as they had studied together under al-Shaykh al-Qāḍī Ḥamīd al-Dīn Nagori Kunjshikan.[9] From time to time, the sulṭān sent Nūr Quṭb al-'Ālam gifts. It was a tradition in the Islamic world at that time to send princes to a madrasa or to different famous 'ulamā' for their formal education.

One of the most renowned sufīs of the Chistiyya order with great political influence in Bengal, Nūr Quṭb al-'Ālam soon faced opposition from Raja Kans (Ganesh), an influential Bengali *zamindar* (feudal landlord) of Bhaturia, who gradually took over power from the Muslim rulers. His harsh policy towards Muslims in general provoked great discontent. Raja Kans even killed some great saints, including Pīr Badr al-Islam and his son Shaykh Mu'īn al-Dīn Fayḍ al-Islām and once commanded a riverboat loaded with 'ulamā' to be sunk.

Alarmed by Raja Kans's anti-Muslim policies, Nūr Quṭb al-'Ālam appealed to Ibrahīm Sharqī, the sulṭān of Jaunpur in Bihar, to come and rescue the Muslims in Bengal. In one of his letters to the sulṭān, Nūr Quṭb al-'Ālam expressed concern about Raja Kans' rise to power and about his hostile policy towards Muslims. Sulṭān Ibrahīm Sharqī subsequently sought advice from Ahshraf Jahāngīr Simnānī, another great sufi saint of the time, with whom Nūr Quṭb al-'Ālam maintained close ties and exchanged letters. In his reply to the sulṭān, Simnānī urged him to march on the capital of Bengal to dislodge Raja Kans from power and the sulṭān acted accordingly. The matter was finally settled through an agreement, according to which Raja's son had to convert to Islam. The sulṭān was annoyed by this settlement prompted by the shaykh and returned to Jaunpur. Subsequently, Raja broke the agreement and exiled the shaykh's son Shaykh Anwar and nephew Shaykh Zāhid to Sonargā'on.[10]

Nūr Quṭb al-ʻĀlam was a great Islamic scholar and writer. One of his works was a commentary and translation of a collection of *ḥadīth* entitled *Anīs al-Ghurabāʼ*. Ten of his letters to various people have been brought to light and copied by ʻAlīm al-Dīn (known as Nūr Pandawī) in 1241/1826. They seem to have been written to his son Shaykh Anwar, although the name is never mentioned.[11] Among the students of Nūr Quṭb al-ʻĀlam were Shaykh Kāku who lived in Lahore (d. 1416), Shams al-Dīn of Ajmer (d. 1476) and Shaykh Ḥusām al-Dīn of Manikpur (d. 1477).

Nūr Quṭb al-ʻĀlam established in Pandua a charity hospital and a free kitchen for the poor and destitute.[12] His fame as a great spiritual mentor spread beyond Bengal. In central India, his name is still invoked in a special Urdu prayer for healing of stomach ache, the text of which is:

بایاں ہاتھ بجر ہاتھ بھسم کردی پیت کا بھات
بھائی صاحب نور قطب عالم پندوی کی دھائی ھی

Translation:

Through the intercession of the sufi brother Nūr Quṭb al-ʻĀlam, it is prayed that may the massage by the left hand help the digestion of rice in the stomach and heal the ache.

Sources disagree about the year that Nūr Quṭb al-ʻAlam died. According to *Mir'at al-Asrār*, the shaykh died on the ninth of Dhū 'l-Qaʻda 818/1415, according to Blochmann 851 (1447), according to Abū 'l-Faḍl 808/1405, according to Abd al-Ḥaq Dehlavī 813/1410, according to the *Khazinat al-Aṣfiyya* 851/1447 and according to the khādim's (attendants) of the dargāh 818/1415, though none of these dates matches the date recorded in the present inscription. The shaykh was buried at Chhotī Dargāh (also known as Shayt Hazari Dargāh) in Pandua. Among other points of interest at the dargāh are the *chilla khānah* of Nūr Quṭb al-ʻĀlam, the public kitchen, *sijdahgāh* (praying station), the Qāḍī Nūr Masjid, the Mitha Tālāb (sweet-water tank), Bihisht ka Darwāza (door to Paradise), Kālā Paththar (black stone), the tombs of Sher Khān, Shaykh Afqah, Shaykh Anwar and Shaykh Zāhid, the Bībī Mahal and Musāfir Khāna, in addition to a stone capital of an unidentified pillar and a few copper drums still lying in the complex.

(52) Masjid inscription of Sulṭān Maḥmūd Shāh in Gaur dated 863 (1458–1459)

ORIGINAL SITE: An unidentified Masjid somewhere in Gaur. **CURRENT LOCATION:** Mahdipur High School Museum, inventory no. 16, Post Office: Mahdipur, Police Station: English Bazar, District: Malda, West Bengal. **MATERIAL, SIZE:** Black basalt; 12 × 17.5 inches. **STYLE, NO. OF LINES:** A local variety of Bihārī in mirror reverse style; three lines. **REIGN:** Sulṭān Maḥmūd Shāh (841–864/1437–1460). **LANGUAGE:** Arabic. **TYPE:** Foundation inscription of a masjid. **PUBLICATION:** Pratip Kumar Mitra, 'Three Unnoticed Inscriptions of the Sultans of Bengal', *Journal of Bengal Art*, 3

(1998): 173–177; idem, 'Late Dr. Z. A. Desai and the Provisional Study of Some New Inscriptions of the Bengal Sultans', *Indo-Iranica, the Quarterly Organ of the Iran Society* (Iran Society, Kolkata), 58(3 & 4) (September–December 2005): 26–29.

Text:

L-1 بسم الله الرحمن الرحيم نصر من الله وفتح قريب
L-2 الله اعلى وأحمده تعالى
L-3 [بني هذا] المسجد في {ال} عهد ناصر الدنيا والدين أبو المظفر محمود شاه السلطان خلّد الله ملكه بنا كرده في التاريخ ثلث وستين وثمانماية

Translation:

L-1 In the name of Allah, the Merciful and Compassionate. Help from Allah and the victory is nearing.
L-2 Allah is the Most Exalted, and I praise Him, the Most High.
L-3 This masjid was built during the reign of Nāṣir al-Dunyā wa 'l-Dīn Abū 'l-Muẓaffar Maḥmūd Shāh, the sulṭān, may Allah perpetuate his kingdom. It was constructed during eight hundred and sixty-three.

Discussion:

This inscription was found by Nimai Goswami in a place known as Qadamtala near Beki village in the suburb of Gaur, and was donated to school museum of Mahdipur village. In this inscription, we find that the textual contents of the first half of the inscription on the right side in the first two lines have been repeated again in a reverse order on the left side to produce a mirror image effect. The Qur'ānic word *qarīb* in the middle of the first line has been repeated several times for further calligraphic stylizing. This is perhaps the first inscription so far discovered in Bengal where the artist has attempted mirror reverse calligraphic style; this style is not common in the calligraphic tradition of Islamic architecture. While the inscription records the construction of a masjid during the reign of Maḥmūd Shāh, it does not record any other name.

(53) An undated bridge inscription of Sulṭān Maḥmūd Shāh in Gaur

ORIGINAL SITE: An unidentified bridge in Gaur. **CURRENT LOCATION:** Mahdipur High School Museum, inventory no. 26, Mahdipur Post Office, English Bazar Police Station, Malda district, West Bengal. **MATERIAL, SIZE:** Black basalt; 11 × 19 inches. **STYLE, NO. OF LINES:** Monumental *thulth* in Bengali *ṭughrā'*; one line. **REIGN:** Sulṭān Maḥmūd Shāh (841–864/1437–1460). **LANGUAGE:** Arabic and Persian. **TYPE:** Bridge inscription. **PUBLICATION:** Pratip Kumar Mitra, 'Three Unnoticed Inscriptions of the Sultans of Bengal', *Journal of Bengal Art*, 3 (1998): 173–177; idem, 'Late Dr. Z. A. Desai and the Provisional Study of Some New Inscriptions of the Bengal Sultans', *Indo-Iranica, the Quarterly Organ of the Iran-Society* (Iran Society, Kolkata), 58(3 & 4) (September-December 2005): 26–29.

Figure 6.5 Bridge inscription (Mahdipur High School Museum, inventory no. 26, Mahdipur Post Office, English Bazar Police Station, Malda District, West Bengal) (source: copyright by author).

Text:

[في] زمن السلطان العادل ناصر الدنيا والدين أبو المظفر محمود شاه السلطان اين پل بنا كرده خان أعظم وخاقان معظم

Translation:

During the reign of the just Sulṭān Nāṣir al-Dunyā wa 'l-Dīn Abū 'l-Muẓaffar Sulṭān Maḥmūd Shāh, the sulṭān, Khān al-A'ẓam Khaqān Mu'aẓẓam had this bridge constructed.

Discussion:

This fragmentary inscription was unearthed by Shri Lakshmi Kanta Sarkar during the cultivation of his land near Mahdipur village in the suburb of Gaur, and was donated subsequently by him to the village school museum. The elegant calligraphy of this inscription suggests that the elite class in Gaur patronized calligraphers and calligraphic activities during this period, in addition to be funding benevolent works. This is the third inscription during the reign of Maḥmūd Shāh that records construction of a bridge. Like his predecessors, it seems that this benevolent sulṭān was also engaged in carrying out numerous public works during his reign which, in way, helped the dissemination of Islam in the region.

(54) Masjid inscription in Bara dated 864 (1460)

ORIGINAL SITE: An unnamed Sultanate mosque in the village of Balanagar, popularly known as Qasba-e-Bara in Birbhum district, West Bengal. **CURRENT LOCATION:** Affixed to the wall of the mausoleum of a saint at the village of Balanagar. **MATERIAL, SIZE:** Black basalt; 42 × 11 inches. **STYLE, NO. OF LINES:** *Naskh* of a local variety; four lines. **REIGN:** Sulṭān Bārbak Shāh (864–878/1460–1474). **LANGUAGE:** Arabic. **TYPE:** Foundation inscription of a congregational mosque. **PUBLICATION:** S. Ahmad, *Inscriptions of Bengal*, 70–71; Dani, *Bibliography of Muslim Inscriptions*, 22; Y. K. Bukhari, 'Four Unpublished Arabic Inscriptions of Sulṭān Barbak Shāh of Bengal' *EIAPS* (1953–54): 21–22, pl. VIII (a); A. Karim, *Corpus of Inscriptions*, 150–152.

Text:

L-1 قال النبي صلى الله عليه وسلم من بنى مسجدا في الدنيا بنى الله تعالى [له] في الجنة قصرا بكل ذراع من المسجد بني في عهد [ال]سلطان العادل ركن الدنيا والدين أبو<أبي> المظفر باربكشاه ابن محمود شاه السلطان

L-2 باني هذا المسجد خانأعظم وخاقان معظم الغ اجلكا خان ابن تربت خان سرگماشته قصبه دهاخا خاص لإمام مولانا المشهور بقاضي ابن قاضي أحمد ابن شيخ علاول في التاريخ الحادي من شهر جمادى الأول سنة أربع وستين وثمانماية

Translation:

L-1 The Prophet, peace and blessings of Allah be on him, said, 'Whoever builds a mosque in the world, Allah the Most High builds for him in Paradise a palace for every cubit of the mosque.' It was built during the reign of the just Sulṭān Rukn al-Dunyā wa 'l-Dīn Abū 'l-Muẓaffar Bārbak Shāh ibn Maḥmūd Shāh al-Sulṭān.

L-2 The builder of this mosque is Khān A'ẓam wa Khāqān Mu'aẓẓam Ulugh Ajalka Khān ibn Turbat Khān, Sar-e-Gumāshta of the Qaṣba of Dhakha. [This mosque is] especially [dedicated] to Imām Mawlānā, known as Qāḍī ibn Qāḍī Aḥmad ibn Shaykh 'Alāwal on the date, the first of the month of Jumād al-Awwal, the year eight hundred and sixty-four [23 February 1460].

Discussion:

The text of the *ḥadīth* quoted in the inscription differs slightly from the usual wording in the other inscriptions of Bengal as it contains the additional phrase, the reward of a palace in Paradise for each cubit of a mosque built. The builder of the mosque is Ulugh Ajalka Khān, the chief tax collector in the Qaṣba (township) of Dhakha. The name Dhakha may refer to an administrative unit in the northwest part of Bengal where the present inscription was discovered. The other possible explanation is that Ulugh Ajalka Khān once served as a tax collector in Dhakha itself (i.e. the present capital of Bangladesh), in which case, this is the first inscription to record the name of Dhakha. The *qāḍī* for whom this mosque was built was also an *imām* and *mawlāna* attached to this mosque. His grandfather, Shaykh ‘Alāwal, was probably the sufi saint who is mentioned in the Bania Pukur inscription dated 743/1342, and who was the father of Nūr Quṭb al-‘Ālam (see also ins. dated 863/1459).

(55) Masjid inscription in Mahi Santosh dated 865 (1460)

ORIGINAL SITE: An unnamed Sultanate mosque in the present district of Nawgaon in North Bengal. **CURRENT LOCATION:** Affixed to the shrine of Mahi Santosh on the eastern bank of the river Atrai at Mahiganj village in the present police station of Patnitola, Nawgaon district, Bangladesh. **MATERIAL, SIZE:** Black basalt; 36 × 11 inches. **STYLE, NO. OF LINES:** Not known; two lines. **REIGN:** Sulṭān Bārbak Shāh (864–878/1460–1474). **LANGUAGE:** Arabic. **TYPE:** Foundation inscription of a mosque. **PUBLICATION:** Blochmann, *JASB* (1873): 272–273; *JASB* (1875): 290–292; Buchanan, *Eastern India*, 667; *List of Ancient Monuments in Rajshahi Division* (Calcutta: Government of Bengal Public Works Department, 1896), 14, no. 13; S. Ahmad, *Inscriptions of Bengal*, 73–75; Dani, *Bibliography of Muslim Inscriptions*, 23–24, no. 32; A. Karim, *Corpus of Inscriptions*, 154–156.

Text:

قال النبي صلى الله عليه وسلم من بنى {الـ}مسجد[ا] في الدنيا بنى الله [له] سبعين قصرا في الجنة بنى المسجد في زمن الملك
العادل السلطان ابن السلطان ركن الدنيا والدين أبو<أبي> المجاهد باربكشاه السلطان ابن محمود شاه السلطان الباني خان
المعظم الغ اقرار خان بواسطة خان معظم اشرفخان خمس وستين وثمانماية

Translation:

The Prophet, peace and the blessings of Allah be on him, said, ‘Whoever builds a mosque in the world, Allah builds seventy palaces for him in Paradise.’ The mosque was built during the time of the just Sulṭān Rukn al-Dunyā wa ’l-Dīn Abū ’l-Mujāhid Bārbak Shāh ibn Maḥmūd Shāh al-Sulṭān. The builder is Khān al-Mu‘aẓẓam ’Ulugh Iqrār Khān through [the good office] of Khān Mu‘aẓẓam Ashraf Khān, [in the year] eight hundred and sixty-five.

Discussion:

Mahi Santosh is a place of great antiquity where many Islamic and pre-Islamic relics can still be found. According to a local tradition, it was ruled by a Hindu chief during the Muslim conquest of Bengal who defeated the Muslim commander Muḥammad Shīrān Khaljī and killed him in a battle. One tomb in this shrine complex is identified as the grave of Shīrān Khaljī.

(56) Masjid inscription in Gaur from the reign of Barbak Shāh dated 865 (1460)

ORIGINAL SITE: An unnamed Sultanate mosque in Gaur. **CURRENT LOCATION:** Indian Museum, Calcutta, inv. no. 11. **MATERIAL, SIZE:** Black basalt; 45 × 14 inches. **STYLE, NO. OF LINES:** Bihārī in Bengali *ṭughrā'* decorative style; one line. **REIGN:** Sulṭān Bārbak Shāh (864–878/1460–1474). **LANGUAGE:** Arabic. **TYPE:** Commemorative inscription of a mosque. **PUBLICATION:** Blochmann, *JASB*, XLIII (1874): 282–295, pl. 1; S. Ahmad, *Inscriptions of Bengal*, 75–76; Dani, *Bibliography of Muslim Inscriptions*, 22; Desai, *EIAPS* (1955–56): 13–14; C. Dutt, *Inscriptions in the Indian Museum*, 14; A. Karim, *Corpus of Inscriptions*, 156–157.

Text:

قال النبي عليه السلام من بنى مسجدا في الدنيا بنى الله تعالى له قصرا في الجنة بني المسجد في زمن الملك العادل الأكرم وهو
السلطان بن السلطان ركن الدنيا والدين أبو المجاهد باربكشاه السلطان بن محمود شاه السلطان وبانيه خان معظم خرشيد خان
سرنوبت غير محليان في العاشر من جمادى الأول سنة خمس وستين وثمانماية

Translation:

The Prophet, peace be upon him, said, 'Whoever builds a mosque in the world, Allah the Exalted builds a palace for him in Paradise.' The mosque was built during the time of the just, sublime king who is al-Sulṭān ibn al-Sulṭān Rukn al-Dunyā wa 'l-Dīn Abū 'l-Mujāhid Bārbak Shāh ibn Maḥmūd Shāh the sulṭān; and the builder is Khān Mu'aẓẓam Khūrshīd Khān Sar-i-Nawbat-i-Ghayr-i-Maḥalliyān (Commander of the Royal Guard outside of the palace), on the tenth of Jumād al-Awwal, [in the] year eight hundred and sixty-five.

(57) Chehil Ghāzī Masjid inscription in Dinajpur dated 865 (1460)

ORIGINAL SITE: A ruined Sultanate mosque near the shrine of Chehil Ghāzī, four miles north of Dinajpur town in Bangladesh. **CURRENT LOCATION:** Dinajpur Museum in the Dinajpur town in Bangladesh. **MATERIAL, SIZE:** Black basalt; 22 × 10 inches. **STYLE, NO. OF LINES:** Not known. **REIGN:** Sulṭān Bārbak Shāh (864–878/1460–1474). **LANGUAGE:** Arabic. **TYPE:** Commemoration of the construction of a mosque and renovation of a shrine adjacent to it. **PUBLICATION:** Blochmann, *JASB*, XLII (1873): 272–274; *List of Ancient Monuments in Rajshahi Division* (Calcutta: Government of Bengal Public Works Department, 1896): 16; S. Ahmad, *Inscriptions of Bengal*, 71–73; Dani, *Bibliography of Muslim Inscriptions*, 23, no. 33; *Islāmī Bishwakosh*, 11 (Dhaka: Islamic Foundation, 1992), s.v. 'Chehil Ghāzī' by A. K. M. Ayub Ali, 33–35; A. Karim, *Corpus of Inscriptions*, 152–154.

Text:

بسم الله الرحمن الرحيم نصر من الله وفتح قريب وبشر المؤمنين فالله خير حافظا وهو ارحم الراحمين بناء المسجد في {ال}عهد
السلطان ابن [ال]سلطان ركن الدنيا والدين أبو<أبي> المجاهد باربكشاه سلطان خلد الله ملكه وسلطانه بحكم إشارة خان أعظم
وخاقان معظم پهلوي العصر والزمان الغ إقرار خان سر لشكر ووزيرباني خير مسجد مذكور ومرمت كردهُ روضة خان أعظم
وخاقان معظم الغ نصرت خان جنگدار وشقدار معاملات جورو برور ومحلهاء ديگر
في التاريخ السادس وعشرمن {ال}شهر {ال}صفر ختمه الله بالخير والظفر
شهور سنة خمس وستين وثمانماية

Translation:

In the name of Allah, the most kind and merciful. 'Help from Allah and nearing victory; so convey to the believers the happy news' [Qur'ān 61:13]. 'Allah is the best to take care of and He is the most kind among all the mercifuls' [Qur'ān 12:64]. The construction of the mosque [took place] during the time of al-Sulṭān ibn al-Sulṭān Rukn al-Dunyā wa 'l-Dīn abū 'l-Mujāhid Bārbak Shāh Sulṭān, may Allah perpetuate his authority, at the direction of the great khān and exalted *khāqān*, Pahlawī al-'Aṣr wa 'l-Zamān (i.e. the Persian monarch-like-king of the age and time) Ulugh Iqrār Khān, chief of the army and vizier. The builder of this benevolent work, the said mosque, and the one who repaired [the] shrine is the great khān and sublime *khāqān* Ulugh Nuṣrat Khān jangdār (warrior) and *shiqdār* (lit. land measurer) of the affairs of Jor and Baror and several other areas, on the date of the sixteenth of the month of Ṣafar, may Allah complete it with grace and success, [in] the months of [the] year eight hundred and sixty-five [1 December 1560].

Discussion:

Another inscription in the same mosque, as described by Westmacott, reads as follows:

اين نقشئه مهر نبوت كه درميان دوشانه مبارك محمد مصطفى صلي الله عليه وسلم بود

(This is a facsimile of the Prophetic seal which was between the two shoulders of Muḥammad, the chosen one, may Allah bless him.)The title Pahlawī al-'Aṣr wa 'l-Zamān appears in several inscriptions of Bengal. Pahlawī was the name of one of the most renowned imperial dynasties of ancient Persia. The word is thus used in constructing the title Pahlawī al-'Aṣr wa 'l-Zamān as an epic simile for a valorous and glorious personality.

Shiqdār was (and continues to be to the present day) the official title for those responsible for land measurements and allotments. Shiq (from *shaq* meaning land) seems to be originally derived from a Turkic dialect. Turkic elements from Central Asia were quite dominant in the early part of Muslim rule in Bengal. Many Turkish names and titles, such as *ulugh* (great), *ṭughril* (hawk), *tughān* (falcon) can often be found in Muslim inscriptions of Bengal in that period. The word *shaq* can also be found in Arabic, meaning fraction or broken part (of land).

This mosque is one of the oldest architectural remains in the area. It is popularly known as Chehil Ghāzī Masjid or mosque of forty martyrs who died in a war with a local Hindu ruler while carrying out their mission of preaching Islam. There is a small graveyard adjacent to the mosque.

(58) An unidentified Masjid inscription found in Mahisantosh dated 867 (1463)

ORIGINAL SITE: An unnamed masjid that once stood on the site of a newly built masjid at the archaeological site in Mahisantosh, Naogaon district, Bangladesh. **CURRENT LOCATION**: Paharpur Museum, Naogaon district, Bangladesh. **MATERIAL, SIZE**: Black basalt; 44 × 17 inches. **STYLE, NO. OF LINES**: *thulth* in Bengali *ṭughrā'*; two lines. **REIGN:** Rukn al-Dunyā wa 'l-Dīn Bārbak Shāh (864–878/1460–1474). **LANGUAGE**: Arabic. **TYPE:** Commemorative inscription of a mosque. **PUBLICATION**: Sulṭān Ahmed, 'A New Light on the Jami' Masjid of Mahisantosh', *Journal of the Pakistan Historical Society*, vol XLVI(2) (1998): 63.

Text:

L-1 لا اله الله محمد الرسول الله قال النبي عليه السلام من بنى مسجدا في الدنيا بنى الله سبعين قصرا له في الجنة بنى هذا المسجد الملك العادل

L-2 السلطان بن السلطان ركن الدنيا والدين ابو المظفر باربكشاه السلطان ابن محمود شاه السلطان *وبانيه* خان الأعظم خاقان المعظم ألغ حسن خان سنة سبع وستين وثمانماية

Translation:

L-1 There is no God but Allah, (and) Muḥammad is his messenger. The Prophet, peace be upon him, said, 'whoever builds a masjid in the world, Allah builds for him seventy palaces in Paradise'. The just king,

L-2 the sulṭān, son of the sulṭān, Rukn al-Dunyā wa 'l-Dīn, Abū 'l-Muẓaffar Bārbak Shāh al-Sulṭān, son of Maḥmūd Shāh al-Sulṭān build this masjid. Its constructor was the great khān and honoured *khāqān* 'Ulugh Ḥasan in the year eight hundred and sixty-seven.

Discussion:

This inscription was originally found in 1994 in the debris of a ruined Sultanate masjid on which a temporary thatched roof village mosque had been raised before a few years. The upper portion of the left corner is slightly broken evenly.

(59) Masjid inscriptions in Hatkhola, Sylhet dated 868 (1463)

ORIGINAL SITE: An unnamed Sultanate mosque near Anair Haor in the Bhanga subdivision of Sylhet district. **CURRENT LOCATION:** Fixed on a mosque wall at Hatkhola in Sylhet district eighteen miles from Karimganj railway. **MATERIAL, SIZE:** Not known; 27 × 12 inches. **STYLE, NO. OF LINES:** *ijāza* in Bengali *ṭughrā'* decorative style; one line. **REIGN:** Sulṭān Bārbak Shāh (864–878/1460–1474). **LANGUAGE:** Arabic. **TYPE:** Commemorative inscription. **PUBLICATION:** S. Ahmad, *EIM* (1935–36): 57–58, pl. XXXVIII (a); S. Ahmad, *Inscriptions of Bengal*, 76–77, pl. 23; Dani, *Bibliography of Muslim Inscriptions*, 24, no. 34; Sayyid Murtaḍā 'Alī, *Ḥaḍrat Shāh Djalāl O Sileter Itihās* (Dhaka, 1988); A. Karim, *Corpus of Inscriptions*, 157–158, pl. 18 (c).

Text:

قال النبي عليه السلام من بنى مسجدا بنى الله تعالى [له] قصرا في الجنة في زمن الملك العادل باربكشاه سلطان بن محمود شاه
سلطان بناه خان معظم خرشيد خان نوبت عالي محليان في الخامس من شهر صفر سنة ثمان وستين وثمانماية

Translation:

The Prophet, peace be upon him, said, 'Whoever builds a mosque, Allah the Exalted builds a palace for him in Paradise.' Khān Mu'aẓẓam [the exalted khān] Khūrshīd Khān Nawbat-i-'Ālī Maḥalliyān [the chief of the palace guards] built this during the time of the just king Bārbak Shāh Sulṭān ibn Maḥmūd Shāh Sulṭān on the fifth of the month of Ṣafar, [in the] year eight hundred and sixty-eight [19 October 1563].

Discussion:

This inscription was uncovered by a farmer while ploughing his land at Anair Haor (name of a lake) in the Bhanga subdivision of Sylhet district. It is probably the earliest known Islamic inscription in Sylhet, the eastern hinterland of Bengal. Its provenance suggests that Barbak Shāh's kingdom extended in the northeast as far as the Kachar district of Assam. It is written in a Bengali style of *ṭughrā'*. Sayyid Murtaḍā 'Alī mentions another inscription from the same period that was found in this area.

(60) Masjid inscription in Deotala dated 868 (1464)

ORIGINAL SITE: An unnamed Sultanate mosque at Deotala, fifteen miles north of Pandua in Dinajpur district. **CURRENT LOCATION:** Affixed to a relatively small modern mosque near the Chilla Khāna of Shāh Jalāl at Deotala village, Dinajpur district. **MATERIAL, SIZE:** Black basalt; not known. **STYLE, NO. OF LINES:** *ruq'a* in Bengali *ṭughrā'* style; two lines. **REIGN:** Sulṭān Bārbak Shāh (864–878/1460–1474). **LANGUAGE:** Arabic. **TYPE:** Commemorative inscription of a mosque. **PUBLICATION:** Blochmann, *JASB*, XLIII (1874): 296–297; Cunningham, *ASR*, XV (1879–80): 94–95; A. A. Khān, *Memoirs of Gaur*, 167–169; R. D. Banerji, *Banglar Itihas*, pt. II, 211; S. Ahmad,

Inscriptions of Bengal, 77–79; A. Karim, *Corpus of Inscriptions*, 158–60, pl. 19 (a); Dani, *Bibliography of Muslim Inscriptions*, 24–25.

Text:

L-1 قال الله تعالى أجعلتم سقاية الحاج وعمارة المسجد الحرام كمن آمن بالله واليوم الآخر وجاهد في سبيل الله لا يستوون عند الله والله لا يهدي القوم الظالمين قال النبي صلى الله عليه وسلم من بنى مسجدا في الدنيا بنى الله تعالى[له] سبعين قصرا في الجنة بنا هذه<بني هذا> المسجد الجامع بقصبئه تبريزاباد خان الأعظم وخاقان المعظم ناصح الملوك

L-2 والسلاطين كافي العصر والزمان الغ مرا بطخان دامت معاليه في زمن الملك العادل الباذل الفاضل العالم ركن الدنيا والدين أبو<أبي> المظفر باربكشاه السلطان بن محمود شاه السلطان خلد الله ملكه وسلطانه وأعلى أمره وشأنه في الخامس من رجب رجب قدره سنة ثمان وستين وثمانماية

Translation:

L-1 Allah the Exalted said, 'Do you reckon that the offering of water to pilgrims and inhabiting the holy mosque is the same as belief in Allah and the last day and struggle in the path of Allah? Not equal are they in Allah's sight. And Allah does not guide those people who are transgressors' [Qur'ān 9:19]. The Prophet, peace and the blessings of Allah be upon him, said, 'Whoever builds a mosque in the world, Allah the Exalted builds seventy palaces for him in Paradise.' The great khān and sublime *khāqān* Nāṣiḥ al-Mulūk

L-2 wa 'l-Salāṭīn (lit. adviser to the kings and sulṭāns), Kāfī al-'Asr wa 'l-Zamān (lit. suitable for the age and time) Ulugh Murābiṭ Khān built this congregational mosque in the *qasbah* of Tabrīzabād, may his highness be perpetuated, during the time of the just, the benevolent, the wise scholar Rukn al-Dunyā wa 'l-Dīn Abū 'l-Muẓaffar Bārbak Shāh al-Sulṭān ibn Maḥmūd Shāh al-Sulṭān, may Allah perpetuate his kingdom and authority and elevate his affairs and position, on the fifth of [the month of] Rajab, may its position be exalted [in the calender], the year eight hundred and sixty-eight [19 March 1464].

Discussion:

Another masjid inscription in Deotala dated 978/1571 currently affixed to the same mosque also records the name Tabrizabad, a name given to the town of Deotala, after an early sufi saint Shaykh Jalāl al-Dīn Tabrīzī who lived in the area.

(61) Masjid inscription from Ghaibi Dighi in Sylhet from the reign of Bārbak Shāh dated 868 (1464)

ORIGINAL SITE: A no longer extant Sultanate mosque near Ghaibi Dighi in Sylhet. **CURRENT LOCATION:** Not known. **MATERIAL, SIZE:** Not known. **STYLE, NO. OF LINES:** Not known. **REIGN:** Sulṭān Bārbak Shāh (864–878/1460–1474). **LANGUAGE:** Arabic. **TYPE:** Commemorative inscription of a mosque. **PUBLICATION:** Sayyid Murtaḍā 'Alī, *Ḥaḍrat Shāh Djalāl*

O Sileter Itihas (Dhaka, 1988): 207; Shamsuddin Ahmad, 'Some Inscriptions from Sylhet', *Bangladesh Archaeology*, 1(1) (1984): 51.

Text:

L-1 قال النبي صلى الله عليه وسلم من بنى مسجدا بنى الله تعالى سبعين قصرا [له]في الجنة
[بني في زمن سلطان] العهد والزمان

L-2 السلطان بن السلطان ركن الدنيا والدين ابو المظفر باربكشاه السلطان

L-3 ابن محمود شاه السلطان بنا كرده . . . . مادر خانأعظم خاقان معظم خانجهان رحمة خان و في التاريخ
شهور سنة ثمان وستين وثمانماية

Translation:

L-1 The Prophet, peace and blessings of Allah be upon him, said, 'Whoever builds a mosque, Allah, the Almighty, will build [for him] seventy palaces in Paradise.' [During the reign of the sulṭān of] the age and time,

L-2 the sulṭān, son of the sulṭān, Rukn al-Dunyā wa 'l-Dīn, Abū 'l-Muẓaffar Bārbak Shāh al-Sulṭān

L-3 son of Maḥmūd Shāh al-Sulṭān. [This mosque was] built by ... the mother of the great Khān and honoured *Khāqān* Khān Jahān Raḥmat Khān during the months of the year eight hundred and sixty-eight.

(62) Masjid inscription in Peril dated 869 (1465)

ORIGINAL SITE: An unnamed Sultanate mosque in Dhaka district. **CURRENT LOCATION:** Affixed to a tomb at the village of Peril in Dhaka district. **MATERIAL, SIZE:** Black basalt; 24 × 11 inches. **STYLE, NO. OF LINES:** Bengali *ṭughrā'*; one line. **REIGN:** Sulṭān Bārbak Shāh (864–878/1460–1474). **LANGUAGE:** Arabic. **TYPE:** Commemorative inscription of a mosque. **PUBLICATION:** Y. K. Bukhari, 'Four Unpublished Arabic Inscriptions of Sulṭān Bārbak Shāh of Bengal', *EIAPS* (1953–54): 22; Dani, *Bibliography of Muslim Inscriptions*, 25, no. 30; S. Ahmad, *Inscriptions of Bengal*, 79–80; A. Karim, *Corpus of Inscriptions*, 160–161.

Text:

قال النبي عليه السلام من بنى مسجدا في الدنيا بنى الله له قصرا في الجنة في زمن الملك العادل باربك شاه سلطان بن محمود شاه
سلطان بناكرده مجلس خرشيد سر نوبت غير محليان في الخامس [من] شهر شوال سنة تسع وستين وثمانماية

Translation:

The Prophet, peace be on him, said, 'Whoever builds a mosque in the world, Allah builds for him a palace in Paradise.' During the time of the just king Bārbak Shāh Sulṭān ibn Maḥmūd Shāh Sulṭān, Majlis Khurshīd (the Office of Khurshid) Sar-e-Nawbat-e-Maḥalliyān [Chief of the guards of the royal house] built it on the fifth of the month of Shawwāl, year eight hundred and sixty-nine [31 May 1565].

Discussion:

Though originally a mosque inscription, this inscription is currently attached to a tomb. There is a strong resemblance between this inscription and the Hatkhola masjid inscription in Sylhet dated 868/1463 in both the calligraphic execution and contents. Both inscriptions record Khurshīd Khān as a patron. The name of Khurshīd Khān also appears in some other inscriptions including mentioning the Sharqī Sulṭān Maḥmūd in Bhagalpur.

(63) Masjid inscription in Gaurai dated 871 (1466–1467)

ORIGINAL SITE: A Sultanate mosque in Gaurai, Mymansing district, Bangladesh. **CURRENT LOCATION:** Probably in situ. **MATERIAL, SIZE:** Basalt; 23 × 17 inches. **STYLE, NO. OF LINES:** *ijāza* in Bengali *ṭughrā'* decorative style; three lines. **REIGN:** Sulṭān Bārbak Shāh (864–878/1460–1474). **LANGUAGE:** Arabic. **TYPE:** Foundation inscription of a mosque. **PUBLICATION:** Y. K. Bukhari, *EIAPS* (1953–1954): 22–23; Dani, *Bibliography of Muslim Inscriptions*, 26; S. *Ahmad, Inscriptions of Bengal*, 83–85; A. Karim, *Corpus of Inscriptions*, 164–165.

Text:

L-1 قال الله تعالى إنما يعمر مساجد الله من آمن بالله واليوم الآخر وقال النبي صلى الله عليه وسلم من بنى مسجدا لله بنى الله له بيتا في الجنة في نوبت سلطان

L-2 العهد والزمان ركن الدنيا والدين أبو<أبي> المظفر باربكشاه سلطان ابن محمود شاه سلطان خلد الله ملكه وسلطانه وأعلى أمره وشأنه بنى المسجد العالي المخصوص بعناية الله

L-3 المتعالي المخاطب بخطاب مجلس عالي جعل الله دولته ثابتة الأركان راسخة البنيان تم البنا مع التجصيص والتذهيب في التاسع والعشرين من شهر المبارك رمضان سنة إحدى [و] سبعين وثمانماية

Translation:

L-1 Allah the Great said, 'Only those build mosques for Allah who believe in Allah and the last day' [Qur'ān 9:18]. The Prophet, peace and blessings of Allah be upon him, said, 'Whoever builds a mosque for Allah, Allah builds for him a house in Paradise.' During the suzerainty of Sulṭān

L-2 al-'Ahd wa 'l-Zamān Rukn al-Dunyā wa 'l-Dīn Bārbak Shāh Sulṭān ibn Maḥmūd Shāh Sulṭān, may Allah perpetuate his kingdom and his authority and elevate his affairs and his position. He who is favoured with the providence of the Most High and is addressed with the title *majlis-i-'ālī*

L-3 built this lofty mosque by the grace of Allah; may Allah consolidate his rule firmly on pillars and steady in foundation. The construction was completed with plaster and gilding on the twenty-ninth of the blessed month of Ramaḍān, the year eight hundred and seventy-one [4 May 1467].

Discussion:

There is a single-domed ancient brick mosque in Gaurai whose façade is decorated in exquisite terracotta. Though architecturally the mosque resembles the late-Mughal regional style of Bengal (especially the Shāyistakhānī style), it is difficult to establish the exact date when it was built. Most likely, the inscription was found in this mosque. It is also possible that the Mughal administrator built a new mosque on the site of a ruined Sultanate mosque. Interestingly, the inscription mentions the plaster and gilt works of the building, a technique that was quite popular for monumental architecture during that period.

(64) Monumental Gate (Nim Darwaza) inscription at Miyaneh Dar in Gaur Citadel dated 871 (1466–1467)

ORIGINAL SITE: The second gate of Miyaneh Dar (middle gates), commonly known as Nim Darwaza (halfway entrance) in Gaur, in the police station of Ingrez Bazar in Malda district, West Bengal. **CURRENT LOCATION:** Lower panel, in almost intact form, is fixed over an arch of the façade of a newly built jāmi‘ masjid (still under construction) locally known as Minarwali Masjid (or Indarawala Masjid), Mahdipur village, Malda district. A tiny fragment of the first part of the inscription, with which the upper panel of the text started, has been found and preserved by Sadeq Shaykh, Honorary Curator of Gaur Social Welfare Mission Museum (Registered with Department of Art and Culture under Government Art and Antiquities Rule 10=973, Lalbazar, P.O.: Uttar Mahdipur, registration no. S-85650). Strangely enough, another stray fragment was located by the author almost nineteen miles (thirty kilometres) away southeast of Gaur in Qadi Para village in Barogharia union, Chapai Nawabganj district, Bangladesh. **MATERIAL, SIZE:** Black basalt; 111 × 16 inches (size of the lower panel only). **STYLE, NO. OF LINES:** *rayḥānī* (akin to monumental *thulth*) and *ṭughrā'* interchangeably in sixteen rectangular panels in each line; two lines (the upper-line, except two tiny portions at the beginning, is currently missing). **REIGN:** Bārbak Shāh (864–878/1460–1474). **LANGUAGE:** Arabic (except for a few Persian words at the end). **METER:** *Baḥr al-Basīt.* (مستفعلن فاعلن مستفعلن فاعلن) The meter scheme is not properly observed throughout. A number of verses are thus broken or faulty. **TYPE:** Commemorative inscription of a monumental entrance at a palace garden. **PUBLICATION:** Siddiq, *Riḥla ma‘a 'l-Nuqūsh al-Islāmiyya fī 'l-Bangl*, 431–432; idem, ‘Calligraphy and Islamic Culture’, *Bulletin of School of Oriental and African Studies*, 68(1) (2005): 21–58.

Text of the first fragment:

بعدَ المحَامِدِ رَنَّ الإنسُ وَالجَانُ
ابنٌ تَقَدَّمَ عن حَدَثٍ وعن قُرَنٍ

Translation:

(Beginning of the first line at the upper panel):
After praises, as (both) human beings and *jinns* resounded,
A son (i.e. the author of these verses) came forward to narrate the happenings about the surroundings.

Text of the second fragment in the upper panel (could not be deciphered properly):

و تر هـ بعده . . . . . .
اذ أول . . . في
أوصا . لكل . . . عدويه
وأوحى

Figure 6.6 Commemorative inscriptions (Nim Darwaza (halfway entrance) in Gaur, in the police station of Ingrez Bazar in Malda district, West Bengal) (source: copyright by author).

Details of the epigraphic text of lower panel:

ما أَمَّهُ مُقتِرٌ يَرجُو سَمَاحَتَه
إلاّ وَلِّي قَادِمٌ وهو غَنِيٌّ
وَدَارُهُ مالَها ثَانٍ فَاقَ دَائِماً
وَمُصَّرَ عَهدُهُ أمناً و هُدى
تَرُوقُ مِن حُسنِهَا فَمَا رَأى أحَدٌ
بِحُسنِهَا مثلاً عَلَتْ مَكَانَتُهُ
أَزْرَى بِنا هَا عمَّار الدُّنيا مُشَيِّدِيْن
مَا زَرَتْ سَنَاْ فِي جَنَّةِ عَدنِ
لِلدَّارِ بَابٌ وَسِيعٌ مُشرِفٌ سِمَه
فينتصرُ بنصرةِ اللهِ خُلِّدَ سلطانُهُ
إحدى وسبعونَ عاماً وثمانمايةٍ
فإنَّ تاريخَ ذلِكَ ذَا شَرَفُ
فاللهَ أسأَلُه تشييدَ مِلكَتِهِ
مخلدٌ وحدَهُ في الأرضِ مباركُ
در دور سلطنت شاه جهانپناه
ركن الدنيا والدين أبو المظفر باربكشاه
[السلطا] ن خُلّد ملكه وسلطانه
بناء ميانه در بسنة احدى وسبعين [و] ثما[نماية]

Translation of the verses inscribed on the lower panel (second line of the Nim Darwaza inscription):

> Whenever a needy person approaches him cherishing his kindness,
> (Due to his graciousness,) he returns with riches after coming here.
> His dwelling is unmatched (there is no other of its kind), as it has stood the test of time,
> His reign is well settled in peace and with righteousness.
> It (the edifice) excels in its charms that none has seen before,
> With its exemplary beauty, indeed its position is marvelled.
> Its building has humbled architects and builders of the world,
> Like the illuminating glamour of Paradise in Eden.
> For this dwelling, there is a monumental entrance, a symbol of vigilance,
> With God's help, he is always victorious; may his kingdom be perpetuated.
> The year eight-hundred-and-seventy-one,
> Indeed this date is of great honour.
> Thus I seek from Allah furtherance of His gift,
> Who alone is the Sustainer on this blessed earth.
> In the era of the Sultanate of Shāh Jahān-Panāh [the refuge of the universe],
> Rukn al-Dunyā wa 'l-Dīn Abū 'l-Muẓaffar Bārbak Shāh Sulṭān.
> May his kingdom and authority be long lasting,
> Along with the building of Miyanah Dar, in the year eight-hundred-and-seventy-one.

Discussion:

Both this inscription and its counterpart at Chand Darwaza (ins. no. 65) can be considered among the finest and most exquisite examples of Arabic inscriptions of the AH ninth century (CE fifteenth century) in the Islamic world. Their beautifully structured rhyme in elegant Arabic literary style suggests that Arabic had a strong impact on the cultural life of Sultanate Bengal and that it was taught in the madrasas of this region with great depth. In composition, the literary style of these verses resembles the *Qaṣīda al-Burda* of Imām al-Buṣīrī. However, since the purpose of these texts is commemorative inscriptions, the exactness of meter (*Baḥr al-Basīṭ*) could not be observed throughout.

The Nim Darwaza inscription was discovered by the author in a locally constructed mosque in the village of Mahdipur, which rose out of the ruins of the once-thriving capital of Muslim Bengal, Gaur. Though the Muslim rulers of Bengal shifted their capitals several times from Gaur to other places such as Pandua, Tanda, Rajmahal, Dhaka and Murshidabad, this ancient city completely lost the patronage of its ruling class towards the end of the sixteenth century. Consequently, its population dwindled rapidly. According to a number of early English visitors, such as Franklin, Creighton and Orme, the city in the late eighteenth and early nineteenth centuries had turned into a deserted wasteland enclosed in deep and thick jungles and inhabited by wild beasts.[13] The population of this area grew only after independence in 1947 as a result of the sudden influx of Hindu refugees (particularly certain middle caste Hindus such as Gowala or milkmen) to the region. Most houses in the village of Mahdipur, as well as in the other villages of the area, are constructed with bricks unsparingly pillaged from the magnificent Sultanate buildings of the Muslim capital of Gaur, once named Jannatabad (lit. an abode in Paradise) by the second Mughal emperor, Humayun. This age-old custom became a common practice in the area, which robbed this ancient capital of most of its superb architectural heritage. Famous for their solidness, outer gilt and ornamentation, these bricks (particularly the enamelled ones) were highly prized and were well sought after for new construction even in many distant cities such as Kolkata, the colonial capital of India. With the passage of time, these bricks earned the special name, 'Gauriyo Bricks'.

The inscription is almost identical to the Chand Darwaza inscription of Bārbak Shāh in the same location, now preserved in the University Museum at the University of Pennsylvania in Philadelphia, in its layout, decorative pattern, literary style, date and every other aspect. Thus, it can be surmised that both of these inscriptions once decorated the façades of the two identical entrances of the Sultanate palace complex of Gaur. Both were located midway between the Dakhil Darwaza (to the extreme north of the citadel) and the private palace of the sulṭāns (in the centre of the Badshahi citadel complex facing the old and original channel of the then mighty River Bhagirathi to the west, which has since dried up). These two entrances are mentioned in both of these separate inscriptions as 'Mianehdar', a clear reference to the monumental entrances in the middle of a scenic paved thoroughfare leading to the interior of the Sultanate palace. These entrances were ornately decorated, as can be seen in an illustration of Chand Darwaza drawn by Henry Creighton towards the end of the eighteenth century. A rectangular form of the size of the present inscription is clearly visible in the illustration just above the second arch in the arcade of Chand Darwaza.[14] An inscription, dated AH 871, was seen by Creighton in the debris of the ruined parts of the entrance.[15] He moved this inscription, along with a number of other valuable antiques, from the area to his Nilkuthi (English indigo factory) in Goamaloty, two or three miles north of Dakhil Darwaza. This was the first collection of Bengal antiquities ever made, and it in effect turned his Nilkuthi into a sort of small museum in the vicinity, noted by several European visitors to the area including Buchanan Hamilton. Remains of Creighton's Nilkuthi still exist at the same site in Goamaloty, though no trace of his collections can be found anymore at the site. Although Creighton went to Bengal as a fortune seeker who exploited every means to increase indigo production for a maximum profit, often at the expense of local farmers, he gradually fell in love with the ruins of Gaur.[16]

Shayam Prasad, a *munshī* (scribe/clerk) and a local assistant to William Franklin (an English regulating officer of Bhagalpur), also noticed the inscription of Chand Darwaza. Not surprisingly, he found its writing extremely intricate, yet stylistically very elegant. After much effort and with great difficulty, he deciphered it quite accurately.[17] The whole complex, according to Munshi Shayam Prasad, was popularly known as Qil'a Dawlatkhāna Bādshāhī (royal residential palace and citadel). Both Chand Darwaza and Nim Darwaza led to Maḥal Khās Badshāhī (Ḥawelī Khāṣ, according to Franklin) or the private palace of the sulṭāns. The private palace was divided into several wings: Diwān Khāna (popularly known as Darbār Maḥal) or the royal court (mentioned as the Public Hall of Audience by Franklin), followed by Jalwa Khāna or Khāṣ Maḥal (mentioned as the Dwelling House of the Sovereign by Franklin, probably the royal chambers), Begum Maḥal (the imperial harem) and Khazāna Kothri (treasury). The complex served as the main palace of the later Ilyās Shāhī rulers of Bengal; a significant part of the palace, particularly Chand Darwaza and Nim Darwaza, was constructed during the reign of Barbak Shah. The main road passing through these monumental gates was flanked by extensive gardens, orchards, canals and artificial lakes, as mentioned in both these inscriptions.

The Chand Darwaza inscription was also seen by Major Franklin, as mentioned in his journal.[18] Around December 1810, he found it in Goamaloti and took possession of it,[19] a common practice among European amateur antique collectors of that time. Franklin also collected a number of valuable Islamic manuscripts from the mosques and khanqas of Gaur and Pandua, as did Francis Buchanan Hamilton (see *A Geographical, Statistical and Historical Description of the District or Zilla of Dinajpur*)[20] around the same period. Among these manuscripts, one in Persian (unfortunately long lost) that he claimed to have procured from Perua (Pandua), seems to be the main source for his reconstruction of the chronology of Muslim rule in Bengal.[21] When he finally returned to England, he carried with him most of his antique collections. How he transported these tablets (including the one now in Philadelphia, measuring 97 × 35.5 inches) from Gaur to his country home in England remains a mystery. These large, bulky stone slabs were first moved from their original location in Gaur by Creighton to a Nilkuthi at Goamaloty towards the end of eighteenth century using bull-carts. When Franklin found them in Creighton's abandoned Nilkuthi in Goamaloty in December 1810 while visiting Gaur he took possession of them. In a subsequent monsoon season, when the dried channel of the Bhagirathi river near the Nilkuthi swelled with water, Franklin managed to send all these inscriptions, along with his own collections, directly to Calcutta in a large boat, from where they were finally shipped to England some time towards the end of the 1820s when he left Bengal for good. He donated a number of them to the British Museum, most of which are now stored in its basement depository. When the author examined these inscriptions in 1982, he found Franklin's name (exact text: 'Presented by Colonel Franklin') incised in Latin characters on the upper rims of a number of them.[22]

The present location of the rest of his collections is unknown; some could be stored unnoticed in the basements or attics of obscure English country houses and their value unknown by the householders. This has been the case with a large number of antiques of Bengal acquired by British collectors during the eighteenth and nineteenth centuries. A rare exception, however, was the inscription of Chand Darwaza, which somehow passed into the hands of Thomas Hope, a famous collector of Greek and Roman vases and sculpture. The inscription remained with the descendants of Thomas Hope at his country estate at Deepdene, near Dorking, Surrey (acquired by Hope in 1807), until the Hope collections were auctioned by Christie's in 1917. The plaque bearing the inscription was purchased by H. Kevorkian, a US art dealer, in London the same year; he sold it finally to the University Museum in Philadelphia in 1924.[23] Unfortunately, Franklin's most valuable collection, the Persian manuscript on Bengal history that he procured in Perua (in Pandua), has not yet come to light; if still extant, it might be able to provide much valuable information on early Muslim rule in Bengal which is not sufficiently available elsewhere.

Franklin, does not refer to the second entrance as Nim Darwaza. Rather he describes the entrance as another gateway, opposite Chand Darwaza, built of bricks and beautifully decorated with flowered work. The entrance was about twenty-five feet high and the arch, through which one could enter, was fifteen by six feet in breadth, which Franklin identified as the entrance to Khazana Kothri (the Sultanate treasury). The inscriptions over the gate (which undoubtedly include the inscription that is now fixed on Minarwali Masjid in Mahdipur), had already been carried away.[24]

While the Chand Darwaza inscription in the University Museum in Philadelphia remains intact, the Nim Darwaza inscription is badly damaged; the upper portion containing the first line has almost been lost. Thanks to the Muslim villagers of Mahdipur village, because of their reverence for Arabic writing, the lower-part (containing the second line) was saved. Fortunately, a tiny fragment of the upper portion (i.e. first line) was found by an amateur archaeologist from the village, who saved it for a local museum in the village. Another fragment of the upper part was located recently by the author, nearly nineteen miles (approximately thirty kilometres) south from its original site in the Qadi Para jāmi' masjid in Barogharia village, Chapai Nawabganj district in Bangladesh. In all probability, the inscription somehow survived in its original (complete) form for a considerable period. Its upper part was probably broken while the villagers attempted to move this huge inscription to the Minarwali Masjid. According to a local tradition, a Hindu farmer from the nearby Kumarpara suburb of Dakhshin Mahdipur discovered the inscription while ploughing near Gunmant Masjid. After he moved it to his house, a series of misfortunes befell his household. Consequently, the farmer decided to place the inscription in the village mosque where it was later fixed on the wall. Unfortunately, the rest of the upper part of the inscription (except the two tiny fragments mentioned above) have not been found to date. The length of the second inscription is slightly (almost thirteen inches) larger than its counterpart in the University Museum in Philadelphia. The height of the remaining half portion (i.e. sixteen inches) suggests that, together with the upper line, the total height of the inscription would have been between thirty-four and thirty-six inches. Owing to some damage to the rim that occurred either because of the chiselling process to fit it to its current location or to some other factors, the existing portion of this black basalt slab has lost certain parts of its text, particularly in its upper border. In addition, parts of its rims have been lost because of the manner of affixation of the inscription within a concrete wall, as well as because of the application of whitewash while the building was being painted.

The text of this inscription is divided into sixteen vertical rectangular panels representing two different elaborate calligraphic styles interchangeably placed in each panel, the very open style of *rayḥānī* (akin to monumental bold *thulth*) in one panel and the compact style of *ṭughrā'* in the next. Unlike the distinctive traditional Bengali *ṭughrā'* style often characterized by the unbroken repetition of elongated verticals which are found in most of the Sultanate inscriptions of Bengal, *ṭughrā'* in this inscription rather resembles the decorative style of Mamluk *ṭughrā'* (found, for instance, in the door panels of Umayyad mosques in Damascus), and, to a lesser extent, the Ottoman *ṭughrā'*. The varying rhythm of the calligraphic programme and its symmetrical contrast make this inscription exceptionally graceful.

(65) Gate inscription of Chand Darwaza at Miyaneh Dar in Gaur dated 871 (1466–1467)

ORIGINAL SITE: Chand Darwaza of Miyaneh Dar (middle gateway) leading to the Sultanate private palace within the compound of the royal citadel in Gaur. **CURRENT LOCATION:** University Museum, Philadelphia, Pennsylvania. **MATERIAL, SIZE:** Black basalt; 97 × 35.50 inches. **STYLE, NO. OF LINES:** *ṭughrā'* and *rayḥānī* (akin to monumental *thulth*); two lines. **REIGN:** Sulṭān Bārbak Shāh (864–878/1460–1474). **LANGUAGE, METER:** Arabic; *Baḥr al-Basīṭ*. **TYPE:** Commemorative inscription of a monumental entrance. **PUBLICATION:** Cunningham, *Archaeological Survey Report*, 15, 53; Ravenshaw, *Gaur*, 19; A. A. Khan, *Memoirs of Gaur*, 56–58; Nabih A. Faris and G. C. Miles, 'An Inscription of Barbak Shah of Bengal', *Ars Islamica*, VI (1940): 141–147; Dani, *Bibliography of Muslim Inscriptions*, 26–27; S. Ahmad, *Inscriptions of Bengal*, 85–88; A. Karim, *Corpus of Inscriptions*, 165–168.

Text:

On the top of the inscriptional panels at the centre of the upper decorative border line:

بسم الله الرحمن الرحيم

The main Arabic text of the inscription:

الحَمْدُ لِلّهِ ذي الآلاءِ والمِنَنِ
رَبٌّ تنزَّهَ عن نومٍ وعَنْ وَسَنِ
ثم الصَلوٰةُ على المختارِ من مُضَرِ
خيرِ الأنامِ النبيِّ السيِّدِ المدَنِ
محمدٌ خاتمِ الرُسْلِ الكِرَامِ ومَنْ
لولاهُ سُبُلُ الهُدَىْ والحقِّ لَمْ تَبِنِ
وآلِهِ مَعَدِنِ التَقْوَىْ وصُحْبَتِهِ
الطَّايِعِيْ اللّهَ في سِرٍّ وفي عَلَنِ
وبَعَدُ أُثْنِيْ على جَوَّادِ رحمَتِهِ
أزْرَىْ بِجُوْدِ السَّحَابِ الهاطلِ الهَتِنِ
الشاهِ سلطانَ ركنِ الدِّينِ والدنياْ
سلطانِنا باربكشاهِ العليِّ الفَطِنِ
ابنِ الذي شاع في الأمصارِ بِأَبِهِ
سلطانِ محمودِ شاه العادلِ الحسَنِ
هل في العراقين سلطانٌ لهُ كَرَمٌ
كباربكشاهِ وفي الشامِ واليمنِ
كلا فما في بلادِ اللّهِ قَطُّ لـهُ
في البذْلِ مِثْلٌ فهذا واحدُ الزَّمَنِ
ودارُهُ كالجِنَانْنِ را{يـ} [ئـ]قٌ نزِهٌ
ومُجْلِبٌ لِلغِنَىْ ومُذْهِبُ الشَّجَنِ
نهرٌ جَرَىْ تحتَها كالسلسبيلِ له
أَجْنَاءُ دُرٌّ قَلَتْ بالفقر والمِحَنِ
بابُهُ راحةٌ للرُّوحِ ريحاناً
لذي الحبيبِ وللأعداءِ كالشَّطَنِ
بابٌ عليٌّ مَسْرَحٌ نَشِيْطٌ سَمَّهِ
ميانه در وهى دخولُ خاصٌ أَمَنِ
إحدى وسبعون والثمانمئة سنَاْ
ذاك مبناهُ زمانُ العيشِ والأَوَنِ
فاللّهَ أسألُهُ تخليدَ دولتِهِ
ما غرَّدَ الطيرُ في روضٍ على فَنَنِ
در دورِ سلطنتِ شاهِ جهانپناه
ركنِ الدنيا والدينِ أبو المظفر باربكشاه
سلطان خلَّد اللهُ ملكَهُ وسلطانَهُ
بناء ميانه در بسنةِ إحدى وسبعون وثمانماية شده است

Translation:

Top:
In the name of Allah, the Compassionate, the Merciful.

Upper panel:

Praise be to Allah, Source of munificence and grace,
A Lord Who neither slumbers nor sleeps.

Then may blessings be upon the elect of Muḍar,
The best of creation, the Prophet, the Medinian leader.
Muḥammad, the seal of the noble prophets,
Without whom the path of righteousness and truth would not have become known.
And upon his family, the fountainhead of piety, and upon his companions,
Who are obedient unto Allah in private and in public.
Then I sing the praise of one whose generosity,
Surpasses the beneficence of clouds heavily laden with moisture.
The shāh, Sulṭān Rukn al-Dunyā wa 'l-Dīn,
Our Sulṭān Barbāk Shāh, the sublime, the wise.
The son of the one whose domain has spread over many metropolises,
Sulṭān Maḥmūd Shāh, the just, the handsome.
Is there in the two Iraqs a sulṭān as generous,
As Bārbak Shāh, yea in Syria and in Yaman?

Lower panel:

No! There is not unto him in all Allah's land,
An equal in generosity, for he is unique, unparalleled in his time.
His abode is like unto a garden, tranquil and pleasing,
It gathers joy and dispels sorrow.
A watercourse flows beneath it, resembling the waters of Paradise,
The fruits which take away all poverty and pain.
Its gate provides refuge, like fragrant basil to the soul,
To friends, while to foes it is forbidden and remote.
A 'lofty gate', refreshing and cheerful, called,
Miyaneh Dar (Middle Gate), set apart as a private and secured entrance.
In the year eight hundred and seventy-one,
A time of prosperity and peace.
I therefore pray to Allah to perpetuate his dominion,
As long as birds on treetops alight and sing.
In the era of the Sultanate of the Shāh Jahān-Panāh [the refuge of the universe],
Rukn al-Dunyā wa 'l-Dīn Abū 'l-Muẓaffar Bārbak Shāh Sulṭān, may Allah prolong
His kingdom and authority. The building of Miyaneh Dar [took place] in the year eight hundred and seventy-one.

Discussion:

This inscription (which has been discussed in detail in the previous [Nim Darwaza, no. 65] inscription), once decorated the famous monumental entrance Chand Darwaza located at 'Mianeh Dar' that passed through the royal garden leading towards the later Ilyās Shāhī palace within the compound of the royal citadel in Gaur. Chand Darwaza was built during the reign of Barbak Shah.

(66) Salik Masjid inscription in Bashirhat dated 871 (1467)

ORIGINAL SITE: A Sultanate mosque, known as Salik Masjid at present, in the town of Bashirhat, district of Chabbish Parganah, West Bengal. **CURRENT LOCATION:** Affixed to the same mosque after its renovation where probably it still remains. **MATERIAL, SIZE:** Black basalt; 13 × 6 inches. **STYLE, NO. OF LINES:** Bihārī; two lines. **REIGN:** Sulṭān Bārbak Shāh (864–878/1460–1474). **LANGUAGE:** Arabic. **TYPE:** Commemorative inscription of a mosque. **PUBLICATION:** Khan Hamidul Haque, 'Letter to the Editor', *Statesman* (Calcutta: 15 December 1909); Rai Manmohan Chakraverty Bahadur, *Proceedings of JASB*, VI (1910): 29, fig. 5; R. D. Banerjee, *Journal of Bihar and Orissa Research Society*, IV (1918): 179–180, pl. II; Dani, *Bibliography of Muslim Inscriptions*, 27–28; S. Ahmad, *Inscriptions of Bengal*, 88–90; Muhammad Mujibur Rahman, *Bangla Bhasay Qur'ān Charcha* ([Bengali Text] Dhaka: Islamic Foundation, 1982), 80–89; A. Karim, *Corpus of Inscriptions*, 169–170.

Text:

L-1 لا إله إلا الله محمد رسول الله بنى هذا المسجد بجلس

L-2 المعظم والمكرم بجلس أعظم دامت عظمته سنة إحدى وسبعين وثمانماية

Translation:

There is no God but Allah, Muḥammad is His messenger. The sublime and gracious *majlis*, Majlis A'ẓam, may his greatness continues, had this mosque constructed in the year eight hundred and seventy-one.

Discussion:

Mawlavi M. Abdul Wathiq, a legal practitioner at Diwani Court in Bashirhat and an Arabic teacher at Bashirhat High School, read the entire inscription for the first time as reported by Khan Hamidul Haque in a 'Letter to the Editor' in the daily *Statesman* in Calcutta (5 December 1909). Interestingly, this letter also included an English translation of the inscription. Shortly afterwards, Mawlavi M. Abdul Wathiq also published for the first time a photograph of the mosque as well as the inscription on the first page of his Bengali translation of the last part of the Qur'ān. The inscription itself is located at the top of the central miḥrāb of a Sultanate mosque that once had six domes resting on huge granite pillars. Most of the materials of the mosque seem to have been taken from the ruins of nearby ancient Hindu temples during its original construction. Situated at the centre of the Bashirhat town of 24 Parganah district, about forty miles from Kolkata, this historic mosque has lost much of its original character in the process of a series of renovations carried out from time to time since the nineteenth century.

(67) Masjid inscription of Barbak Shāh from Tezpur dated 872 (1468)

ORIGINAL SITE: A ruined Sultanate mosque near Atiya Masjid in the village of Tezpur in the Tangail district, Bangladesh. **CURRENT LOCATION:**

Bangladesh National Museum, inv. no. 81.640 (in addition to inv. no. 70.1350). **MATERIAL, SIZE:** Black basalt; 23 × 20 inches. **STYLE, NO. OF LINES:** A local variety of Bihārī in Bengali *ṭughrā'*; four lines. **REIGN:** Sulṭān Bārbak Shāh (864–879/1459–1474). **LANGUAGE:** Arabic with a few Persian idioms in the last line. **TYPE:** Foundation inscription containing the 'throne verse' from the Qur'ān and a reference to the construction of a congregational mosque. **PUBLICATION:** Enamul Haque, *Islamic Art in Bangladesh: Catalogue of a Special Exhibition in Dacca Museum* (Dhaka: Dhaka Museum, 1978), 25, 68–70; Shamsuddin Ahmad, 'Arabic and Persian Inscriptions from Sylhet', *Bangladesh Archaeology*, 1(1) (1979): 152–153; *Bangladesh District Gazetteer: Tangail* (Dhaka, 1983); A. Karim, *Corpus of Inscriptions*, 522–523; Siddiq, *Riḥla ma'a 'l-Nuqūsh fī 'l-Bangāl*, 162.

Text:

L-1 لا اله الا الله محمد رسول الله لا اله الا هو الحي القيوم لا تاخذه سنة و لا نوم له ما في السموات و ما في الارض
من ذا الذي يشفع عنده الا باذنه يعلم

L-2 ما بين ايديهم و ما خافهم و لا يحيطون بشيء من علمه {له} الا بما شاء وسع كرسيه السموات و الارض و لا يوده
حفظهما و هو العلي العظيم لا اكراه

L-3 في الدين قد تبين الرشد من الغي فمن يكفر بالطاغوت و يومن بالله فقد استمسك بالعروة الوثقي لانفصام لها و الله
سميع {ال}عليم تاريخ نهم

L-4 سال كرسي سلامت سلطان بن سلطان ركن الدنيا و الدين ابو المظفر باربك شاه سلطان بن محمود شاه سلطان اين
مسجد جامع بنا كرد بليار خان

Translation:

L-1 There is no God but Allah alone, [and] Muḥammad is His messenger. Allah; there is no God but He, the Living, the Everlasting. No slumber can seize Him, nor sleep. To Him belongs all that is in the heavens and the earth. Who is there that shall intercede with Him without His permission? He knows

L-2 what lies before them and what is after them, and they cannot comprehend anything of His knowledge except what He wishes. His throne extends over the heavens and the earth and He feels no fatigue in guarding them for He is the All-high and the All-glorious. There is no compulsion

L-3 in the religion; for the truth stands out clearly from misguidance. Whoever rejects evil and brings faith in Allah, he indeed grasps the most trustworthy handclasp that never breaks. Allah hears and knows everything. During the ninth

L-4 year of the unimpaired throne of sulṭān [corresponding to the beginning of 872/1467], son of sulṭān, Rukn al-Dunyā wa 'l Dīn, Abū 'l-Muẓaffar, Bārbak Shāh Sulṭān son of Maḥmūd Shāh Sulṭān, this jāmi' masjid was founded by Bilyār Khān.

Discussion:

The text appears to be a purely religious, consisting of verses (including the Throne Verse) from the Qur'ān. At the end, however, there is a reference to the construction of a congregational mosque. The inscription seems to have been produced locally without any patronage from the ruling class. Its calligraphy is mediocre like a few other inscriptions of this period (e.g. Salik Masjid inscription in Bashirhat dated 871/1467).

Inspired by the prevailing *ṭughrā'* style in the region, it seems that the calligrapher tried to create something new. There are quite a few orthographic and grammatical errors in the text. In the Qur'ānic verses of this inscription, for instance, there is an error in the second line in the word *'ilmihi*, where two unnecessary letters joined at the end can be deciphered as *lahu*. Similarly the Arabic definite article *al-* has been added to the divine adjective *'Alīm* (at the end of third line), which is also a grammatical mistake.

Though the epigraphical text does not record any date, it does mention the name of the contemporary sulṭān, Barbak Shāh, who ruled Bengal around 864–879 (1459–1474). The name of the builder of the mosque is recorded as Bilyār Khān, about whom nothing is known from other sources.

Enamul Haque vaguely suggests the existence of another identical inscription (inv. no. 70.1350) in the collection of Bangladesh National Museum, Dhaka. But unfortunately no other information could be procured about inv. no. 70.1350. It is possible that when describing the present inscription, he mistakenly identified it as inv. no. 70.1350.

(68) An unidentified Masjid inscription of Bārbak Shāh currently preserved at Dinajpur Museum dated 875 (1470)

ORIGINAL SITE: An unnamed masjid somewhere in Dinajpur district, Bangladesh. **CURRENT LOCATION:** Dinajpur Museum, Dinajpur city, Bangladesh. **MATERIAL, SIZE:** Black basalt; not known. **STYLE, NO. OF LINES:** A crude form of local *naskh*; five lines. **REIGN:** Rukn al-Dunyā wa 'l-Dīn Bārbak Shāh (864–878/1460–1474). **LANGUAGE:** Arabic. **TYPE:** Commemorative inscription of a mosque. **PUBLICATION:** M. Y. Siddiq, 'Inscriptions as an Important Means for Understanding History of the Muslims', *Journal of Islamic Studies*, 20(2) (May 2009).

Text:

L-1 نصر من الله وفتح قريب وبشّر المؤمنين بسم الله الرحمن الرحيم قال الله الله خير حافظا وهو أرحم الراحمين

L-2 بناء المسجد في {ال} عهد السلطان ابن السلطان ركن الدنيا والدين أبو المجاهد باربكشاه سلطان

L-3 . . . . خلّد الله ملكه وسلطانه بحكم وإشارة خان أعظم خاقان معظم بهلوى العصر والزمان

L-4 . . . . وبنى هذا المسجد المذكور خان أعظم وخاقان معظم ألغ نصر خان جنگدار

L-5 . . . في التاريخ السادس والعشرين من الشهر الصفر ختمه الله بالخير والظفر في شهور سنة خمس وسبعين وثمانمأة

Translation:

L-1 Help from Allah and the victory is nearing. So convey the good news to the believers. In the name of Allah, the most kind, and the most gracious. Allah said, 'Allah is the best protector, and He is the most kind of the kind.'

L-2 Construction of this masjid (took place) during the reign of the sulṭān, the son of sulṭān, Rukn al-Dunyā' wa 'l-Dīn Abū 'l-Mujāhid Bārbak Shāh Sultan,
L-3 […] may Allah perpetuate his kingdom and his authority, due to the order and indication of the great Khān, the honourable Khāqān, Bahlawī 'l-Aṣr wa 'l-Zamān.
L-4 […] Khān A'ẓam Khaqān Mu'aẓẓam Ulugh Naṣr Khān Jangdār constructed it
L-5 in the date twenty six of Ṣafar, May Allah complete it with felicity and success, during the year eight hundred and seventy-five.

Discussion:

This inscription is currently preserved at Dinajpur museum. It does not represent any high calligraphic standard. Somewhat far from the capital of Gaur, the masjid perhaps failed to attract any royal patronage. A significant portion of the inscription at the bottom on the right side has been worn away by time, making its complete and proper deciphering impossible. The name of the patron of the masjid is, unfortunately, eroded. But it appears from his titles, 'Khān A'ẓam Khaqān Mu'aẓẓam Bahlawī al-'Aṣr wa 'l-Zamān', that he enjoyed a high official status in the state and was in a position to order the construction of a masjid. The person who executed the order and supervised its construction, was a local army officer who bore a popular military title in Bengal 'Jangdār'.

(69) Masjid inscription from Bayang dated 876 (1471)

ORIGINAL SITE: A Sultanate mosque in a small village known as Bayang nearly eight miles from Mirzaganj in the district of Barisal in Bangladesh. **CURRENT LOCATION:** Indian Museum, Calcutta, inv. no. 12. **MATERIAL, SIZE:** Black basalt; 25 × 10 inches. **STYLE, NO. OF LINES:** *Naskh*; two lines. **REIGN:** Sulṭān Bārbak Shāh (864–878/1460–1474). **LANGUAGE:** Arabic. **TYPE:** Commemorative inscription of a mosque. **PUBLICATION:** W. N. Lees, *JASB*, XXIX (1860): 406–407, pl. 1; Z. A. Desai, *EIAPS* (1955–1956): 15–16; Dani, *Bibliography of Muslim Inscriptions*, 25; S. Ahmad, *Inscriptions of Bengal*, 81–83; C. Dutt, *Inscriptions in the Indian Museum*, 15, no. 14; A. Karim, *Corpus of Inscriptions*, 171–173.

Text:

L-1 قال النبي صلى الله عليه وسلم من بنى مسجدا بنى الله له في الجنة سبعين قصرا بني هذا المسجد في عهد السلطان الأعظم ركن الدنيا والدين
L-2 أبي المظفر باربكشاه بن محمود شاه السلطان بناه خان معظم أجيال خان ابن محمد و بنى بأمر ملك مظهرالدين مؤرخا في سنة شهورست و سبعين و ثمانماية

Translation:

The Prophet, peace and blessings of Allah be upon him, said, 'Whoever builds a mosque, Allah will build for him seventy palaces in Paradise.' This mosque was built during the time of the great Sulṭān Rukn al-Dunyā wa 'l-Dīn Bārbak Shāh ibn Maḥmūd Shāh. Khān Mu'aẓẓam Ajyāl Khān ibn Muḥammad built it. And it was built at the order of Malik Maẓhar al-Dīn, dated in the month of [the] year eight hundred and seventy-six.

Discussion:

The architectural remains of Khān Jahān 'Alī, particularly Shāit-Gumbuj Masjid and its epigraphical evidence (see ins. no. 50, dated 863/1459) indicate the strong Muslim presence in the southern parts of Bengal towards the middle of the fifteenth century. The provenance of this inscription further suggests that the rule of the Muslim sulṭāns of Bengal during the reign of Bārbak Shāh extended almost up to the coastal region of the Bay of Bengal, and most likely included northern and eastern parts of the Sundarban. The ancient Harikela kingdom (known to Muslim geographers as Harkand, from which comes Baḥr al-Harkand, the early Arabic name for Bay of Bengal) once existed in this region. The tiny Hindu kingdom of Chandradvīpa (Deva dynasty) that emerged towards the end of the thirteenth century and lasted until the end of the sixteenth century probably co-existed in certain parts of this region along with Muslim rule.

(70) Masjid inscription in Mahisantosh dated 876 (1471–1472)

ORIGINAL SITE: An unnamed Sultanate masjid near the Shrine of Mahisantosh at Mahiganj village, Nawgaon district, Bangladesh. **CURRENT LOCATION:** Affixed to a shrine at Mahisantosh in Mahiganj village, Nawgaon district, Bangladesh. **MATERIAL, SIZE:** Not known; 17 × 8.50 inches. **STYLE, NO. OF LINES:** Not known; two lines. **REIGN:** Sulṭān Bārbak Shāh (864–878/1460–1474). **LANGUAGE:** Arabic. **TYPE:** Foundation inscription of a mosque. **PUBLICATION:** Blochmann, *JASB*, XLIV (1875): 291; Dani, *Bibliography of Muslim Inscriptions*, 28, no. 42; S. Ahmad, *Inscriptions of Bengal*, 90–91; A. Karim, *Corpus of Inscriptions*, 170–171.

Text:

L-1 قال عليه السلام . . . . . .

L-2 بنى المسجد خان الأعظم والمعظم الغ . . وزير شهر مشهور باربك أباد مكن (مسكن؟) ست وسبعين]و[ثمانماية

Translation:

The sublime and exalted Khān Ulugh built this mosque ... [he] was the vizier of the famous city of Bārbakabād Makan [in the year] eight hundred [and] seventy-six.

Discussion:

The text indicates that Mahisantosh was given the name of Bārbakabād during the reign of Sulṭān Bārbak Shāh and that it continued in use during the Mughal period. According to the *A'in-i-Akbarī*, Bārbakabād was a sarkar (an administrative unit) that comprised thirty-eight *maḥal*s and it covered roughly parts of the present districts of Dinajpur, Rangpur, Bogra, Rajshahi and Pabna.

(71) An unidentified Sultanate masjid inscription from Gaur from the reign of Sulṭān Bārbak Shāh dated 877 (1473)

ORIGINAL SITE: An unidentified masjid somewhere in Gaur, Malda district, West Bengal. **CURRENT LOCATION:** Affixed to the eastern wall of a newly constructed Masjid in the village of Harugram, Malda district, West Bengal. **MATERIAL, SIZE:** Black basalt; 26 × 8.5 inches. **STYLE, NO. OF LINES:** Bengali *ṭughrā'* style; one line. **REIGN:** Sulṭān Bārbak Shāh (864–878/1459–1474). **LANGUAGE:** Arabic, with a few Persian words at the end. **TYPE:** Commemorative inscription of a masjid. **PUBLICATION:** M. Y. Siddiq, 'Calligraphy and Islamic Culture', *Bulletin of the School of Oriental and African Studies*, 68(1) (2005): 21–58; S. P. K. Mitra, 'Late Z. A. Desai and the Provisional Study of Some New Inscriptions', *Indo-Iranica*, 58(3 & 4) (September–December 2005): 26–29.

Text:

قال النبي صلى الله عليه وسلم من بنى لله مسجدا في الدنيا بنى الله تعالى له سبعين قصرا في الجنة بنى هذا المسجد في عهد
السلطان ابن السلطان ركن الدنيا والدين أبو المظفر باربكشاه ابن السلطان محمود شاه خلد ملكه بنا كرد اين مسجد خان محمد
سعيد في سنة سبع وسبعين ثمانماية

Translation:

The Prophet, peace and blessings of Allah be upon him, said, 'Whosoever builds a mosque in this world for the sake of Allah, Allah, the Exalted, will build for him seventy palaces in Paradise.' This masjid was built during the era of al-Sulṭān ibn al-Sulṭān Rukn al-Dunyā wa 'l-Dīn Abū 'l-Muẓaffar Bārbak Shāh al-Sulṭān, son of al-Sulṭān Maḥmūd Shāh. Khān Muḥammad Sa'īd built this masjid in the year eight hundred and seventy-seven.

Discussion:

The upper part of this inscription, above the main body of the Arabic text, has been decorated with beautiful ornamental designs, namely floral, vegetal and geometrical motifs. In middle of this rich decorative background the Arabic phrase *yā Allāh* (يا الله Oh God) is inscribed, flanked by the divine adjective *yā Fattāḥ* (يا فتاح Oh Opener) on both sides. The stone tablet seems to be a part of a calligraphic ornamentation of an edifice (most likely a masjid) somewhere in

Gaur. The edifice was erected under the patronage of a person whose name can barely be read. Perhaps one may read it conjecturally as Khān Muḥammad Sa'īd. Since the patron had the resource to build a mosque in the area, it is reasonable to assume that he enjoyed a high position during that period. Unfortunately, nothing more is known about him. Calligraphically the inscription represents a rather simple variety of Bengali *ṭughrā'* style compared with some other monumental inscriptions of Gaur from this period.

(72) Masjid inscription in Hathhazari dated 878 (1473)

ORIGINAL SITE: A no longer extant Mughal mosque near the town of Hathazari, district of Chitagong, Bangladesh. **CURRENT LOCATION:** Affixed to the wall of a relatively modern mosque built on the site of an ancient mosque known as 'Alāwal Khān Masjid in Hathazari. **MATERIAL, SIZE:** Not known. **STYLE, NO. OF LINES:** A local variety of *ijāza*; two lines. **REIGN:** Sulṭān Bārbak Shāh (864–878/1460–1474). **LANGUAGE**: Arabic, mixed with a few Persian phrases. **TYPE:** Commemorative inscription. **PUBLICATION:** R. D. Banerjee, *Journal of Bihar and Orissa Research Society*, IV (1918): 181, fig. III; Dani, *Bibliography of Muslim Inscriptions*, 28, no. 43; S. Ahmad, *Inscriptions of Bengal*, 91; A. Karim, *Corpus of Inscriptions*, 173–174.

Text:

On the top of the inscription at the centre:

L-1 يا مفتح الأبواب إنه

بتاريخ بيست و پنجم ماه مبارك رمضان سنة ثمان وسبعين وثمانماية في عهد سلطان ركن الدنيا والدين أبو<أبي>
المظفر باربكشاه السلطان

L-2 ابن محمود شاه السلطان خلد الله ملكه وسلطانه هذا المسجد مجلس أعلى عليه الرحمة والغفران بنا كرده راستخان

Translation:

Top: O the Opener of the door; indeed He.

L-1 On the date of twenty-fifth of the blessed month of Ramaḍān [in the] year eight hundred and seventy-eight, in the era of Sulṭān Rukn al-Dunyā Dīn wa 'l-Dīn Abū 'l-Muẓaffar Bārbak Shāh al-Sulṭān

L-2 ibn Maḥmūd Shāh al-Sulṭān, may Allah prolong his power and dominion. Rāst Khān Majlis A'lā (the great council), [divine] mercy and forgiveness be on him, built this mosque.

Discussion:

This inscription indicates the extent of Muslim rule during the reign of Bārbak Shāh, which had reached Chittagong at the southernmost tip of Bengal, the most important seaport in the Bay of Bengal at that time.

(73) Masjid inscription in Kalna dated 878 (1473–1474)

ORIGINAL SITE: A ruined mosque in Kalna, Burdwan district, West Bengal. **CURRENT LOCATION:** Indian Museum, Calcutta, inv. no. 15. **MATERIAL, SIZE:** Sandstone; 27 × 14 inches. **STYLE, NO. OF LINES:** *thulth*; four lines. **REIGN:** Sulṭān Bārbak Shāh (864–878/1460–1474). **LANGUAGE:** Arabic. **TYPE:** Commemorative inscription. **PUBLICATIONS:** S. Ahmad, *EIM* (1933–1934): 1–2; Dani, *Bibliography of Muslim Inscriptions*, 42; S. Ahmad, *Inscriptions of Bengal*, 138–40; C. Dutt, *Arabic and Persian Inscriptions in the Indian Museum*, 20; A. Karim, *JASP*, XIII(3) (December 1968): 319–328; Desai, 'Correct Attribution of the Two So-Called Inscriptions of Nasir al-Din Maḥmūd Shāh', *JASBD*, XXIII(1) (April 1978): 11–17; A. Karim, *Corpus of Inscriptions*, 174–179.

Text:

In the middle at the top:

L-1 بسم الله الرحمن الرحيم
الله لا إله إلا هو الحي القيوم لا تأخذه سنة ولا نوم له ما في السبموات <السموات> وما في الأرض من ذا الذي يشفع عنده إلا بإذنه يعلم

L-2 ما بين أيديهم وما خلفهم ولا يحيطون بشيء من علمه إلا بما شاء وسع كرسيه السمواة <السموات> والأرض ولا يؤده حفظهما وهو العلي العظيم

L-3 لا إكراه في الدين قد تبين الرشد من الغي فمن يكفر بالطاغوة <بالطاغوت> ويؤمن بالله فقد استمسك بالعروة الوثقى لا [ا]نفصام لها والله

L-4 سميع عليم بنى هذا المسجد دولت خان ابن حسين خان في عهد السلطان ابن السلطان ناصر أميرالمؤ منين باربك شاه السلطان بادشاه غازي خلد الله ملكه وسلطانه نمقها في التاريخ سنة ثمان و سبعين و ثمانماية

Translation:

In the middle at the top: In the name of Allah, the Most Compassionate and Merciful.

L-1 'Allah; there is no God but He, the Living, the Everlasting. No slumber can seize Him, nor sleep. To Him belongs all that is in the heavens and the earth. Who is there that shall intercede with Him without His permission? He knows

L-2 what lies before them and what is after them, and they cannot comprehend anything of His knowledge except what He wishes. His throne extends over the heavens and the earth and He feels no fatigue in guarding them for He is the All-high and the All-glorious.

L-3 There is no compulsion in the religion, for the truth stands out clearly from misguidance. Whoever rejects evil and brings faith in Allah, he indeed grasps the most trustworthy handclasp that never breaks. Allah

L-4 hears and knows everything' [Qur'ān 2:255–256]. Dawlat Khān ibn Ḥusayn Khān built this mosque during the reign of the sulṭān, son of the sulṭān,

Nāṣir Amīr al-Mu'minīn Bārbak Shāh al-Sulṭān Pādshāh Ghāzī, may Allah perpetuate his kingdom and sovereignty, [he] embellished it on the date, the year eight hundred and seventy-eight.

Discussion:

This epigraphical text inscribed on sandstone has worn away, rendering it difficult to decipher. The portion containing the date of the inscription at the end is particularly unclear. Its conjectural reading places the inscription in the reign of Sulṭān Bārbak Shāh. However, most titles used in the inscription, such as *nāṣir amīr al-mu'minīn* do not appear commonly in Sulṭān Bārbak Shāh's other inscriptions.

(74) An undated inscription from Ghazipur

ORIGINAL SITE: Ghazipur in Uttar Pradesh, India. **CURRENT LOCATION:** State Museum, Lucknow, India. **MATERIAL, SIZE:** Not known. **STYLE, NO. OF LINES:** Monumental *thulth*; two lines. **REIGN:** Bārbak Shāh (864–879/1459–1474). **LANGUAGE:** Arabic. **TYPE:** Foundation inscription. **PUBLICATION:** Y. K. Bukhari, 'Inscriptions from the State Museum, Lakhnow', *EIAPS* (1955–56): 47–48, pl. XII; M. R. Tarafdar, 'Epigraphic and Numismatic Notes Bearing on the History of Pre-Mughal Bengal', *JASBD*, XX(3) (December 1975): 2–3; A. Karim, *Corpus of Inscriptions*, 179–180.

Text:

L-1 . . . . خاناعظم وخاقان معظم مكرم صاحب السيف والقلم
L-2 پهلوى عصر والزمان الغ اقرار خان سلمه الله تعالى فى الدارين . . . .

Translation:

L-1 . . . The sublime khan and the exalted and gracious *khāqān* Ṣāḥib al-Sayf wa 'l-Qalam
L-2 Pahlawī al-'Aṣr wa 'l-Zamān Ulugh Iqrār Khān, may Allah protect him in both worlds . . .

Discussion:

The name of the patron, Iqrār Khān, appears in three more inscriptions from different places during the reign of Bārbak Shāh. Discovery of this inscription in Ghazipur indicates that the territory of the Bengal Sultanate during this period extended in the northwest up to Ghazipur area in the present state of Uttar Pradesh in India.

(75) An unidentified Sultanate masjid inscription from Gaur dated 879 (1474)

ORIGINAL SITE: An unidentified Sultanate masjid in Gaur, Malda district, West Bengal, India. **CURRENT LOCATION:** Affixed to the southern wall of a recently constructed Masjid in the village of Harugram near Gaur. **MATERIAL, SIZE:** Black basalt; 23.5 × 12.5 inches. **STYLE, NO. OF LINES:** Monumental *thulth* in Bengali *ṭughrā'*; one line. **REIGN:** Sulṭān Shams al-Dunyā wa 'l-Dīn Abū 'l-Muẓaffar Yūsuf Shāh (879–886/1474–1481). **LANGUAGE:** Arabic. **TYPE:** Commemorative inscription of a masjid. **PUBLICATION:** Siddiq, 'Calligraphy and Islamic Culture: Reflection on Some New Epigraphic Discoveries in Gaur and Pandua', *Bulletin of the School of Oriental and African Studies*, 68(1) (2005): 21–58; S. Pratip Kumar Mitra, 'Late Dr. Z. A. Desai and the Provisional Study of Some New Inscriptions of the Bengal Sultans', *Indo-Iranica, the Quarterly Organ of the Iran-Society* (Iran Society, Kolkata), 58(3 & 4) (September–December 2005): 26–29.

Text:

قال النبي عليه السلام من بنى مسجدا لله بنى الله تعالى له سبعين قصرا في الجنة بنى هذا المسجد في عهد السلطان شمس الدنيا
والدين أبو المظفر يوسف شاه السلطان ابن باربكشاه السلطان ابن محمود شاه السلطان وقد بنى هذا المسجد الملك المعظم المكرم
ناظر خان في سنة تسع وسبعين وثمانماية

Translation:

The Prophet, peace be upon him, said, 'Whosoever builds a mosque for the sake of Allah, Allah, the exalted, will build for him seventy palaces in Paradise.' This masjid was built during the era of Sulṭān Shams al-Dunyā wa 'l-Dīn Abū 'l-Muẓaffar Yūsuf Shāh al-Sulṭān, son of Sulṭān Bārbak Shāh al-Sulṭān, son of Maḥmūd Shāh al-Sulṭān. Al-Malik al-Mu'aẓẓam al-Mukarram Nāẓir Khān built this masjid in the year eight-hundred-and-seventy-nine (CE 1474).

Discussion:

This inscription belongs to the period of Shams al-Dunyā wa 'l-Dīn abū 'l-Muẓaffar Yusuf Shāh who ruled Bengal for about six years (879–886/1474–1481). He was the third ruler in the line of the restored Ilyās Shāhī dynasty (841–993/1437–1487). The last few words, containing important historical clues, namely the date, have been damaged with the passage of time. Therefore, my reading of the date at the end of the text of this inscription is conjectural.

(76) Faqīr Muḥammad Masjid inscription in Shank Mohan dated 879 (1474)

ORIGINAL SITE: An unnamed Sultanate mosque in the locality known as Shank Mohan (Shaykh Maḥalla) in the old quarters of Malda town in West

Bengal. **CURRENT LOCATION:** Probably in situ. **MATERIAL, SIZE:** Black basalt; 30 × 66 inches. **STYLE, NO. OF LINES:** Not known. **REIGN:** Sulṭān Yūsuf Shāh (879–886/1474–1481). **LANGUAGE:** Arabic. **TYPE:** Foundation inscription. **PUBLICATION:** Blochmann, *JASB*, XLIII (1874): 297–298; Cunningham, *ASR*, 15: 77–78; Beverage, 'Khurshid-i-Jahan-Numa of Sayyid Ilahi Baksh', *JASB*, LXIV (1895): 199–200; A. A. Khan, *Memoirs of Gaur*, 147–148; Dani, *Bibliography of Muslim Inscriptions*, 29, no. 44; S. Ahmad, *Inscriptions of Bengal*, 92–94; A. Karim, *Corpus of Inscriptions*, 192–194.

Text:

قال النبي صلى الله عليه وسلم من بنى مسجدا لله بنى الله له قصرا في الجنة مثله بني بأمر السلطان شمس الدنيا والدين
أبو<أبي> المظفريوسف شاه بن باربك شاه ابن محمود شاه السلطان خلد الله ملكه وسلطنته هذا المسجد . . الملك .
. في التاريخ . غرة جمادى الأولى سنة [تسع و ؟] سبعين وثمانماية

Translation:

The Prophet, peace and blessings of Allah be upon him, said, 'Whoever builds a mosque for the sake of Allah, Allah will build for him a palace in Paradise.' This mosque was built by the order of the Sulṭān Shams al-Dunyā wa 'l-Dīn Abū 'l-Muẓaffar Yūsuf Shāh ibn Bārbak Shāh ibn Maḥmūd Shāh the Sulṭān, may Allah prolong his dominion and power.... al-Malik ... on the date first of Jumād al-Ūlā, year eight hundred seventy [nine] ... [1474].

(77) Inscription of an unnamed Sultanate masjid near Gaur dated 879 (1474)

ORIGINAL SITE: An unidentified Sultanate mosque near Gaur. **CURRENT LOCATION:** Gaur Social Welfare Mission Museum. **MATERIAL, SIZE:** Black basalt; 6.5 × 42 inches. **STYLE, NO. OF LINES:** Local Bihārī style; two lines. **REIGN:** Sulṭān Yūsuf Shāh (879–886/1474–1481). **LANGUAGE:** Arabic. **TYPE:** Foundation inscription. **PUBLICATION:** Blochmann, *JASB*, XLIII (1874): 297–298; Cunningham, *ASR*, 15: 77–78; Beverage, 'Khurshid-i-Jahan-Numa of Sayyid Ilahi Baksh', *JASB*, LXIV (1895): 199–200; A. A. Khan, *Memoirs of Gaur*, 147–148; Dani, *Bibliography of Muslim Inscriptions*, 29, no. 44; S. Ahmad, *Inscriptions of Bengal*, 92–94; A. Karim, *Corpus of Inscriptions*, 192–194.

Text:

L-1 بسم الله الرحمن الرحيم لا إله إلا الله ليقول العبد في بد{ى}ء الامال لتوحيد بنظم آلاء الله الخالق مولانا قدير
وموصوف بأوصاف الكمال

L-2 صفات الذات جلال الدنيا والدين . . بركات <ة> اين مهر شاهان مصر ذوانفصال هو الحي القيوم .
. عنايت مجلس الشرف ليست عين جنات بالمحال تمت هذا المسجد مجلس الشرف . هم الرجل شايعاً بالنظم في
عهد فيروز . شهر مبارك شهر رمضان سنة تسع وسبعين وثمانماية

Translation:

L-1 In the name of Allah, the Compassionate, the Merciful. There is no God but Allah. The servant says in Bad'i 'l-'Amāl (lit. in the beginning of the hopes) that ... and the One who is attributed with the qualifications of perfection...

L-2 ...He is the Living and Everlasting ... Janāb-i-Majlis al-Sharf (i.e. his excellency of the council of honour) ... the fountain of bounties ... Majlis al-Sharf built this mosque ... the man ... in the blessed month of Ramaḍān in the year eight hundred and seventy-nine.

Discussion:

This inscription as well as the previous inscription were found by Westmacott in the 1870s affixed to an old mosque known as Shank Mohan Masjid in an old quarter of Malda town, known as Shaykh Mahalla in West Bengal. After the collapse of the old mosque, a new mosque was built on the same site. The present inscription remained in the courtyard of the new mosque, somewhat neglected. Around CE 2000, the inscription was moved to Gaur Social Welfare Museum for preservation by its curator Sadeq Shaykh. The text of the inscription could not be deciphered satisfactorily because the writing was badly damaged in a number of places. Part of the date (the number تسع) has been conjecturally read, based on the reign of Sulṭān Yusuf Shāh's rule which started in the year 879 (1474). The inscription records the title of a popular theology book of Ḥanafī *'Aqīda* (foundational theological doctrines) *Bad'i 'l-'Amāl*, which suggests that the Ḥanafī school of *fiqh* was quite popular in the country from the very beginning of the consolidation of Islam in the region.

(78) Masjid inscription from Sultanganj dated 879 (1474)

ORIGINAL SITE: An unnamed mosque in Sultanganj village (bordering Jahanabad), four miles west of Godagari police station, Rajshahi district, Bangladesh. **CURRENT LOCATION:** Varendra Research Museum, inv. no. 2661. **MATERIAL, SIZE:** Black basalt; 25 × 12 inches. **STYLE, NO. OF LINES:** *ijāza* in Bengali *ṭughrā'* style; two lines. **REIGN:** Sulṭān Yūsuf Shāh (879–886/1474–1481). **LANGUAGE:** Arabic. **TYPE:** Foundation inscription of a mosque. **PUBLICATION:** Dani, *Bibliography of Muslim Inscriptions*, 29; S. Ahmad, *Inscriptions of Bengal*, 94–96; A. Karim, *Corpus of Inscriptions*, 181–182.

Text:

L-1 قال النبي عليه السلام من بنى مسجدا بنى الله تعالى [له] سبعين قصرا في الجنة بنى هذا المسجد في عهد السلطان ابن السلطان نبن <ابن> السلطان

L-2 شمس الدنيا والدين أبو <أبي> المظفر يوسف شاه ابن باربكشاه سلطان نبن <ابن>محمود شاه سلطان بنا كرده خان معظم خاقان أعظم الغ صوفيخان بتاريخ تسع وسبعين وثمانماية

The vertical line on the right: و يسبح الرعد بحمده والملائكة من خيفته (13:13)

The vertical line on the left: لا إله إلا الله محمد رسول الله

Translation:

L-1 The Prophet, peace be on him, said, 'Whoever builds a mosque, Allah, the Exalted, will build for him a palace in Paradise.' This mosque was built in the era of the sulṭān son of the sulṭān son of the sulṭān

L-2 Shams al-Dunyā wa 'l-Dīn Abū 'l-Muẓaffar Yūsuf Shāh ibn Bārbak Shāh Sulṭān ibn Maḥmūd Shāh Sulṭān. The great khan, the exalted *khāqān*, Ulugh Ṣufī Khān built it on the date [in the year] eight hundred and seventy-nine.

On the right: The thunder glorifies His praise and [so do] the angels in his fear [Qur'ān 13:13].

On the left: There is no God but Allah and Muḥammad is Allah's messenger

Discussion:

Among the properly dated inscriptions from the reign of Sulṭān Yusuf Shah that have been discoverd so far, this one seems to be the earliest.

(79) Masjid inscription from Puruya dated 880 (1475)

ORIGINAL SITE: An unnamed Sultanate mosque in Puruya near Pandua in Malda district, West Bengal. **CURRENT LOCATION:** Not known. **MATERIAL, SIZE:** Not known. **STYLE, NO. OF LINES:** Not known. **REIGN:** Sulṭān Yūsuf Shāh (879–886/1474–1481). **LANGUAGE:** Arabic. **TYPE:** Foundation inscription. **PUBLICATION:** Franklin, *Journal of a Route from Rajmahal to Gour* (MS no. 19 in India Office Library): 12.

Text:

لا إله إلا الله قال النبي صلى الله عليه وسلم من بنى مسجدا لله بنى الله له قصرا في الجنة بنى هذا المسجد السلطان العادل الباذل
شمس الدنيا والدين أبو المظفر يوسف شاه السلطان بن باربك شاه بن السلطان محمود شاه السلطان خلد الله ملكه وسلطانه
وأعلى الله أمره وشانه في مجلس الدين هو أعلى المجالس كان ذلك الباب في التاريخ يوم الجمعة أربعة وعشرين شهر رجب سنة
ثمانين وثمانماية من هجرة النبي صلى الله عليه وسلم

Translation:

There is no God but Allah. The Prophet, peace and the blessings of Allah be upon him, said, 'Whoever builds a mosque for the sake of Allah, Allah will build for him a palace in Paradise.' The just and benevolent Sulṭān Shams al-Dunyā wa 'l-Dīn Abū 'l-Muẓaffar Yusuf Shāh al-Sulṭān, ibn Bārbak Shāh al-Sulṭān, ibn Maḥmud Shāh al-Sulṭān, may Allah make his kingdom and his authority everlasting and promote his status and prestige, built this mosque. [In the time of] Majlis al-Dīn, who holds the highest nobility, that the gate was built, on the date: the day of Friday, the twenty-fourth of the month of Rajab, in the year eight hundred and eighty from the Hijra of the Prophet, peace and blessings of Allah be upon him.

Discussion:

This inscription is not mentioned in any other sources. Franklin saw it affixed to the miḥrāb of a mosque in the compound of the mausoleum of Shaykh Nūr Quṭub al-'Ālam in Puruya near Pandua in Malda district. Perhaps he took it with him to England along with other antiquities. Unfortunately, no other information is available about this transcription.

(80) Inscription of a religious edifice in Pichhli Gangarampur, Malda dated 881 (1476)

ORIGINAL SITE: An unnamed religious edifice in Pichhli Gangarampur village near a meander of Kalindri river, about ten kilometres northwest of Malda town, West Bengal. **CURRENT LOCATION:** B. T. College, Malda town. **MATERIAL, SIZE:** Probably basalt; 35.5 × 18 inches. **STYLE, NO. OF LINES:** Upper panel as well as first section on the right side of lower panel in Bihari style executed in the traditional Bengali *ṭughrā'* decorative pattern while the rest of the lower panel in *ijāza* of a local variety; two major lines (panels). **REIGN:** Sulṭān Yusuf Shāh (879–886/1474–1481). **LANGUAGE:** Arabic and Persian. **TYPE:** Commemorative inscription of a religious edifice. **PUBLICATION:** *Annual Report on Indian Epigraphy for 1987–88*, no. 193 (New Delhi, 1999): 75; S. P. K. Mitra, 'Z. A. Desai and the Provisional Study of Some New Inscriptions', *Indo-Iranica*, (Kolkata), 58(3 & 4) (September-December 2005): 22–26.

Figure 6.7 Commemorative inscription (Pichhli Gangarampur village, west of Malda town, West Bengal) (source: Archaeological Survey of India).

Text:

Upper (main) line:

[السلطا]ن[ا]بن السلطان ابن السلطان شمس الدنيا والدين أبوالمظفر يوسف شاه سلطان ابن باربكشاه سلطان نبن محمود شاه
سلطان خلد الله ملكه وسلطانه و أعلى أمره وشأنه وأعزّ جنده وبرهانه بناه معالي السراج دخولي قطب الأ[مراء]و ز

Right side of lower line (first panel):

[حفظ]الله تعالى أهل البنغ من الفساد وسرد ذلك إلى يوم التناد وتمّ في يوم العاشر من جماد الأخرى لسنة إحدى وثمانين وثمانماية

Middle panel of lower line:

التاريخ المثنوي
بالتوحيد البا[ر] ي
ونعت النبي
ومدح الأمر وثناء
العام الكاتب القائم
[لـ]كل بادشاه

Second half on the left side of lower line (last panel):

از خدائی خالق أرض وسماء بر وبحر وكوه هامون وها<هوا>   مسجد و محراب و [منبر]
مرسل إنس مقتدى أو مقتدا ز أمرحق آمد أساس دين نهاد   اين خرا ب اباد ا زو
داد فرمان ودين أحمدي   تا أساسي نو برار د سرمدي   كوتوال شهر ملك[بنگال؟]– –

Translation:

Upper (main) line:
[The sulṭā]n – son of the sulṭān – son of the Sulṭān Shams al-Dunyā wa 'l-Dīn Abū 'l-Muẓaffar Yusuf Shāh Sulṭān ibn Bārbak Shāh Sulṭān ibn Maḥmūd Shāh Sulṭān, may Allah make his kingdom and authority everlasting, and exalt his status and prestige and strengthen his army and authority. His highness Sirāj al-Dakhūlī (Chief of Internal Affairs), Quṭb al-Umarā' (the pole of the chiefs), built this (masjid?).

Right side of lower line (first panel):
May the Almighty Allah save the inhabitants of Bang (Bengal) from turmoil; and may it sustain till the day of judgement. It was completed on the tenth day of Jumād al-'Ukhra in the year eight hundred and eighty-one (30 September 1476).

Middle panel of lower line:
The codified date in verses, through (the blessing of) the unity of the Creator, and the praise of the Prophet, and the appreciation of the work, and the admiration of the year, the ever-alert scribe for every monarch.

Second half on the left side of lower line (last panel):
From the God, the creator of the earth and the heaven

The land and the sea and the mountain and the desert and the air
Mosque, miḥrāb (and minbar [pulpit])
The Prophet for the followers and the followed ones among human being
The divinely ordained foundation of the religion was laid down
May this wild region be inhabited through His (grace)
He (God) issued the decree (that imbued) the splendour of the religion of Aḥmad (the Prophet Muḥammad)
So that a new enduring habitation may evolve (down the line)
(Issued by the) Kotwāl of the city, Malik

Discussion:

Discovered by Shri Kamal Basak of B. T. College, Malda towards the end of 1976, the present inscription seems to be the central part of a quite large inscription of the period as some texts are clearly missing on both right as well as left sides. The incomplete Persian metrical verses on the lower left of the last panel indicate the loss of at least three more verses that seemingly completed the existing three halves of hemistiches in the original rhythmic scheme of the text. The use of Persian for epigraphic texts in Bengal remained somewhat limited during the Sultanate period. Thus the Persian text in this inscription is in a way a departure from common practice of the period.

There are clear indications in the text (such as the words *masjid* and *miḥrāb* in the last panel) that the inscription belonged to a large religious complex of a newly built city, not far from Gaur and Pandua. But what makes it more interesting is that this is one of the earliest inscriptions to mention the name *Bang* (the early name of Bengal). The epigraphic text also indicates the efforts of the Muslim rulers of the region to legitimize their rule through proclamation of their Islamic mission in the face of the constant challenges (as indicated through the use of the word الفساد [lit. turmoil]) that the newly evolving political establishment was encountering during this period from outside as well as from inside.

While the calligraphy of the upper line as well as the first panel (on the right) of the lower line indicates that it was executed by an accomplished artist, the rest of the writing on the left side of the lower line seems to be completed unprofessionally by an unskilful local scribe as it contains some orthographic sloppiness and calligraphic mediocrity.

(81) Masjid inscription in Gaigharh in Sylhet dated 881 (1476)

ORIGINAL SITE: Khojar Masjid (Mosque of the Eunuch) in the Mauza of Gaigharh, three miles southwest of Maulvi Bazar district in Sylhet Division, Bangladesh. **CURRENT LOCATION:** Probably in situ. **MATERIAL, SIZE:** Not known. **STYLE, NO. OF LINES:** Not known. **REIGN:** Sulṭān Yūsuf Shāh (879–886/1474–1481). **LANGUAGE:** Arabic. **TYPE:** Commemorative inscription. **PUBLICATION:** Sayyid Murtaḍā ʻAlī, *Ḥaḍrat Shāh Jalāl O Sileter Itihās*, 207.

Text:

قال الله تعالى . . . و قال النبي صلى الله عليه وسلم من بنى مسجدا في الدنيا بنى الله له سبعين قصرا في الجنة بنى هذا المسجد في عهد السلطان شمس الدنيا والدين [أبو المظفر] يوسف شاه بن باربكشاه السلطان بن محمود شاه السلطان وباني هذا المسجد الوزير المشهور مجلس العالم بن موسي بن حاجي أمير في سنة واحد وثمانين وثمانماية الهجرية

Translation:

Allah the Exalted said,… and the Prophet, peace and the blessings of Allah be on him, [said,] 'Whoever builds a mosque in the world, Allah will build for him seventy palaces in Paradise.' Sulṭān Shams al-Dunyā wa 'l-Dīn [Abū 'l-Muẓaffar] Yūsuf Shāh ibn Bārbak Shāh al-Sulṭān ibn Maḥmūd Shāh al-Sulṭān built this mosque. The builder of this mosque was the famous vizier Majlis al-'Ālam, the son of Mūsā ibn Ḥājī Amīr; in the year eight hundred and eighty-one Hijra.

Discussion:

The walls and façades of this dilapidated mosque are richly decorated with various decorative motifs commonly found in the ancient and medieval Hindu temples in the area.

(82) A Masjid inscription at the mausoleum complex of Shāh Shafī' al-Dīn in Hoogly dated 882 (1477)

ORIGINAL SITE: An unnamed Sultanate mosque in Chhoto Panduah in Hoogly district, West Bengal, India. **CURRENT LOCATION:** Affixed to the central arch of the tomb of Shāh Shafī 'al-Dīn in the same town. **MATERIAL, SIZE:** Probably grey basalt; unknown. **STYLE, NO. OF LINES:** *naskh* in Bengali *ṭughrā'*; four lines. **REIGN:** Sulṭān Yusuf Shāh (879–886/1474–1481). **LANGUAGE:** Arabic. **TYPE:** Commemorative inscription. **PUBLICATION:** Blochmann, *JASB*, XXXIX (1870): 300; idem. *JASB*, XLIV (1875): 275–276, pl. VI (1); Cunningham, *ASR*, 1 (1882): 124–126; Dani, *Bibliography of Muslim Inscriptions*, 30–31; S. Ahmad, *Inscriptions of Bengal*, 97–100; A. Karim, *Corpus of Inscriptions*, 182–184.

Text:

L-1 قال الله تعالى و أن المساجد لله فلا تدعوا مع الله أحدا وقال عليه السلام من بنى مسجدا في الدنيا بنى الله له في الآخرة سبعين قصرا بنى المسجد في عهد {ال}سلطان

L-2 الزمان المؤيد بتأييد الديان خليفة الله بالحجة والبرهان السلطان ابن السلطان ابن السلطان شمس الدنيا والدين أبو <أبي> المظفر يوسف شاه السلطان ابن باربكشاه

L-3 السلطان ابن محمود شاه السلطان خلد الله ملكه وسلطانه بنى هذا {ال} مجلس المجالس مجلس [ال] معظم المكرم صاحب السيف والقلم مهدي العصر والزمان الغ مجلس أعظم سلمه

L-4 الله تعالى في الدارين مؤرخا في اليوم الرابع الغرة من شهر محرم سنة اثني <اثنتي> وثمانين وثمانماية و تمّ <تم> بالخير

Translation:

L-1 Allah the Exalted said, 'Verily the mosques are for Allah, so do not invoke anyone with Allah.' And the Prophet, peace be on him, said, 'Whoever builds a mosque in the world, Allah will build for him a palace in the hereafter.' This mosque was built in the reign of Sulṭān
L-2 al-Zamān, al-Mu'yyad bi Tā'yīd al-Dayyān, Khalīfat Allah bi-'l-Ḥujja wa 'l-Burhān, the sulṭān, son of the sulṭān, son of the sulṭān
L-3 Shams al-Dunyā wa 'l-Dīn Abū 'l-Muẓaffar Yusuf Shāh al-Sulṭān ibn Bārbak Shāh al-Sulṭān ibn Maḥmūd Shāh al-Sulṭān, may Allah make his kingdom and authority everlasting. Majlis al-Majālis (the council of the councils) the sublime and exalted Majlis, Ṣāḥib al-Sayf wa 'l-Qalm (the man of sword and pen), Mahdī al-'Aṣr wa 'l-Zamān (rightly guided of the time and age), Ulugh Majlis A'ẓam, may Allah the Exalted protect him
L-4 in both worlds. Dated Wednesday, the first of the month of Muḥarram, [in] the year eight hundred and eighty-two [15 April 1477]; may it end well.

Discussion:

The Shāh Shafī' al-Dīn mausoleum complex has a number of inscriptions, the most important of which is an inscription dated 882/1477 from the reign of Sulṭān Yusuf Shāh (879–886/1474–1481). In this inscription, the long titles of Ulugh (the builder of the masjid) suggest that he was a noble who held a high position in the state. There are three other undated religious inscriptions in the compound containing mostly religious messages.

(83) Masjid inscription from Gaur dated 883 (1477)

ORIGINAL SITE: Either Chamkatti Masjid or Mahajantola Masjid in Gaur. **CURRENT LOCATION:** British Museum, inv. nos OA+64851/1 and OA+6485/1. **MATERIAL, SIZE:** Black granite; the slab is broken into two pieces – the first (OA+64851/1) is 57 × 20 inches, the second (OA+6485/1) is 46 × 20 inches. **STYLE, NO. OF LINES:** *thulth* in Bengali *ṭughrā'*; one line. **REIGN:** Sulṭān Yūsuf Shāh (879–886/1474–1481). **LANGUAGE:** Arabic. **TYPE:** Commemorative inscription. **PUBLICATION:** W. Franklin, *Journal of a Route from Rajmahal to Gaur* (MS in India Office Library): 8; Shayam Prasad, *Ahwal-i-Gaur wa Pandua*, 17; Creighton, *Ruins of Gaur*, pl. 30; Cunningham, *ASR*, XV (1882): 60–61; Ravenshaw, *Gaur*, 30; Dani, *Bibliography of Muslim Inscriptions*, 30, no. 47; S. Ahmad, *Inscriptions of Bengal*, 96–97; S. M. Hasan, 'Two Bengal Inscriptions in the British Museum', *Journal of the Royal Asiatic Society of Great Britain and Ireland* (October 1966): 141–147; Mohammad Yusuf Siddiq, *al-Nuqūsh al-Kitābiyya 'alā' 'l-'Amā'ir al-Islāmiyya fī 'l-Bangāl*, MA Dissertation, Umm al-Qura University, Makkah, 1984, 89–93; idem., *Darāsāt al-Nuqūsh al-'Arabiyya fī 'l-Hind*, PhD Dissertation, Umm al-Qura University, Makkah, 1987, 97–99; A. Karim, *Corpus of Inscriptions*, 184–185.

Figure 6.8 Commemorative inscription (British Museum, inv. nos OA+64851/1 and OA+6485/1) (source: author's own image).

Text:

قد بنى هذا المسجد الجامع السلطان أعظم المعظم شمس الدنيا والدين أبو المظفر يوسف شاه السلطا[ن] ب[ن]
[بار]بكشاه [ال]سلطان ابن محمود شاه السلطان خلد الله ملكه وسلطانه بتاريخ غرة ماه محرم ثلا[ث] [و]ثمانين وثمانماية

Translation:

L-1 The great sublime Sulṭān Shams al-Dunyā wa 'l-Dīn Abū 'l-Muẓaffar Yūsuf Shāh al-Sulṭān

L-2 ibn Bārbak Shāh al-sulṭān ibn Maḥmūd Shāh al-Sulṭān, may Allah perpetuate his kingdom and his authority, built this congregational mosque dated the first of the month of Muḥarram, [in the year] eight hundred and eighty-three [4 April 1478].

Discussion:

This inscription was taken to England by Major William Franklin along with a number of other inscriptions. There is confusion about its provenance. While some sources attribute it to the Chamkatti Masjid, according to others, the inscription belonged to the Mahajantola Masjid.

(84) Waqf inscription of a Masjid in Tilapara, Sylhet dated 884 (1479)

ORIGINAL SITE: An old Sultanate mosque in Tilapara village of Mukhtarpur Parganah in the district of Sylhet, Bangladesh. **CURRENT LOCATION:** Probably in situ. **MATERIAL, SIZE**: Not known. **STYLE, NO. OF LINES:** Not known. **REIGN:** Sulṭān Yusuf Shāh (879–886/1474–1481). **LANGUAGE:** Arabic. **TYPE:** Endowment inscription. **PUBLICATION:** Sayyid Murtaḍā 'Alī, *Ḥaḍrat Shāh Jalāl O Sileter Itihās*, 207.

Text:

قال الله تعالى و أن المساجد لله [فلا تدعوا مع الله أحدا] وقال عليه السلام من بنى مسجدا في الدنيا بنى الله له قصرا في الجنة
بنى المسجد في عهد السلطان العادل شمس الدنيا والدين [أبي المظفر] يوسف شاه السلطان ابن باربكشاه السلطان ابن محمود
شاه السلطان وبنى هذا المسجد وزيره ملك سكندر مؤرخا في العاشرمن شهر ربيع الأوّل سنة اربع وثمانين وثمانماية الهجرية والذي
يضرّ هذا الوقف او يحاول امتلاكه، فسوف يكون مردودا او مثل ولد الحمار عند الله

Translation:

Allah the Exalted said, 'Verily the mosques are for Allah, [so do not invoke anyone with Allah].' And the Prophet, peace be on him, said, 'Whoever builds a mosque in the world, Allah will build for him a palace in the hereafter.' This mosque was built in the era of the just Sulṭān Shams al-Dunyā wa 'l-Dīn [Abū 'l-Muẓaffar] Yusuf Shāh ibn Bārbak Shāh al-Sulṭān ibn Maḥmūd Shāh al-Sulṭān. It was his vizier, Malik Sikandar, who built it on the tenth of Rabī' al-Awwal of the month of Muḥarram, [in] the year eight hundred and eighty-four. Anyone who harms the endowed property of this mosque or usurps it, in the sight of Allah, he would be like the one rejected or like the progeny of a donkey.

(85) Masjid inscription from Ḥaḍrat Pandua dated 884 (1479)

ORIGINAL SITE: A no longer extant Sultanate mosque in Ḥaḍrat Pandua, Malda. **CURRENT LOCATION:** Indian Museum, Calcutta. **MATERIAL, SIZE:** Not known. **STYLE, NO. OF LINES:** *rayḥānī* in Bengali *ṭughrā'* style; one line. **REIGN:** Sulṭān Yūsuf Shāh (879–886/1474–1481). **LANGUAGE:** Arabic. **TYPE:** Foundation inscription of a masjid. **PUBLICATION:** Blochmann, *JASB*, XLII (1873): 276; Cunningham, *ASR*, XV (1882): 85; Ravenshaw, *Gaur*, 50, no. 5, pl. 47; A. A. Khan, *Memoirs of Gaur*, 116; Dani, *Bibliography of Muslim Inscriptions*, 31–32; S. Ahmad, *Inscriptions of Bengal*, 100–103; Chinmoy Dutt, *Arabic and Persian Inscriptions in the Indian Museum*, 16; A. Karim, *Corpus of Inscriptions*, 185–186.

Text:

قال النبي صلى الله عليه وسلم من بنى مسجدا لله بنى الله له قصرا في الجنة بنى هذا المسجد في زمن السلطان العادل الباذل شمس
الدنيا والدين أبو<أبي> المظفر يوسف شاه سلطان بن باربك شاه سلطان بن محمود شاه سلطان خلد الله ملكه وسلطانه مجلس
المجالس مجلس أعلى أعلاه الله تعالى شانه في الدارين وكان ذلك في التاريخ [من] هجرة النبي صلى الله عليه وسلم في يوم الجمعة
(من) عشرين شهر رجب رجب قدره سنة أربع وثمانين وثمانماية

Translation:

The Prophet, peace and the blessings of Allah be on him, said, 'Whoever builds a mosque for the sake of Allah, Allah will build for him a palace in Paradise.' The mosque was built in the reign of the just and benevolent Sulṭān Shams al-Dunyā wa 'l-Dīn Abū 'l-Muẓaffar Yūsuf Shāh al-Sulṭān ibn Bārbak Shāh al-Sulṭān ibn Maḥmūd Shāh al-Sulṭān, may Allah make his kingdom and authority everlasting, [by] Majlis wa Majālis Majlis A'lā', may Allah the Exalted make his position high in both abodes. And this took place on the date of the Hijra of the Prophet, peace and blessing of Allah be upon him, on Friday, the twentieth of the month of Rajab whose position is distinguished, [in the] year eight hundred and eighty-four [7 October 1479].

Discussion:

Though a mosque inscription, it was found fixed on the east wall of the kitchen of Shaykh Nūr Quṭub al-ʻĀlam at Pandua. The actual name of patron is not mentioned in this epigraphic text. His title *majlis al-majālis majlis aʻlā'* (council of the councils of highest council), however, suggests that he was an influential official of the royal court.

(86) Masjid inscription in Shāh Jalāl Mausoleum in Sylhet from the reign of Yusuf Shāh dated 884 (1479)

ORIGINAL SITE: A no longer extant masjid in *Dighi* Mahalla quarter near the mausoleum of Shāh Jalāl in Sylhet city, Bangladesh. **CURRENT LOCATION:** Affixed to the outer side of the northern wall of a mosque within the mausoleum complex of Shāh Jalāl in Sylhet, Bangladesh. **MATERIAL, SIZE:** Black basalt; 52 × 16 inches. **STYLE, NO. OF LINES:** Monumental *thulth* in Bengali *ṭughrā'*; one line. **REIGN:** Sulṭān Yusuf Shāh (879–886/1474–1481). **LANGUAGE:** Arabic. **TYPE:** Commemorative inscription. **PUBLICATION:** Blochmann, *JASB*, XLII (1873): 277–281; Dani, *Bibliography of Muslim Inscriptions*, 29; S. Ahmad, *Inscriptions of Bengal*, 109–112; A. Karim, *Corpus of Inscriptions*, 194; Sayyid Murtaḍā ʻAlī, *Ḥaḍrat Shāh Djalāl O Sileter Itihās* (Dhaka, 1988): 207.

Text:

قال الله تعالى وان المساجد لله وقال النبي صلى الله عليه وسلم من بنى مسجدا لله بنى الله له قصرا في الجنة قد بنى هذا المسجد الجامع السلطان العادل شمس الدنيا والدين أبو المظفر يوسف شاه السلطان بن باربكشاه السلطان بن محمود شاه السلطان خلد الله ملكه وسلطانه وباني هذا المسجد المجلس الأعظم والمعظم الدستور الساعي في الخيرات والمبرات المجلس الأعلى حفظه الله تعالى عن الآفات والعاهات و تمّ بناء الدّار في شهر ربيع الآخر سنة أربع وثمانين وثمانماية من الهجرية النبوية

Translation:

Allah, the exalted, said, 'Surely all the mosques belong to Allah.' The Prophet, peace and the blessings of Allah be on him, said, 'Whoever builds a mosque for the sake of Allah, Allah will build for him a palace in Paradise.' The just Sulṭān, Shams al-Dunyā wa 'l-Dīn Abū 'l-Muẓaffar Yusuf Shāh al-Sulṭān ibn Bārbak Shāh al-Sulṭān ibn Maḥmūd Shāh al-Sulṭān constructed this congregational mosque. The builder of this mosque is al-Majlis al-Aʻẓam wa 'l-Muʻẓẓam al-Dastūr al-Sāʻī fi 'l-khayrāt wa 'l-mubirrāt al-Majlis al-Aʻla'. May Allah the exalted save him from troubles and grieves. Construction of this edifice was completed in the month of Rabīʻ al-Ākhir in the year eight hundred and eighty-four Hijra.

Discussion:

Sayyid Murtaḍā ʻAlī mentions several other inscriptions that exist in the present division of Sylhet, including those which are found in the compound of Shāh

Jalāl's mausoleum. The provenance of such a large number of Islamic inscriptions and the spread of mosque architecture in the area indicate the gradual rooting of Islam at the grassroots level in this easternmost corner of Bengal. Details of these inscriptions are discussed in several other places of this book.

(87) Darsbari Masjid and Madrasa inscription from 'Umarpur dated 884 (1479)

ORIGINAL SITE: A Masjid and Madrasa complex near the village of 'Umarpur in the vicinity of Gaur. **CURRENT LOCATION:** Indian Museum, Calcutta, inv. no. 3239. **MATERIAL, SIZE:** Black basalt; 41 × 27 inches. **STYLE, NO. OF LINES:** *thulth* in Bengali *ṭughrā'*; one line. **REIGN:** Sulṭān Yūsuf Shāh (879–886/1474–1481). **LANGUAGE:** Arabic. **TYPE:** Commemorative inscription. **PUBLICATION:** Beveridge, 'Khurshīd-i-Jahān-Numa of Sayyid Ilahi Baksh', *JASB*, LXIV (1895): 222–223; Cunningham, *ASR*, XV (1882): 76, pl. XXII; Ravenshaw, *Gaur*, 76, pl. 49; A. A. Khan, *Memoirs of Gaur*, 76–77, pl. III; Dani, *Bibliography of Muslim Inscriptions*, 31; S. Ahmad, *Inscriptions of Bengal*, 104–106; Chinmoy Dutt, *Arabic and Persian Inscriptions in the Indian Museum*, 17; A. Karim, *Corpus of Inscriptions*, 186–188.

Text:

قال الله تعالى وأن المساجد لله فلا تدعوا مع الله احدا وقال النبي صلى الله عليه وسلم من بنى مسجدا لله بنى الله له قصرا في الجنة
مثله قد بنى هذا المسجد الجامع السلطان الأعدل الأعظم مالك الرقاب والأمم السلطان بن السلطان بن السلطان شمس الدنيا
والدين أبو المظفر يوسف شاه السلطان بن باربكشاه السلطان بن محمود شاه السلطان خلد الله ملكه وسلطانه وأفاض على
العالمين إحسانه وبره في سنة أربع وثمانين وثمانماية الهجرية

Translation:

Allah the Exalted said, 'Verily the mosques are for Allah, so do not invoke anyone with Allah.' And the Prophet, peace and blessing of Allah be on him, said, 'Whoever builds a mosque for the sake of Allah, Allah will build for him the same in Paradise.' The just and great sulṭān, Mālik al-Riqāb wa 'l-'Umam, the sulṭān, son of the sulṭān, son of the sulṭān, Shams al-Dunyā wa 'l-Dīn Abū 'l-Muẓaffar Yūsuf Shāh al-Sulṭān ibn Bārbak Shāh al-Sulṭān ibn Maḥmūd Shāh al-Sulṭān, may Allah make his kingdom and authority everlasting and fill the universe with his generosity and benevolence, built this congregational mosque in the year eight hundred and eighty-four hijra.

Discussion:

Munshī Ilāhi Bakhsh found this inscription in a large dilapidated brick mosque near the village of 'Umarpur in the vicinity of Gaur. The entire complex, of which the mosque formed an important part, was known as *Darsbari* (the house for education). Its madrasa inscription is dated 909/1503.

(88) Sona Masjid inscription dated 885 (1480)

ORIGINAL SITE: Sona Masjid (Golden mosque) probably in Gaur, in the district of Malda. **CURRENT LOCATION:** British Museum. **MATERIAL, SIZE:** Black basalt slab; broken into five pieces; the first portion (inv. no. OA+6416) is 19 × 6 inches, second portion (inv. no. OA+6017 EA) is 23 × 19 inches, third portion (inv. no. OA+6017 EA) is: 19 × 17 inches, fourth portion (inv. no. OA+6414) is 19 × 10 inches, fifth portion (inv. no. OA+6414) is 39 × 19 inches. **STYLE, NO. OF LINES:** *thulth* in Bengali *ṭughrā'* decorative feature; one line. **REIGN:** Sulṭān Yūsuf Shāh (879–886/1474–1481). **LANGUAGE:** Arabic. **TYPE:** Commemorative inscription. **PUBLICATION:** Ravenshaw, *Gaur*, 56; Franklin, *Journal of a Route from Rajmahal to Gour* (MS no. 19 in India Office Library): 7; S. M. Hasan, *Glimpses of Muslim Art and Architecture*, 12; Siddiq, *al-Nuqūsh al-Kitābiyya 'alā' 'l-'Amā'ir al-Islāmiyya fī 'l-Bangāl*, MA Dissertation, Umm al-Qura University, Makkah, 1984, 79–83; A. Karim, *Corpus of Inscriptions*, 191–92; Siddiq, 'Arabic Calligraphy in the Early Inscriptions', *Muslim Education Quarterly*, 2(3) (1985): 77–88.

Text:

السلطان الأعظم المعظم السلطان ابن السلطان ابن السلطان شمس الدنيا والدين أبو المظفر يوسف شاه ابن السلطان باربكشاه
ابن السلطان محمود شاه السلطان خلد الله ملكه وسلطانه تاريخ يوم الإثنين أربعة عشر في شهر محرم سنة خمس وثمانين وثمانماية

Translation:

The sublime and great sulṭān, al-Sulṭān ibn al-Sulṭān ibn al-Sulṭān Shams al-Dunyā wa 'l-Dīn Abū 'l-Muẓaffar Yūsuf Shāh, son of the Sulṭān Bārbak Shāh, son of the Sulṭān Maḥmūd Shāh, the sulṭān, may Allah make his kingdom and authority everlasting, on the date Monday, the fourteen of the month of Muḥarram, the year eight hundred and eighty-five [27 March 1480].

Discussion:

Ravenshaw attributed this inscription to a place known as Purua (near Pandua). According to Franklin, however, this inscription belonged to Sona Masjid or Golden Mosque (probably nearby Gaur), Malda, which seems to be more plausible. On the raised border of one fragment of this stone inscription, we find an engraving in Roman characters which says, 'Presented by Colonel Franklin'. This suggests that the inscription was brought to England by Major Franklin, who gave it to the British Museum. The bold *thulth* calligraphy of this inscription is outstanding.

(89) Tantipara Masjid inscription in Gaur dated 885 (1481)

ORIGINAL SITE: Tantipara masjid in Gaur. **CURRENT LOCATION:** Fixed over the doorway of the courtyard of the Qadam Rasul Shrine in Gaur.

MATERIAL, SIZE: Black basalt; 28 × 13 inches. **STYLE, NO. OF LINES:** *naskh*; two lines. **REIGN:** Sulṭān Yūsuf Shāh (879–886/1474–1481). **LANGUAGE:** Arabic. **TYPE:** Foundation inscription. **PUBLICATION:** Blochmann, *JASB*, XLII (1873): 277; Beveridge, *JASB*, LXIV (1895): 217–218; Cunningham, *ASR*, XV (1882): 61–62; Ravenshaw, *Gaur*, 22, pl. 48; P. Horn, *Epigraphia Indica*, II: 284; A. A. Khan, *Memoirs of Gaur*, 62–63; Dani, *Bibliography of Muslim Inscriptions*, 32; S. Ahmad, *Inscriptions of Bengal*, 106–108; S. M. Hasan, *Glimpses of Muslim Art and Architecture*, 10–12; A. Karim, *Corpus of Inscriptions*, 188–189.

Text:

L-1 قال النبي صلى الله عليه وسلم من بنى مسجدا لله بنى الله تعالى له سبعين قصرا في الجنة بنى هذا المسجد في عهد
السلطان ابن السلطان ابن السلطان شمس الدنيا والدين أبو <أبي> المظفر

L-2 يوسف شاه السلطان ابن باربكشاه السلطان ابن محمود شاه السلطان بنى هذا المسجد خان أعظم وخاقان معظم
مرصاد خان اتابك رايت أعلى بتاريخ هزدهم ماه مبارك رمضان سنة خمس وثمانين وثمانماية

Translation:

L-1 The Prophet, peace and the blessings of Allah be upon him, said, 'Whoever builds a mosque for the sake of Allah, Allah the Exalted will build for him seventy palaces in Paradise.' The mosque was built in the era of the sulṭān son of the sulṭān son of the sulṭān Shams al-Dunyā wa 'l Dīn Abū 'l-Muẓaffar

L-2 Yūsuf Shāh al-Sulṭān ibn Bārbak Shāh al-Sulṭān ibn Maḥmūd Shāh al-Sulṭān. The great khān and sublime *khāqān* Mirṣād Khān Atābak Ra'yat-i-A'lā (lit. the guardian of the exalted banner) built this mosque on the date of eighteen of the blessed month of Ramaḍān [in the] year eight hundred and eighty-five [21 November 1480].

Discussion:

The builder of this mosque, Mirṣād Khān, in this inscription has been given the title *Atābak Ra'yat-i-A'lā* (guardian of the exalted banner). This is a rare title in the inscriptions of Bengal. It appears that Mirṣād Khān held the high office of keeper of the royal standard in the government.

(90) A Sultanate inscription from the Khānqāh of Shāh Baghdādi in Mirpur dated 885 (1480)

ORIGINAL SITE: An unnamed Sultanate mosque near the mausoleum of Shāh Baghdādi in Mirpur near Dhaka, Bangladesh. **CURRENT LOCATION:** Fixed slightly above a later Persian inscription dated 1221 (1806) in the mausoleum of Shāh Baghdādī in Mirpur near Dhaka. **MATERIAL, SIZE:** Black basalt; 42 × 24 inches. **STYLE, NO. OF LINES:** *thulth* in Bengali *ṭughrā'* with some features of Bihārī style of calligraphy; three lines. **REIGN:** Yūsuf Shāh (879–886/1474–1489). **LANGUAGE, METER:** Main text in Arabic; the Persian couplet at the end in *baḥr Mutaqārib* (فعولن فعولن فعولن فعول). **TYPE:** Commemorative inscription of a mosque. **PUBLICATION:** Blochmann, *JASB*, XLIV (1875): 293–294; Dani, *Bibliography of Muslim Inscriptions*, 32 and 124; S. Ahmad, *Inscriptions of Bengal*, 108–109; A. Karim, *Corpus of Inscriptions*, 189–191.

Text:

Upper panel:

قال الله تعالى إنما يعمر مساجد الله من آمن بالله واليوم الآخر وأقام الصلاة وآتى الزكاة ولم يخش إلا الله فعسى أولئك أن
يكونوا من المهتدين قال النبي عليه السلام من بنى مسجدا في الدنيا بنى الله له سبعين بيتا في الجنة

Lower panel:

L-1 بانى هذا المسجد في عهد {ال} سلطان السلاطين ظل الله في العالمين خليفة الله في الأرضين الأ عظم والمعظم السلطان
ابن السلطان ابن السلطان شمس الدنيا والدين أبو<أبي> المظفر يوسف شاه السلطان ابن باربكشاه السلطان ابن
محمود شاه السلطان خلد الله ملكه وسلطانه وأعلى أمره وشأنه الملك الأعظم

L-2 . . . خاقان المعظم پهلوي العصر والزمان . . و الصلاة و السلام علي محمد النبي و آله [و صحبه أجمعين]
مؤرخا في التاريخ سنة خمس وثمانين وثمانماية
كسى راكه خيرى بماند روان   دمادم رسد رحمتش برروان

Translation:

Upper panel:

Allah the Great said, ‘Mosques of Allah are inhabited only by those who believe in Allah and the last day and establish prayer and offer prescribed charity and fear none but Allah; it is they who are expected to be truly guided’ [Qur’ān 9:18]. The Prophet, peace be upon him, said, ‘Whomsoever builds a mosque, Allah will build for him seventy houses in Paradise.’

Lower panel:

L-1 During the period of the king of kings, Ẓill Allah fī ’l-‘Alamīn (i.e. shadow of Allah among the creatures), Khalīfat Allah fī ’l-Arḍayn (i.e. vicegerent of Allah in the worlds), the mightiest and the respected one, the sulṭān, son of the sulṭān [who was also] son of a sulṭān, Shams al-Dunyā wa ’l-Dīn, Abū ’l-Muẓaffar Yūsuf Shāh al-Sulṭān, son of Bārbak Shāh the sulṭān, son of Maḥmūd Shāh the sulṭān, may Allah perpetuate his kingdom and rule and elevate his affairs and status. The builder of this mosque is the greatest malik,…

L-2 the honourable *khāqān*,… Pahlawī al-‘Aṣr wa ’l-Zamān (i.e. Pahlawī of the time and the age),… the blessing and peace be on Muḥammad, the Prophet and his family … (It was) dated as a day in the year eight hundred and eighty-five.

Allah's mercy reaches every moment to the soul of the one,
Whose benevolent works continue producing good even after him.

Discussion:

This is the main inscription of a Sultanate mosque that disappeared long ago. Currently, the inscription is affixed above a Persian inscription (dated 1221/1806) on an inner wall of the mausoleum of Shāh Baghdādi in Mirpur near Dhaka.

The present inscription is a typical fifteenth century Sultanate inscription of Bengal, where a long text is crowded into a relatively short space. In addition, the forms of the letters are often twisted into the Bengali *ṭughrā'* style. There are several floral and foliated motifs blended harmoniously into the calligraphic design. One such flower-like motif is quite apparent at the end of the Qur'ānic verse in the first line. The heart-shaped motif inside the letter *nūn*, the last letter of the same Qur'ānic verse, can also be seen in many other Bengali inscriptions of this period. Another foliated motif is entwined with the letters *lām-alif* of the word *al-salāt* in the same verse. There is also a chain-like motif on the top of the letter *qāf*, the very first letter of the first line. The complex calligraphic layout of the inscription renders the text difficult to decipher.

The surface of the slab is divided into two equal parts by a raised border. The upper half has a single line of writing containing a Qur'ānic verse and a *ḥadīth* which are separated by a raised vertical line. The lower half is further divided into two lines of writing much smaller in size than the upper half, and correspondingly more difficult to decipher. Certain portions of the writing, especially at two corners of the slab, are slightly eroded due to the passage of time.

The text records the construction of a mosque in 885 (1480); after some dilapidation, the mosque was probably changed into a mausoleum, and in that form still exists. Though some of the titles of the patron can be read from the inscription, the portion containing his name could not be deciphered properly. The titles of the patron suggest that he must have been a high-ranking official serving in the area. The text ends with a couplet taken from the famous Persian classical *Bustān* of Shaykh Sa'dī, a poet popular throughout the Persian cultural belt of the Islamic world.

(91) Faqirer Masjid inscription in Hathazari from the reign of Yūsuf Shāh

ORIGINAL SITE: Faqīrer Masjid, Hathazari, Chittagong district, Bangladesh. **CURRENT LOCATION:** Probably in situ. **MATERIAL, SIZE:** Black basalt; 51 × 18 inches. **STYLE, NO. OF LINES:** *naskh* in Bengali *ṭughrā'*; two lines. **REIGN:** Sulṭān Yūsuf Shāh (879–886/1474–1481). **LANGUAGE:** Arabic. **TYPE:** Commemorative inscription. **PUBLICATION:** A. Karim, *JASP*, XII, 111 (December 1967): 221–332, pl. 2; A. Karim, *Corpus of Inscriptions*, 194–96.

Text:

. . . السلطان شمس الدنيا والدين أبو المظفر يوسف شاه بن باربكشاه . .

Translation:

. . . the Sulṭān Shams al-Dunyā wa ’l-Dīn Abū ’l-Muẓaffar Yūsuf Shāh ibn Bārbak Shāh.

Discussion:

Some parts of the inscription have been damaged. Others, especially at the beginning and the end, are unfortunately, covered by bricks.

(92) An undated Masjid inscription from the reign of Sulṭān Yūsuf Shāh found at the Shrine of Boamaloti near Gaur

ORIGINAL SITE: An unnamed masjid near the Shrine of Boamaloti in the suburb of Gaur, Malda district, West Bengal, India. **CURRENT LOCATION**: Shrine of Sayyid Aḥmad Maloti at the village of Jaygirtola (near Dakhshin Lakhshipur [Mu’aẓẓampur]), Kaliachak Police Station, Malda district, West Bengal, India. **MATERIAL, SIZE:** Black basalt; not known. **STYLE, NO. OF LINES**: *thulth* in Bengali *ṭughrā’*; one line. **REIGN**: Shams al-Dunyā wa ‘l-Dīn Abū ’l-Muẓaffar Yūsuf Shāh (879–886/1474–1481). **LANGUAGE**: Arabic. **TYPE:** Commemorative inscription of a mosque. **PUBLICATION**: M. Y. Siddiq, ‘Inscriptions as an Important Means for Understanding History of the Muslims’, *Journal of Islamic Studies*, 20(2) (May 2009), 213–250.

Figure 6.9 Commemorative inscription (Shrine of Boamaloti in the suburb of Gaur, Malda district, West Bengal) (source: author’s own image).

Text:

قال النبي عليه السلام من بنى مسجدا لله [في الدنيا] بنى الله له (سبعين) قصرا في الجنة بنى في عهد السلطان الأعظم شمس الدنيا
والدين أبو المظفر يوسف شاه السلطان ابن باربكشاه السلطان ابن محمود شاه السلطان

Translation:

The Prophet, upon him be peace, said, ‘Whoever builds a mosque for the sake of Allah [in this world], Allah will build for him [seventy] palaces in Paradise.’

It was built during the reign of Shams al-Dunyā wa 'l-Dīn Abū 'l-Muẓaffar Yūsuf Shāh al-Sulṭān ibn Bārbak Shāh al-Sulṭān ibn Maḥmūd Shāh al-Sulṭān...

Discussion:

This inscription was discovered by the author in 2005 at the Shrine of Boamalati in the suburb of Gaur.

(93) Masjid inscription in Bandar dated 886 (1481)

ORIGINAL SITE: A Sultanate masjid at Bandar on the bank of the Tribeni canal, opposite Khizrpur, near Dhaka, Bangladesh. **CURRENT LOCATION:** Probably in situ. **MATERIAL, SIZE:** Black basalt; not known. **STYLE, NO. OF LINES:** *thulth* in Bengali *ṭughrā'*; three lines. **REIGN:** Sulṭān Fatḥ Shāh (886–893/1481–1488). **LANGUAGE:** Arabic. **TYPE:** Commemorative inscription. **PUBLICATION:** Blochmann, *JASB*, XLII (1873): 282–283; Dani, *Bibliography of Muslim Inscriptions*, 34; S. Ahmad, *Inscriptions of Bengal*, 113–114; A. Karim, *Corpus of Inscriptions*, 196–198.

Text:

L-1 قال الله تعالى وأن المساجد لله فلا تدعوا مع الله أحدا قال النبي صلى الله عليه وسلم من بنى مسجدا بنى الله له قصرا في الجنة بنى هذا المسجد

L-2 المبارك الملك المعظم بابا صالح في زمان السلطان ابن السلطان جلال الدنيا والدين أبو <أبي>المظفر فتح شاه السلطان

L-3 ابن محمود شاه السلطان خلد الله ملكه وسلطانه في تاريخ أول شهر ذي القعدة سنة ست وثمانين وثمانماية من الهجرة النبوية

Translation:

L-1 Allah the Exalted said, 'And verily the mosques are for Allah, so do not invoke anyone with Allah.' The Prophet, peace and the blessing of Allah be upon him, said, 'Whoever builds a mosque, Allah will build for him a palace in Paradise.' Al-Malik al-Mu'aẓẓam [the exalted lord] Bābā Ṣāliḥ built this auspicious mosque

L-2 in the reign of al-Sulṭān ibn al-Sulṭān Jalāl al-Dunyā wa 'l-Dīn Abū 'l-Muẓaffar Fatḥ Shāh the sulṭān

L-3 ibn Maḥmūd Shāh al-Sulṭān, may Allah make his kingdom and authority everlasting, on the date, on the first of the month of Dhū 'l-Qa'da, [in the] year eight hundred and eighty-six Hijra.

Discussion:

The name of the patron of the mosque, Bābā Ṣāliḥ, combines Bengali (*bābā* in Bengali and a number of South Asian languages as well as in some colloquial Arabic and Persian dialects means father) and Arabic (*sāliḥ* in Arabic means pious), indicating the fusion between the two cultures through Arab/Islamic influence from the west. Three more inscriptions from the reign of Ḥusayn Shāh (Masjid ins., Azimnagar, dated 910/1504; Masjid ins., dated 911/1505; Tombstone of Ḥajjī Bābā Ṣāliḥ, Sonārgā'on, dated 912/1506) also record Bābā Ṣāliḥ's name. It seems that Bābā Ṣāliḥ was an official of high rank in the government, as he bore the title 'Malik'. In addition to building a mosque at Bandar in Dhaka district as recorded in the present inscription, he also established another mosque in 1504 in Azimnagar in Dhaka. In the last days of his life, he visited Makkah and Madinah for Ḥajj as was customary with rich Muslims in Bengal. He died in 912/1506.

(94) Masjid inscription in Pathantola dated 887 (1482)

ORIGINAL SITE: An unnamed Sultanate mosque in the Pathantola quarter of Dhamrai village, twenty miles north of Dhaka, Bangladesh. **CURRENT LOCATION:** Probably fixed on the wall of a newly constructed local mosque in Pathantola in Dhamrai. **MATERIAL, SIZE:** Black basalt; not known. **STYLE, NO. OF LINES:** Bihārī in Bengali *ṭughrā'*; two lines. **REIGN:** Sulṭān Fatḥ Shāh (886–893/1481–1488). **LANGUAGE:** Arabic. **TYPE:** Foundation inscription. **PUBLICATION:** Blochmann, *JASB*, XLI (1872): 109–110; Dani, *Bibliography of Muslim Inscriptions*, 34; S. Ahmad, *Inscriptions of Bengal*, 117–118; A. Karim, *Corpus of Inscriptions*, 199–201.

Text:

L-1 قال الله تعالى إنما يعمر مساجد الله من آمن بالله واليوم الآخر قال النبي صلى الله عليه وسلم من بنى مسجدا لله بنى الله له بيتا في الجنة [بني] هذا المسجد في زمن سلطان العهد والزمان المؤيد بتأييد الرحمن غوث الإسلام والمسلمين السلطان ابن السلطان جلال الدنيا

L-2 والدين أبو<أبي> المظفر فتحشاه سلطان بن محمود شاه السلطان خلد الله ملكه وسلطانه وأعلى أمره وشأنه بنى هذا المسجد المبارك للإسلام والمسلمين ظهير الملة والدين ملك الملوك اخوند شير مير بحر أسكنه الله تعالى في الجنة العاشر من جماد الأول سنة سبع وثمانين وثمانماية

Translation:

Allah the Great said, 'Only those build the mosques of Allah who believe in Allah and the last day' [Qur'ān 9:18]. The Prophet, peace and the blessings of Allah be on him, said, 'Whomsoever builds a mosque for Allah, Allah will build for him a house in Paradise.' This mosque was built in the reign of Sulṭān al-'Ahd wa 'l-Zamān (i.e. sulṭān of the age and time), al-Mu'ayyad bi Ta'yīd al-Raḥmān, Ghawth al-Islām wa 'l-Muslimīn (i.e. succour of Islam and the Muslims), the sulṭān, son of the sulṭān Jalāl al-Dunyā wa 'l-Dīn Abū 'l-Muẓaffar Fatḥ Shāh Sulṭān ibn Maḥmūd Shāh al-Sulṭān, may Allah make his kingdom and authority everlasting and elevate his prestige and status. Ẓahīr al-Millat wa 'l-Dīn Malik al-Mulk Akhund Sher, Mīr-i-Baḥr built this auspicious mosque for Islam and the Muslims, may Allah the Exalted provide him a dwelling in

Paradise, on the tenth of Jumād al-Awwal, [in the] year eight hundred and eighty-seven [27 June 1482].

Discussion:

This inscription was found by J. Wise in a private house in the village of Dhamrai in the Pathantola locality, twenty miles north of Dhaka. The patron of the mosque, Akhūnd Sher, had the title Mīr-i-Baḥr (admiral of the fleet), an important position particularly in the southern riverine part of the Bengal delta where the inscription was found. Akhūnd Malik's other title *zahīr al-millat wa 'l-dīn* (supporter of the nation and religion) also indicates the important role he played in the defence of the Sultanate.

(95) An inscription of the Khānqāh of Mawlānā 'Aṭā' Waḥīd al-Dīn from Deotala dated 887 (1482)

ORIGINAL SITE: Mausoleum of Mawlānā 'Aṭā' Waḥīd al-Dīn located adjacent to his *zāwiya* (khānqāh) in Deotala, Dakhshin Dinajpur district (in West Bengal), India. **CURRENT LOCATION:** Varendra Research Museum, Rajshahi, inv. no. 1460. **MATERIAL, SIZE:** Black basalt; 23 × 10 inches. **STYLE, NO. OF LINES:** Pseudo – *Muḥaqqaq*; three lines. **REIGN:** Sulṭān Fatḥ Shāh (886–893/1481–1488). **LANGUAGE:** Arabic. **TYPE:** Commemorative inscription recording the renovation of a religious edifice. **PUBLICATION:** S. Sharaf-ud-Din, *Varendra Research Society's Monographs*, 6 (March 1935): 3–4, pl. 2; Cunningham, *ASR*, XV (1882): 97–99; Dani, *Bibliography of Muslim Inscriptions*, 34–35; S. Ahmad, *Inscriptions of Bengal*, 115–116; A. Karim, *Corpus of Inscriptions*, 198–199.

Text:

L-1 بنى هدم هذا العمارة<عمارة هذه> الحجرة في عهد مخدوم المشهور مولانا

L-2 عطا وحيد الدين في {ال}عهد السلطان الأعظم جلال الدنيا والدين أبو <أبي>

L-3 ا لمظفر فتحشاه سلطان ابن محمود شاه سلطان التاريخ في شهور سنة سبع [و] ثمانين وثمانماية

Translation:

L-1 The ruins of this building, the *ḥujra* (monastery), were reconstructed at the time of the famous Makhdūm (spiritual leader) Mawlānā

L-2 'Aṭā Waḥīd al-Dīn during the reign of the great Sulṭān Jalāl al-Dunyā wa 'l-Dīn Abū

L-3 'l-Muẓaffar Fatḥ Shāh Sulṭān ibn Maḥmūd Shāh Sulṭān; dated in the months of the year eight hundred and eighty-seven.

Discussion:

This inscription originally belonged to the mausoleum of Mawlānā Aṭā Waḥīd al-Dīn located adjacent to his khānqāh near a huge pond, known as Dhaldighi in Deotala, Dakhshin Dinajpur district (in West Bengal). The inscription was brought to Rajshahi by E. H. Rudoch where it was left unattended in the bungalow of the magistrate of Rajshahi district for a number of years. Later on, the inscription was taken to a local mosque at Hatem Khān, from where it was finally transferred to Varendra Research Museum. A famous Muslim scholar and sufi-saint of his age, Shaykh 'Atā Wahīd al-Dīn was known as the Quṭb al-Awliyā' (pole of the friends of Allah). He was very popular and highly respected because of his vast learning and exemplary piety. Mawlānā established a seminary at Gangarampur after settling there with his followers. Over time, this institution received the attention and patronage of a number of Muslim rulers. The grammatical errors and the crude calligraphic appearance in the epigraphic text suggest that the inscription was laid out locally by an inexpert. All we can surmise from it is that a khānqāh was reconstructed at the site of a dilapidated monastery during the life of the Mawlānā that coincided with the reign of Sulṭān Fatḥ Shāh. The tomb of Mawlānā and ruins of an old mosque can still be seen near the tank.

(96) Adam Shāhīd Masjid inscription in Rampal dated 888 (1483)

ORIGINAL SITE: A no longer extant Sultanate masjid in Rampal (Bikrampur) in Dhaka district, Bangladesh. **CURRENT LOCATION:** Main entrance of Bābā Ādam Shāhīd mosque in Rampal (Bikrampur) in Dhaka district, Bangladesh. **MATERIAL, SIZE:** Not known. **STYLE, NO. OF LINES:** Bihārī in Bengali *ṭughrā'* decorative style; two lines. **REIGN:** Sulṭān Fatḥ Shāh (886–893/1481–1488). **LANGUAGE:** Arabic. **TYPE:** Commemorative inscription. **PUBLICATION:** Blochmann, *JASB*, XLII (1873): 284–285; (1889): 23; Asutosh Gupta, 'Ruins and Antiquities of Rampal', *JASB*, LVII (1889): 17–27, pl. V; Cunningham, *ASR*, XV (1882): 135; Dani, *Bibliography of Muslim Inscriptions*, 35; S. Ahmad, *Inscriptions of Bengal*, 118–120; A. Karim, *Corpus of Inscriptions*, 201–203.

Text:

L-1 قال الله تعالى وأن المساجد لله فلا تدعوا مع الله أحدا قال النبي صلى الله عليه وسلم من بنى مسجدا في الدنيا بنى الله له قصرا في الجنة بنى هذا المسجد

L-2 الجامع الملك المعظم ملك كافور في زمان السلطان ابن السلطان جلال الدنيا والدين أبو<أبي> المظفر فتحشاه السلطان ابن محمود شاه السلطان في تاريخ أوسط شهر رجب سنة ثما[ن] وثمانين و ثمانماية

Translation:

L-1 Allah the Exalted said, 'And verily the mosques are for Allah, so do not invoke anyone with Allah.' The Prophet, peace and the blessings of Allah be upon him, said, 'Whoever builds a mosque in the world, Allah will build for him a palace in Paradise.' The exalted al-Malik Kāfur built this congregational mosque

L-2 in the reign of the sulṭān, son of the sulṭān Jalāl al-Dunyā wa 'l-Dīn Abū 'l-Muẓaffar Fatḥ Shāh al-Sulṭān ibn Maḥmūd Shāh al-Sulṭān in the middle (approximately fifteenth) of the month of Rajab, [in the] year eight hundred and eighty-eight [August 1483].

Discussion:

The mosque on which the inscription is affixed is known as Bābā Ādam Shahīd Masjid. No reliable information is available about Bābā Ādam. His place of origin was supposedly somewhere near Vikrampur, in the Munshiganj district. Local folk tradition suggests that Ballalasena, the Hindu king in the area, was his contemporary. When Bābā Ādam died, he was buried in a grave at Rampal near the mosque, built by Malik Kāfur in 1483. His *astanah* (monastery) was located near Rampal, in Abdullapur.[25] He is mentioned by Ananda Bhatta in his biographical work *Ballala Charita.*

(97) Masjid/Madrasa inscriptions in Sonārgā'on dated 889 (1483–1484)

ORIGINAL SITE: A no longer extant Sultanate masjid-cum-madrasa complex in Yusufganj village, not far from the present Mughrapara Shahi Masjid in the present village of Mughrapara near Sonārgā'on, district of Dhaka, Bangladesh. **CURRENT LOCATION:** Graveyard near the Mughrapara Ilyās Shāhī masjid in the village of Mughrapara near Sonārgā'on, district of Dhaka, Bangladesh. **MATERIAL, SIZE:** Black basalt; 14 × 9 inches. **STYLE, NO. OF LINES:** Pseudo *thulth* in Bengali *ṭughrā'*; three lines. **REIGN:** Sulṭān Fatḥ Shāh

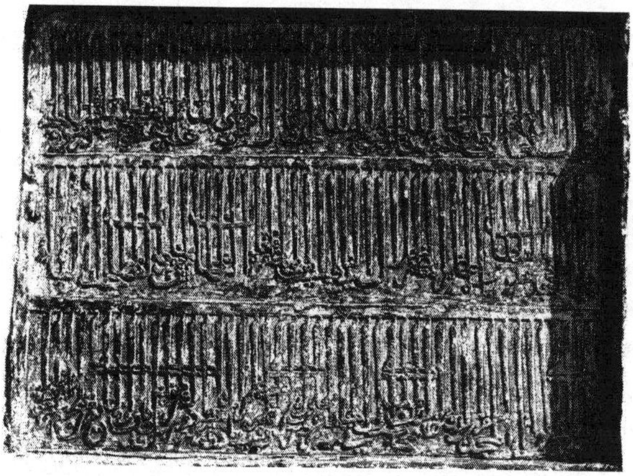

Figure 6.10 Commemorative inscription (Mughrapara near Sonārgā'on, district of Dhaka, Bangladesh) (source: author's own image).

(886–893/1481–1488). **LANGUAGE:** Arabic. **TYPE:** Commemorative inscription. **PUBLICATION:** Blochmann, *JASB*, XLII (1873): 285–286; Cunningham, *ASR*, XV (1882): 141; Dani, *Bibliography of Muslim Inscriptions*, 35–36; S. Ahmad, *Inscriptions of Bengal*, 121–122; A. Karim, *Corpus of Inscriptions*, 203–205, Md. Abu Musa, *History of Dhaka through Inscriptions and Architecture* (Dhaka: Department of Archaeology, Ministry of Cultural Affairs, Government of the People's Republic of Bangladesh, 2000), 52–53.

Text:

L-1 قال الله تعالى وأن المساجد لله فلا تدعوا مع الله أحدا وقال النبي صلى الله عليه وسلم من بنى مسجدا بنى الله له سبعين قصرا في الجنة

L-2 بنى هذا المسجد في عهد السلطان الأعظم المعظم جلال الدنيا والدين أبو<أبي > المظفر فتح شاه السلطان ابن محمود شاه السلطان خلد الله

L-3 ملكه وسلطانه باني المسجد مقرب الدولة والملك والدين السلطاني جامدار غير محلى وسر لشكر ووزير إقليم معظما باد و نيز مشهور محمود آباد وسر لشكر تهانه لاود كان ذلك في التاريخ من المحرم سنة تسع وثمانين وثمانماية

Translation:

L-1 Allah the Exalted said, 'And verily the mosques are for Allah, so do not invoke anyone with Allah.' The Prophet, peace and the blessings of Allah be upon him, said, 'Whoever builds a mosque, Allah will build for him seventy palaces in Paradise.'

L-2 This mosque was built in the reign of the great and exalted Sulṭān Jalāl al-Dunyā wa 'l-Dīn Abū 'l-Muẓaffar Fatḥ Shāh al-Sulṭān ibn Maḥmūd Shāh al-Sulṭān, may Allah make his kingdom and authority everlasting.

L-3 The builder of the mosque is Muqarrab al-Dawla wa 'l-Mulk wa 'l-Dīn al-Sulṭāni Jāmdār Ghayr-maḥallī and sar-e-lashkar (chief of army) and vizier of the iqlīm (district) of Mu'aẓẓamabād, also known as Maḥmūdābād, and chief of the army of thāna (precinct/police station) Lāwud. This took place on the date Muḥarram, [in the] year eight hundred and eighty-nine [February 1484].

Discussion:

This inscription was found in a graveyard near the Mughrapara Shāhi masjid in the village of Mughrapara near Sonārgā'on, district of Dhaka. It records the term *thana* (county/borough) which used to be, and continues to be to this day, the very basic administrative unit in Bengal, and throughout South Asia. In addition to the sulṭāns of Bengal, Mughal and British rulers also used the term for the same purpose. There are a few other Islamic inscriptions in the area, particularly in the Moghrapara jāmi' masjid, such as two undated inscriptions containing *ḥadīth*s (one of them referring to the importance of education), one from the reign of Ḥusayn Shāh now fixed above the northern miḥrāb of Moghrapara jāmi' masjid, dated 899/1493 and one inscription dated 1112/1700.

(98) Gunmant Masjid inscription in Gaur dated 889 (1484)

ORIGINAL SITE: Gunmant Masjid in Gaur. **CURRENT LOCATION:** Not known. **MATERIAL, SIZE:** Black basalt; not known. **STYLE, NO. OF LINES:** *ijāza*; two lines. **REIGN:** Sulṭān Fatḥ Shāh (886–893/1481–1488). **LANGUAGE:** Arabic.**TYPE:** Commemorative inscription of a masjid. **PUBLICATION:** Cunningham, *ASR*, XV (1882): 65, pl. XXIII; A. A. Khan, *Memoirs of Gaur*, 85–87; P. Horn, *Epigraphia Indica*, II: 87; Dani, *Bibliography of Muslim Inscriptions*, 36, no. 58; S. Ahmad, *Inscriptions of Bengal*, 122–124; A. Karim, *Corpus of Inscriptions*, 205–207.

Text and translation:

For the detailed view, complete text and translation of the epigraph, please see the beginning of Chapter 5.

Discussion:

The inscription was found by Cunningham lying near the Gunmant Masjid in Gaur in the 1870s, though its present whereabouts is not known. Most Ilyās Shāhī rulers were great patrons of learning and many (e.g. Sulṭān Ghiyāth al-Dīn A'ẓam Shāh who studied under al-Shaykh al-Qāḍī Ḥamīd al-Dīn Nagori Kunjshikan; see also the jāmi' masjid gate inscription in Naswa Gali dated 863/1459) went to madrasas for their formal education. The royal titles in this inscription, such as *qahramān al-mā' wa 'l-ṭin* (the authority amidst water and soil), *kāshif asrār al-Qur'ān* (the one who reveals the secrets of the Qur'ān), *'ālim 'ulum al-'ādyān wa 'l-'ābdān* (scholar of the science of religions and physiology) suggest that not only did Fatḥ Shāh know *'ulūm al-tafsīr* (exegesis of Qur'ān) and *'ulūm al-'adyān* (science of religion), but he was also interested in anatomy and physiology.

(99) Masjid inscription from Gaur dated 889 (1484)

ORIGINAL SITE: An unidentified Sultanate mosque near Ḥusaynī Dālān in Katra (fort) in Gaur. **CURRENT LOCATION:** Indian Museum, Calcutta, inv. no. 16. **MATERIAL, SIZE:** Black basalt; 25 × 9 inches. **STYLE, NO. OF LINES:** *thulth* in Bengali *ṭughrā'*; one line. **REIGN:** Sulṭān Fatḥ Shāh (886–893/1481–1488). **LANGUAGE:** Arabic. **TYPE:** Commemorative inscription of a mosque. **PUBLICATION:** Cunningham, *ASR*, XV (1882): 78; Ravenshaw, *Gaur*, 76, pl. 49, no. 8; Blochmann, *JASB*, XLIII (1874): 299–300, pl. I; Desai, *EIAPS* (1955–1956): 16–17; Dani, *Bibliography of Muslim Inscriptions*, 39; S. Ahmad, *Inscriptions of Bengal*, 133–134; C. Dutt, *Arabic and Persian Inscriptions in the Indian Museum*, 18, no. 16; A. Karim, *Corpus of Inscriptions*, 219–220.

Text:

قال النبي عليه السلام من بنى في الدنيا مسجدا بنى الله له سبعين قصرا مثله في الجنة وقد بني هذا المسجد في زمن السلطان العادل سيف الدنيا والدين أبو <أبي> المظفر فيروز شاه سلطان خلد الله ملكه وسلطانه باني هذا المسجد مجلس شهالا خالد و هو سعيد بالدين في شهور سنة تسع وثمانين وثمانماية

Translation:

The Prophet, peace be upon him, said, 'Whomsoever builds a mosque in the world, Allah will build for him seventy palaces in Paradise.' This mosque was built in the reign of the just and benevolent Sulṭān Sayf al-Dunyā wa 'l-Dīn Abū 'l-Muẓaffar Fīrūz Shāh Sulṭān, may Allah make his kingdom and authority everlasting. The builder of this mosque is Majlis Shihālā Khālid who is fortunate in religion, during the months of the year eight hundred and eighty-nine.

Discussion:

Originally this inscription belonged to a Sultanate mosque in Gaur. It was discovered, however, in the Ḥusaynī Dalān (Ḥusaynīyya or the place of mourning of the Shī'a) in the building complex known as Katra (an inn) near Gaur in old Malda. The portion containing the date of the inscription, especially the first unit (conjecturally read as تسع), is not clear. Thus the inscription raises a few problems for the chronological ordering of the rulers during the period since it suggests that Fīrūz Shāh started exerting his authority and power towards the middle of Sulṭān Fatḥ Shāh's reign, as he assumed the title sulṭān as early as 889/1484. It seems that the death of Sulṭān Yusuf Shāh led to differences of opinion among the nobles which resulted in intrigue and conspiracies, followed by a series of revolts, usurpations and political assassinations. According to *Riyāḍ al-Salāṭin*, on the death of Sulṭān Yūsuf Shāh, his son Sikandar Shāh was raised to the throne, but was deposed after only a few days. The throne was then offered by the nobles to Fatḥ Shāh. Fatḥ Shāh ascended to the throne in 886/1481 and was assassinated at the beginning of 893/1487 by an Abyssinian palace guard named Sulṭān Shahzāda who proclaimed himself as Sulṭān Bārbak Shāh. But towards the end of the same year (in 893/1487), he, too, was assassinated. Finally, Malik 'Andīl, another influential member of the royal court of Abyssinian origin, established his supremacy as the ruler of Bengal. This inscription suggests that some kind of palace conspiracy started developing during the reign of Sulṭān Fatḥ Shāh and continued for some length of time.

(100) Masjid inscription from Birol dated 889 (1484)

ORIGINAL SITE: An unidentified Sultanate mosque near the village of Birol, Dinajpur district, Bangladesh. **CURRENT LOCATION:** Varendra Research Museum, Rajshahi, Bangladesh (inv. no. 1443). **MATERIAL, SIZE:** Black basalt; 23 × 10 inches. **STYLE, NO. OF LINES:** A local variety of Bihārī; three lines. **REIGN:** Sulṭān Fatḥ Shāh (886–893/1481–1488). **LANGUAGE:** Arabic. **TYPE:** Commemorative inscription of a mosque. **PUBLICATION:** S. Sharaf-ud-Din, 'Birol Inscription of Sayfuddin Firoz Shāh', *Varendra Research Society's Monographs*, 6 (March 1935): 1–2; Dani, *Bibliography of Muslim Inscriptions*, 38; S. Ahmad, *Inscriptions of Bengal*, 128–130; A Karim, 'A Fresh Study of Birol Inscription', *JASBD*, XVII(1) (1972): 10–11; Muhammad Nizamuddin, *Journal of the Varendra Research Museum*, 5 (1976–1977): 87–93; A. Karim, *Corpus of Inscriptions*, 184–185.

Text:

L-1 قال الله تعالى إنما يعمر مساجد الله من آمن بالله واليوم الآخر وأقام الصلاة وآتى الزكاة ولم يخش إلا الله فعسى أولئك أن يكونوا من المهتدين

L-2 قال النبي صلى الله عليه وسلم من بنى مسجدا بنى الله له في الجنة قصرا – في عهد السلطان سيف الدنيا والدين أبو < أبي> المظفر فيروز شاه سلطان خلد الله ملكه وسلطانه

L-3 بنى هذا المسجد خان أعظم المعظم بحر المعاني حاتم الثاني محب العلماء والفقراء المخاطب بخطاب قيران خان سلمه الله تعالى في التاريخ الثاني والعشر من جماد الآخر سنة تسع وثمانين وثمانماية

Translation:

L-1 Allah the Great said, 'Only those build the mosques of Allah who believe in Allah and the last day and establish prayer and offer prescribed charity and fear none but Allah; it is they who are expected to be truly guided' [Qur'ān 9:18].

L-2 The Prophet, peace and the blessings of Allah be upon him, said, 'Whomsoever builds a mosque, Allah will build for him a palace in Paradise.' During the reign of al-Sulṭān Sayf al-Dunyā wa 'l-Dīn Abū 'l-Muẓaffar Fīruz Shāh Sulṭān, may Allah make his kingdom and authority everlasting,

L-3 the sublime [and] exalted Khān Baḥr al-Ma'ānī (lit. sea of meaningful qualities) Ḥāṭim al-Thānī (the second Ḥātim [an exemplary figure] in benevolence) Muḥibb al-'Ulamā' wa 'l-Fuqarā (the lover of scholars and destitute) styled Qīrān Khān, may Allah the Exalted protect him, built this mosque on the date of twelfth of Jumād al-'Akhir [in the] year eight hundred and eighty-nine [July 1484].

Discussion:

Malik 'Andīl was recorded as a sulṭān in the previous inscription (no. 100) dated 889/1484 as he assumed the title *sulṭān sayf al-dunyā wa 'l-dīn abū 'l-muẓaffar firūz shāh*. The present inscription further attests that he never gave up his claim as sulṭān. Thus in 12 Jumāda 'l-'Ākhira 889 (July 1484) during the reign of Fatḥ Shāh, he was trying to establish his authority actively by pronouncing himself a sulṭān.

(101) Challa Masjid inscription in Gaur dated 889 (1484)

ORIGINAL SITE: Challa mosque in the village of Mahdipur, Gaur. **CURRENT LOCATION:** Not known. **MATERIAL, SIZE:** Not known; 67 × 4 inches. **STYLE, NO OF LINES:** Not known. **REIGN:** Sulṭān Fatḥ Shāh (886–893/1481–1488). **LANGUAGE:** Arabic. **TYPE:** Commemorative inscription. **PUBLICATION:** P. Horn, *Epigraphia Indica*, II: 287–288; S. Ahmad, *Inscriptions of Bengal*, 125–126; A. Karim, *Corpus of Inscriptions*, 208–209.

Text:

. . . جلال الدنيا والدين أبو المظفر فتح شاه السلطان ابن محمود شاه السلطان خلد الله ملكه وسلطانه وأعلى أمره وشأنه بسعي خان الأعظم وخاقان المعظم الواثق بالملك المنان خان معظم دولتخان وزير لشكر تقبل الله منه في سنة تسع . . . .

Translation:

...Jalāl al-Dunyā wa 'l-Dīn Abū 'l-Muẓaffar Fatḥ Shāh Sulṭān ibn Maḥmud Shāh al-Sulṭān, may Allah perpetuate his kingdom and authority and make his position and prestige high. [It took place] through the effort of the exalted khān and the sublime khāqān al-Wāthiq bi 'l-Malik al-Mannān (the one who trusts the king, the beneficent) Khān al-Mu'aẓẓam Dawlat Khān, defence minister, may [Allah] accept from him [this deeds], in the year [eight hundred and eighty] nine.

Discussion:

Dawlat Khān also appears in the Gunmant Masjid inscription (located near the present Mahdipur village) in Gaur dated 889/1484 as *wazīr-i-lashkar* or chief of the army (lit. defence minister).

(102) Masjid inscription in Mahdipur dated 891 (1486)

ORIGINAL SITE: An unidentified Sultanate mosque in Gaur, probably near the present village of Mahdipur. **CURRENT LOCATION:** Fixed above the lintel of a small gate at the extreme south of the *qibla* wall of a recently constructed mosque, known as Bara Jāmi' Masjid, in the village of Mahdipur, near Gaur. **MATERIAL, SIZE:** Black basalt; 52 × 10 inches. **STYLE, NO. OF LINES:** *naskh* in Bengali *ṭughrā'* decorative style; single line divided into four rectangular panels. **REIGN:** Sulṭān Fatḥ Shāh (886–893/1481–1488). **LANGUAGE:** Arabic. **TYPE:** Commemorative inscription of a mosque. **PUBLICATION:** P. Horn, *Epigraphia Indica*, II: 287–288; Dani, *Bibliography of Muslim Inscriptions*, 36–37, no. 59; S. Ahmad, *Inscriptions of Bengal*, 124–125; A. Karim, *Corpus of Inscriptions*, 207–208.

Text:

First panel:

قال الله تعالى إنما يعمر مساجد الله من آمن بالله واليوم الآخر وأقام الصلاة وآتى الزكاة ولم يخش إلا الله فعسى أولئك أن يكونوا من المهتدين

Second panel:

وقال الله تعالى وأن المساجد لله فلا تدعوا مع الله أحدا وقال النبي صلى الله عليه وسلم من بنى مسجدا لله تعالى بنى الله له بيتا في الجنة

Third panel:

بني هذا المسجد في عهد السلطان ابن السلطان جلال الدنيا والدين أبو < أبي> المظفر فتحشاه السلطان ابن محمود شاه السلطا
ن

Fourth panel:

قد بناه السيد الأعظم سيد دستور بن سيد راحت بالحسنة ثمر جعله سر گنبد مولانا برخوردار ابن خانمعظم تاج خان في شهر رمضان المبارك سنة إحدى وتسعين وثمانماية

Translation:

First panel:
Allah the Great said, 'Only those build the mosques of Allah who believe in Allah and the last day and establish prayer and offer prescribed charity and fear none but Allah; it is they who are expected to be truly guided' [Qur'ān 9:18].

Second panel:
And Allah the Exalted said, 'And verily the mosques are for Allah, so do not invoke anyone with Allah.' The Prophet, peace and the blessings of Allah be upon him, said, 'Whosoever builds a mosque for the sake of Allah the Exalted, Allah will build for him a house in Paradise.'

Third panel:
This mosque was built during the reign of the sulṭān, son of the Sulṭān Jalāl al-Dunyā wa 'l-Dīn Abū 'l-Muẓaffar Fatḥ Shāh al-Sulṭān ibn Maḥmūd Shāh al-Sulṭān.

Fourth panel:
The great lord Sayyid Dastur ibn Sayyid Rāhat, may he bring forth good deeds, built the crown of this dome of Mawlānā Barkhurdār ibn Khān Mu'aẓẓam Tāj Khān, in the blessed month of Ramaḍān [in the] year eight hundred and ninety-one [September 1486].

Discussion:

This inscription records the construction of a dome on the mausoleum of Mawlānā Barkhurdār in Gaur. Nothing is known about Mawlānā Barkhurdār. But his title, *mawlānā* (lit. our lord), suggests that he was a known religious personality of the time. Epigraphic evidence, such as this inscription, suggest that the capitals of Bengal, particularly Gaur and Pandua, attracted many 'ulamā' during the Sultanate and Mughal periods.

(103) Masjid inscription from Rohanpur dated 891(1486)

ORIGINAL SITE: An unidentified Sultanate mosque in Rohanpur near Gaur, Bangladesh. **CURRENT LOCATION:** Varendra Research Museum, Rajshahi, Bangladesh (inv. no. 2852). **MATERIAL, SIZE:** Black basalt; 24 × 14 inches. **STYLE, NO. OF LINES:** *naskh* with some elements of *thulth* in the decorative style of Bengali *ṭughrā'*; two lines. **REIGN:** Sulṭān Fatḥ Shāh (886–893/1481–1488). **LANGUAGE:** Arabic, except for two Persian words, *binā kardah*, at the end. **TYPE:** Commemorative inscription. **PUBLICATION:** Yakub Ali, 'Two Unidentified Inscriptions', *Bangladesh Historical Studies*, VIII–X (1984–86): 18–25; Yakub Ali, *Journal of the Institute of Bangladesh Studies*, XI (1988): 12–13, pl. 1; A. Karim, *Corpus of Inscriptions*, 524–525.

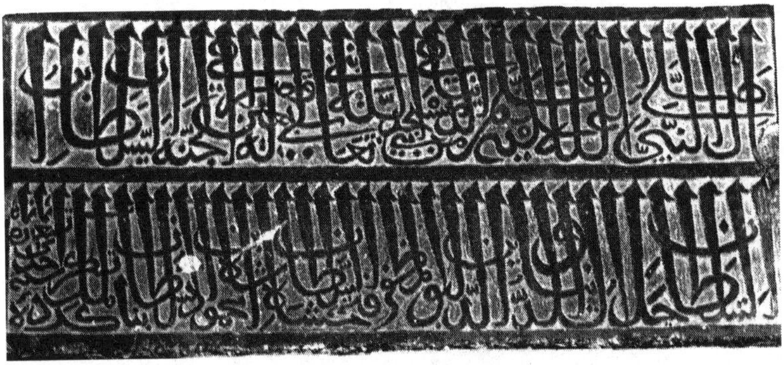

Figure 6.11 Commemorative inscription (an unidentified Sultanate mosque in Rohanpur near Gaur, Bangladesh) (source: author's own image).

Text:

L-1 [قا] ل النبي صلى الله عليه وسلم من بنى مسجدا في الدنيا بنى الله تعالى له سبعين قصرا في الجنة السلطان ابن

L-2 السلطان جلال الدنيا والدين أبو المظفر فتحشاه السلطان ابن محمود شاه السلطان بنا كرده ملك تكر سنة إحدى [و] تسعين [و] ثمانماية

Translation:

L-1 The Prophet, peace and the blessings of Allah be upon him, said, 'Whosoever builds a mosque on earth, Allah will make for him seventy palaces in Paradise.' [During the reign of] the sulṭān, son of

L-2 the sulṭān, Jalāl al-Dunyā wa 'l-Dīn Abū 'l-Muẓaffar Fatḥ Shāh, the sulṭān, son of Maḥmūd Shāh the sulṭān, Malik Thakur built [this mosque in the] year eight hundred [and] ninety-one.

Discussion:

This inscription was discovered in a village near Rohanpur in Chapai Nawabganj district, not far from Gaur. The black basalt stone slab is slightly broken on its right side, but this has not caused much damage to the text. As in most other inscriptions in Bengal, the text has been rendered in a raised form. Elements of both *naskh* and *thulth* styles are visible in its calligraphy. The bold calligraphy of this inscription bears some similarity to many of the inscriptions engraved on Mamluk metalwork in Egypt. The traditional calligraphic features of the period, especially the elongation of verticals in symmetrical order, are also apparent.

(104) Masjid inscription in Satgaon dated 892 (1487)

ORIGINAL SITE: An unidentified Sultanate mosque near Satgaon in Hoogly district, West Bengal, India. **CURRENT LOCATION:** Not known. **MATERIAL, SIZE:** Not known. **STYLE, NO OF LINES:** *naskh*; not known. **REIGN:** Sulṭān Fatḥ Shāh (886–893/1481–1488). **LANGUAGE:** Arabic. **TYPE:** Commemorative inscription of a mosque. **PUBLICATION:** Blochmann, *JASB*, XXXIX (1870): 293–294, pl. 1; R. D. Banerjee, *Sahitya Parisad Patrica*, XV (1316 Bengali year): 30–31; Dani, *Bibliography of Muslim Inscriptions*, 37; S. Ahmad, *Inscriptions of Bengal*, 126–127; A. Karim, *Corpus of Inscriptions*, 210–211.

Text:

قال الله تعالى وأن المساجد لله فلا تدعوا مع الله أحدا وقال النبي صلى الله عليه وسلم من بنى مسجدا في الدنيا بنى الله له في الجنة
قصرا بني المسجد في عهد الملك العادل الباذل جلال الدنيا والدين أبو <أبي> المظفر فتح شاه سلطان ابن محمود شاه سلطان
خلد الله ملكه بنى المسجد المجيد العظيم صاحب السيف والقلم الغ مجلس نورسرلشكر ووزير عرصه ساجلا منكهباد وشهر
مشهور شملا باد وسر لشكر تهانه لاويلا ومحرربك عرصه ومحل هاديگرسلمه الله تعالى في الدارين مؤرخا في الرابع من المحرم سنة
اثنين وتسعين وثمانماية بخط عبد ضعيف آخوند ملك

Translation:

Allah the Exalted said, 'And verily the mosques are for Allah, so do not invoke anyone with Allah.' The Prophet, peace and the blessings of Allah be upon him, said, 'Whoever builds a mosque in the world, Allah will build for him a palace in Paradise.' The mosque was built in the reign of the just and benevolent king Jalāl al-Dunyā wa 'l-Dīn Abū 'l-Muẓaffar Fatḥ Shāh Sulṭān ibn Maḥmūd Shāh Sulṭān, may Allah perpetuate his kingdom. Ṣāḥib al-Sayf wa 'l-Qalam Ulugh Majlis Nūr, chief of army and vizier of the *'arṣa* (province) Sajlā Mankhabād and the famous city of Shimlabād and chief of army of the *thānā* of Lawela and

Muḥarrir Bayk (chief registrar) of the *'arṣa* and *maḥall* (administrative unit) of Ḥadīgar, may Allah the exalted protect him in both worlds, dated fourth of Muḥarram [in the] year eight hundred and ninety-two [1 January 1487], in the handwriting of the humble servant Akhund Malik.

Discussion:

Blochmann found this inscription near the mausoleum of Jamāl al-Dīn in the village of Trishbigha near Satgaon, in Hoogly district. The patron of the mosque, Ulugh Majlis Nūr, must have been a very important and influential official, as he held a number of important positions in the administration. The name of the calligrapher (i.e. Ākhund Malik) is mentioned in this inscription, which is rather unusual in the Islamic inscriptions of Bengal.

(105) A Waqf inscription of a Masjid from Gaur dated 893 (1489)

ORIGINAL SITE: An unidentified Sultanate mosque in Gaur. **CURRENT LOCATION:** British Museum (inv. no. 2299). **MATERIAL, SIZE:** Black basalt; 25 × 11 inches. **STYLE, NO. OF LINES:** *thulth* in Bengali *ṭughrā'* decorative style; two lines. **REIGN:** Sulṭān Fatḥ Shāh (886–893/1481–1488). **LANGUAGE:** Arabic. **TYPE:** A *waqf* (endowment) inscription of a mosque with a Qur'ānic verse. **PUBLICATION:** S. M. Hasan, *JASP*, XIII(1) (April 1968): 49–55; S. M. Hasan, *Glimpses of Muslim Art and Architecture*, 14–20; Siddiq, 'Arabic Calligraphy in the Early Inscriptions', *Muslim Education Quarterly*, 2(3) (1985): 77–88; idem, *al-Nuqūsh al-Kitābiyya 'alā' 'l-'Amā'ir al-Islāmiyya fī 'l-Bangāl*, MA Dissertation, Umm al-Qura University, Makkah, 1984, 69–73; A. Karim, *Corpus of Inscriptions*, 211–212.

Text:

L-1 فمن بدله بعد ما سمعه فإنما إثمه على الذين يبدلونه إن الله سميع عليم بنى هذا المسجد للصلوات الخمس لسبحان الله في عهد السلطان ابن السلطان جلال الدنيا

L-2 والدين أبو <أبي> المظفر فتحشاه ابن السلطان محمود {ا} شاه السلطان خلد الله ملكه {ن} بالاف الأمان منصور بن ملك تكر في <ا> لتاريخ سنة ثلاث وتسعين وثمانماية

Translation:

L-1 'If anyone changes the bequest after hearing it, the guilt shall be on those who make the change, for Allah hears and knows [all things]' [Qur'ān 1:181]. Manṣūr ibn Malik Thakur built this mosque for the five-times [daily] prayers for Allah, praise be to Him, in the reign of the sulṭān, son of the sulṭān Jalāl al-Dunyā

L-2 wa 'l-Dīn Abū 'l-Muẓaffar Fatḥ Shāh, son of Maḥmūd Shāh the sulṭān, may Allah make his kingdom everlasting with thousands of protection, dated [in the] year eight hundred and ninety-three.

Discussion:

This inscription suggests that Sulṭān Fatḥ Shāh's rule in Bengal extended beyond the year 892/1487, contrary to what most historians have thought. According to this epigraphical record, his rule must have continued till the beginning of the year 893/1488. Two previous inscriptions (both dated 889/1484), one from a ruined mosque near Ḥusaynī Dālān in Katra (fort) in Gaur and the other from an unidentified Sultanate mosque somewhere near the village of Birol in Dinajpur district (currently at Varendra Research Museum, Rajshahi, inv. no. 1443), record Sayf al-Dunyā wa 'l-Dīn Fīrūz Shāh as sulṭān as early as 889/1484, posing a number of problems for the chronology of the rulers. Not only do the two earlier inscriptions suggest that Sayf al-Dunyā wa 'l-Dīn Fīrūz Shāh declared himself a sulṭān towards the middle of Fatḥ Shāh's rule, but they also do not leave any room for an interim period of rule by the Abyssinian palace guard Sulṭān Shāhzāda, who masterminded the assassination of Fatḥ Shāh in a palace conspiracy according to most accounts. One possible explanation could be that the founder of the mosque, Manṣūr ibn Malik, was expressing his allegiance in this inscription to the assassinated Sulṭān Fatḥ Shāh at a time when there was no central authority in Gaur. The other plausible possibility is that Fatḥ Shāh's rule ended in the early part of the year 893/1488 when he was assassinated by Sulṭān Shahzāda. Another contestant for power, Malik 'Andīl (known later on as Fīrūz Shāh), who had been proclaiming himself sulṭān since 889/1484, seized this opportunity to occupy Gaur and overthrew Sulṭān Shahzāda. Thus, it seems, that Fīrūz Shāh was actually tempted to the throne during the reign of Sulṭān Fatḥ Shāh. Malik Thakur, who was the father of Manṣūr, mentioned in the inscription as the patron of the mosque, has also been mentioned in a mosque inscription dated 891/1486 from Rohanpur (currently preserved at Varendra Research Museum, Rajshahi, inv. no. 2852).

The message of the verse selected for the inscription is quite appropriate since it enjoins the people of the area not to bring any change to the original character of the mosque or its endowment.

(106) Inscription of an unidentified monument (probably a madrasa) in Gaur during the reign of Fatḥ Shāh

ORIGINAL SITE: An unidentified Sultanate monument (probably madrasa) nearby the royal citadel of Gaur. **CURRENT LOCATION:** Mahdipur High School, Uttar Mahdipur, English Bazar Police Station, Malda district. **MATERIAL, SIZE:** Black basalt; 18 × 29 inches. **STYLE, NO. OF LINES:** *ijāzah* in Bengali *ṭughrā'* decorative style; two lines. **REIGN:** Sulṭān Fatḥ Shāh (886–893/1481–1488). **LANGUAGE:** Persian. **TYPE:** Eulogistic inscription that probably belonged to an educational institution (namely, madrasa). **PUBLICATION:** S. Pratip Kumar Mitra, 'Late Dr. Z. A. Desai and the Provisional Study of some New Inscriptions of the Bengal Sultans', *Indo-Iranica, the Quarterly Organ of the Iran-Society* (Iran Society, Kolkata), 58(3 & 4) (September-December 2005): 26–29.

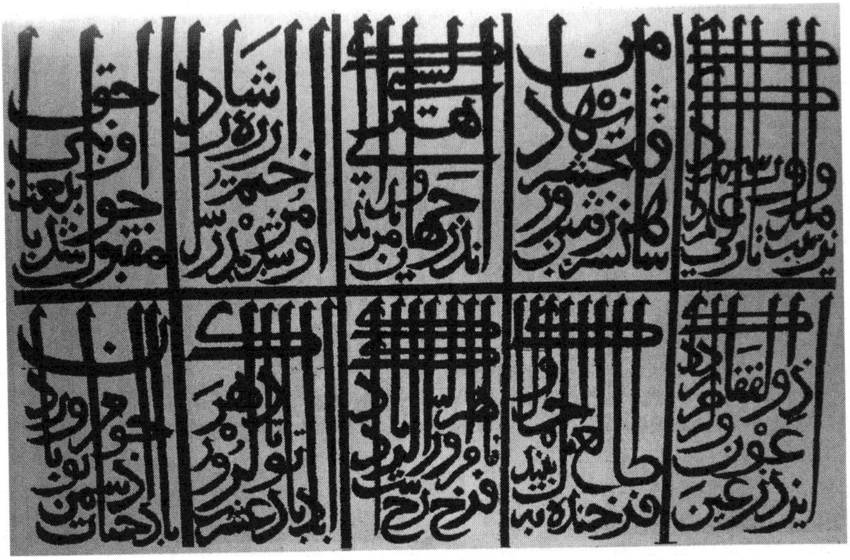

Figure 6.12 Commemorative inscription (an unidentified Sultanate monument from the royal citadel in Gaur) (source: author's own image).

Text:

L-1 ترتیب ملك وتازگي علم ورسم داد
شاهنشه زمین وزمن فتحشه نهاد
اندر جهان مرید ولی اند هر کسي
او شد مرید ختم رسل از ره رشاد
مقبول حق چو او شد[ه] با بیعت نبی

L-2 ایزد ز عین عون وکرم ذوالفقار داد
فرخنده طالع به امل وبیند جمال او
فرخ رخ است هر که ورا نام کرد یار
آباد باد عشرت تو با و کرور دهر
یادا حیات دشمن تو با مرور یاد

Translation:

L-1 Emperor of the earth and times Fatḥ Shāh implemented the orderliness of the kingdom, the renaissance of knowledge and the tradition of justice
While everyone in the world is a disciple of a saint, he (i.e. the emperor Fatḥ Shāh) has become disciple of the last Prophet (Muḥammad) through choosing the right path.
By expressing his adherence to the Prophet, he has become a favourite of the Ultimate Reality (The God)

L-2 God, through His kindness and graciousness has given him Dhū 'l-Fiqār (the sacred sword).

Fortunate is he who sees his beauty with cheerfulness; and with whosoever he befriended, has a happy countenance.

May your joy endure through the passage of Time! May the life of your enemy turn into a passing wind.

Discussion:

This inscription containing Persian verses in the eulogy of Sulṭān Fatḥ Shāh is a unique one for this period both calligraphically as well as linguistically. Its scheme of dividing each of the two lines of writing into five calligraphic panels has somewhat resemblance with two Arabic inscriptions (nos 65 and 66) of Bārbak Shāh from Miyanah Dar of the royal citadel in Gaur, dated 871 (1466–1467). On the other hand, its use of Persian (and that too in poetry form) surely makes it an exceptional one as Arabic was the commonly used language for architectural inscriptions during this period. There is a strong possibility that the present slab actually formed a part of a larger inscriptional scheme, like the two inscriptions of Miyanah Dar dated AH 871 (nos 65 and 66), though no other part of the inscription has been discovered so far. Signs of a sculptural image of a Hindu deity with attendants under a niche flanked by two rows of eight *jyotiska-devas* (subsidiary deities) on the reverse of this inscription suggests that the stone slab was picked up from the ruins of an ancient Hindu temple in the area.

Inscriptions of the so-called Ḥabashī rulers of Abyssinian origin

(107) Masjid inscriptions at Chapai dated 893 (1487–1488)

ORIGINAL SITE: A Sultanate masjid in Chapai-Maheshpur village in Gobratala Union, Palsha Post Office, Chapai Nawabganj district, Bangladesh.

Figure 6.13 Commemorative inscription (Chapai-Maheshpur village in Gobratala Union, Palsha Post Office, Chapai Nawabganj district, Bangladesh) (source: author's own image).

CURRENT LOCATION: In situ. **MATERIAL, SIZE:** Black basalt; 43 × 17. **STYLE, NO. OF LINES:** Bold *thulth*; two lines. **REIGN:** Sayf al-Dunyā wa 'l-Dīn Abū 'l-Muẓaffar Fīrūz Shāh (893–896/1488–1490). **LANGUAGE:** Arabic. **TYPE:** Monumental inscription of a masjid. **PUBLICATION:** Muhammad Abdul Qadir, 'Eight Unpublished Sultanate Inscriptions of Bengal', *Journal of Bengal Art*, 4(2) (1999): 235–261.

Text:

L-1 قال عليه السلام من بنا مسجدا لله بنا الله له مثله في الجنة
L-2 بنا <بنى> هذا المسجد المعظم مجلس المكرم مجلس اعلى عرف خواص خان ۸۹۳

Translation:

L-1 [The Prophet], peace be upon him, said, 'Whosoever builds a masjid for the sake of Allah, Allah will build for him the same in Paradise.'
L-2 Known as Khawāṣ Khān, the honourable and respected majlis (royal council member/courtier) of the higher majlis built this magnificent masjid in the year 893 (1487–1488).

Discussion:

This inscription is fixed above the lintel of the middle entrance of a three-domed traditional Sultanate masjid in the village of Chapai. Like many other Sultanate mosques of this period, the middle dome of this mosque is slightly larger than the other two domes on either side. There are four tiny closed minarets (*chatris* in South Asian architectural terminology) on all four corners of the mosques. Though the original structure of the masjid was fairly intact until very recently, local residents in the area have recently started renovating it without taking into consideration the original character of the monument. Quite recently, a madrasa has been haphazardly added adjacent to the mosque. Originally, the mosque was built at a very strategic location on the bank of the mighty river Mahananda overlooking a vast area. Presumably it also served as a resting place from time to time for the passing Sultanate naval fleet (known as *nawwara*) on the Mahanada river.

The bold *thulth* calligraphy in this inscription has been further decorated with a variety of floral and vegetal motifs appearing on the upper parts of each line. The date has been recorded in numerals, an uncommon feature in the Islamic inscriptions of Bengal during this period.

The patron of this mosque, seems to have served more than one sulṭān, as his name also appears in another inscription during the reign of Ḥusayn Shāh. It is interesting to notice that the name of the ruling Sulṭān Sayf al-Dīn Fīrūz Shāh was not mentioned in this inscription, perhaps indicating some hesitation on the part of Khawāṣ Khān to publically recognize the rule of the new sulṭān of Abyssinian origin who had just occupied the throne through a palace power struggle.

(108) Gate inscription from Garh Jaripa dated 893 (1487)

ORIGINAL SITE: Garh Jaripa, Sherpur, Mymansingh district, Bangladesh. **CURRENT LOCATION:** Indian Museum, inv. no. 14. **MATERIAL, SIZE:** Granite; 50 × 23 inches. **STYLE, NO OF LINES:** *naskh*, four lines. **REIGN:** Sulṭān Fīrūz Shāh (892–896/1487–1490). **LANGUAGE:** Arabic. **TYPE:** Construction of a gateway for a fort. **PUBLICATION:** Blochmann, *JASB*, XLIII (1874): 300; Z. A. Desai, *EIAPS* (1955–1956): 17–18, pl. V(a); Dani, *Bibliography of Muslim Inscriptions*, 39–40; S. Ahmad, *Inscriptions of Bengal*, 134–137; C. Dutt, *Arabic and Persian Inscriptions in the Indian Museum*, 19, no. 17; M. R. Tarafdar, *JASBD*, XX(3) (December 1975): 3–4; A. Karim, *Corpus of Inscriptions*, 220–222.

Text:

Four corners — ابو بكرصديق   عمر خطاب عثمان عفان على مرتضى

Right side — ....زور

که یکتن ببردیم باخود بکور

L-1 بسم الله الرحمن الرحيم لا إله إلا الله محمد رسول الله لا إله إلا الله

L-2 محمد رسول الله اللهم صل على محمد المصطفى وعلى المرتضى

L-3 والفاطمة الزهرا والحسن [ال] مجتبى والحسين الشهيد بكربلا وزين العابدين علي وباقر المحمد وجعفر الصادق وموسى الكاظم والعالي رضا ومحمد التقي وعلي النقي

L-4 والحسن [ال] عسكري والمحمد المهدي بني باب الحصار في زمن سلطان العهد والزمان سيف الدنيا والدين أبو<أبي>المظفر فيروز شاه السلطان خلد الله ملكه وسلطانه وتم بنيان هذا الباب في الأربع من محرم سنة ثلاث وتسعين وثمانماية

Translation:

Corners: Abu Bakr Siddiq, ‘Umar Khaṭṭab, ‘Uthmān ‘Affān, ‘Alī Murtaḍā…

L-1 In the name of Allah, the Compassionate, the Merciful. There is no God but Allah, Muḥammad is Allah's messenger. There is no God but Allah,

L-2 Muḥammad is Allah's messenger. O Allah, bless Muḥammad al-Muṣṭafā (the chosen one) and ‘Alī al-Murtaḍā

L-3 and Fāṭima al-Ẓahrā and al-Ḥasan al-Mujtabā and al-Ḥusayn, the martyr of Karbala, and Zayn al-‘Abidīn ‘Alī and Bāqir al-Muḥammad and Ja‘far al-Ṣādiq and Musā al-Kāẓim and al-‘Alī Riḍa and Muḥammad al-Taqī and ‘Alī al-Naqī

L-4 and al-Ḥasan al-‘Askarī and al-Muḥammad al-Mahdī. The gate of the enclosure (castle) was built in the reign of Sulṭān al-‘Ahd wa ’l-Zamān Sayf al-Dunyā wa ’l-Dīn Abū ’l-Muẓaffar Fīruz Shāh al-Sulṭān, may Allah make his kingdom and authority everlasting. The construction of the gate of this enclosure (fortified wall) was completed on the fourth of Muḥarram, [in the] year eight hundred and ninety-three [20 December 1487].

Discussion:

While the masjid inscription dated 889/1484 found near Ḥusaynī Dalan in Gaur and the masjid inscription dated 889/1484 from Birol indicate that Sayf al-Dunyā wa 'l-Dīn Fīruz Shāh pronounced himself as sulṭān as early as 889/1484, the date of this inscription further indicates that he never gave up his claim to be sulṭān during the last four years of Fatḥ Shāh's rule.

While the epigraphic text contains the names of the twelve Shi'ī imams, it also contains the names of the first four rightly guided caliphs highly respected by the Sunnis in the same epigraphic text. Accommodation of the two different sectarian beliefs of Islam in the same inscription suggests a good degree of religious tolerance and co-existence, a social phenomenon that generally prevails in Bengali society to this day.

(109) Masjid inscription in Aqaliyya dated 893 (1488–1489)

ORIGINAL SITE: An unnamed Sultanate masjid in Aqaliyya village, Sylhet district, Bangladesh. **CURRENT LOCATION**: A new mosque built on Sylhet-Sunamganj highway, about three miles away from Sylhet town, Bangladesh. **MATERIAL, SIZE**: Black basalt; not known. **STYLE, NO. OF LINES**: *thulth* in Bengali *ṭughrā'*; three lines. **REIGN**: Sayf al-Dunyā wa 'l-Dīn Abū 'l-Muẓaffar Fīrūz Shāh (893–896/1488–1490). **LANGUAGE**: Arabic. **TYPE:** Commemorative inscription of a mosque. **PUBLICATION:** Muhammad Abdul Qadir, 'Eight Unpublished Sultanate Inscriptions of Bengal', *Journal of Bengal Art*, 4(2) (1999): 235–261.

Text:

L-1 شهد الله أنه لا اله إلا هو والملائكة وأولوا العلم قائما بالقسط لا إله إلا هو العزيز الحكيم. فالله خير حافظا وهو أرحم الراحمين

L-2 السلطان سيف الدنيا والدين ابو المظفر (فيروز) شاه السلطان خلد الله

L-3 . . . . سنة ثلث و تسعين وثمانماية

Translation:

L-1 Allah bears witness that there is no God but He (Himself), and the angels, and those having knowledge, firmly sticking to justice; indeed none has the right to be worshipped but He (Allah), the All-Mighty, the All-Wise (Qur'ān 3:18). Allah is the best of protectors, and He is the Most Kind among the compassionates (Qur'ān 12:64).

L-2 Sulṭān Sayf al-Dunyā wa 'l-Dīn Abū 'l-Muẓaffar (Firūz) Shāh May Allah perpetuate (his rule and kingdom)

L-3 (in) the year eight hundred and ninety-three (1488).

Discussion:

This inscription was originally found in the debris of a ruined Sultanate masjid near where the present mosque was built. The lower portion of the right corner of this inscription is badly damaged. Due to long exposure to saltpetre, the surface of the inscription, namely the writing, has been largely eroded, rendering the deciphering of the text very difficult. The three lines of text are separated by two distinct raised borderlines. Since the beginnings of the last two lines are completely eroded, reading of this epigraphic text is largely conjectural.

Due to the decaying condition of the inscription, the local masjid committee decided to encase it with cement for future preservation. This resulted in concealing the text completely at one point. In order to obtain a rubbing of the inscription, the cement had to be removed, causing further damage to the inscription.

(110) Masjid inscription in Goamalati dated 894 (1489)

ORIGINAL SITE: A no longer extant Sultanate masjid in Goamaloti near Gaur. **CURRENT LOCATION:** Not known. **MATERIAL, SIZE:** Granite; not known. **STYLE, NO. OF LINES:** *naskh*; one line. **REIGN:** Sulṭān Fīrūz Shāh (892–896/1487–1490). **LANGUAGE:** Arabic. **TYPE:** Commemorative inscription. **PUBLICATION:** Blochmann, *JASB*, XLIII (1874); Ravenshaw, *Gaur*, 74, pl. 48; Dani, *Bibliography of Muslim Inscriptions*, 38–39, no. 62; S. Ahmad, *Inscriptions of Bengal*, 131–132; A. Karim, *Corpus of Inscriptions*, 222–223.

Text:

قال النبي صلى الله عليه وسلم من بنى مسجدا في الدنيا بنى الله تعالى له سبعين قصرا في الجنة بنى هذا المسجد . . . . الغ
أعظم وخاقان معظم بهلوي عصر سر نشين خرمسر مخلص خان عالي . . . في عهد [ال]سلطان الأعظم والمعظم العادل
الباذل سيف الدنيا والدين أبو<أبي> المظفر فيروز شاه السلطان خلد الله ملكه وسلطانه وأعلى أمره وشأنه في الخامس من شهر
صفر سنة أربع وتسعين وثمانماية

Translation:

The Prophet, peace and blessings of Allah be upon him, said, 'Whosoever builds a mosque in the world, Allah will build for him seventy palaces in Paradise.' The sublime Ulugh and exalted Khāqān, Pahlawi-i-'Aṣr, Sar Nashīn (humble/one who exhibits goods to the people of a caravan) Khuramsar Mukhliṣ Khān 'Ālī...; during the reign of great, sublime, just and benevolent Sulṭān Sayf al-Dunyā wa 'l-Dīn Abū 'l-Muẓaffar Fīrūz Shāh Sulṭān, may Allah make his kingdom and authority everlasting and keep his position and prestige high, on the fifteenth of the month of Ṣafar (in the) year eight hundred and ninety-four [24 January 1489].

Discussion:

This inscription originally belonged to a beautiful ten-domed mosque built with brick and stone, as recorded by Westmacot in the 1870s in a report to the Asiatic Society of Bengal.

(111) Masjid inscription in Kalna dated 895 (1489)

ORIGINAL SITE: A ruined Sultanate mosque in Kalna, Burdwan district, West Bengal, India. **CURRENT LOCATION:** Indian Museum, Calcutta, inv. no. 15. **MATERIAL, SIZE:** Black basalt, 21 × 7 inches. **STYLE, NO. OF LINES:** *naskh*; not known. **REIGN:** Most likely during the reign of Sulṭān Firūz Shāh (892–896/1487–1490). **LANGUAGE:** Arabic. **TYPE:** Commemorative inscription. **PUBLICATION:** Banerjee, *Journal of Bihar and Orissa Research Society*, IV (1918): 181–182; Dani, *Bibliography of Muslim Inscriptions*, 39; S. Ahmad, *Inscriptions of Bengal*, 132–133; A. Karim, *Corpus of Inscriptions*, 229–230.

Text:

قال النبي [عليه] السلام من بنى مسجدا [في الدنيا بنى الله (له) سبعين قصرا في الجنة بنى في عهد] السلطان فيروز [شاه]
السلطان خلد الله ملكه وسلطانه . . الغ علي ظفر خان . . خان . . الغ . . خمس وتسعين وثمانماية

Translation:

The Prophet, peace be upon him, said, 'Whosoever builds a mosque in the world, Allah will build for him seventy palaces in Paradise.' Ulugh 'Alī Ẓafar Khān … Khān … Ulugh … built [this mosque] in the reign of the Sulṭān Fīrūz Shāh – may Allah make his kingdom and authority everlasting – [in the year] eight hundred and ninety-five.

Discussion:

This inscription is often confused with the Masjid inscription now preserved in Shāh Majlis Dargāh dated 897/1491–1492. It is quite likely that this inscription is one of the three inscriptions taken to the court building at Kalna about a century ago, before it was given to the Indian Museum.

(112) Undated inscription of Fīrūz Minār in Goamaloti, Gaur

ORIGINAL SITE: Fīrūz Shāh Minār in Goamaloti, Gaur. **CURRENT LOCATION:** British Museum, inv. no. OA+6415. **MATERIAL, SIZE:** Black basalt; 18 × 10 inches. **STYLE, NO. OF LINES:** *thulth* in Bengali *ṭughrā'*; single line. **REIGN:** Most likely the reign of Sulṭān Sayf al-Dunyā wa 'l-Dīn Firūz Shāh (892–896/1487–1490). **LANGUAGE:** Arabic. **TYPE:** Commemorative inscription. **PUBLICATION:** S. M. Hasan, 'A Sulṭān Fīrūz Shāh II Fragment', *Asian*

Review (Arts and Letters), n.s. 2(2) (August, 1965): 79–83; W. Franklin, *Journal of a Route from Rajmahal to Gour*, MS in India Office Library, 16; A. Karim, *Corpus of Inscriptions*, 226–227.

Text:

. . . . .الموید بتاید<المؤيد بتأييد> الديان المجاهد في سبيل الرحمن خليفة
الله بالحجة والبرهان سيف الدنيا [والد]ين . . . .

Translation:

...al-Mu'ayyad bi Ta'yīd al-Dayyān, al-Mujāhid fī Sabīl al-Raḥmān, Khalīfat Allah bi 'l-Ḥujjat wa 'l-Burhān, Sayf al-Dunyā wa 'l-Dīn...

Discussion:

This is one of the inscriptions taken to England by Franklin and donated by him to the British Museum.

(113) Masjid inscription in Chunakhali dated 896 (1490)

ORIGINAL SITE: An unidentified Sultanate mosque near Chunakhali in Murshidabad district, West Bengal, India. **CURRENT LOCATION:** Affixed to the shrine of Masnad-i-A'lā at Chunakhali. **MATERIAL, SIZE:** Not known. **STYLE, NO. OF LINES:** *thulth* in *ṭughrā'* decorative features; not known. **REIGN:** Sulṭān Sayf al-Dunyā wa 'l-Dīn Fīrūz Shāh (892–896/1487–1490). **LANGUAGE:** Arabic. **TYPE:** Commemorative inscription. **PUBLICATION:** Beveridge, *Proceedings of the Asiatic Society of Bengal* (1873): 55; Dani, *Bibliography of Muslim Inscriptions*, 42; S. Ahmad, *Inscriptions of Bengal*, 140–141; Z. A. Desai, 'The So-called Chunakhali Inscription', *JASBD* (Humanities), XXVI–VI (1979–1981): 11–20; A. Karim, *Corpus of Inscriptions*, 223–226.

Text:

L-1 قال الله تعالى وأن المساجد لله فلا تدعوا مع الله أحدا وقال النبي عليه السلام من بنى مسجدا في الدنيا بنى الله له سبعين
قصرا في الجنة بنى هذا المسجد في زمن السلطان العادل
L-2 الباذل سيف الدنيا والدين أبو<أبي> المظفر فيروز شاه السلطان خلد الله ملكه وسلطانه [ال] مجلس المعظم المكرم
مجلس باربك أدام الله معاليا مؤرخا في الثاني من المحرم سنة ست وتسعين وثمانماية

Translation:

Allah the Exalted said, 'And verily the mosques are for Allah, so do not invoke anyone with Allah.' The Prophet, peace be upon him, said, 'Whosoever builds a mosque in the world, Allah will build for him seventy palaces in Paradise.' The sublime and honoured majlis (council), Majlis-i-Bārbak, may Allah keep him always venerable, built this mosque in the reign of the just and benevolent Sulṭān Sayf al-Dunyā wa 'l-Dīn Abū 'l-Muẓaffar Fīrūz Shāh al-Sulṭān, may Allah make his kingdom and authority everlasting, dated on second of Muḥarram [in the] year eight hundred and ninety-six [5 November 1490].

Discussion:

Around 1873, Beveridge found the inscription on the shrine of Masnad-i-A'lā at Chunakhali where it still remains.

(114) Masjid inscription in Devikot dated 896 (1490–1491)

ORIGINAL SITE: An unnamed Sultanate mosque near the shrine of Shāh 'Atā' at Devikot in the Dakhshin Dinajpur district, West Bengal. **CURRENT LOCATION:** Affixed to the right wall by the door of the shrine of Shāh 'Aṭā' near Dhol Pukur at Devikot. **MATERIAL, SIZE:** Not known; 23 × 12 inches. **STYLE, NO. OF LINES:** A crude form of local *thulth*; three lines. **REIGN:** Sulṭān Shams al-Dīn Muẓaffar Shāh (896–899/1491–1494). **LANGUAGE:** Arabic. **TYPE:** Commemorative inscription. **PUBLICATION:** Blochmann, *JASB*, XLII (1873): 289–290; and XLI (1872): 107; Cunningham, *ASR*, XV (1882): 98–99; G. Yazdani, *EIM* (1929–30): 11–12, pl. VII (B); Dani, *Bibliography of Muslim Inscriptions*, 43; S. Ahmad, *Inscriptions of Bengal*, 143–144; A. Karim, *Corpus of Inscriptions*, 227–228.

Text:

L-1 بنى هذه . . العمارة المسجد في عهد المخدوم المشهور
L-2 قطب أوليا مخدوم مولانا عطا طيب الله ثرا[ه] وجعل الجنة مثواه في عهد
L-3 شمس الدنيا والدين أبو<أبي> النصر مظفر شاه سلطان خلد الله ملكه وسلطانه في التاريخ ست وتسعين و [ثمانماية

Translation:

L-1 The edifice of this ... mosque was constructed during the time of the famous *makhdūm* (Sufi master)
L-2 Quṭb-i-Awliyā' Makhdūm Mawlānā 'Aṭā', may Allah let him rest in peace and make Paradise his abode, in the reign of
L-3 Shams al-Dunyā wa 'l-Dīn Abū 'l-Naṣr Muẓaffar Shāh Sulṭān, may Allah make his kingdom and authority everlasting, on the day [of the year] eight hundred and ninety-six.

Discussion:

Mawlānā 'Aṭā' died long before the reign of Sulṭān Muẓaffar Shāh (896–899/1491–1494). This inscription was probably inscribed to commemorate the renovation of the mosque that once served as the centre of *da'wah* (Islamic propagation) activities of Mawlānā in the area.

(115) Masjid inscription in Champanagar dated 897 (1491)

ORIGINAL SITE: An unnamed Sultanate mosque near Champanagar, Bhagalpur district, Bihar, India. **CURRENT LOCATION:** Jāmi‘ Masjid in Champanagar, Bhagalpur district, Bihar, India. **MATERIAL, SIZE:** Black basalt; 29 × 10 inches. **STYLE, NO. OF LINES:** *naskh*; two lines. **REIGN:** Sulṭān Shams al-Dīn Muẓaffar Shāh (896–899/1491–1494). **LANGUAGE:** Arabic. **TYPE:** Commemorative inscription. **PUBLICATION:** A. A. Kadiri, ‘Inscriptions of the Sulṭāns of Bengal from Bihar’, *EIAPS* (1961): 37–38, pl. XI (b); Dani, *Bibliography of Muslim Inscriptions*, 137; S. Ahmad, *Inscriptions of Bengal*, 144–145; Q. Ahmad, *Inscriptions of Bihar*, 98–99; A. Karim, *Corpus of Inscriptions*, 228–229.

Text:

L-1 بسم الله الرحمن الرحيم قال النبي عليه السلام من بنى مسجدا في {ال} دارالدنيا بنى الله له في الآخرة سبعين قصرا .
في[عهد]. المالك الواثق بتأييد الرحمن

L-2 شمس الدنيا والدين أبو<أبي> النصر مظفر شاه السلطان خلد الله ملكه وسلطانه باني خير خان أعظم معتبر خان
كار فرمان بازو راي هاٹ مؤرخا في العاشر من المحرم المكرم سنة سبع وتسعين وثمانماية

Translation:

L-1 In the name of Allah, the Compassionate, the Merciful. The Prophet, peace be upon him, said, ‘Whoever builds a mosque in the worldly abode, Allah will build for him seventy palaces hereafter.’ This mosque was built in the reign of al-Mālik al-Wāthiq bi Tā’yīd al-Raḥmān (the lord who trust in the support of the Most Merciful)

L-2 Shams al-Dunyā wa ’l-Dīn Abū ’l-Naṣr Muẓaffar Shāh al-Sulṭān, may Allah perpetuate his kingdom and authority. The builder of [this] benevolent [deed] is the sublime khan Mu‘tabar Khān, Kar-i-Farmān (administrator) of Bazurai Hāt; dated the tenth of the revered [month of] Muḥarram, [in the] year eight hundred and ninety-seven [13 November 1491].

Discussion:

This provenance of this inscription serves as further evidence that the Bengal Sultanate continued to extend into Bihar during this period. The place name itself, Bazurai Hāt, is interesting, as the suffix, *Hāt*, means ‘market’ in Bengali. A large number of place names during this period used the suffix *Hāt*. This suggests a gradual expansion of market activities after the arrival of Islam in the region. Bengal’s gradual assimilation into the greater economic framework of the Islamic world consequently made this region an integral part of Islamic civilization.

(116) A commemorative inscription of an unidentified Sultanate masjid in Gaur dated 897 (1490–1491)

ORIGINAL SITE: An unidentified Sultanate masjid in Gaur, Ingrez Bazar police station, Malda district, West Bengal, India. **CURRENT LOCATION:** Gaur Social Welfare Mission Museum. **MATERIAL, SIZE:** Black basalt; 26 × 10 inches. **STYLE, NO. OF LINES:** Plaited *thulth* in monumental Bengali *ṭughrā'*; one line. **REIGN:** Sulṭān Shams al-Dunyā wa 'l-Dīn Abū 'l-Naṣr Muẓaffar Shāh [Sīdī Badr] (896–898/1491–1493). **LANGUAGE:** Arabic. **TYPE:** Commemorative inscription of a masjid. **PUBLICATION:** M. Y. Siddiq, 'Calligraphy and Islamic Culture', *Bulletin of the School of Oriental and African Studies*, 68(1) (2005): 21–58.

Figure 6.14 Commemorative inscription (Sultanate Masjid in Gaur, Ingrez Bazar police station, Malda District, West Bengal) (source: author's own image).

Text:

قال النبي صلى الله عليه وسلم من بنى مسجدا لله بنى الله له سبعين قصرا في الجنة في عهد [ال] سلطان شمس الدنيا والدين
أبو<أبي> النصرمظفر شاه سلطان [بنى] هذا المسجد الملك الماس سلمه الله تعالى في الدارين وذلك في التاريخ عشرين ماه
شعبان قدره سنة سبع وتسعين وثمانماية

Translation:

The Prophet, peace and blessings of Allah be upon him, said, 'Whosoever builds a mosque for the sake of Allah, Allah will build for him seventy palaces in Paradise.' During the era of Sulṭān Shams al-Dunyā wa 'l-Dīn Abū 'l-Naṣr Muẓaffar Shāh Sulṭān, al-Malik Almās (built) this masjid, may the Almighty Allah keep him in peace in both of the abodes (worlds). This was (done) in the date, the twentieth of the month of Sha'bān, the year eight hundred and ninety-seven.

Discussion:

This newly discovered inscription is an exemplary piece of Islamic calligraphy from the reign of Sulṭān Shams al-Dunyā wa 'l-Dīn Abū 'l-Naṣr Muẓaffar Shāh, during whose brief rule the Bengal Sultanate was extended from Champaran,

Bihar to Kalna, Burdwan. Sulṭān Shams al-Dunyā wa 'l-Dīn Abū 'l-Naṣr Muẓaffar Shāh was the last sulṭān of the four so called Ḥabashī (Abyssinian) rulers who reigned Bengal for a very short transitional period between the restored Ilyās Shāhī dynasty and the Ḥusayn Shāhī dynasty, for approximately six years during 893–898/1487–1493.

In the calligraphy of this inscription, we find a continuation of the distinctive Sultanate decorative style that prevailed in the earlier Sultanate inscriptions, particularly featured in the elongation of vertical letters (i.e. *alif*, *lām* etc.), their arrangement in a symmetrical order, and the superimposition of the horizontally elongated Arabic preposition *fī* at the top. The text in the inscription is slightly ungrammatical, as the verb *buniya* (constructed by) is missing before the phrase *hādhā 'l-masjid* (this mosque). The title *al-malik* (king/lord) used before the name of the patron of the masjid, Almās, seems to have been used to convey the meaning of a powerful lord in the Sultanate court, and clearly not to mean a king.

(117) Masjid inscription from Kalna dated 897 (1490–1491)

ORIGINAL SITE: An unnamed Sultanate mosque at Kalna in the district of Burdwan, West Bengal, India. **CURRENT LOCATION:** Indian Museum, Calcutta, inv. no. 6063. **MATERIAL, SIZE:** Grey granite; 22 × 9 inches. **STYLE, NO. OF LINES:** *naskh*; two lines. **REIGN:** Sulṭān Muẓaffar Shāh (896–899/1491–1494). **LANGUAGE:** Arabic. **TYPE:** Foundation inscription. **PUBLICATION:** Blochmann, *JASB*, XLI (1872): 331; T. Bloch, *Annual Report of the Archaeological Survey of India: Bengal Circle, Part II (1903–4)*, 4, pl. II; A. Wali, *Bengal Past and Present*, XIV (January-July 1917): 100–101; Z. A. Desai, *EIAPS* (1955–1956): 19–20; S. Ahmad, *Inscriptions of Bengal*, 132–133; C. Dutt, *Arabic and Persian inscriptions in the Indian Museum*, 21, no. 19; A. Karim, *Corpus of Inscriptions*, 229–230.

Text:

قال النبي عليه السلام من بنى مسجدا في الدنيا بنى الله [له] سبعين قصرا في الجنة بني هذا المسجد في زمن السلطان العادل مظفر
شاه السلطان و باني الخير . . مؤرخا في شهور سنة سبع وتسعين وثمانماية

Translation:

The Prophet, peace be upon him, said, 'Whosoever builds a mosque in the world, Allah will build for him seventy palaces in Paradise.' This mosque was built in the era of the just Sulṭān Muẓaffar Shāh al-Sulṭān, the builder of the charitable [deed]...; dated in the month of [the] year eight hundred and ninety-seven.

Discussion:

This inscription originally belonged to a no longer extant Sultanate mosque. It was found in the shrine of Shāh Majlis at Kalna.

(118) Jāmi‘ Masjid inscription from Chapai Nawabganj dated 898 (1492)

ORIGINAL SITE: An unnamed Sultanate jāmi‘ masjid, probably near Gaur, Chapai Nawabganj district, Bangladesh. **CURRENT LOCATION:** Malda Museum (formerly B. R. Sen Museum), West Bengal, India. **MATERIAL, SIZE:** Not known. **STYLE, NO. OF LINES:** *thulth* in Bengali *ṭughrā'*; one line. **REIGN:** Sulṭān Muẓaffar Shāh (896–899/1491–1494). **LANGUAGE:** Arabic. **TYPE:** Foundation inscription. **PUBLICATION:** *Proceedings of the Asiatic Society of Bengal* (1890): 242; A. A. Khan, *Memoirs of Gaur*, 33; Yazdani, *EIM* (1929–30): 13; Dani, *Bibliography of Muslim Inscriptions*, 43, no. 71; S. Ahmad, *Inscriptions of Bengal*, 147–148; A. Karim, *Corpus of Inscriptions*, 232–233.

Text:

قال النبي صلى الله عليه وسلم من بنى مسجدا ويبتغي به وجه الله بنى الله {الله} له بيتا مثله في الجنة في عهد السلطان الأعظم شمس الدنيا والدين أبو<أبي> النصر مظفر شاه السلطان خلد الله ملكه وسلطانه بنى هذا المسجد الجامع [ال]مجلس المعظم والمكرم مجلس الغ خرشيد دام علوه في العاشر من ربيع الأول سنة ثمان وتسعين وثمانماية

Translation:

The Prophet, peace and the blessings of Allah be upon him, said, ‘Whoever builds a mosque seeking favour of Allah, Allah will build for him a house of a similar kind in Paradise.’ During the reign of the great king Shams al-Dunyā wa ’l-Dīn Abū ’l-Naṣr Muẓaffar Shāh al-Sulṭān, may Allah perpetuate his kingdom and authority. The builder of this congregational mosque is the sublime and honoured council Majlis Ulugh Khurshīd, may his greatness continue,– on the tenth of Rabī‘ al-Awwal [in the] year eight hundred and ninety-eight [5 January 1493].

Discussion:

This inscription was incidentally found in a jungle near Chapai Nawabganj, about twenty miles southeast of Gaur, by a *faqir*.

(119) Inscription of Chilla Khāna of Nūr Quṭb al-‘Ālam in Ḥaḍrat Pandua dated 898 (1493)

ORIGINAL SITE: Chilla Khāna of Nūr Quṭb al-‘Ālam in Choto Dargāh at Ḥaḍrat Pandua in Malda district. **CURRENT LOCATION:** In situ. **MATERIAL, SIZE:** Black basalt; not known. **STYLE, NO. OF LINES:** *thulth* in Bengali *ṭughrā'*; one line. **REIGN:** Sulṭān Muẓaffar Shāh (896–899/1491–1494). **LANGUAGE:** Arabic. **TYPE:** Commemorative inscription. **PUBLICATION:** Blochmann, *JASB*, XLII (1873): 290–291; Cunningham, *ASR*, XV (1882): 84; Ravenshaw, *Gaur*, 77, pl. 49 (no. 9); A. A. Khan, *Memoirs of Gaur*, 114–115;

Dani, *Bibliography of Muslim Inscriptions*, 44; S. Ahmad, *Inscriptions of Bengal*, 145–147; A. Karim, *Corpus of Inscriptions*, 230–232.

Text:

L-1 قال الله تعالى إن أول بيت وضع للناس للذي ببكة مباركا وهدى للعالمين فيه آيات بينا[ت] مقام إبراهيم ومن دخله كان آمنا ولله على الناس حج البيت من استطاع إليه سبيلا ومن كفر فإن الله غنى عن العالمين بنى في {ال}بيت الصوفية {ال}روضة قطب الأقطاب قتيل محبت وهاب شيخ المشائخ حضرت شيخ نور الحق والشرع والدين سيد نور قطب عالم قدس الله العزيز سره ونوّر الله قبره

L-2 بنى هذا البيت في عهد السلطان العادل الباذل الفاضل غوث الإسلام والمسلمين شمس الدنيا والدين أبو<أبي> النصر مظفر شاه سلطان خلد الله ملكه وسلطانه وأعلى أمره وشأنه بنى هذا البيت في خلافة شيخ الإسلام والمسلمين شيخ المشائخ ابن شيخ المشايخ شيخ محمد غوث سلمه الله تعالى دائما مورخا السابع {ال}عشر من شهر رمضان المبارك في سنة ثمان وتسعين [و] ثمانماية

Translation:

L-1 Allah the Exalted said, 'Verily the first house [of worship] set up for mankind was in Bakkah (Makkah), full of blessing and guidance for the universe. In it are clear signs, the place of Abraham. And whoever enters it attains security. And pilgrimage to the house [of Allah] is a duty owed to Allah by any human being who can afford the journey; but whoever disbelieves, Allah is surely independent of all beings' [Qur'ān 4:96–97]. The abode of, sufis and the rawḍa (shrine) for Quṭb al-Aqṭāb Qatīl Maḥabbat Wahhāb Shaykh al-Mashāyikh Ḥaḍrat Shaykh Nūr al-Ḥaqq wa 'l-Shar' wa 'l-Dīn Sayyid Nūr Quṭb 'Ālam, may the Almighty Allah sanctify his soul and enlighten his grave.

L-2 The house was built in the reign of the just, benevolent and outstanding Sulṭān Ghawth al-Islām wa 'l-Muslimīn Abū 'l-Naṣr Muẓaffar Shāh Sulṭān, may Allah perpetuate his kingdom and authority and promote his status and prestige. This house was built during the *khilāfa* (spiritual succession) of Shaykh al-Islām wa 'l-Muslimīn, Shaykh al-Mashāyikh, who himself was the son of Shaykh al-Mashāyikh, Shaykh Muḥammad Gawth, may Allah the Exalted always protect him; dated the seventeen of the blessed month of Ramaḍan in the year eight hundred and ninety-eight [8 July 1493].

Discussion:

Muḥammad Gawth was a descendant of Nūr Quṭb al-'Ālam (whose details can be found in an inscription dated 863/1459) and a spiritual successor from the same family line belonging to Chishtiya sufi order. From the title Shaykh al-Mashāyikh ibn Shaykh al-Mashāyikh, it seems that he was one of the sons of Nūr Quṭb al-'Ālam whose name can only be found in this inscription.

Notes

1 Abdul Karim, *Social History of the Muslims in Bengal* (Chittagong: Baitush Sharaf Islamic Research Institute, 1985): 142–143.
2 *Encyclopaedia of Islam*, 2nd edn, s.v. 'Sātgā'on'.
3 For details on the history of Satgaon, Rakhal Das Bandyopādhyāya, 'Saptagrāma or Sātgānw', *JASB*, 7 (July 1909): 245–262; G. Crawford, 'Satgaon and Tribeni', *Bengal Past and Present*, III (January-April 1909): 18–26.
4 *Encyclopaedia of Islam*, 2nd edn, s.v. 'Sātgā'on'.
5 Ghulam Saqlayn, *Bangladesher Sufi-Sadhak* (Dhaka: Islamic Foundation, 1987): 78–82.
6 Enamul Haque, *Islamic Art Heritage of Bangladesh* (Dhaka: Bangladesh National Museum, 1983): 40–101.
7 *Encyclopaedia of Islam*, 2nd edn, s.v. 'Sundarban'.
8 Ghulam Saqlayn, *Bangladesher Sufi-Sadhak*, 191–196.
9 Mohar Ali, *History of the Muslims of Bengal*, vol. 1A: 42.
10 Abdul Karim, 'Nur Qutub Alam's letter on the ascendency of Ganes', *Abdul Karim Sahitya-Visharad Commemorative Volume*, ed. M. Enamul Haq (Dhaka: Asiatic Society of Bangladesh, 1972): 335–343; Ghulam Hussain Salim, *Riyazu-s-Salatin*, English trans. Abdus Salam, 108.
11 S. H. Askari, 'New light on Rajah Ganesh and Sultan Ibrahim Sharqi of Jaunpur from contemporary correspondence of two Muslim saints', *Bengal Past and Present*, 57(130) (1948): 38–39.
12 M. Saghīr al-Dīn Mian, *Gowre Muslim Sāshan wo Nūr Quṭb al-'Ālam* (Dhaka: Islamic Foundation, 1991): 36–37; Abdul Karim, *Social History of the Muslims in Bengal*, 142–143.
13 Orme, *Gowre: Description of its ruins with four inscriptions taken in Arabic*, MS in India Office Library, London, MS (EUR) No. 65:25; Henry Creighton, *The Ruins of Gaur* (London: Black, Parbury, & Allen, 1817): 2–7.
14 Creighton, *The Ruins of Gaur*, pl. 3.
15 Ibid., pl. 3 (description).
16 Creighton lived in the area for almost twenty years (1787–1807). His book, published posthumously, was the first full account of Gaur with many rich illustrations, and is still considered a valuable primary source. The epitaph on his grave (grave no. 150, located at the northeast of the graveyard) in Babulbona, Bahrampur, West Bengal (unfortunately stolen a few years ago) recorded the following: 'HENRY CREIGHTON OF GOAMALOTY, Date of Death: 2nd October, 1807, Age – 44 years; FIRST INSTITUTOR OF A NATIVE SCHOOL, FOR INSTRUCTING POOR CHILDREN IN THEIR OWN LANGUAGE'. Thus, in addition to being an amateur archaeologist, a natural artist and an accomplished indigo planter, he was also one of the very few pioneers who ventured to set up a vernacular primary school for poor local students. The use of Bengali language for basic education was, indeed, a revolutionary idea at that time.
17 Munshī Shayam Prasad, *Aḥwal-i-Gaur wa Pandua*, India Office Library, MS 2841, ed. Ahmad Hasan Dani and published as an 'Appendix to *Muslim Architecture of Bengal*' (Dacca: Asiatic Society of Bengal, 1961): 14–15.
18 William Franklin, *Ruins of Gaur*. Written in 1810, it was sent by Major Franklin (then a regulating officer stationed at Bhagalpur) from Bhagalpur to the Court of the Directors for Conducting the Affairs of the United East India Company, along with a map, a few drawings (map and drawings have long since disappeared) of the celebrated city of Gaur, and a covering letter dated 12 April 1812. See India Office Library, London, MS No. 19; the printed version of which is now preserved in the map room of the India Office Library, London. MS No. C506=W 5761. The book was printed in 1910 in Shillong as an official document (reference no.: E. B. & A. S. P. O. (R. & A.)

No. 76-100-9-3-1910 – G.N.K.). It was acquired by India Office Library on 3 June 1910. Franklin joined the 19th Regiment of Native Infantry in 1788, became Lieutenant in 1789, Captain in 1803, Major in 1810, Lieutenant Colonel in 1814 and finally retired as a Colonel in 1824.

19 Franklin, *Ruins of Gaur*, MS No. C506=W 5761: f. 3.

20 *A Geographical, Statistical and Historical Description of the District or Zilla of Dinajpur in the Province or Subah of Bengal* (Calcutta, 1833).

21 Franklin, *Ruins of Gaur*, MS No. C506=W 5761: f. 3.

22 One such example is Firūz Mīnār inscription of Sulṭān Sayf al-Dīn Fīrūz Shāh (British Museum inventory no. OA+6415).

23 Nabih A. Faris and G. C. Miles, 'An Inscription of Bārbak Shāh of Bengal', *Ars Islamica*, VI (1940): 141–147.

24 Franklin, *Ruins of Gaur*, f. 4.

25 M. A. Rahim, *Social and Cultural History of Bengal*, 79–80.

Bibliography

Primary sources

Arabic, Persian or Urdu

Abu ’l-faḍl ‘Allāmī. *A’īn-i-Akbarī*, 3 vols, Lucknow: Nawal Kishor, 1869. English edition: vol. 1, trans. H. Blochmann, ed. D. C. Phillott; vols. 2 and 3 trans. H. S. Jarrett, ed. Jadunath Sarkar, 2nd edn, Calcutta: Asiatic Society of Bengal, 1927. Reprint – New Delhi: Oriental Books Reprint Corp., 1977–1978.

‘Alī, Munshī Rahmān. *Tawarīkh-i-Dhaka*, Dhaka, 1910.

Balkhī, Muẓaffar Shams. *Maktubat-i-Muzaffar Shams Balkhi*, Persian MS Khuda Bakhsh Oriental Public Library, Patna. Acc. No. 1859.

Chisti, ‘Abd al-Rahman. *Mir’at al-Asrar*, Persian MS Dhaka University Library, Dhaka. MS No. 16 AR Persian MS Dhaka Aliya Madrasa, Dhaka. MS No. MA 12/19–20. Persian MS Khuda Bakhsh Oriental Public Library, Patna. MS No. 204. Compiled 1654.

Chisti, ‘Abd al-Rahman. *Mir’at-i-Madar*, MS Dhaka University, Dhaka. No. 217.

Habib al-Rahman, Hakim. *Asudgan-i-Dhaka*, Dhaka, 1946.

Ilāhī Bakhsh, Munshī Sayyid (al-Husaynī Awrangzebadi). *Khurshid-i-Jahān-i-Numā*, Extracts related to the history of Bengal discussed by Henry Beveridge in ‘Notes on Khurshid-I-Jahan-I-Numa of Ilahi Baksh’, *Journal of the Asiatic Society of Bengal*, LXIV (1895).

Isfahani, Muhammad Sadiq. *Ṣubḥ-i-Ṣādiq*, Relevant portions translated into English by A. Halim, *Journal of Pakistan Historical Society*, 1, part IV (1953): 339–356.

Khan, Hamid Allah. *Aḥādīth-i-Khwānīn* (*Tarīkh-i-Hamīdī*), Calcutta, 1871.

Khan, Hamid Allah. *Iḥata-i-Ḥāṣirah Li-Khazānah-i-Amirah*, MS Chittagong Islamic Intermediate College, Chittagong.

Ma‘sum, Muhammad. *Tārīkh-i-Shāh Shujā’*, MS India Office Library. MS No. 533.

Muradullah, Shah, *Athār-i-Maner*, Bankipur, 1367.

Nathan, Mirza. (‘Alā’ al-Dīn Shihāb Khān Isfahānī). *Bahāristān-i-Ghaibi*. Sup. Pers. MS Bibliotheque nationale, Paris. MS No. 252. Trans. Mu’ayyid al-Islam Borah, 2 vols, Gauhati, Assam: Government of Assam Press, 1936.

Prasad, Munshi Shayam. *Aḥwal-i-Gaur wa Pandua*, MS now preserved in the map-room of the India Office Library, London, MS No. C506=W 5761, and MS 2841 (probably printed in Bhagalpur in 1812, and was reprinted in Shillong in 1910 [under the reference: E. B. & A. S. P. O. (R. & A.) No. 76-100-9-3-1910 – G.N.K.). Published by Ahmad Hasan Dani as an Appendix to *Muslim Architecture of Bengal*, Dacca: Asiatic Society of Bengal, 1961.

Salim (Zaydpuri), Sayyed Ghulam Husayn. *Riyāḍ al-Salāṭīn*, Originally written in 1788, Calcutta: Asiatic Society of Bengal, 1893. Persian text ed. and trans. into English by Abdus Salām, Calcutta, 1904. Trans. into Bengali by Akbaruddin, Dhaka, 1974.

Samarqandi, Qadi Rukn al-Din. *Ḥauḍ al-Ḥayāt*, ed. Yusuf Husain. 'Haud al-hayat: La Version arabe de l'Amratkund', *Journal Asiatique*, 113 (October-December 1928): 291–344. *Baḥr al-Ḥayāt*. Persian MS India Office Library, London, MS No. 2002.

Shattari, Pir Muhammad. *Risala al-Shuhada*, ed. and trans. G. H. Damant, *Journal of the Asiatic Society of Bengal*, 3 (1874): 215–230.

Sirāj al-Dīn, Mawlānā Minhāj al-Dīn. *Ṭabaqāt-i-Nāṣirī.* ed. al-Ḥay Ḥabībī, Kabul, AH 1342.

Taish, Rahman 'Ali. *Tawarīkh-i-Dhaka*, ed. Rahmat Ali, Arrah, 1910.

Tālish, Shihāb al-Din Ibn Muhammad Wali. *Tarikh-i-Mulk-i-Assam*, or *Fathiyah-i-'Ibrayah*, Persian MS Bodleian Library, Oxford, MS Or. 589. Extracts trans. H. Blochmann, 'Koch Bihar. Koch Hajo, and Assam in the 16th and 17th Centuries, According to Akbarnamah, the Padshanamah, and the Fathiyah I 'Ibriyah', *Journal of the Asiatic Society of Bengal*, 41(1) (1872): 49–101.

South Asian (mainly Bengali)

Aghfar, Abdul. *Tarafer Itihasa*, Calcutta, 1294 Bengali year (1887).

Hoq, M. Enamul. *Vange Sufi Prabhav*, Calcutta, 1935.

Hoq, M. Enamul. *Muslim Bangla Sahitya*, Dhaka: Pakistan Publications, 1955.

Hoq, M. Enamul. *Purbo Pakistane Islam*, Dhaka, 1948.

Hoq, M. Enamul and A. Karim. *Arkan Rajsabhay Bangla Sahitya*, Calcutta, 1935.

Karim, Abdul. *Banglar Itihas: Sultani Amol*, 2nd edn, Dhaka, 1987.

Maulik, Ksitish, ed. *Prachin Purba Banga Gitika*, 7 vols, Calcutta: Mukherjee Publishers, 1972.

Mukhopadhaya, Sukhamay. *Banglay Muslim Adhikarer Adiparva*, Calcutta, 1988.

European/Western languages (mainly English)

Ahmad, Qeyamuddin. *Corpus of Arabic and Persian Inscriptions of Bihar*. Patna: Jayaswal Research Institute, 1973.

Ahmad, Shamsuddin. *Inscriptions of Bengal*, vol. IV, Rajshahi: Varendra Research Museum, 1960.

Anonymous. 'Ruins of Gaur (Abstracted from "Friend of India", No. VIII)', *Asiatic Journal and Monthly Register*, VII (1819–1820).

Blaves. *Theatrum Orbis Teatrum* (comprising maps of Bengal), vol. 11, Amsterdam, 1650.

Creighton, Henry. *The Ruins of Gaur*, London: Black, Parbury, & Allen, 1817.

Dani, Ahmad Hasan. *Bibliography of the Muslim Inscriptions of Bengal, Down to 1538*, Appendix to the *Journal of the Asiatic Society of Pakistan*, 2. Dacca: Asiatic Society of Pakistan, 1957.

Fadl, Abul. *Ain-I-Akbari*, trans. Henry Blochmann, Lahore: Qausain, 1975.

Franklin, Major William. *Ruins of Gaur* (written in 1810, it was sent by Franklin from Bhagalpur to the Court of the Directors for Conducting the Affairs of the United East India Company, ETC along with a map, a few drawings of the celebrated city of Gour and a covering letter dated 12 April 1812). MS India Office Library, London, MS No. 19.

Franklin, Major William. *Journal of a Route from Rajmahal to Gaur*. The printed version of the above-mentioned MS, now preserved in the map-room of the India Office Library, London. MS No. C506=W 5761 (it was printed in 1910 in Shillong for official preservation purpose of the document [under the reference: E. B. & A. S. P. O. (R. & A.) No. 76-100-9-3-1910 – G.N.K. acquired by India Office Library in London on 3 June 1910).

Karim, Abdul. *Corpus of the Arabic and Persian Inscriptions of Bengal*, Dhaka: Asiatic Society of Bangladesh, 1992.

Khan, M. Abid Ali. *Memoirs of Gaur and Pandua*, ed. and revd H. E. Stapleton, Calcutta: Bengal Secretariat, 1931. Reprint – New Delhi: Asian Publication Services, 1980.

Khan, M. Abid Ali. *Short Notes on the Ancient Monuments of Gaur and Pandua*, Malda, 1913.

Orme. *Gowre: Description of its Ruins with Four Inscriptions taken in Arabic*, MS India Office Library, London. MS No. 65:25.

Ravenshaw, J. H., *Gaur; Its Ruins and Inscriptions*, London, 1878.

Répertoire chronologique d'épigraphie arabe, 16 vols, Cairo, 1931–1964.

Secondary sources

Abd al-Alim, A. K. M. 'Calligraphy in East Pakistan', *Pakistan Quarterly* XI, no, 3 (1959): 46–51.

Ahmad, Mufti Azharuddin, *History of Shah Jalal and His Khadims*. Sylhet, 1914.

Ahmad, Qeyamud-Din. 'A New Inscription of Sikandar Shah of Bengal from Bihar', *EIAPS* (1963, published in 1965): 1–4, pl. I (a).

Ahmad, K. and A. Muqtadir. *Catalogue of the Arabic and Persian Manuscripts in the Library of the Calcutta Madrasah*. Calcutta, 1905.

Ahmed, Nizamuddin. *Bagerhat Monuments*. Dhaka: Department of Archaeology and Museum, 1980.

Ahmed, Shamsuddin. 'Some Unpublished Inscriptions of Bengal', *EIM* (1933–1934): 1–9, pl. I–III.

Ahmed, Shamsuddin. 'Three Inscriptions of Bengal', *EIM* (1935–1936): 57–60.

Ahmed, Shamsuddin. 'Two Inscriptions from Sherpur, Bogra District, Bengal', *EIM* (1937–1938): 17–20, pl. IV.

Ahmed, Shamsuddin. 'Navagram Inscription of Nusrat Shah, Bengal', *EIM* (1937–1938): 37–38.

Ahmed, Shamsuddin. 'A Rare Unpublished Inscription of Ilyas Shah of Bengal', *EIM* (1939–1940): 7–9, pl. IV (a).

Ahmed, Shamsuddin. 'Inscriptions from Provincial Museum Lukhnow', *EIM* (1939–1940): 26–29.

Ahmed, Shamsuddin. 'Muslim Calligraphy', in *Cultural Heritage of Pakistan*, Karachi: 1955.

Ahmed, Shamsuddin. *Inscriptions of Bengal*, vol. IV. Rajshahi: Varendra Research Museum, 1960.

al-Basha, Hasan. 'Ahmiyat Shawahid al-Qubur ka Masdarin li Tarikhi al-Jazirah al-'Arabiyyah', *Majallat Darasat Tarikh al-Jazirah al-'Arabiyyah* [Riyadh University Press] 1, no. 1 (AH 1399): 81–83.

Alamgir, Khoundkar. *Sultanate Architecture of Bengal: Analysis of Architectural and Decorative Elements*. Delhi: Kaveri Books, 2011.

Ali, A. K. M. Yaqub. 'Two Unpublished Arabic Inscriptions', *Journal of the Varendra Research Museum* 6 (1980–1981): 101–108.

Ali, A. K. M. Yaqub. 'A Study of Mural Calligraphy in Bengal: Based on Selected Muslim Epigraphs', *Journal of Varendra Research Museum* (University of Rajshahi) 7 (1981–1982): 173–182.

Ali, A. K. M. Yaqub. 'Two Unidentified Inscriptions', *Bangladesh Historical Studies* (1984–1985): 18–25.

Ali, A. K. M. Yaqub. *Select Arabic and Persian Epigraphs*. Dhaka: Bangla Academy, 1988.

Ali, A. K. M. Yaqub. *Muslim Mudra O Hastalikhan Shilpa*. Dhaka: Islamic Foundation Bangladesh, 1989.

Ali, A. K. M. Yaqub. 'Calligraphy on Stone Inscriptions of Bengal Sultanate', *Islamic Culture* 68, no. II (1994): 67–83.

Ali, Muhammad Mohar. *History of the Muslims in Bengal (600–1170/1203–1757)*, 6 vols. Riyadh: Imam Muhammad Ibn Sa'ud Islamic University, 1985.

Al-Ma'sumi, M. Saghir Hasan. 'Sunargaon's Contribution to Islamic Learning', *Islamic Culture* (1953): 8–17.

Asher, Catherine B. 'Inventory of Key Monuments', in *The Islamic Heritage of Bengal*, ed. George Michell. Paris: UNESCO, 1984: 37–140.

Asher, Catherine B. 'The Mughal and Post-Mughal Periods', in *The Islamic Heritage of Bengal*, ed. George Michell, Paris: UNESCO, 1984: 37–140.

Asher, Frederick M. ed. *Indian Epigraphy: Its Bearing on the History of Art*. Varanasi (printed in New Delhi): American Institute of Indian Studies, 1985.

Ashfaque, S. M. *Lalbagh Fort, Monuments and Museum*. Karachi: Ministry of Education, 1970.

Askari, Khan Sahib Syed Hasan. 'New Light on Rajah Ganesh and Sultan Ibrahim Sharqi of Jaunpur from Contemporary Correspondence of Two Muslim Saints', *Bengal Past and Present* 57 (1948): 32–39.

Askari, Khan Sahib Syed Hasan. 'The Correspondence of Two 14th Century Sufi Saints of Bihar with the Contemporary Sovereigns of Delhi and Bengal', *Journal of Bihar Research Society* 42, no. 2 (1956): 177–195.

Bahadur, Sayed Zahiruddin Khan. 'The Bogra Inscription', *Journal of the Bhiar and Orissa Research Society* 4 (1918): 357–60.

Bandyopadhdhay, Rakhal. 'Septagrama or Satgawn', *JASB* (1909): 245–262.

Banerji, R. D. 'Some Unpublished Records of the Sultans of Bengal', *Journal of the Bihar and Orissa Research Society* 4 (1918): 178–190.

Bendrey, V. S. *Studies in Muslim Inscriptions, with Special Reference to the Inscriptions Published in Epigraphia Indo-Moslemica (1907–38)*. Bombay: Karnatak Publishing House, 1944. Reprint. Delhi: Anmol, 1986.

Berchem, Max Van. 'Note on the Graffiti of the Cistern at Wady el-Joz', *Palestine Exploration Fund Quarterly Statement* (1915): 85–90, 195–198.

Beveridge, Henry. 'The Antiquities of Bagura (Bogra)', *JASB* 47, no. 1 (1878): 88–95.

Beveridge, Henry. 'Inscription of Chunakhali Murshidabad', *Proceedings of the Asiatic Society of Bengal* (1893): 55–59.

Bhattasali, Nalini Kanta. 'Antiquity of the Lower Ganges and its Courses', *Science and Culture* 7, no. 5 (1941): 233–239.

Bhattasali, Nalini Kanta. *Coins and Chronology of the Early Independent Sultans of Bengal*. Cambridge: W. Heffer & Sons, 1922. Reprint. New Delhi: Indological Book Corporation, 1976.

Bhattyacharya, A. K. 'An Arabic Inscription of Gaur, District Maldah, Bengal', *Indian Historical Quarterly* 26 (1950): 173–183.

Bhattyacharya, A. K. 'A Study in Muslim Calligraphy in Relation to Indian Inscriptions', *Indo-Iranica* IV, nos 2–3 (1950–1951): 13–23.

Bhattyacharya, A. K. 'Two Unpublished Arabic Inscriptions of Nusrat Shah from Santoshpur, District Hooghly, Bengal', *EIAPS* (1951–1952): 24–27, pl. XI (a).

Bhattyacharya, A. K. 'An Unpublished Arabic Inscription on a Jaina Image from Maldah, Bengal', *JASB (in Letters Section)* 18 (1953): 9–12.

Birt, Bradley. *The Romance of an Eastern Capital (Dacca).* London: Smith & Company, 1904.

Bloch, T. 'A Note on Two New Inscriptions of Alauddin Hussein Shah', *JASB* n.s., 5 (1909): 260–261, pl. VIII.

Blochmann, H. *JASB* XLI (1872): 106.

Blochmann, H. 'Contributions to the Geography and History of Bengal (Mohammadan Period)', *JASB* 42, no. 3 (1873): 209–273; 43, no. 3 (1874): 280–309.

Bukhari, Y. K. 'Four Unpublished Arabic Inscriptions of Bengal', *EIAPS* (1953–1954): 18–23.

Bukhari, Y. K. 'Inscriptions from Gomti Gate Museum, Gaur', *EIAPS* (1955–1956, published in 1960): 43–48.

Bukhari, Y. K. 'A Rare Manuscript on Calligraphy', *Islamic Culture* XXXVII (1963): 92–99.

Chabra, B. C. 'Ten Years of Indian Epigraphy (1937–46)', *Ancient India* 5 (1949): 46–61.

Choudhry, Mohammad Ismail. *Catalogue of the Arabic and Persian Inscriptions in the Prince of Wales Museum, Bombay.* Bombay: Government Central Press, 1925.

Choudhry, Sibdas. *Bibliography of Studies in Indian Epigraphy (1926–50).* Baroda: Oriental Institute, 1966.

Cope, H. 'Public Inscriptions at Lahore', *JASB* XXVII (1858): 308–313.

Cunningham, Alexander. 'Report of a Tour in Bihar and Bengal in 1879–80 from Patna to Sonargaon', In *ASR* vol. XV. Calcutta: Superintendent Government Printing Press, 1882.

Dani, Ahmad Hasan. 'Early Muslim Contact with Bengal', *Proceedings of the Pakistan History Conference* (1951).

Dani, Ahmad Hasan. 'A Specimen of the Calligraphy in Dacca Museum', *Museum Journal of Pakistan* IV (1952): 28–31.

Dani, Ahmad Hasan. *Bibliography of Muslim Inscriptions of Bengal* (published as an appendix to *Journal of the Asiatic Society of Pakistan*) 2 (1957).

Dani, Ahmad Hasan. *Muslim Architecture of Bengal.* Dacca: Asiatic Society of Bangladesh, 1961.

Dani, Ahmad Hasan. 'Inscriptions in the Peshawar Museum', *Ancient Pakistan* II (1964): 125–135.

Desai, Ziauddin Ahmad. 'Some New Data Regarding the Pre-Mughal Rulers of Bengal', *Islamic Culture* 32, no. 3 (July 1958): 195–207.

Desai, Ziauddin Ahmad. 'Arabic and Persian Inscriptions from the Indian Museum Calcutta', *EIAPS* (1955–1956, published in 1960): 1–32.

Desai, Ziauddin Ahmad. 'Inscriptions from the Assam Provincial Museum, Gauhati', *EIAPS* (1955–1956, published in 1960): 33–34.

Desai, Ziauddin Ahmad. 'Epitaphs from Cambay, Gujrat', *EIAPS* (1971): 1–65.

Desai, Ziauddin Ahmad. 'Correct Attribution of the Two So-Called Inscriptions of Nasirud-din Mahmud Shah II of Bengal', *EIAPS* (1973): 26–35, pls. III (c) and IV (a).

Desai, Ziauddin Ahmad. 'The So-Called Chunakhali Inscription of Nasirud-din Mahmud Shah II of Bengal', *EIAPS* (1973): 36–43, pl. IV (b).

Desai, Ziauddin Ahmad. 'Correct Attribution of the Two So-Called Inscriptions of Nasiruddin Mahmud Shah II of Bengal', *JASBD* XXIII, no. 1 (April 1978): 1–17.

Desai, Ziauddin Ahmad. *JASBD* XXIII, no. 1 (April 1979): 1–17.

Desai, Ziauddin Ahmad. 'The So-Called Chunakhali Inscription of Nasirud-din Mahmud Shah II of Bengal', *JASBD* (Humanities) XXIV–VI (1979–1981): 11–19.

Desai, Ziauddin Ahmad. 'A Note on the Mandaran (Hooghly District) Inscription of Husain Shah', *Journal of the Varendra Research Museum* 6 (1980–1981): 15–22.

Desai, Ziauddin Ahmad. 'Some Aspects of the Arabic and Persian Inscriptions of Bengal', *Journal of the Varendra Research Museum* 7 (1981–1982): 126–140.

Desai, Ziauddin Ahmad. 'An Early Thirteenth Century Inscription from West Bengal', *EIAPS* (1975, published in 1983): 6–12, pl. 1(b).

Digby, Simon. 'The Fate of Daniyal, Prince of Bengal, in the Light of an Unpublished Inscription', *Bulletin of the School of Oriental and African Studies* 38 (1973): 588–602.

Doley, Sir Charles. *Antiques of Dacca*. London: Landseer, 1814.

Dutt, Chinmoy. *Catalogue of Arabic and Persian Inscriptions in the Indian Museum*. Calcutta: Indian Museum, 1967.

Eaton, Richard M. *The Rise of Islam and the Bengal Frontier, 1204–1760*. Berkeley, CA: University of California Press, 1993.

Ettinghausen, R. 'Arabic Epigraphy: Communication or Symbolic Affirmation', in *Near Eastern Numismatics, Iconography, Epigraphy and History: Studies in Honor of George C. Miles*, ed. D. K. Kouymjian (Beirut: American University of Beirut, 1974): 297–317.

Faris, Nabih A. and George C. Miles. 'An Inscription of Barbak Shah of Bengal', *Ars Islamica* 7, no. 2 (1940): 141–147.

Firminger, Walter K. 'The Antiquities of Kalna', *Bengal Past and Present* XIV (1917): 99–105 (with 2 plates).

Firminger, Walter K. 'The Antiquities of Pandua', *Bengal Past and Present* XIV (1917): 106–114.

Ghafur, M. Abdul. 'A Persian Inscription of Shah Hasan Argun', *JASP* 7, no. 2 (December 1962): 277–288.

Ghafur, M. Abdul. 'Fresh Light on the Sultan-Ganj Inscription of Sultan Jalal al-din Muhammad Shah', *JASP* VIII, no. 1 (June 1963): 55–65.

Ghafur, M. Abdul. 'Epigraphy in Pakistan' in *The Cultural History of Pakistan*. Lahore, 1966: 61–65.

Glazier, E. Z. *Report on the District of Rangpur*. Calcutta, 1873: 107–110.

Government of Bengal, Public Works Department. *List of Ancient Monuments in Rajshahi Division, Revised and Corrected up to 31st August 1895*. Calcutta: Bengal Secretariat Press, 1896.

Gupta, Kamalakanta. *Copper-Plates of Sylhet*, vol. 1. Sylhet: Lipika Enterprises, 1967.

Habibullah, A. B. M. ed. *Nalini Kanta Bhattshali Commemoration Volume*. Dhaka: Dacca Museum, 1966.

Habibullah, A. B. M. 'An Unpublished Inscription from Sitalmat', *Bangladesh Lalit Kala* 1, no. 2 (July 1975): 89–94.

Hamilton, Francis Buchanan. *A Geographical, Statistical and Historical Description of the District or Zilla of Dinajpur in the Province or Soubah of Bengal*. Calcutta, 1833.

Haque, Enamul. *Islamic Art in Bangladesh*. Dhaka: Dacca Museum, 1978.

Haque, Enamul. 'Samrat Akbarer Rajyatvakāler tiṇti aprakāshita shilāḷīpi (in Bengali)', *Itihas*, year 12, issue 1–3 (1978), Dhaka.

Haque, Enamul. *Islamic Art Heritage of Bangladesh.* Dhaka: Bangladesh National Museum, 1983.
Haque, Enamul. *The Art Heritage of Bangladesh.* Dhaka: ICSBA, 2007.
Hasan, Perween. *Sultans and Mosques: The Early Muslim Architecture of Bangladesh.* London: Tauris, 2007.
Hasan, Sayed Mahmudul. 'A Sultan Firoz Shah 11 Fragment', *Asian Review* n.s. 11 (1965): 79–83.
Hasan, Sayed Mahmudul. 'Two Bengal Inscriptions in the Collection of the British Museum', *Journal of the Royal Asiatic Society* (1966): 141–147.
Hasan, Sayed Mahmudul. 'An Unpublished Inscription of Fateh Shah of Bengal in the British Museum', *JASP* XIII, no. 1 (April 1968): 49–55.
Hasan, Sayed Mahmudul. 'An Inscription of Alauddin Husein Shah, King of Bengal', *Proceedings of All India Oriental Conference* (1970?): 260–262.
Hasan, Sayed Mahmudul. *Mosque Architecture of Pre-Mughal Bengal.* Dhaka: University Press Limited, 1979.
Hasan, Sayed Mahmudul. *Muslim Monuments of Bangladesh.* Dhaka: Islamic Foundation, 1980 (1400).
Hasan, Sayed Mahmudul. *Glimpses of Muslim Art and Architecture.* Dhaka: Islamic Foundation, 1983.
Horn, Paul. 'Muhammadan inscriptions from Bengal (with facsimiles)', *Epigraphia Indica*, II.
Horvitz, J. 'List of Published Mohammadan Inscriptions of India', *EIM* (1909–1910): 30–144.
Hunter, W. W. *A Statistical Account of Bengal.* London, 1876.
Husain, Saiyid Aulad. *Echoes from Old Dacca.* Dhaka, 1909.
Husain, A. B. M., Harunur M. Rashid, Abdul Momin Chowddhury, Abu A. Imamuddin, eds. *Gawr-Lakhnawti.* Dhaka: Asiatic Society of Bangladesh, 1997.
Hussain, S. S. 'Some More New Inscriptions of Husain Shah from West Bengal', *EIAPS* (1975, published in 1983): 31–38, plates IV (a & b), V (a & b) and VI (a & b).
Husain, Saiyid Aulad. *Notes on the Antiquities of Dacca.* Dhaka, 1904.
Hussain, Syed Ejaz. *The Bengal Sultanate: Politics, Economy and Coins.* Delhi: Manohar, 2003.
Hussain, Syed Ejaz. 'Kings and Coins: Money as the State Media in the Indian Sultanates', in *Coins in India: Power and Communication*, ed. Himanshu Prabha Ray. Mumbai: Marg Publications, 2006: 56–65.
'Inscription from Chakdah', *Nadiyah Sahitya Parisad Patricia* (1323 Bengali Year): 257–258.
'Inscription from Jhilli, Murshidabad', *Sahitya Parisad Patricia* (1357 Bengali Year): 81.
'Inscription from Madrasa Tribeni', *Sahitya Parisad Patricia* XV: 24–25.
'Inscription from Satgaon, Hoogly', *Sahitya Parisad Patricia* XV: 26–27 and 30–31.
Ishaque, M. 'Arabic and Persian Inscriptions from the B. R. Sen Museum, W. Bengal', *EIAPS* (1956–1957, published in 1960): 37–42.
Kaderi, A. A. 'Inscriptions of the Sultans of Bengal from Bihar', *EIAPS* (1961): 35–44, pl. XI (a and b), XII (a and b), XIII (a and b), XIV (a, b and c), XV (a and b).
Karim, Abdul. 'A Note on the First Muslim Conquest of Satgaon and Zafar Khan Ghazi, the Conqueror', *Proceedings of the Pakistan History Conference*, 1956.
Karim, Abdul. *Social History of the Muslims of Bengal (Down to A.D. 1538).* Dhaka, 1959.

Karim, Abdul. 'An Unpublished Sultanate Inscription and a Mughal Mosque of Chittagong', *JASP* IX, no. 2 (December 1964): 23–30.
Karim, Abdul. *Dacca, The Mughal Capital*. Dhaka: Asiatic Society of Pakistan, 1964.
Karim, Abdul. 'The Inscriptions of Khan Muhammad Mirdha Mosque at Dacca', *JASP* XI, no. 2 (August 1966): 143–151.
Karim, Abdul. 'The Inscription of Khan Mohammad Mirdha Mosque in Dhaka', *JASP* XI, no. 2 (1967): 143–151, pls I and II.
Karim, Abdul. 'Some Inscriptions of Dacca', *JASP* XII, no. 2 (August 1967): 289–303.
Karim, Abdul. 'Two Hitherto Unnoticed Sultanate Mosques of Chittagong', *JASP* XII, no. 3 (December 1967): 321–332.
Karim, Abdul. 'A Fresh Examination of the Inscriptions Attributed to Mahmud Shah', *JASP* XIII, no. 3 (December 1968): 138–140.
Karim, Abdul. 'Mughal Nawara in Bengal', *JASP* XIV, no. 1 (April 1969).
Karim, Abdul. 'A Fresh Study of the Biral Inscription of Saif al-Din Firuz Shah', *JASBD* XVII, no. 1 (April 1972): 1–10.
Karim, Abdul. 'A Notes on the Navagram Inscription of Nusrat Shah', *JASBD* XVII, no. 2 (August 1972): 1–8.
Karim, Abdul. 'Nur Qutb Alam's Letter on the Ascendancy of Ganesa', in *Abdul Karim Sahitya-Visarad Commemoration Volume*, ed. Muhammad Enamul Haq. Dacca: Asiatic Society of Bangladesh, 1972: 335–343.
Karim, Abdul. 'Date of Bakhtiyar Khilji's Conquest of Nadia', *JASBD* (Humanities) XXIV–VI (1979–81): 1–10.
Karim, Abdul. 'The First and Only Discovered Inscription of Ghiyath al-Din Bahadur Shah', *Journal of the Varendra Research Museum* 6 (1980–1981): 5–9.
Karim, Abdul. 'Shahpur Inscription of Sultan Ghiath Al-Din Mahmud Shah', *JASBD* (Humanities) XXX, no. 2 (December 1985): 1–8.
Karim, Abdul. 'Gaur o Panduar Itihas', *Bangladesh Asiatic Society Patrica* 7 (December 1989): 1–78.
Karim, Abdul. *Corpus of the Arabic and Persian Inscriptions of Bengal*. Dhaka: Asiatic Society of Bangladesh, 1992.
Khan, M. F. 'Three New Inscriptions of Alauddin Hussein Shah', *EIAPS* (1961): 23–28.
Khan Bahadur, Maulvi Zafar Hasan. 'Muslim Calligraphy', *Indian Arts and Letters* 9 (1935).
Khare, G. H. 'Notes on the Indo-Muslim Epigraphy', *Annals of Bhandarkar Oriental Research Institute* 40 (1959): 158–159.
Khatun, M. 'A Persian Inscription in the Indian Museum, Calcutta, from Murshidabad', *EIAPS* (1959–1960): 23–26, pl. VII (a).
Law, N. N. *Promotion of Learning in India during Muhammad Rule by Muhammadans*. London, 1916.
Lowick, Nicholas W. 'The Horseman Type of Bengal and the Question of Commemorative Issues', *Journal of the Numismatic Society of India* 35 (1973): 196–208.
Martin, Montogomery, ed. *History, Antiquities, Topography and Statistics of Eastern India*, 3 vols. London: William H. Allen, 1836–1838.
Maitra, Akshay Kumar. 'Historical Antiquities of Rahshahi', *Bengal Past and Present* XXVIII (1924): 37–41.
Majumdar, Nani Gopal. *Inscriptions of Bengal*, ed. Ksitish Maulik, vol. 3. Rajshahi: Varendra Research, 1929.
Melik, Beglaroff and Joseph Daviditch. *Archaeological Survey of Bengal: Report for 1888*. Calcutta: Catholic Orphan Press, 1888.

Michell, George, ed. *The Islamic Heritage of Bengal*. Paris: UNESCO, 1984.

Mir, Zahan. 'The Islamic Section of the Varendra Research Museum', *Museum Journal of Pakistan* (Peshawar) IV (1952): 7–27.

Mitra, S. Pratip Kumar. 'Bibliography on the Inscriptions of Bengal', *Our Heritage* 14 (January 1966): 1–12.

Mitra, S. Pratip Kumar. 'Late Dr. Z. A. Desai and the Provisional Study of Some New Inscriptions of the Bengal Sultans', *Indo-Iranica, the Quarterly Organ of the Iran-Society* (Iran Society, Kolkata) 58, nos 3 & 4 (September-December 2005): 26–29.

Mohammad, Syed. 'An Inscription of Alauddin Hussain Shah, King of Bengal of 1509–10 A.D. at Nawdah near Barh in Patna District', *Proceedings of the 6th All-India Oriental Conference* (1930): 181–184.

Mukherji, Ramaranjan and Sachindra Kumar Maitry. *Corpus of Bengal Inscriptions Bearing on History and Civilization of Bengal*. Calcutta: Firma K. L. Mukhpadhyay, 1967.

Nasib, Akhtar. 'The Inscription of Mubarak Manzil in Hugli District', *Journal of the Pakistan Historical Society* 18 (1970): 110–114.

Nizamuddin, Muhammad. 'Fresh Light on Biral Inscription of Sultan Saif al-Din Firuz Shah', *Journal of the Varendra Research Museum* 5 (1976–1977): 87–93.

Odud, Abdul. 'The Historic Mosques of Dacca', *Islamic Culture* (April 1933): 823–837.

O'Malley, L. S. S. *Bengal District Gazetteers, Murshidabad*, vol. 32 *of Bengal District Gazetteers*. Calcutta: Bengal Secretariat Book Depot, 1914.

O'Malley, L. S. S. *Rajshahi, Vol. 33* of *Bengal District Gazetteers*. Calcutta: Bengal Secretariat Book Depot, 1916.

Qadir, Muhammad Abdul. 'The Newly Discovered Madrasah Ruins at Gaur and its Inscription', *JASBD* (Humanities) XXIV–VI (1979–1981): 20–90.

Qadir, Muhammad Abdul. 'Gadagram Inscription and Advent of the Muslims in Bengal', *JASBD* (Humanities) XXVIII, no. II (December 1983): 83–96.

Rahim, Muhammad Abdur. *Social and Cultural History of Bengal*, 2 vols. Karachi, 1963, 1967.

Rahman, Sayed Mustafizur. *Islamic Calligraphy in Medieval India*. Dhaka: University Press Limited, 1979.

Roy, N. B. 'Shadipur Inscription of Sultan Ghiyasuddin Mahmud Shah', *Journal and Proceedings of the Asiatic Society of Bengal* 17 (1951): 217–218.

Sanyal, N. B. *A Descriptive Catalogue of Inscriptions in the Museum*. Rajshahi: Varendra Research Museum, 1926.

Schimmel, A. *Calligraphy and Islamic Culture*. New York: New York University Press, 1984.

Sharaf-ud-Din, S. 'Biral Inscription of Sayfuddin Firoz Shah: A.H. 880', 'Rajshahi Inscription of Jalaluddin Fath Shah', and 'Rajshahi Inscription of Ghiyathuddin Bahadur Shah', *Varendra Research Society's Monographs* no. 6, Rajshahi: Varendra Research Society (March 1935): 1–2, 3–4 and 18–21.

Siddiq, Mohammad Yusuf. *The Encyclopaedia of Islam*, new edn. Leiden: E. J. Brill, 1997–2002: s.v. 'Ruhmi', 'Satga'on', 'Sikandar Shāh', 'Sonārgā'on', 'Sundarban', 'Sylhet', 'Tirhut', 'Tribeni', 'Tītūmīr', 'Ṭughrā' in Muslim India' and 'Yāghistān'.

Siddiq, Mohammad Yusuf. *al-Nuqūsh al-Kitābiyya 'alā' 'l-'Amā'ir al-Islāmiyya fī 'l-Bangāl*. MA Thesis,. Makkah: Umm al-Qura University, 1984.

Siddiq, Mohammad Yusuf. 'Arabic Calligraphy in the Early Inscriptions', *Muslim Education Quarterly* 2, no. 3 (1985): 77–88.

Siddiq, Mohammad Yusuf. 'The Development of Arabic Script' (written in Arabic under the title: al-Kitaba al-'Arabiyya), *Majalla al-Jami'a al-Salafiyyah* (May, June 1987): 44–54.

Siddiq, Mohammad Yusuf. 'The City of Gaur: the First Islamic Capital of Bengal' (written in Arabic under the title: Madinat al-Ghawr, al-'Asima al-Islamiyya al-Ula fi Bilad al-Bangal), *Al-Manhal* 48, no. 455 (July-August 1987): 40–43.

Siddiq, Mohammad Yusuf. 'The Early Contacts Between Arabia and Bengal' (written in Arabic under the title: al-Silat al-Mubakkira bayna 'l-'Arab wa 'l-Bangal), *Majalla al-Jami'a al-Salafiyyah* (September 1987): 11–15.

Siddiq, Mohammad Yusuf. *Darāsāt al-Nuqūsh al-'Arabiyya fī 'l-Hind*. PhD Dissertation, Makkah: Umm al-Qura University, 1987.

Siddiq, Mohammad Yusuf. 'The Significance of the Study of Arabic Inscriptions' (written in Arabic under the title: Ahmiyyat Darasāt al-Nuqūsh al-'Arabiyyah) *Al-Manhal* 49, no. 264 (July-August 1988): 90–97.

Siddiq, Mohammad Yusuf. 'Tughra and its Usage in the Arabic Inscriptions' (written in Arabic under the title: al-Ṭughrā' wa Istikhdamuha fi 'l-Kitabat al-'Arabiyya) *al-Faysal* 148 (1989): 95–100.

Siddiq, Mohammad Yusuf. 'An Epigraphical Journey to an Eastern Islamic Land', *Muqarnas: An Annual on Islamic Art and Architecture* 7 (1990): 83–108.

Siddiq, Mohammad Yusuf. 'Arabic Scripts in India' (written in Arabic under the title: al-Khuṭūṭ al-'Arabiyya fi 'l-Hind) *al-Manhal* 53, no. 489 (July-August 1991): 40–45; and 53, no. 490 (August-September 1991): 18–22.

Siddiq, Mohammad Yusuf. 'Epigraphy and Islamic Culture', *Muslim Education Quarterly* 8, no. 4 (1991): 52–73.

Siddiq, Mohammad Yusuf. 'Epigraphy and Islamic Culture', *Muslim Education Quarterly* 9, no. 2 (1992): 57–78.

Siddiq, Mohammad Yusuf. 'Literary Evaluation of the Arabic Epigraphical Texts in the Indian Subcontinent' (written in Arabic under the title: al-Taqyīm al-Adabi li 'l-Nuqūsh al-'Arabiyyah al-Warida fi 'l-Nuqūsh al-Hindiyya), *Sawt al-Umma* (August 1992): 49–53.

Siddiq, Mohammad Yusuf. *Studies in Islamic Civilization and Culture* (written in Arabic under the title: *Darasat fi 'l-Thaqafah wa 'l-Ḥadar al-Islamiyya*). Kushtia: Islamic University, 1992.

Siddiq, Mohammad Yusuf. *Arabic and Persian Texts of the Islamic Inscriptions of Bengal*. Watertown, MA: South Asia Press, 1991 (2nd edn 1992).

Siddiq, Mohammad Yusuf. 'Arabic Script and its Cultural Implications' (written in Arabic under the title: al-Khaṭṭ al-'Arabī wa Atharuhu 'l-Ḥaḍārī), *al-Jami'a al-Islamiyya* 2 (April-June 1994): 173–204.

Siddiq, Mohammad Yusuf. 'Growth of Art and Architecture in Bengal during Islamic Rule' (written in Arabic under the title: al-Nahda al-Fanniyya wa 'l-Mi'mariyya fi 'l-Bangal ibban al-hukm al-Islami), *al-Manhal* (October-November 1994): 290–293.

Siddiq, Mohammad Yusuf. 'Masjid, Madrasah, Khanqah and Bridge: Reflections on Some Islamic Inscriptions', *Journal of the Asiatic Society of Bangladesh* 42, no. 2 (December 1997): 167–185.

Siddiq, Mohammad Yusuf. 'The Rise of Islam and Articulation of a New Order', *Journal of the Asiatic Society of Bangladesh* 45, no. 1 (June 2000): 1–20.

Siddiq, Mohammad Yusuf. 'Arabic Writings' (written in Arabic under the title: al-Khaṭṭ al-'Arabī), *al-'Arabiyyāh* 3, no. 4 (2002).

Siddiq, Mohammad Yusuf. 'An Ecological Journey in Muslim Bengal', in *Islam and*

Ecology: A Bestowed Trust, ed. Richard C. Foltz. Cambridge, MA: Harvard University Press, 2003: 451–462.

Siddiq, Mohammad Yusuf. *An Epigraphical Journey through Muslim Bengal* (written in Arabic under the title: *Riḥla Ma'a al-Nuqūsh al-Kitābiyyah al-Islāmiyyah fī Bilād al-Bangāl* رحلة مع النقوش الإسلامية في بلاد البنغال: دراسة تاريخية وحضارية، دمشق: دار الفكر). Damascus: Dār al-Fikr, 2004.

Siddiq, Mohammad Yusuf. 'Origin of Arabic Script' (written in Arabic under the title: Nash'at al-Khaṭṭ al-'Arabī), *Manār al-Islām* 8, no. 3 (2004).

Siddiq, Mohammad Yusuf. 'Epigraphy as a Source for the Study of Islamic Culture', *Journal of the Asiatic Society of Bangladesh* (Golden Jubilee Volume) 50, nos 1–2 (2005): 113–140.

Siddiq, Mohammad Yusuf. 'Calligraphy and Islamic Culture: Reflection on Some New Epigraphic Discoveries in Gaur and Pandua', *Bulletin of the School of Oriental and African Studies* 68, no. 1 (2005): 21–58.

Siddiq, Mohammad Yusuf. 'Mosque as a Form of Socio-Cultural Expression', *Journal of the Asiatic Society of Bangladesh* 52, no. 2 (December 2007): 197–212.

Siddiq, Mohammad Yusuf. 'Advent of Islam in Bengal', *Dhaka University Journal for Islamic Studies* 1, no. 1 (2007).

Siddiq, Mohammad Yusuf. 'Calligraphy as Cultural Expression in Bengal' in *History, Civilization and Culture of Barind Region of South Asia: Professor Yaqub Ali Felicitation Volume*, ed. Shahnawaz and M. Salih (written in Bengali under the title: *Barendra Barennya*). Dhaka: Somoy Prokashan (2007): 507–520.

Siddiq, Mohammad Yusuf. 'Khan Jahan 'Ali Mausoleum Complex Inscriptions at Khalifatabad', *Journal of Bengal Art* 9–10 (2007): 167–185.

Siddiq, Mohammad Yusuf. 'Calligraphy as an Art in the Architectural Inscriptions', *Jihāt al-Islām* (published by Faculty of Islamic Studies, University of the Punjab, Lahore) 1, no. 2 (January-June 2008): 81–110.

Siddiq, Mohammad Yusuf. 'Cultural Continuity in the Medieval World of Islam', *University of Sharjah Journal of Humanities and Social Sciences* 5, no. 2 (June 2008): 41–67.

Siddiq, Mohammad Yusuf. 'Calligraphy as an Art in Architectural Inscriptions', *Jihat al-Islam* (published by Faculty of Islamic Studies, University of the Punjab) 1, no. 2 (June 2008): 81–110.

Siddiq, Mohammad Yusuf. 'Bengal in the Light of its Arabic Inscriptions' (written in Arabic under the title: الإسلام في البنغال عبر العصور من خلال نقوشها العربية) *Jihat al-Islam* (published Faculty of Islamic Studies, University of the Punjab) 2, no. 1 (July-December 2008): 151–170.

Siddiq, Mohammad Yusuf. 'Islamic Inscriptions and their Cultural Implication', in *Studies in Indian Epigraphy: Journal of the Epigraphical Society of India*. ed. S. Subramonia Iyer. Delhi: Caxton Publication, 2008: viii, 17–21.

Siddiq, Mohammad Yusuf. 'Splendour of the Adina Masjid Inscriptions at Pandua', in *Abdul Karim Commemoration Volume*. ed. Shamsul Hossain. Dhaka: Adorn Publication, 2008.

Siddiq, Mohammad Yusuf. 'Inscriptions as an Important Means for Understanding History of the Muslims', *Journal of Islamic Studies* 20, no. 2 (May 2009): 213–250.

Siddiq, Mohammad Yusuf. 'Splendor of Islamic Civilization and Culture' (written in Arabic under the title: روائع الحضارة والثقافة الإسلامية في بلاد البنغال من خلال نقوشها الإسلامية) *al-Qalam* (published by the Department of Islamic Studies, University of the Punjab) 13, no. 13 (June 2009): 416–445.

Siddiq, Mohammad Yusuf. 'Importance of Epigraphy in Islamic Civilization and Culture' (written in Urdu under the title: (تاریخ و تهذیب مین کتبه شناسی کی اهمیت) *Fikr-O-Nazr*) (published by Islamic Research Institute, International Islamic University, Islamabad) 47, no. 1 (July-September 2009): 86–135.

Siddiq, Mohammad Yusuf. 'Islamic Inscriptions of South Asia and their Cultural Implications' (written in Arabic under the title: (الكتابات الإسلامية في جنوب آسيه وأثرها الحضاري مع العناية الخاصة بالنقوش العربية في البنغال) *al-Adwa'* (published by Shaykh Zayed Islamic Centre, University of the Punjab) xxiv, no. xxxii (December 2009): 185–210.

Siddiq, Mohammad Yusuf. 'Eden Garden and Paradisiacal River in Worldly Palaces: Water Cosmology in Some Arabic Verses in Gaur (Bengal) and Granada (Andalusia)', *Journal of Bengal Art* 11 (2009): 227–236.

Siddiq, Mohammad Yusuf. *Historical and Cultural Aspects of the Islamic Inscriptions of Bengal: A Reflective Study of Some New Epigraphic Discoveries*. Dhaka: International Centre for the Study of Art, 2009.

Siddiq, Mohammad Yusuf. 'Splendour of Writing in Muslim Bengal Architecture', in *Abhijñān: Studies in South Asian Archaeology and Art History of Artifacts, Felicitating A.K.M. Zakariah*, ed. Shahnaj Husne Jahan. Oxford: British Archaeological Reports (BAR), John and Erica Hedges Ltd, 2009), 130–143.

Siddiq, Mohammad Yusuf. 'Epigraphy in the World of Islam: Some Newly Discovered Inscriptions', *Prtnatattva (Journal of Archaeology)* 16 (June 2010): 45–62.

Siddiqi, W. H. 'Two Inscriptions of Sultans of Bengal from Uttar Pradesh', *EIAPS* (1961): 45–48, pl. (a) and (b).

Siddiqi, W. H. 'Three Mughal Inscriptions from Kesiari, West Bengal', *EIAPS* (1961): 69–73, pl. XXII (b), XXIII (a and b).

Sinha, Sutapa. *Gold Coins in the Collection of the Asiatic Society*. Kolkata: The Asiatic Society, 2010.

Sircar, D. C. *Some Epigraphical Records of the Medieval Period from Eastern India.* New Delhi: Abhinav Publications, 1979.

Skelton, Robert and Francis Mark, eds. *Arts of Bengal*. London: Whitechapel Art Gallery, 1979.

Sourdel-Thomine. 'Inscriptions Seljoukides et salles a couples de Qazwin en Iran', *Revue de Etudes Islamiques* 42 (1974): 3–43.

Stapleton, H. E. *JASB* n.s. VI (1910): 144–145.

Stapleton, H. E. 'Coins of Danujmardanna Deva and Mahendra Deva, Two Hindu Kings of Bengal', *JASB* Numismatic Number, n.s. 26, no. 2 (1930): 5–13.

Stewart, Sir Charles. *History of Bengal*. London, 1813.

Taifoor, Syed Muhammad. *Glimpses of Old Dhaka*, 2nd edn. Dhaka: S. M. Perwez Publisher, 1956.

Tarafdar, Mumtazur Rahman. *Husain Shahi Bengal, 1494–1538 A.D.: A Socio-Political Study*. Dhaka: Asiatic Society of Pakistan, 1965.

Tarafdar, Mumtazur Rahman. 'Epigraphic and Numismatic Notes Bearing on the History of Pre-Mughal Bengal', *JASBD* XX, no. 3 (December 1975): 1–22.

Walsh, Major J. H. Tull. *A History of Murshidabad District (Bengal) with Biographies of some of its Noted Families*. London: Jarrold & Sons, 1902.

Wilson, C. R. *List of Inscriptions on Tombs or Monuments in Bengal Possessing Historical Archaeological Interest*. Calcutta: Bengal Public Works Department, 1886.

Yazdani, G. 'A New Inscription from Nusrat Shah of Bengal', *EIM* (1911–1912): 5–7.

Yazdani, G. *EIM* (1913–1914): 29–30, pl. V.

Yazdani, G. 'Two Inscriptions of King Hussein Shah of Bengal from Tribeni', *EIM* (1915–1916): 10–14.
Yazdani, G. 'Inscriptions of Khalji Sultan of Delhi and their Contemporaries of Bengal', *EIM* (1917–1918): 8–42.
Yazdani, G. 'An Inscription of S. Hussein Shah of Bengal from the Village of Margram, Murshidabad', *EIM* (1933–1934): 23–24.
Yazdani, G. 'Some Inscriptions of the Mosalman Kings of Bengal', *EIM* (1937–1938): 52–59.
Zahiruddin, Khan Bahadur Sayed. 'The Bogra Inscription', *Journal of Bihar and Orissa Research Society* 4 (1918): 357.
Zakaria, A. K. M. 'Mahalbari Inscription of Husain Shah', *JASBD* XXII, no. 1 (April 1977): 20–25.

Index

Abbasid (dynasty) 11, 28, 38, 77, 81–3, 85, 95; Abbasid caliphs 75, 80, 89
Abbina (a region bordering Bengal mentioned by ibn Khurradādhbih) 28
Abd al-Ḥaq Dehlavī 163
ʻAbd al-Ṣamad Shīrāzī 124
ʻAbd al-Wahhāb, Shaykh Muḥammad ibn (founder of Wahhābī movement) 42
Abdul Wali, Khan Sahib Moulvi 5
Abdul Wathiq, Mawlavi M. (Arabic teacher of Bashirhat) 184
ʻAbdus al-Jahshiyārī, Abū ʻAbd-Allah Muḥammad ibn (author of *Kitāb al-Wuzarā' wa 'l-Kuttāb*) 78
[ibn] Abī Sharf (early Arab poet) 74
Abraham (Ibrāhīm) 139; Abraham and Moses [Mūsā] (prophets in Abrahimic traditions) 66
Abū 'l-Faḍl (vizier) 16, 33
Abū 'l-Fatḥ Ṭughril al-Sulṭānī 96
Abū 'l-Fatḥ Yuzbak al-Sulṭānī 98–9
Abū 'l-Ma'ālī 102
Abū 'l-Misk (a title given to slave officials) 74
Abū 'l-Mujāhid (title) 83, 123, 126, 128, 132, 140, 167–9, 187
Abū 'l-Muẓaffar (ʻvictoriousʼ, title) 35, 59, 73, 81–2, 91, 98, 101–3, 105, 114–16, 118, 121, 132–8, 142, 144–5, 147–50, 152, 154–5, 161, 164–6, 170, 172, 173, 177, 183, 185, 189–90, 193–4, 196, 198, 200–8, 210–13, 215–16, 218–21, 223–4, 228–31, 234
Abū Muḥammad ʻAbd-Allah ibn Muslim al-Dīnūrī (famous as ibn Qutayba, author of *Adab al-Kātib*) 78
Abyssinian slaves (four sultans of African origin in Bengal) 73
Acre (a city in Palestine) 11
Ādam Shahīd, Bābā 214–15
'Aḍd al-Islām wa 'l-Muslimīn 149
Adina masjid of Pandua (one of the largest mosques of South Asia) 47, 83, 126–30, 212, 252
Afrīdī 55–6
[ibn] Aḥamd al-Tarūjī, Aḥmad ibn Sulaymān (traveller from Alexandria) 38
Ahl al-Ḥadīth 41, 55n45, 56n49
ahl al-suffa 64, 92
Aḥmad Khān Sarwar, Ulugh Aʻẓam 146
Aḥmad ibn Mājid 29
Ahmad, Qeyamuddin 6, 56, 95, 117, 124
Ahmad Shāh, Sulṭān Abū 'l-Muẓaffar Shams al-Dunyā wa 'l-Dīn 138–9, 149
Ahmed, Maulvi Shamsud-Din (epigraphist) 6
aḥqar al-khalā'iq (title) 81
A'in-i-Akbarī 189
Ajalka Khān ibn Turbat Khān, Khān Aʻẓam wa Khāqān Muʻaẓẓam Ulugh 166
Ajyāl Khān ibn Muḥammad, Khān Muʻaẓẓam 188
Akbar (Mughal emperor) 6, 33–4, 49, 62, 113
Akhī Sirāj al-Dīn 121
Akhund Sher Mīr-i-Baḥr, Ẓahīr al-Millat wa 'l-Dīn Malik al-Mulk 212–13, 224
aʻlā āthār al-masjid (lit. who has exalted the influence of the masjid) 56
[al]-Aʻlā, Ṣāḥib al-Qalam 77
al-ʻĀlam, Nūr Quṭb 37–8, 58–60, 65, 75, 81, 121–2, 139–40, 160–3, 167, 238–9, 249
ʻAlā' al-Dunyā' wa 'l-Dīn (a title) 88–9; *see also* Ḥusayn Shāh (ʻAlā' al-Dunyā' wa 'l-Dīn)

'Alā' al-Ḥaq', Shaykh 57, 65, 120–2, 162
alam (name) 73
'Alāwal Khān Masjid 190
Alexander 76, 103; Alexander the Great, Macedonian conqueror 76; Dhū 'l-Qarnayn 76; Sikandar 76, 103
Alhambra Palace in Granada 17–18, 20
'Alī al-Naqī 229
'Ālī al-Shān Sharf al-Zamān 141–2
'Alī Mardān Khaljī (the second Muslim ruler of Bengal who proclaim himself sultan) 2, 29, 35; Sulṭān 'Alā' Dīn wa Dunyā' 1–2, 13, 29, 33, 35, 37, 40, 65, 83–4, 87–91, 95, 103
'Alī, Mawlānā 'Ināyat 41, 56
'Alī, Mawlānā Kirāmat 42
Alī, Mawlānā Wilāyat 41, 56
'Alī Mech (tribal leader) 36
'Alī Murtaḍā 229
'Alī Musā Sulṭān 139
'Alī Qulī Bayg (Iranian origin Shī'ī elite) 81
'Ali Raja 71n28
'Alī Riḍa 229
Ali, Sayyid Mujtaba (author of a famous Bengali travelogue *Deshe-Bideshe*) 44
'Alī Sher ibn 'Iwaḍ Burhān-i-Amīr al-Mu'[minīn] 92
'ālim (Islamic scholar) 21, 68, 72–3, 186, 217
'Alīm al-Dīn 163; *see also* Nūr Pandawī
'Ālim 'Ulūm al-'Adyān wa 'l-'Abdān 72–3, 217
'āliya madrasa (Islamic higher seat of learning) 52, 242
Almās, al-Malik 236
alqāb (plural of *laqab*) 79
al-Alqāb al-Islāmiyyah 86n8
[*al-*]*Alqāb al-Islāmiyyah fī 'l-Tārīkh wa 'l-Wathā'iq wa 'l-Āthār* (Arabic book on Islamic titles) 78
al-alqāb al-makāniyya (positional titles) 79
al-alqāb al-mashriqiyyah 75
'amālas (scholars) 108
Ambhua (a village in Birbhum district) 55
Ambila 56
al-Amīn (title) 77
Amīr al-Mu'minīn 79–80, 102; Burhān-Amīr al-Mu'minīn 80; *qasīm amīr al-mu'minīn* 89; Nāṣir Amīr al-Mu'minīn 98–9, 102, 105, 148, 192
amīr-i-akhūr (superintendent of the royal stable) 96
amma ba'd 149
Amrit-Kunda (The Eternal Lake) 66
Anair Haor 170–1
Ananda Bhatta 215
Andalusian 74
Andrās 28
Anīs al-Ghurabā' 163
Anwār al-Ḥaq Shahīd 121
Aqaliyya village (Sylhet) 230
[*al-*] *'Aqd al-Thamīn* 55
[*al-*] *'Arab wa 'l-'Ajm* 82
Arabian desert 47
Arabian peninsula 42, 81
Arakan (a region in Myanmar bordering Bangladesh) 29–30, 32, 34, 44, 54
Archaeological Survey of India 5, 18, 72, 106, 197, 237
'arṣa 112, 151, 223–4
Aryan race 62
Aryan Vedic culture 47
Aryan Vedic religion 66
Ascalon (Tomb place of Ḥusayn) 14
ashraf (nobles) 40
Ashraf Jahāngīr Simnānī 122
al-'Askarī, Abū 'l-Hilāl 77
[*al-*]*asmā' al-Ḥusnā'* (the beautiful names of God) 14, 156
Assam (an eastern region and state in India) 29, 32, 36, 43, 67, 132–3, 171, 242–3, 246
'Aṭā' Waḥīd al-Dīn, Mawlānā 123–4, 213–14, 234; *see also* Makhdūm Mawlānā; Quṭb al-Awliyā'
Āthār (used in modern Arabic to mean archaeology) 9
al-Āthār al-Bāqiya 85n2
[ibn al-]'Athīr 11
Atiya Masjid 184
aṭraf 40; *see also ajlaf*; *arzal; mlechcha*
Atrai (river) 27, 167
Aulad Husain, Khan Bahadur 155
awqāf (endowments) 51
Awr Khān Aybak 96
Awrangzebādī, Sayyid Munshī Ilāhī Bakhsh al-Ḥusaynī 4, 205; *see also* Ilāhī Bakhsh; *Khūrshīd-i-Jahān Numā*
Awrangzib (Mughal emperor) 75
Ayat-Allāh 81
Aybak, Quṭb al-Dīn (sultan) 82, 90; *see also* Quṭb al-Dīn
Ayyubid era 82
A'ẓam Khān 121
A'ẓam Shāh, al-Sulṭān Ghiyāth al-Dīn (ruler of Bengal) 24, 37, 50, 54, 66, 73, 132–4, 162, 217

Azarbayjan 11
Azimnagar (village near Dhaka) 39, 212

Bāb al-Salām 50
Bāb al-Sharī'a ('the Gate of Justice', Alhambra, Andalusia) 19
Babar (Mughal emperor) 15
Babri masjid (Ayodha, India) 25
Bāburnāma (autobiography of Babar in Persian) 15
Badaon 96
Bad'i 'l-'Amāl 195
Badr al-Islam Pīr 162
Badr-i-'Ālam Ṣūfī 113
Bādshāh 80, 112; Pādshāh 80, 84, 192
badshāh-e-ahle īmān (monarch of the believers) 95
Badshah Kā Takht 129–30
Bagha Masjid 24
Baghdad 51, 74–5, 80, 83, 89, 207, 209
Bahādur Shāh, Sulṭān 83–4, 117–18, 249
Bahāristān-e-Ghaybī 121
Bahlawī 'l-'Aṣr wa 'l-Zamān (title) 187
Baḥr al-Basīṭ 17, 175, 177, 181
Baḥr al-Harkand (early Arabic name for the Bay of Bengal) 27
Baḥr al-Ma'ānī (a title) 219
baḥr Mutaqārib 208
Baḥr Shalāhaṭ (the Strait of Malacca) 33
Bahrām Aytgīn Sulṭānī 76, 104
Bahrām Eytgin, Ḥajjī 81
Bahrām ibn Ḥājjī 117
Bahrām Saqqā' 48, 70–1
baḥth (religious debates) 42
Baisgazi Wall of Gaur 18, 25
Bā'ith al-'Adl wa 'l-'Iḥsān 123
Bajur Agency 55
Bakht Bīnat, Musammat 153
Bakhtiyār Khaljī, Ikhtiyār al-Dīn Muḥammad 13, 16, 89
Balban, Sulṭān Ghiyāth al-Dīn 103
Balbani Dynasty 37
Baliaghata village (near Jangipur, Murshidabad district) 142–3
Balkā Khān Khaljī 3; Dawlāt Shāh 88; Malik Ikhtiyār al-Dīn Balkā Khān Khaljī 94
Balkhī, Muẓaffar Shams 37, 54n42–55n42, 66, 122, 242
Ballaharā (Raja Ballahrāya of the Rāṣṭrakūṭa dynasty of the Deccan) 28
Ballala Charita 215
Bandar (*thana* in Dhaka district) 39, 211–12
Banerji, R.D. 5, 151, 171
Banga (Southern Bengal) 27–8, 243
Bāngarh 90, 105
Bangla Bhasay Qur'ān Charcha (Bengali text) 184
Bania Pukur (near Kolkata) 120–1, 167
Bāqir al-Muḥammad 229
Bara (village) 146
Bara Jāmi' Masjid 220
Barailiwī, Sayyid Aḥmad 42, 55
baraka 10, 15
Barakatra (monument) 17, 25
Baramatyabari 13
Bārbak Shāh (Sultan) 5, 6, 18–20, 83, 88, 151, 153, 166–75, 177–9, 181, 183–94, 196, 198, 200–8, 210, 211, 218, 227, 233, 241n23, 247; Bārbakabād (city named after Bārbak Shāh) 188–9
Barbosa (Portuguese merchant) 33
Bareilliwī, Sayyid Aḥmad 42
Bari Dargah 76, 91, 95
Barind 27; *see also* Gaur; Gowḍa
Barkhurdār ibn Khān Mu'aẓẓam Tāj Khān, Mawlānā 221–2
Baro Gharia 40
Barr wa Baḥr 82
Bārsbāy (Sulṭān in Egypt) 38
Bashirhat (town in Chabbish Parganah) 184, 186
basmala 4, 88, 127, 158
Bāsiṭ al-'Adl wa 'l-Iḥsān 146
Bāsiṭ al-'Amn wa 'l-'Amān 147
[ibn] Baṭṭūṭa (traveller) 14, 24, 27, 33, 65, 112
Baya Chakara 25
al-Bayrūnī 74; Abū Rayḥān al-Bīrūnī 85n3
Bazurai Hāt 235
Beg (title) 75
Begum Maḥal 179
Bengal: Bang 198–9; Bangala (the province of Bengal during Muslim period) 29; Banglā 27, 74; Bangladesh 2, 3, 6, 7, 24n17, 25n20, 27–9, 39, 52n2, 84, 87, 90–1, 94, 98–9, 104, 109, 111–12, 117, 119n7, 135–7, 147–9, 155–6, 160, 166–8, 170–1, 173–5, 180, 184–8, 190, 195, 199, 200, 204, 207, 209, 211–12, 214–16, 218, 222, 227, 229, 230, 238, 240n5; Bay of Bengal 29, 32, 44–5; Bengal delta 40, 48; Bengali bazaar culture 80; Bengali Islamic culture 38; Bengali language 37, 240n16; Bengali literature 39; Bengali madrasas 38; Bengali Muslim 3, 7, 29,

Bengal *continued*
33, 34, 36, 47, 67, 81, 135; Bengali Muslim Dynasty 38; Bilād-i-Bang 28; East Bengal 43; Islam in Bengal 27–57; *see also* Bengali *ṭughrā*
Berchem, Max Van (Swiss orientalist) 12, 24
Beveridge, Henry 4–5
Beverly, H. 42, 56
bhadrolok (gentry in Bengal [Hindu version of *ashraf*]) 40–1
Bhāgal Khān 25n18, 71n15
Bhagirathi (river) 29, 152
Bhakti movements 70
bhikshu 64
Bhojar Brahmin 66, 90
Bhoura 102
Bībī Mahal 163
Bihar (state of India) 22, 25, 28, 33, 39, 54, 59, 69, 76, 79, 81, 84, 88, 95–6, 100
Bihārī (regional calligraphic style) 7, 59, 88, 134–6, 144, 155–6, 161, 163, 168, 184–5, 194, 197, 208, 212, 214, 218
Bihisht ka Darwāza 163
Bilād-i-Bang 28
Bilyār Khān 185–6
bīmāristān (hospitals) 44
binā kardah 222
binā al-khayr 109
Birol (Dinajpur district) 218
bi-shara' 68
Boa Malati 31, 48; Boamaloti 210
Book of Government or *Rules for Kings, The* 85n4
Bosworth, C.E. 78
Bourke, Walter M. 5
Brahman Kshatriya (high Hindu caste) 35
Brahmaputra (river) 36
British India 43, 55
British Museum 5, 25, 54, 89, 100, 119, 179, 201–2, 206, 224, 232–3, 241, 248
Buddhism 28, 35, 62
Buddhist Monastery 64
Bughrā Khān, Nāsir al-Dīn Maḥmūd 103
Bular Ati (Satkhira district, Bangladesh) 40
Bunair (near Swat valley) 55–6
Buno (forest people) 40
Burarchar 24–5, 81
Burhān Amīr al-Mu'minīn 98
Burj al-Mā' (lit. Tower of Water) 19
[al-]Burj al-Qamarī (lit. 'Moon Tower') 19
Bustān 209
Būyīds 74
Byzantine civilizations 76

Cairo (city) 38, 64
Calcutta madrasa 52, 244; Calcutta 'Ālia Madrasa 52; 'Ālia University 52
Caliphate 41, 83
Caspian Sea 64
Central Asia 13, 16, 21, 32, 34, 37–8, 43–5, 50–1, 55, 57, 64, 68, 76, 93, 97, 101, 122, 135, 169
Challa mosque 220
Chamar (low caste tribe assigned to leather works, shoemakers) 30
Chamarqand (Afghanistan) 41, 55–6
Chamkatti Masjid (Gaur) 201–2
Champanagar (Bihar) 124, 235
Champaran (district in Bihar) 102
Chancellery script (Islamic calligraphy) 21, 77
Chānd Darwāza (royal entrance and a lofty gate to the Bādshāhī citadel in Gaur) 17, 19–20, 88, 177–81, 183
Chandra dynasty 28
Chandradvipa 27, 188
Chapai-Maheshpur village (Chapai Nawabganj district, Bangladesh) 227
Chapai Nawabgnaj (district in Bangladesh) 29
chāshnigīr (taster of royal food) 96
Chattapadhdhay, Sharat Chandra (popular Bengali writer) 43, 56, 70, 71
Chehil Ghāzī Masjid 35, 168, 170
Chhoto Sona Masjid (Chapai Nawabganj district, Bangladesh) 24n6
Chilla Khāna (place for meditation for the Sufis) 139–40, 163, 171, 238
Chistiyya order 162, 239
Chittagong (district in Bangladesh) 27–8, 32–4, 36–7, 48, 50, 54–5, 57, 190, 209, 240, 242, 249
Chota Pandua (in the present district of Hooghly) 50, 108, 153
Choti Dargah of Bihar Sharif 113–14
Choto Pheni estuary 28
Christian missionary 31
Christian usage 68
Chunakhali (Murshidabad district, West Bengal) 233–4
Churihatta (quarter in old Dhaka) 29
'Codovascam' (a name Portuguese gave to Chittagong) 34
Comilla (district in Bangladesh) 27
Court of Lions (Alhambra, Granada, Andalusia) 18

Court scribes 74
cowrie-shells (used for monetary transaction) 112
Creighton, Sir Henry 4, 178, 201, 240, 243
Creolized forms 68
Cunningham, Sir Alexander 5

Ḍābiṭ Aṭrāf al-Umam (title used by some sultans) 146
ḍabṭ al-nafs 69
Dahlawi 112–13; *see also* Dalwi
Dahum (geographic name of Bengal in Arabic sources) 27; *see also* Ruhmī
Dakhil Darwaza (Gaur) 178
Damdama 98, 105
Danbāl Bādshāh (Prince Dānyāl) 112
Dani, A.H. 5–6, 100–1, 111
Dār al-Khayrāt 50, 108, 114–15, 153
Dār al-'Ulūm in Deoband 51
Darbhanga (Persian *Dār-i-Bang*, gateway to Bengal) 102
dars-bāris (schools) 49
Dars-i-Niẓāmi 51
Darsbari Masjid 205
al-Dastūr 204
da'wah (Islamic propagation) 68–9, 234
dawla (state, used also as part of title) 82; Mu'aẓẓam al-Dawla 82
Dawlat Khān 73, 191, 220
Dawlat Khān (al-Wāthiq bi 'l-Malik al-Mannān, Khān al-Mu'aẓẓam) 73, 191, 220
Dawlat Shāh ibn Mawdūd 94
Delhi (Indian capital) 3, 14, 23, 31, 35–7, 39, 51, 54n34, 54n35, 56n47, 80, 82, 84, 89–97, 101–4, 113–14, 118n1, 119n5, 125, 135, 160–1, 197, 242, 244–5, 248, 252–4; Delhi Museum 54
Deotala (in Dinajpur) 171–2, 213–14
Desai, Ziauddin (epigraphist) 5
Deva dynasty 28, 188
Devikot (capital of Sultan Ala Din) 27, 31, 36, 65, 90, 104, 118, 122, 124, 234
Dhaka 5–6, 15–16, 24n17, 25n20, 27, 33, 36, 39, 43, 47, 50, 52n2, 54n29, 56n52, 71n28, 87, 95, 99, 109, 111, 125, 166; Dacca 26, 53, 56, 99, 111, 137, 139, 153, 155, 185
Dhaldighi 124, 214
Dharmapāla (Budhdhist king of Bengal) 27
dhimmī 67
Dhū 'l-Fiqār 227
Dhū 'l-Wizāratayn (title of lisān al-Dīn al-Khaṭīb) 18
dīn al-fiṭra 59, 61–3
al-Dīn, Mawlawī Naṣīr 55
al-Dīn Muḥammad, Sultan Jalāl 34, 38, 80, 134–7, 139, 149, 247
al-Dīn, Mulla Niẓām 51
Dinajpur (district in Bangladesh) 3, 5, 35, 50, 124, 168, 171, 179, 186, 189, 218, 225, 241n20, 247; Dakhshin Dinajpur (Southern Dinajpur) 65, 76, 90, 97, 104, 122, 213–14, 234; Dinajpur Museum 168, 186–7
Dīnār Khān, Ulugh Khān Mu'aẓẓam 137
Dīr 55
District Collectorate Record Rooms 48
Diva-Sing 122
Diwān Khāna 179; *see also* Darbār Maḥal
Dīwān al-Dast al-Sharīf 77
Diwan al-'Insha' (chiefs of the state secretariat) 21, 76–8, 85
Dīwān al-Kitāba 77
Dīwān al-Mukātibāt 77
Dīwān al-Ṭughrā' 77
diwān-i-risāla (institution for religious matters,
endowments and grants etc. [e.g. *madad-i-ma'āsh*]) 17
Ḍiyā' al-Dawla wa 'l-Dīn 103
Diyār Suknāt (probably Samataṭa region/ Sylhet district) 28
Diyaṟa 53
Diyār-e-Bangālah (Bangāla) 29
Dohar in Bengal 17, 24–5, 71, 81
Dom (low caste Hindu tribe engaged in various menial jobs) 30
Dost Muḥammad 56
Dudu Miah (son of Ḥājjī Sharī'at Allah) 42
Dummanpal (ruler) 28
Dunyā 83
al-dunyā wa 'l-dīn 82

East India Company 40, 44, 51, 240, 243
Eden 177
Egypt 24, 38, 63, 74, 76–8, 80, 82, 84, 97, 223
Ekdala (medieval sultanate fort) 27, 36
Epigraphia Indica 5
Epigraphia Indica, Arabic and Persian Supplement 6
Epigraphia Indo-Moslemica 5, 245
eulogists 74
euphemism 73

European colonial power 85

Faḍl-Allah Gosain 100
Fakhr Salāṭīn Ādam 147
Fanā' al-Birka ('Court of the Cistern' in Alhambra, Granada) 19
Fanā' al-Rayḥān (Rayḥān [lit. basil/mint] Court in Alhambra, Granada) 19
Faqīr 59, 64–5, 68, 92, 193, 238
Faqīrer Masjid 209
Farā'iḍī movement (religious movement by Ḥājjī Sharī'at Allah) 42
farmans 78
al-Fāsī, Qāḍī Muḥy al-Dīn 'Abd al-Qādir al-Ḥusaynī 51
al-Fāsī, Taqī al-Dīn 11, 24n9, 50, 55, 57
Fatḥ Shāh, Sulṭān 38, 73, 211–27, 230, 250
'fātiḥ Kāmrū wa Kāmtah bi 'awn Allah al-Ḥannān al-Mannān' (title of Ḥusayn Shāh) 84
Fāṭima (the daughter of the Prophet) 85; Fāṭima al-Ẓahrā 229
Fatimid 78; Fatimid era 76–7; Fatimid rule in Egypt 76
al-Fawā'id fī Uṣūl 'ilm al-Baḥr wa 'l-Qawā'id (a book by Captain Aḥmad ibn Mājid) 29
Fazlul Haque 74; *see also* 'Sher-i-Bangla'
fiqh 50–1, 109, 195
First World War 56
Fīrūz Eytgīn al-Sulṭānī 102
Fīruz Khān 139
Fīrūz Shāh Minār (Goamaloti, Gaur) 232
Fīrūz Shāh Sulṭān Shams al-Dīn 89, 108, 111–17, 218, 229, 232; Sayf al-Dunyā wa 'l-Dīn Fīrūz Shāh 219, 225, 228, 230–1, 233–4, 241, 249–50
Fīruz Tughluq 125
Fitch, Ralph (English traveller, visited Bengal during 1585–1586) 33
Franklin, Major William (British collector of Islamic inscriptions of Bengal) 4, 202
fuqahā' (jurists) 108

Gaigharh (Maulvi Bazar district, Bangladesh) 199
Gandak river (Monghyr district, Bihar, India) 101
Ganesh (Raja Kans, a Bengali landlord during the rule of Aẓam Shāh) 34, 135, 149, 162, 240, 245; *see also* Raja Ganesh
Gangarampur 97–9, 124, 214
Ganges (river) 17–18, 27, 18, 33, 53–4, 122, 245
Gangetic delta (mainly the southernmost part of Bangladesh) 27
Garden of Eden (earthly embodiment of the paradisal garden) 18
Garh Jaripa (Sherpur District, Bangladesh) 24, 229
Gauhati (capital of Assam) 32, 132, 242, 246
Gaur (capital of various sultans of Bengal): *Gaur; Its Ruins and Inscriptions* 5, 125; Gaur Social Welfare Mission Museum 140, 175, 194, 236; 'Gauriyo Bricks' 178; *see also* Barind; Gowḍa
Gaurai (in Mymansing district) 174–5
Ghagra (Mymansingh district, Bangladesh) 147
Ghaibi Dighi (Sylhet, Bangladesh) 172
Ghawth al-Islām wa 'l-Muslimīn (popular title for sultans) 140, 212, 239
ghāzī ('victorious', 'conqueror', a title) 65; al-Ghāzī 84, 103, 105, 118, 147
al-Ghāzī fī Ẓill-Allah (title for sultan) 147
Ghazī Pīr (Shrine of Ghazī Pīr, Shibganj Police Station, Nawabganj district, Bangladesh) 137–8
Ghāzī, Shāh Ismā'īl (legendary saint) 65
Ghazipur (Uttar Pradesh, India) 192
Ghaznah (capital of early Ghaznavid rulers) 80, 90, 97; Ghaznavid period 91
Ghiyāth al-Islām wa 'l-Muslimīn (title used by some rulers in Bengal) 96
Ghoraghat (famous for a madrasa in Mughal period) 50
globalization 17, 23, 85
Goamaloty (Gaur, Malda district, West Bengal) 178–9
Godagari (a police station [*thana*] in Rajshahi, Bangladesh) 87, 135, 195
Govinda Chandra (mentioned in the Tirumalai Sanskrit ins.) 28; *see also* Rajendra-Cola dynasty (*c.*1021–1023)
Gowḍa 27; *see also* Gaur; Barind
Granada (famous Muslim Capital in Andalusia) 17–18, 25, 253
Greek and Roman vases and sculpture 180
Gunbad (Gonbuj in Bengali, dome) 123
Gunmant mosque (Gaur) 73; Gunmant Masjid 180, 217, 220
Gur-i-Mīr (medieval Islamic architectural complex in Samarqand) 16
Guru–disciple relationship (Hindu tradition adopted by some sufis in South Asia) 70

Habānaq (mentioned by [ibn] Baṭṭūṭa, probably Sylhet) 27; *see also* Śrihaṭṭa (in Sanskrit); Suknāt; Sylhet
Ḥabashī rulers (four slave sultans of Bengal of African origin) 237; Ḥabshīs 38; *see also* Abyssinian slaves
Ḥabībī, 'Abd al-Ḥay 23n2, 52
Hadda Mulla, Najm al-Dīn 56
hādhā 'l-masjid 237
Ḥadīgar 224
ḥadīth (sayings of the Prophet) 7, 14–15, 21, 64, 66, 70n6, 83, 88, 92–3, 106, 109, 111, 158, 163, 166, 209, 216; *see also* Ahl al-Ḥadīth
Ḥaḍrat Muḥammad Kabīr Sāḥib 131
Ḥaḍrat Pandua 50, 58, 75, 125, 129, 130, 139–40, 161, 203, 238
Ḥaḍrat Shaykh 239
Ḥāfiz Bilād-Allah (title used by some sultans) 81
hagiographic literature 65; biographic literature 65
Ḥajji (one who has performed pilgrimage) 25, 37, 39, 42, 55–6, 71, 81, 117, 212
Ḥājjī al-Ḥaramayn wa Zā'ir al-Qadamayn (title used by Ḥājjī Bābā Ṣāliḥ) 39; *see also* Ṣāliḥ
Ḥajji Muḥammad 71n28
Hakimpur (village in Jessore) 41
Hall of Ambassadors (Alhambra, Granada, Andalusia) 18
Ḥāmī Bilād Ahl al-Islām wa 'l-Muslimīn (protector of the lands of Islam and the Muslims) 59; Ḥāmī al-Bilād 123
Ḥamīd al-Dīn Nagori Kunjshikan, al-Shaykh al-Qāḍī 73, 162, 217
Hamilton, Francis Buchanan (author of *A Geographical, Statistical and Historical Description of the District or Zilla of Dinajpur*) 3, 5, 179, 241, 247
Ḥanafī *fiqh* 51, 67; jurisprudence 67; jurist 66–7; school of jurisprudence 67
Haq, Enamul 33, 54, 99, 156, 185–6, 240, 249
Haque, Khan Hamidul 184
al-Ḥaram al-Makkī 50
Harikela (Chittagong area in the early period, Sylhet in the later period) 27–8, 188
Harkand (early Arabic term for Chittagong and Sylhet) 27, 188
Harugram (Malda district) 189, 193
Hārūn al-Rashīd 28
[al-]Ḥasan al-'Askarī 229
al-Ḥasan al-Mujtabā 229
Hasht Kāmhāriyān 112–13
al-Ḥaṣkafī, Shaykh Abu 'l-Ḥasan 'Alī ibn Aḥmad al-Mārdīnī 51
Hastings, Warren 52
Hathazari (Chitagong district) 190; Hathazari madrasa 50
Ḥāṭim Khān's Palace (Bihar Sharif) 81, 113, 116–17
Ḥātim al-Milla (title) 75
Ḥātim al-Ṭā'ī (title) 75
Ḥāṭim al-Thānī (title) 219
Hatkhola (Sylhet district) 170–1, 174
Haveli (Bagerhat, Khulna) 160
Ḥawḍ al-Ḥayāt (Arabic translation of a Sanskit manual) 47, 66, 90
Ḥawelī Khāṣ (private room in the Qil'a Dawlatkhāna Bādshāhī) 179; *see also* Maḥal Khās Badshāhī
Herat (a historical city in Afghanistan) 38, 109
Hilāl Bandah-e-Dargah 150
Hindu holy scriptures 66
Hindu temple 64
Hindu–Muslim encounter 66
Hinduism 21, 28
ḥisba 107, 109
ibn-Hishām 9
Ḥizb-Allah 56
Hooghly (district) 24n6, 108–9, 246–7
Horn, Paul 5, 125
Horseman Type of Bengal, The (coins/numismatic) 54, 118, 249; Horseman Tankah 54; Horseman Tankah of Muhammad bin Sam 162, 217
Horvitz, J. 5–6
Ḥudūd al-'Ālam 28
ḥujra 213
Ḥukūmat-i-Muwaqqata-i-Hind 56
Humāyūn (Mughal emperor) 39, 132, 178
[al-]Ḥummāris (Qāḍī Muḥammad al-Naṣīr) 107; *see also* Muḥammad al-Naṣīr
Husain, S. Aulad 5
Ḥusayn (grandson of the Prophet) 14
Ḥusayn Nawsha-i-Tawḥīd 122
Ḥusayn Shāh (Sultan) 24n6, 38–9, 69, 84–5, 89, 111, 113, 122, 212, 216, 228; Ḥusayn Shāhī (dynasty) 30, 34, 38–9, 113, 237
Ḥusaynī Dalān in Gaur 24, 217–18, 225, 230

*ibāḥī*s 68

ibn al-Sulṭān (royal title meaning 'son of the king') 84, 98, 103, 105, 114, 118, 126, 132, 168–9, 221, 211; *see also* al-Sulṭān ibn al-Sulṭān
Ibrāhīm al-Nakha'ī 67
Ibrāhīm, Prophet 67
Ibrahīm Sharqī (sulṭān of Jaunpur, Bihar) 162
al-ibrīq (jug) 19
al-Idrīsī 28
Ikhtiyār al-Ḥaq wa 'l-Dīn (title) 101–2
Ilāhi Bakhsh, Munshī 4, 205; *see also* Awrangzebādī; *Khūrshīd-i-Jahān Numā*; Sayyid Munshī Ilāhī Bakhsh al-Ḥusaynī
'ilm al-jadal (the art of dialectics) 66
Iltutmish, Shams al-Dīn 82, 94
Ilyās Shāh (Sulṭān) 29, 120, 126
Ilyās Shāhī Dynasty 37–8, 62, 73, 83
Imām al-Būṣīrī 17, 177
Imām Khomeini 81
īmān (faith) 108
'imāra al-mazīda 114
in'āms 69
inā' al-mā' (water vessel) 19
Ināna-sāgara 71n28
India Office Library 4–5, 125, 196, 201, 206, 233, 240–1
indigenization 68
Indonesia 31
Ingrezbazar (Malda, West Bengal) 4, 175–6, 236
Iqrār Khān 151, 153, 167, 169, 192
Iran 16–17, 21, 57, 81, 96, 101
Iraq 20, 67, 183
al-Irshād 66
ibn Isḥāq 9, 23
al-Islām wa 'l-Muslimīn ('shelter of Islam and the Muslims', a title) 59, 92, 96, 118, 140, 149, 152, 212, 239
ithnā 'ashariyya (mainstream Shī'ī sect) 81
'Iwaḍ Khaljī, Sulṭān Giyāthal-Dīn Ḥusām al-Dīn (early sultan of Bengal) 3, 13, 36, 80, 89, 91–5
Iwāns 123
'Izz al-Ḥaq wa 'l-Dīn (title meaning 'the glory of truth and religion') 96
'Izz al-Mulk Malik 'Alā' al-Dunyā' wa 'l-Dīn Jānī 88

Jadu 38, 149; Jadu Sen 135; *see also* Muḥammad Shāh
Ja'far al-Ṣādiq 229
Jahaj Bhangar Ghat ('the landing stage after shipwreck') 32
Jahanabad 87, 89
Jahānniyan Jāmi' Masjid 48
Jahnabi (old channel of Ganges West of Gaur) 29
al-Jahshiyāri 11, 78
Jalāl al-Ḥaq wa 'l-Dīn (the glory of truth and religion) 98
Jale Kumir-Dangay Bagh (Bengali proverb) 7n13
Jalwa Khāna 179; *see also* Khāṣ Maḥal
Jamāl al-Dīn 151, 224; Jamāl al-Dīn, Ḥusayn ibn Sayyid Fakhr al-Dīn 153
Jāmdār Ghayr-Maḥallī 142–4, 151, 216
jāmi' (congregational mosque) 14–15, 47–8, 57n53, 66, 70–1, 79, 90, 102, 106, 126, 147, 150, 155, 170, 175, 180, 185, 216–17, 220, 235, 238
Jam'iyyat al-Anṣār 56
Jān-i-Jānān, shaykh Mirza Maẓhar 71n27
Janāb-i-Majlis al-Sharf 195
janna (garden) 18, 60
Jannatabad (name given to Gaur by Mughal emperor Humāyūn) 178
Jayantia 112
Jaygirtola (village in Malda) 210
[ibn al-]Jayyāb (author of verses inscribed on halls at Alhambra) 19
Jazira al-Ramnī or Jazira al-Rāmī (the city of Lāmurī in Sumatra or Ramu near Cox's Bazar) 33
Jaznagar 112
Jewish tradition 75
Jharkhand 25
Jihād movement (anti-colonial struggles) 41–2, 51, 55–6; *see also* Mawlawī movement
Jirgah 56
Journal of a Route from Raj-mahal to Gaur 4; *The Ruins of Gaur* 4
julūs (titles) 82
Jum'a prayer 45
Junāb al-A'ẓam 149; Junāb al-Mu'aẓẓam 149
Junūd Rabbāniyyah 56
Jurz (Gurjaras of Kanauj) 28
jyotiska-devas (subsidiary deities in Hindu mythology) 227

Ka'ba (centre of the holy mosque in Makkah) 9, 12, 45
al-Kabir (the great, an adjective) 118

Kābulī (a *nisba* [geographical attribution] to Kabul) 15
kāḍī-i-mamālik (Chief Judge of the realm) 17
Kadkhuda (adoption of household/family life in the old Turkish tradition) 65
al-kāf al-thu'bānī (the python shape *kāf*) 95
kāfī 'l-kufāt (honourary title) 74
Kāfūr (camphor-like white and pure) 74
Kagol (Bihar, India) 105
Kālā Paththar 163
al-Kalbī, Muḥammad ibn al-Sā'ib (father of historian ibn-Hishām) 9
Kaliachak (Police Station in Malda district) 210
Kalinga 35
Kalna (Burdwan district, West Bengal) 191, 232, 237
kamar (blacksmiths) 30
Kamarupa 35; Kamarup 66; Kāmrūd 28; Kāmrūn 28
Kamta (tribal zone in the northern area of West Bengal) 54n38, 84, 112–13; *see also* Mech
Kanamah (Hindu Tantrik Yogi) 71n26
Kanja (Ganges river) 27
Karim, Abdul 5
Karnafuli (river) 28, 34
Karnāta dynasty 102
Kāshif Asrār al-Qur'ān (title of Sulṭān Fatḥ Shāh) 71, 73, 217
Kashmir 41, 55–6
Katībah hā (a recent book on Islamic epigraphy of Bengal in Persian) 8n2, 86n20
Katra 150, 218, 225; Barakatra (Mughal architecture in Dhaka) 17, 25, 48
Kaykā'ūs Shāh, Rukn al-Dunyā wa 'l-Dīn 84, 101–6, 109
khādim 74
khādim al-ḥaramayn (title of Saudi king) 74
Khādim al-Nabī (title) 39
[ibn] Khaldūn (famous North African medieval scholar) 45, 63, 71, 74, 78, 85n2
Khālid ibn al-Walīd 121
Khalīfa (a title) 79
Khalīfat-Allah 'Alā 'l-Mukawwanīn (title) 80
Khalīfat Allah bi 'l-Ḥujja wa 'l-Burhān (title) 72, 144–6, 148, 152, 233
Khalīfat Allah fī 'l-Arḍayn (title) 208
Khalifatabad (present Bagerhat) 91, 156, 160, 252
Khaljī (tribe in Afghanistan) 2–3, 6, 13, 16, 29, 31, 35–7, 40, 65, 76, 83, 87, 89, 90–1, 93–5, 102–3, 105, 113, 116, 167, 254; Khaljīstan 35
Khaljistān (original homeland of the Khaljī tribe in Afganistan) 35
khallada Allah mulkahu wa sulṭānahu (pious wishes/prayer formulas for sultan) 85
Khān (title) 73–85
Khan, Abid Ali 4, 97
[al-]Khān al-A'ẓam 131–2, 231; *see also* 'Ulugh Mukhliṣ Khān
Khan, Hamid Allah 5
Khān Jahān in Bagerhat 65, 91, 156–7, 160–1, 173, 188, 252
Khān Khānān al-Sharq wa 'l-Ṣīn 103
[al-]Khān al-Mu'aẓẓam (title) 76; Khān Mu'aẓẓam Ashraf Khān 167; Khān Mu'aẓẓam Khurshīd Khān 144, 168; Khān, Qadr 37
Khān-i-Khānān 102
Khanḍawāla 102
Khanjālī, Pīr 160; Khanjali pond 161
Khānqāh 3, 7, 13, 15–16, 30, 37, 48, 50, 54, 58, 63–4, 69–70, 91–3, 98–9, 100–1, 121, 133–4, 147, 179, 207, 213–14, 251
khāqān ('overlord', popular title) 73, 76, 85, 96, 108, 138, 144, 149, 151, 165–6, 169, 170, 172–3, 187, 192, 196, 207–8, 220, 231; Khāqān al-Zamān (title) 116
khasta (tired) 53
al-Khaṭīb, lisān al-Dīn (Naṣirid vizier) 18, 20
khaṭṭ al-ijāza (calligraphical style) 140
Khawāṣ Khān 228
Khazāna Kothri 179–80
khilāfa 162, 239
khiṭāb (honourary titles in Urdu and Persian languages) 73
al-Khiṭaṭ wa 'l-Āthār 23n4, 25, 86n6
khiṭṭa rifiyya 62
Khojar Masjid 199
Khudā Bakhsh Khān 34
Khulna (district in Bangladesh) 27, 156
Khuramsar Mukhliṣ Khān 231
Khurasan (present region of Afghanistan) 37, 43, 51, 55, 64, 67, 80, 90, 97, 101, 109
ibn Khurradādhbih 28
Khūrshīd-i-Jahān Numā 4, 194, 205; *see also* Awrangzebādī, Sayyid Munshī Ilāhī Bakhsh al-Ḥusaynī

Khusrow Anoshirvan 75
Khusrow-i-Zaman (title) 75, 104
khutba (congregational sermon) 74
Khwāja Jahān (title) 155
Khyber Pakhtunkhwa (province of Pakistan) 55
kiswa (decorated black cloth on the Ka'ba) 12, 24
Kitāb al-Wuzarā' wa 'l-Kuttāb (Arabic source book) 78
Kohin Kā Bāgh (Bhagalpur, Bihar) 145, 154
Kotivarsa 104
kotwāl (jailor) 90, 199; Kotwali Darwaza 53; Kotwali Gate 154; Kotwali mosque 154
kumar (pottery manufacturers) 29
Kufa (city in Iraq) 9
Kūfī (calligraphic style) 7, 10, 23n5, 126–7
Kunjshikan, Shaykh al-Qāḍī Ḥamīd al-Dīn Nagori (academic mentor of Sulṭān A'ẓam Shāh) 73, 93, 162, 217; *see also* Nagori
kunya (agnomen) 73, 79, 82–3

Lādin, 'Usāmah ibn (bin Ladin) 56
Lakhisarai (Monghyr district, Bihar) 57, 79, 102, 106, 109
Lakhmid 9
Lakhnor (town of early Muslim settlement near Rajnagar, in Birbhum district) 93; *see also* Nagor
Lakhnot 36, 90
Lakṣmaṇasena (Hindu king of Sena dynasty, defeated by Bakhtiyār Khaljī in 1205) 28, 35
Lakṣmṇāvatī (somewhere near Gaur where Muslim conquerors first settled) 27
Laor (small kingdom in or around Sylhet) 112
laqab (Arabic term for 'title') 73, 79–81
Laṭīf Khān 59
Lattan mosque (Gaur) 154
Lāwud (*thana* near Sonārgā'on) 216
Lees, Captain W.N. 5
Lohagara (Satkania Thana, Chittagong) 57
Lohānī (Paththān tribe) 55

Ma'ālim al-Kitāba wa Magānim al-'Isāba (by Jamāl al-Dīn 'Abd al-Raḥīm ibn 'Alī ibn al-Shīth) 78
madad-i-ma'āsh (endowment and land grants for religious institutions) 17, 30, 48, 57, 69–71
madhāhib (different Islamic legal schools) 67
Madinah (second most important holy city in Islam) 30, 39, 47, 50–1, 64, 74, 212
madrasa (academic institution) 3, 7, 11, 15–17, 30, 38, 40–1, 44, 48, 53n23, 63, 66, 73, 77, 83, 94–5, 100, 105–7, 109, 115–16, 122, 149, 153, 215, 217, 225, 244, 248, 250–1; darsbari masjid 205; *madrasa-bāri*s 47; Madrasa Dar al-Khayrat 108, 114–15, 153; madrasa masjid 29, 62, 94, 116, 135, 148; Madrasa Muḥsiniyyah 50; Madrasa Raḥmāniya in Delhi 51; al-Madrasa al-Niẓāmiyya 51; al-Madrasa al-Sulṭāniyyah al-Ghiyāthiyyah al-Bangāliyyah 11, 24n10, 50–1; role of madrasa 48–52; *see also* 'āliya madrasa; Calcutta madrasa; Hathazari madrasa
Magh pirates of Arakan 43
Mahajantola Masjid (Gaur) 201–2
Maḥal Khās Badshāhī (private room in the Qil'a Dawlatkhāna Bādshāhī [royal residential palace and citadel]) 179; *see also* Ḥawelī Khāṣ
Mahalla Mandaroga (Bhagalpur, Bihar) 144
Mahanada (river) 53, 102, 228
Mahdipur village (near Gaur) 29, 36, 53, 90, 141, 163–5, 175, 177–8, 180, 220, 225
Maheśa Thākura (founder of a Khanḍawāla Hindu ruling dynasty in Mithila in 1556) 102
Maheshwara (Begusarai, Bihar) 84, 101
Mahi Santosh (Patnitola, Nawgaon district, Bangladesh) 167, 170, 188–9
Maḥmūd Shāh (Sultan) 13–14, 59, 62, 73, 81, 83, 94, 97–8, 139–56
Mainamati (Comilla district, Bangladesh) 26, 28, 53
Majd Kābulī 100–1
[al]-Majlis al-A'la' 204; Majlis al-'Ālam 200; Majlis wa Majālis Majlis A'lā' 203–4; *majlis-i-'ālī* 174; Majlis-i-Bārbak 233; Majlis Manṣūr 149; Majlis Shihālā Khālid 218; Majlis Ṭāhir 159; al-Majlis al-A'ẓam wa 'l-Mu'ẓẓam 204
Makhdūm (sufi title) 81, 91, 121–2, 123, 146, 213–14, 234; *see also* Makhdum Shāh 91, 122; Makhdūm Shaykh 121; Quṭb al-Awliyā'
[al]-Makhṣūṣ bi-'Ināyat Rabb al-'Ālamīn (title) 115

Makkah (holiest city in Islam) 11, 24n10, 30, 38–9, 42, 50–1, 55n42, 74, 121, 201, 206, 212, 224, 239, 250–1
maktab (primary schools) 46, 50
maktūbāt (letters) 37, 66
Maktūbāt-i-Muẓaffar Shams Balkh 55, 242
[al]-Ma'lā 11, 24; *see also* al-Mu'allā
malādh al-warā 53, 108–9
Malaysia 31
Malda (district) 40
malfuẓāt (mystical tracts) 37, 66
malik (lord) 74, 80, 98, 118, 136, 151, 194, 199, 212, 237; Malik 'Andīl 218–19, 225; Malik, Ghazi (ruler of Multan) 14; Malik Mulūk al-Sharq ('the lord of the lords of the East', a title) 97; Mālik Riqāb al-'Umam 103, 115; Malik Sayf al-Dīn Aybak 96; Malik Sikandar (vizier of Sulṭān Yusuf Shāh ibn Bārbak Shāh ibn Maḥmūd Shāh) 203; Malik Thakur 223–5
[al]-Malik al-Mu'aẓẓam (common title appearing in many inscriptions) 39, 211–12; *see also* Ḥājjī Bābā Ṣāliḥ
[al]-Malik Kāfur 215
Maliki school of *fiqh* (jurisprudence) 50
Maloti, Sayyid Aḥmad 210
Mamluk 82, 84
Man Kali Bhita (in Mahasthangarh) 109, 111
Mandaran (village of Hoogly district) 65, 247
Manerī, Shaykh Sharaf al-Dīn Yaḥyā 50
Mangalkot (in the present district of Burdwan) 50
[al]-Manṣūr 103; al-Manṣūr bi-'Ināyat al-Raḥmān 120; Manṣūr ibn Malik Thakur 224
[al]-maqbarah al-mutabarrakah 101
[al]-Maqrīzī, Taqī al-Dīn Aḥmad ibn 'Alī 11, 16, 23n4, 24, 50, 55, 57, 86
[al]-Marāghī, ibn Muḥammad 64, 92, 99; Marāgha 93
Marḥamat 153
mashāyikh (sufi saints) 37, 93; *see also* Shaykh al-Mashāyikh
Mashriq men Islāmī Tahzīb ke Athār (Urdu book on the epigraphy of Muslim Bengal) 6, 8n3, 86n20, 87
masjid: Masjid al-Nabawi (the Prophet's mosque) 47; Masjid-i-Mīr (Mashhad, Iran) 16; *see also* mosque
Masnad-i-A'lā 23, 43, 234
Maṣrif al-Dawla wa 'l-Dīn 118
Mastān, Sa'd-Allah Khān Mulla 56
[ibn] Mas'ūd 67
Mas'ūd ibn Maḥmūd Ghaznavi, Sulṭān 81
Mas'ūd Shāh Jānī 97–8
math (Hindu monastery) 70
Mawlā Mulūk al-Turk wa 'l-'Ajam 103
Mawlānā 23n2, 27, 41–2, 55n45, 56n47, 56n50, 69, 76, 81, 85, 104, 122–4, 166, 167, 213–14, 221–2, 234, 243 (*see also* Munshī); Mawlānā Bhasani (political leader) 42; Mawlawī 3, 69; Mawlawī movement 69, 41 (*see also* Jihād movement)
Maẓāhir al-'Ulūm in Saharanpur 51
Maẓhar al-Dīn, Malik 188
Mech (tribe in Kamta) 35–6, 54, 113; *see also* Kamta
Meghna (river) 28
Memoirs of Gaur and Pandua 4, 125, 244
Methor (toilet cleaners, low caste in Hindu tradition) 30
Miḥrāb 14, 25n30, 38, 45, 106, 107, 126–31, 133–4, 184, 197, 199, 216
[al]-mi'mār (architect or mason) 79
Minarwali Masjid 175, 180; *see also* Indarawala Masjid
Minhāj al-Dīn Sirāj al-Dīn, Mawlānā 23n2, 97
[al]-Minhāj al-Fākhir fī 'Ilm al-Baḥr al-Zākhir 45
Mīr Aghmā 132
Mir Nāmwar Khan 110
Mir'at al-Asrār 163
mirror image (a calligraphic style) 164; mirror reverse calligraphic style 163–4
Mirṣād Khān Atābak Ra'yat-i-A'lā, *khāqān* 207
Mirzā (title) 75; Mirza Nathan 121
Mitha Tālāb 163
Mithila (ancient name of a region in Bihar) 102
Miyaneh Dar (monumental entrance of palace in Gaur) 6, 19, 175, 181, 183
Mlechcha (non-Aryan natives/non-Hindu aborigines) 35, 40, 62, 67
Mohmand Agency (Khyber Pakhtunkhwa, Pakistan) 55–6
Monghyr (district in Bihar) 79, 101–2, 109; Monghyr Fort 69
Mongols 41, 76; Mongol invasion 64
Morocco 77
mosque: Bengali village mosques 47; rural mosques 48; Sultanate mosques 228–49;

mosque *continued*
Umayyad mosques 181; urban mosques 48; vernacular mosques 47; *see also masjid*
[al]-Mu'allā 11; *see also* al Ma'lā'
mu'ayyid al-dīn mehtar mubārak al-khāzin al-sulṭānī (series of titles) 97
[al]-Mu'ayyad bi-Tā'yīd al-Dayyān 146
[al]-Mu'ayyad bi Ta'yīd al-Raḥmān 148
Mu'aẓẓam al-Dīn wa 'l-Dawla 135
Muazzampur (village in Dhaka district) 139
Mubārak, al-Khāzin (the treasurer) 96
Mubarak Shāh, Fakhr al-Dīn (sultan) 33, 37, 65
Mubārakabād (a district near Dhaka during Sultanate period) 155
[*al*]-*mubghiḍ li 'l-kuffār wa 'l-mushrikīn* (adjectives used for Ulugh Khān Jahān) 160
muftī (deliverer of formal legal opinions) 24, 66
Mughaltoli (in old Malda town) 150
Mughīth al-Mulūk wa 'l-Salāṭīn 96
Mughrapara Shahi Masjid (near Sonargaon, Dhaka) 215–16
muḥaddithūn (recognized scholars of the Prophet's traditions) 66
Muḥammad al-Khālidī 121
[al]-Muḥammad al-Mahdī 229
[ibn] Muḥammad al-Marāghī 64, 92
Muḥammad al-Naṣīr (Qāḍī al-Ḥummāris) 107; *see also* al-Ḥummāris, Qāḍī
Muḥammad al-Taqī 229
Muḥammad Bikampruri 114
Muḥammad bin Sam 54n35
Muḥammad ibn al-Qāsim 67
Muḥammad Sa'īd, Khān 189–90
Muḥammad Shāh, Jalāl al-Dīn (sultan) 34, 38, 88, 134–7, 139, 149, 247; Jalāl al-Dīn, Sultan 51, 80, 134–5, 137, 139, 247; *see also* Jadu; Jadu Sen
Muḥammad Shirān (Bakhtiyār's general) 90
Muḥammad Ṭāhir 159, 160–1
Muhammadabad 160
muḥaqqaq (calligraphic style used for Qur'ān) 7, 111, 213
Muḥarrir Bayk 224
Muḥibb al-'Ulamā' wa 'l-Fuqarā 219
Muḥy 'l-Sunna 83
Mu'īn al-Mulūk wa 'l-Salāṭīn (title) 115
mujāhidūn (freedom fighters) 41, 65; al-Mujāhid 83; al-Mujāhid fi Sabīl Allah al-Mannān 83; al-Mujāhid fī Sabīl al-Raḥmān 146
[*al*]-*mukātibāt* 78
[al]-Mukhtaṣ bi 'Inayat al-Ḥannān al-Mannān 147
Mulka 56
Mulla 40–1, 68–9
Mulla Simla 131–2
Mulla Tero Gharia 40
Mulla 'Umar 56
Mullikpur 117
Multan (a historical city in Punjab) 14, 105
mu'mīn (believer) 61
munāẓira 42
Munshī 3, 69, 178; *see also* Mawlawī; Mawlānā
[al]-Muntaṣir billāh, Abū Aḥmad 'Abd-Allah 28
Muqaddima 45, 85n2
Muqarrab al-Dawla wa 'l-Mulk wa 'l-Dīn al-Sulṭāni (title) 216
Murabbī Arbāb al-Yaqīn (title) 115
[al]-Murābiṭ (advance guard on the frontier) 84, 118
[al]-Murāghī, ibn Muḥammad 64, 93
'*murawwiju maḍhab a'immat ithnā 'ashara*' (title) 81
murīd (disciple) 64
murshid (spiritual master) 64
Murshidabad (district in West Bengal) 40
Mūsā (Moses) 67
Musā al-Kāẓim 229
Mūsā ibn Ḥājī Amīr 200
Musāfir Khāna 163
mushābih bi-ahl al-kitāb 66–7
mushrikūn 67
Musla (perhaps the Meghna river) 28
Muslim League 43
Mu'tabar Khān 235
Muẓaffar Shāh, Sulṭān Shams al-Dīn 122, 234–9
Muẓāffar Shams Balkhī 37, 54–5, 66; *Maktubat-i-Muzaffar Shams Balkhi* 242

Nabaz (nickname for enemies) 79
Nadia (district in West Bengal) 29, 90, 249
Nadwat al-'Ulamā' (famous madrasa in Lucknow) 51
Nagor (town of early Muslim settlement near Rajnagar, in Birbhum district) 93; *see also* Lakhnor
Nagori (geographical attribution to Nagor) 73, 93, 162, 217

Nagori, Shaykh al-Qāḍī Ḥamīd al-Dīn (academic mentor of Sulṭān A'ẓam Shāh) 73, 93, 162, 217; *see also* Kunjshikan
Nagri Legend (on Horseman Tankah of Muhammad bin Sam) 54n35
Naohata (Rahjshahi district, Bangladesh) 3
Napit (clan of barbers in low caste Hindus) 30
Naramithla (Arakanese king during ninth/fifteenth century) 34
Narankot (also Narayankot, a fiefdom given to 'Alī Mardān by Bakhtiyār) 90; *see also* Narayankot
nasab (lineage) 73, 79
Nāṣir Ahl al-'Īmān (royal title) 120
Nāṣir Amīr al-Mu'minīn (royal title) 98–9, 103–5, 148, 192
Nāṣir Khān, Al-Malik al-Mu'aẓẓam al-Mukarram 193
Naṣirid (ruling dynasty in Granada) 18
[al]-Naṣrānī, Abū 'l-Naṣr ibn 'Abdūn 76
[al]-Naṣrānī, Fahd ibn Ibrāhīm 76
[al]-Naṣrānī, Sā'id ibn 'Īsā ibn Nasṭūras 77; al-Naṣrānī, Waz'a ibn 'Īsā ibn Nasṭūras 76
'Naswa Gali' (mosque in the Girdi-Qila quarter of old Dhaka) 155
Navagram (village in Pabna District) 62, 148–9
Nawda Burj (Nawdapara, Rohanpur railway station, Chapai Nawabganj district) 53n18; *see also* Shāṛ Burj
Nawdah (the present Mahdipur village and its adjacent areas) 29, 53, 90, 250
Nawdiya (*Navadipa* in Sanskrit) 53
nawkar 74
nawwara 228
Nayabari (near Dhaka) 15–16
Nayk Muḥammad 137
Nilkuthi 178–9
Nim Darwaza (royal entrances to the Bādshāhī citadel in Gaur) 6, 16–20, 88, 175–7, 179, 180, 183
Nimyās 28
nisba (attribution of a person to the place of origin) 15, 21, 64, 73, 79, 93, 101, 105, 113
Niẓām al-Mulk 51, 75, 82
Noakhali (district) 33, 48, 54
North Africa 7, 75, 77, 81
Nūr al-Ḥaqq wa 'l-Shar' wa 'l-Dīn 239
Nūr Jamāl 71n28
Nūr Quṭb al-'Ālam (sufi) 37–8, 58–60, 65, 75, 81, 121–2, 139–40, 160–3, 167, 238–9
Nuṣrat Shāh (Sultan) 14, 81, 153
NWFP (Khyber Pakhtunkhwa) 56

Oinwāra 102
Orissa 25, 28–9, 109, 112–13, 184, 190, 232, 245, 254

Pagla (river) 29
Paharpur (*Vihara*) 28, 170
Pahlawi-i-'Aṣr 231; Pahlawī al-'Aṣr wa 'l-Zamān 169, 192, 208
pāk panj tan (five holy bodies) 15
Pak̲h̲tūns 55
Pakistan 5–6, 26, 43, 53–6, 87, 170, 242–4, 246–50, 253
Pala (dynasty) 10, 21–3, 35, 90, 92
Pan-Islamic 42, 74, 79
Pandua (Muslim capital city of Bengal) 27, 36, 40, 47, 50, 54, 58, 66, 75, 83, 90, 108, 118, 121, 222; Ḥaḍrat Pandua 125, 129–30, 139–40, 161, 203
Panegyrists 74
Pannī 55
Pathantola (in Dhamrai village, Dhaka) 212–13
Paththān 55
Peril (village in Dhaka) 173
Persian traditions 76
Pichhli Gangarampur 197
Pichhli Ghatal (village, Malda district) 97–8
*pīr*s (saints) 65, 68–70
Piyārī Dās Road 24
Prasād, Munshī Shayām (local assistant to William Franklin and scholar of Arabic and Persian) 5, 125, 178, 179, 201, 240
pre-Islamic 3, 21–2, 75, 79, 167
pre-Mughal 7, 22, 84, 125, 192, 246, 248, 253
proselytization 31, 68
Puri (Purushattam-Khśetra in ancient days) 35
Purnabvaba (river) 102
Purua (near Pandua) 206
Pūthī 67

Qadam Rasul 206
Qāḍī (judge) 36, 49, 51, 67, 107, 109, 166
Qāḍī al-Ḥummāris 107
Qāḍī ibn Qāḍī Aḥmad ibn Shaykh 'Alāwal 166
Qāḍī Nūr Masjid 163

Qadi Para (village in Barogharia union, Chapai Nawabganj) 175
Qāḍī Rukn al-Dīn 66, 67
[al]-Qādir, Abbasid caliph 81
Qādiyānī (Mirzā'ī sect of the Punjab) 56
Qahramān al-Mā' wa 'l-Ṭīn (title) 71, 217; *al-Mā' wa 'l-Ṭīn* 82
al-Qā'ida movements 56
Qala'ūn (Mamlūk sultan of Egypt, *c.*1279–1290) 85n1
[al]-Qalqashandi, Shihāb al-Dīn Aḥmad ibn 'Alī (Egyptian author of *Ṣubḥ al-A'shā fī Ṣanā'at al-Inshā'* (A.H. nineth century)) 78, 86n25
Qāqshāl (a *nisba* or geographical attribution) 15
Qarah Khitai (a *nisba* of Ṭughril to a Tatar or Turkish tribe) 96
[al]-Qarshī, Qāḍī Jamāl al-Dīn Muḥammad ibn 'Abd Allāh (academic at al-Madrasa al-Bangāliyyah) 24, 51
Qasaba (main street of medieval Cairo) 85n1
Qasba 146, 160, 166, 172; Qasba-e-Bara (Birbhum district, West Bengal) 166
Qaṣīda al-Burda (famous devotional ode by Imām al-Buṣīrī) 17, 177
qasīm amīr al-mu'minīn (associate of the commander of the faithful) 89
Qaṣūrī, Mawlāna Muḥammad 'Alī 56
Qatīl Maḥabbat Wahhāb (sufi title) 239
qibla (direction to Makkah during prayer) 45, 125–7, 130–1, 220
Qil'a Dawlatkhāna Bādshāhī (royal residential palace in Gaur citadel) 179
Qīrān Khān (builder of a masjd in Birol) 219
Qur'ānic verse 14–16, 21, 39, 60, 64, 70, 88, 93, 99, 127, 129, 131, 156–8, 186, 209, 224
Quṭb al-Aqṭāb (sufi title) 239
Quṭb al-Awliyā' (sufi title) 123, 213–14, 234; *see also* Quṭb al-Awliyā'
Quṭb al-Dīn Aybak 82, 90; *see also* Aybak
Quṭb al-Umarā' (title) 198
Quṭb Mīnār 23n5, 97; Quwwat 82; Qubbat 82

Rāḍh or Rāḍha (region lying to the west of the Hugli-Bhagirathi river) 27
Rahman, Muhammad Mujibur 184
Raḥmat Khān (great Khān and honoured *Khāqān* Khān Jahān as mentioned in ins. 61) 172
Rā'i al-'Ibād (appeared in a few inscriptions as a title of rulers) 123
Raja Ganesh (Raja Kans, a Bengali landlord during the rule of Aẓam Shāh) 135, 149; Raja Kans 162; Raja Kānsa (a misspelling of Sanskrit Ganeśa) 38
Rajendra-Cola dynasty 28; *see also* Govinda Chandra
Rajmahal (Jharkhand, India) 22, 25, 47, 50, 125, 177, 196, 201, 206, 233, 244
Rajshahi (district/city in Bangladesh) 24n6, 25n30, 56, 81, 87, 94, 97–8, 104, 117, 135, 145, 167–8, 189
Rame (Jazira al-Ramnī or Jazira al-Rāmīin Sumatra or Ramu near Cox's Bazar, Bangladesh) 33
Rampal (near Bikrampur, Dhaka) 214–15
Rānī Bībī 144
[al]-rasā'il 78
[ibn] Rashīq 74
Rāst Khān Majlis A'lā 190
Rasūlīd rulers in Yemen 84
Ratnapala 31
Ravenshaw, J.H. 5
rawḍa (shrines associated with saint veneration) 37, 54, 69, 111, 239; *dargāh* 69, 131–2, 139, 163; *mazār* 69
rayḥānī (calligraphic style used for Qur'ān) 7, 122, 156, 175, 181, 203
Reza Shah Pahlawi (Iranian monarch, twentieth century) 74
Rif'at al-Dīn 121, 162; *see also* Rafqat al-Dīn; Rafīq al-Dīn; Shaykh Barkat al-Dīn
Riḥla m'a 'l-Nuqūsh fī 'l-Bangāl (Arabic work on epigraphy of Bengal) 6, 8n2, 86n20, 87, 94, 175, 185, 252
Riqā' (calligraphic style) 7
al-riqā' al-musalsal (calligraphic style) 114
risāla 66
riyā' (eye-service of rituals) 70
Riyāḍ al-Salāṭīn (Persian chronicle on Bengal) 4, 43–4, 218, 243; *see also* Zayedpuri
Rohanpur (railway station in Chapai Nawabganj district, Bangladesh) 29, 222
'Room of the Ship' (part of the compound of Alhambra palace in Granada, Andalusia) 19
Ross, Denison (wrote on inscriptions in *Epigraphia Indo-Moslemica*) 5
Ruhmī (geographic name for Bengal in the early Arabic sources) 28, 52–3, 250; *see also* Dahum

Ruins of Gaur, The 4–5, 122, 178, 240, 243
Rukn al-Danā (title meaning 'support of the commoners') 53n23, 108–9
Rukn al-Dunyā wa 'l-Dīn (title appeared for sultan Kaykā'ūs Shāh) 89, 101–6, 109
[al]-Rukn al-Yamani (Yamani corner of the Ka'aba in the Grand Mosque in Makkah) 50
Rukn Khān 112–13
ruq'a (calligraphic style) 97–8, 114, 171

Sābiqī (traditionalists, *pīr*s, mullas) 68
Ṣadr al-Millat wa 'l-Dīn ('chief among the kings and the sulṭāns', title of an officer) 136
Ṣadr al-Mulūk wa 'l-Salāṭīn (chief among the kings and the sulṭāns, a title of a high officer) 92
sadr al-ṣudūr (controller of *madad-i-ma'āsh*) 17
Safid Buland Gulistan tomb (Farghana valley, Uzbekistan) 13, 91
al-Sāghānī, Shihāb al-Dīn Abū 'l-Khayr Aḥmad ibn Muḥammad (academic at al-Madrasa al-Bangāliyyah, Makkah) 51
Ṣāhib al-'Ahd wa 'l-Zamān (title of Sikandar Shāh) 123
Ṣāḥib al-Sayf wa 'l-Qalam (compound title) 192, 201, 218–19, 223–4; *see also* Ulugh Majlis Nūr, Sāḥib
Ṣāhib al-Tāj wa 'l-Khātim (title used by Kayka'us Shah and by Mahmud Shah) 103, 115, 148
ṣaḥn (courtyard, often found in a traditional mosque) 45, 47
[al]-Sā'ī fi 'l-khayrāt wa 'l-mubirrāt 204
saja' (rhythmic expression, often found in Islamic titles) 82
Sajla (city) 144, 147; Sajla Mankhabad 151, 223
Salafī 42
Salāḥ Jīwand Multānī 105
Ṣāliḥ, Ḥājjī Bābā (his title: 'al-Malik al-Mu'aẓẓam') 39, 211–12; *see also* Khādim al-Nabī
Salik Masjid (Bashirhat, Chabbish Parganah district, West Bengal) 184, 186
Saljūq 75, 84
salsabīl (spring) 18
Samandar 28
Samanids 75
Samarqand 15–16
Samataṭa (Ancient *janapada*) 27–8, 112; *see also* Habānaq; Suknāt; Tripura
Sanad (Mughal land deeds) 48, 55
Sanskrit: inscription 22–3, 28, 32, 64, 92; language 22–3, 25, 27–8, 32, 35–6, 38, 53, 64, 71, 92, 108, 119, 152
sāqi-i-khās (cup-bearer) 96
Sar Nashīn 231
Saraswati 108, 152
Sar-e-Gumāshta 166
Sare-nawbat Ghayr-Maḥalliyān 144, 168
Sarfrāz Khān, Khān Mu'aẓẓam Ulugh 142–4
sar-i-dawāt-dār (keeper of the imperial seal) 96
Sassanid (ancient ruling dynasty in Persia) 37; Sassanian imperial legacy 68
Sātgā'on (famous medieval port and administrative centre in southwestern Bengal) 36–7, 108, 150, 152–3, 223–4, 240n2, 240n3, 240n4, 245, 248, 250
Sayyid Dastur ibn Sayyid Rāhat 221
Schimmel, Annemarie 79
Sena (dynasty) 2, 35–6, 90
sha'ā'ir al-shar' 62
al-Shāfī (title) 77
Shāh (Persian title) 80
Shāh 'Abbās Ṣafawī al-Ḥusaynī 81
Shāh 'Aṭā, Mawlanā 76, 104, 123; Quṭb al-Awliyā' 123, 214
Shāh Baghdādi 207, 209
Shāh Gudā 150
Shāh Jahān (Mughal King Khurram) 81; Shāh Jahān-Panāh 177, 183; Shāh-e-jahān (royal title of sultan 'Alī Mardān Khaljī) 1, 88
Shāh Jalāl 98, 171, 204; Shāykh Shāh Jalāl 111; Shāh Jalāl Mujarrad kunyā'ī 112; *Ḥaḍrat Shāh Jalāl O Sileter Itihās* 199, 202; *History of Shah Jalal and His Khadims* 244
Shāh, Kaykā'us 79, 84, 101–6, 109, 111, 153
Shāh Majlis Dargāh 232
Shāh Makhdūm Dargāh (Rajshahi, Bangladesh) 81
Shāh Nafa 69
Shāh Nūr (sufi) 100
Shāh Safi al-Dīn 105
Shāh Shafī' al-Dīn 200–1
Shāh Shujā' 122
Shāh 'Uthmān 142–3
Shāhanshāh 74

Shāh-i-Bangāliyān (title of sultan Ilyās Shāh) 29
Shahīd, Sayyid Aḥmad 41
Shahīd, Sayyid Ismā'īl 41
Shahr-i-Nawdia (capital of Lakṣmaṇasena, currently Nawdapara, Rohanpur railway station, Chapai Nawabganj district) 28
Shāhzāda Sulṭān 38, 225
Shait Gumbuj masjid (Bagerhat, Bangladesh) 47, 160
Shams al-Dīn (title) 75
Shams al-Dunyā' wa 'l-Dīn (title) 98
Shank Mohan (Malda City, West Bengal) 193
Shāṛ Burj (Nawdapara, Rohanpur railway station, Chapai Nawabganj district) 53n18; *see also* Nawda Burj
al-Sharf al-A'lā fī Dhikr Qubūr Maqbira Bāb al-Ma'lā 24
Sharī'at Allah, Ḥājjī 42
sharī'a (Islamic code of life) 51, 60, 62, 64, 68–9, 107–9, 123, 137, 149
Shāṭī' al-Gangā (bank of the Ganges) 33
Shāṭi'-jām (Chittagong) 28
Shayam Prasad 5, 125, 178–9, 201, 240n17
Shaydā (faqīr revolting against Fakhr al-Dīn Mubārak Shāh) 65
Shāyistakhānī style (Mughal architectural legacy in and around Dhaka) 175
Shaykh Afqah al-Dīn 162; *see also* Shaykh Barkat al-Dīn, Rafqat al-Dīn, Rafīq al-Dīn, Rif'at al-Dīn
Shaykh al-Islām Shaykh Mas'ūd 121
Shaykh al-Mashāyikh 112, 239
[al]-Shaykh al-Qāḍī Ḥamīd al-Dīn Nagori Kunjshikan 162
Shaykh 'Alā' al-Ḥaqq 120–2, 162
Shaykh Anwar 121, 162–3
Shaykh Ḥusām al-Dīn of Manikpur 163
Shaykh Ḥusayn Dhukkarpūsh 122
Shaykh Jalāl al-Dīn Tabrīzī 121, 133–4, 172
Shaykh Kāku 163
Shaykh Mu'īn al-Dīn Fayḍ al-Islām 162
Shaykh Nāṣir al-Dīn Mānikpūrī 122
Shaykh Sa'dī 209
Shaykh Zāhid 121, 162–3
Shayt Hazari Dargāh 163
Shēr Shāh Ābād Parganah 53
Shēr Shāh Sūrī (ruler) 39, 53
Sher-i-Bangla (the Lion of Bengal) 74; *see also* Fazlul Haque
Sherpur 29, 229, 244
Shērshabadiya 53
Shī'a sect 81
Shibganj Police Station (Nawabganj District, Bangladesh) 137–8
[al]-Shībī, Jamāl al-Dīn Muḥammad ibn 'Alī ibn Muḥammad Jamāl al-Dīn al-Makkī al-Qarshī (epigraphist of Makkah, author of *Sharf al-A'lā*, *c.*779–837/1378–1433) 11, 24, 50
Shihāb al-Ḥaq wa 'l-Dīn (title) 104
Shi'ism 10
Shiqdār 137, 169
Shīrān Khaljī, Muḥammad 167
Shīrāzī (*nisba* [geographic attribution] to Shīrāz) 15; [al-]Shīrāzī, Sa'ad al-Dīn Muḥammad (the calligrapher of Barakatra) 25
shīrīn-qalam 124
[al]-Shīth, Jamāl al-Dīn 'Abd al-Raḥīm ibn 'Alī ibn 78
Shiv-Singh 122
Shiva and Shakti (Hindu god and goddess) 35
Short Notes on the Ancient Monuments of Gaur and Pandua (Abid Ali Khan) 4, 244
Sian (Birbhum district, West Bengal) 3, 13, 22, 91; inscription 64; Khānqāh 64
Sidon (historical town in Palestine) 11
[*al*]-*Ṣiḥaḥ al-Sitta* (six most authentic books of the sayings of the Prophet) 111
Sijdahgāh (place for prostration) 163
Sikandar Khān Ghāzī (first Islamic conquerer of Sylhet) 112
Sikandar Shāh (second ruler of the Ilyās Shāhi dynasty) 65, 83, 121–6, 128–32, 218, 244, 250
Sikandar thānī ('the second Alexander', title) 104; Sikandar al-Thānī 76, 103
*Silsilah*s 69
Simarāon (old capital of Tirhut) 102
Simlabād 149
siqāya (water tank, well) 30, 62
Sirāj al-Dakhūlī, (Chief of Internal Affairs during the reign of Sulṭān Yusuf Shāh) 198
Sirāj al-Ḥaqq wa 'l-Shar' wa 'l-Dīn (religious title for Mawlānā 'Aṭā') 123
Sirat Rasūl Allāh (biography of the Prophet by ibn Hisham) 23
Sitalmat (Naogan district, Bangladesh) 15, 16, 91, 98–9, 119, 247
Sitāna 56
Siyāsat Nāma (manual on politics by Nizam al-Mulk) 85n4

sjd (prostration during prayer) 45
Smithsonian Institution (Washington D.C.) 54
Solomon (King Sulaymān in Islamic tradition) 75, 115, 120; *see also* Sulaymān
Sona Masjid 206
Sonārgā'on (Muslim Capital of Bengal) 29, 36–7, 39, 50, 65–6, 109, 121, 162, 212, 215–16, 250
South Asian languages 80
Śrihaṭṭa (Sanskrit name of Sylhet [in Bangladesh], Habānaq according to ibn Baṭṭūṭa, Suknāt in other Islamic sources) 27; *see also* Habānaq ibn Baṭṭūṭa, Suknāt
Stapleton, H.E. 4–5, 162, 244
Ṣūba-i-Bangala (province of Bengal) 29
Ṣubḥ al-A'shā fī Ṣanā'at al-Inshā' (nineth century Hijra work by an Egyptian scholar Shihāb al-Qalqashandi) 78
sufi (Muslim saints) 15, 36–7, 48–50, 60, 64–9, 92–3, 121, 162, 239
Suhma (ancient name of the western region of Bengal) 28
Suknāt (mentioned in *Ṭabaqāt-i-Nāṣirī* for Sylhet or Samataṭa region) 27, 119n19; *see also* Śrihaṭṭa, Habānaq
Sulaymān (King Solomon in Jewish tradition) 75, 115, 120, 147–8; *see also* Solomon
Sulaymān Karrānī (ruler of Bengal) 39
[ibn] Sulaymān, Sulaymān ibn Aḥmad (an early sixteenth century Omani captain who wrote on Bay of Bengal) 33, 45
sulḥ-e-kull or *sulḥ-kul* ('peace with all', a principle followed by some sufis in South Asia) 67, 70
Sulṭān al-'Aṣr wa 'l-Zamān (title for Sulṭān Maḥmūd Shāh) 149
Sulṭān al-Salāṭīn (a title for A'ẓam Shah and some other Sulṭāns) 72, 104, 108
[al]-Sulṭān ibn al-Sulṭān (a royal title meaning 'the king, son of the king') 84, 118, 132, 168–9, 221, 211
[al]-Sulṭān ibn al-Sulṭān ibn al-Sulṭān ('the king, son of the king, [who was also] son of the king') 84, 103, 105; *see also* ibn al-Sulṭān
[al]-Sulṭān Pādshāh Ghāzī (title for Sulṭān Bārbak Shāh) 192
Sultan al-Zamān alladhi Mulkuhu Mulku Sulayman (title of some sultans of Bengal) 75, 120
Sultan al-Zamān bi 'l-'Adl wa 'l-Iḥsān 140
Sultanganj (Islamic archaeological site near Godagari police station, Rajshahi district) 2, 29, 70, 87, 90, 135–6, 195
[al]-Sultanī, Abū 'l-Fatḥ Ṭughril 76, 80, 96; Mughīth al-Dīn 36; Ṭughril 96, 97, 169
Sundarban (in Bangladesh) 27–8, 40, 52, 156, 160, 188, 240, 250
Sunna 41, 83
sūra (chapter of Qur'ān) 156; al-Falaq' 158; al-Fatḥ 130; al-Fatiḥa 127; al-Ikhlās 158; al-Kāfirūn 158; al-Nās' 158; al-Takāthur 158; al-Takwīr 158; al-Kāfirūn 158; 'Repentance (Tawba)' 128
Surtan (probably a misnomer of sultan in Arakanese dialect) 54
Suvarna Chandra (a Hindu king and a follower of Buddha as appeared in Ram-apala Sanskrit copperplate) 35
Swat (mountainous valley in Khyber Pakhtunkhwa, Pakistan) 55–6
Sylhet (Jalālābād, a district) 112
syncretic belief 42
syncretion 67
syncretistic traditions 68–70
Syriac inscription 9

[al]-ta'awwudh (Arabic prayer formula for divine protection from Satan) 158
Ta'ayyunī movement (1800–1873) 56
Ṭabaqāt-i-Nāṣirī (thirteenth century Persian chronicle by Mawlānā Minhāj al-Dīn 'Uthmān Sirāj al-Dīn) 23, 27, 31–2, 36, 52, 113, 116, 119, 243
[al]-Ṭabaṭab'ī al-Sīmnānī (*nisba* [attribution] used for Abu 'l-Qāsim al-Ḥusaynī) 25
Tablīghī Jamā'a (global Islamic movement of South Asian origin) 42
Tabrīzabād (medieval name of Deotala, fifteen miles north of Pandua) 172
Tabrīzī, Jalāl al-Dīn 98, 121, 133–4, 172
tabūt (coffin of Ḥusayn) 23n5, 24n15
Tagore, Rabindra Nath (Bengali literary figure) 43
[al]-tahlīl (foundational religious formula of Islam) 158
Ṭā'ifah (sectarian approach to religion) 69
Taish, Rahmat Ali (author of *Tawarīkh-i-Dhaka*, Arrah 1910) 5
Tāj al-Ḥaq wa 'l-Dīn (a title used for Ḥātim Khan) 114

Tajikas (reference to the Tajiks of Central Asia) 32
al-Tājir, Sulaymān (author of *Akhbār al-Ṣīn wa 'l-Hind* 237/851) 28, 52n9
takhalluṣ 73
Tanda (Muslim capital) 36, 177
Tankah 89
Tantipara masjid (in Gaur) 206
tantric practices 67
taqwa (religious piety) 70
Tarbiyyat Khān 152
[al]-Ta'rīf bi 'l-Muṣṭaliḥ al-Sharīf (book) 79
Ṭarīqah 69; Ṭarīqa Muḥammadiya 41
al-tashahhud 158
Ta-shih 31
Tashrīfiyyah (honourific) 75
taṣliya (a pious wish for the Prophet) 85; *taslīm* 84
Tātār Khān (Caliph) 100–1
tawḥīd (Divine unity) 45, 60, 122
tawqī' (calligraphic style) 88, 94–5, 117
Tawwāma, Shaykh Sharaf al-Dīn Abū 50
tax collector in Dhakha 166
Tezpur (Tangail district, Bangladesh) 184
Throne verse 5, 15, 24, 109–10, 130, 142–3, 185
thulth 7, 10, 88, 94–5, 97–8, 106, 125–30, 138, 141–2, 154, 156, 164, 170, 175, 181, 191–3, 201, 204–7, 210–11, 215, 217, 222–4, 228, 230, 232–4, 236, 238
Thu-ra-tan (Arabic sulṭān) 32, 54
Tibet 28, 31, 36, 90, 100
Tilapara village (in Sylhet) 202
Tīmūr, Amīr (ancestor of Babar) 15
Timurid citadel 109
ṭirāz (highly stylized form of embroidered writing on early Islamic textiles) 12, 24
Tirhut (in Bihar, India) 102, 114, 119, 122, 250
Tishu Lamba (meaning 'the seat of Luma', a Buddhist monastery built by Bakhtiar about eighty miles from Rangpur) 54n36
Tītūmīr (anti-colonial Islamic activist and leader) 42, 56, 69, 250; Sayyid Mīr Nithār 'Alī 42
Treasury inscription 83, 117
Tribeni (ancient place of Hindu pilgrimage and Sanskrit learning) 24n6, 50, 53, 105–6, 108–9, 114, 116, 119, 150, 211, 240, 248, 250, 254; Fīruzābād 108
Tripura (India) 27, 29
Trishbigha (in Hoogly district) 152, 224
Triveni (holy place of the Hindus) 152
Tset-ta-going (Chittagong) 31
Tsu-la-Taing Tsan-da-ya (King) 32
ṭughrā (calligraphic style): Bengali *ṭughrā'* 7, 10, 62, 131, 138–40, 142–3, 146, 148, 155, 161, 164, 168, 170–1, 173–4, 181, 189–90, 193, 195, 197, 200–1, 203–7, 209–12, 214–15, 217, 220, 222, 224–5, 230, 232, 236, 238; Mamluk *ṭughrā'* 181; Ottoman *ṭughrā'* 181
Ṭughril, Mughīth al-Dīn (ruler) 36, 76, 80, 95–7, 169
Tulunid era in Egypt 77
Turk tribes 76; Khatai 76; Tatar 76, 96
Turkey 16
Turkic dialect 169
Turko-Afghan tribes 76; Khaljī 76
Turko-Mongol 64
Tuzuk-i-Bābarī (autobiography of Babar) 15
Twenty Four Parganas in West Bengal, India 27

'ulamā' 20, 36–8, 41–2, 47, 49, 50–1, 62, 66–9, 78, 83, 107, 156, 160, 162, 219, 222
Ulugh Ajmal Khān 151
Ulugh 'Alī Ẓafar Khān 232
'Ulugh Iqrār Khān 167
Ulugh 'Izz al-Dīn 135
Ulugh Khān 103, 105–6
Ulugh Majlis Khān 140
Ulugh Majlis Nūr 223–4; *see also* Sāḥib al-Sayf wa 'l-Qalam
Ulugh Mukhliṣ Khān 131–2, 231; *see also* al-Khān al-A'ẓam
Ulugh Murābiṭ Khān 172
Ulugh Naṣr Khān Jangdār (title: Khān A'ẓam Khaqān Mu'aẓẓam) 187
Ulugh Raḥīm Khān 149
Ulugh Ṣufī Khān 196
Ulugh Taghī Khān ibn Bughrā Khān 125
ulūm al-'adyān 73, 217
'ulūm al-tafsīr 73, 217
[*al*]-*'ulūm al-'aqliyyah* 51
[*al*]-*'ulūm al-ḥadīthah* 51
[*al*]-*'ulūm al-naqliyyah* 51
[*al*]-*'ulamā' al-rāshidūn* 160
'Umar, Caliph 76
'Umar ibn Asad 121; [ibn] 'Umar ibn Asad Khālidī 162
'Umar Khaṭṭab 229
[al]-'Umarī, Shihāb al-Dīn ibn Faḍl-Allah 78
Umayyad period 9

[*al*]-*'Umda al-Mahriyyah fi ḍabt al-'Ulūm al-Baḥriyyah* 45
Umdat al-Biḥār 33
Umm al-Hānī gate 50, 57
ummah (concept about the Muslims as a single united nation) 22, 43, 45, 68, 79–80, 89, 131
[*al*]-*'umrān* (civilization) 45
University Museum in Philadelphia 180
Ūrshīn (Orissa) 28
'Uthmān 'Affān 229

Veda (scripture in the Aryan Vedic religion) 66, 71n27
Vedic religion (early Aryan religious tradition based on scripture) 35–6, 47, 62, 66
vernacular architecture 17, 47, 48, 240n16

waḥdat al-shuhūd (universal evidence of Divine Unity) 60
Wahhābī, (religious movement initiated by Shaykh Muḥammad ibn 'Abd al-Wahhāb in Arabia) 42, 56
Waḥīd al-Muḥaqqiqīn (sufi title for Mawlanā 'Aṭa') 123
[*al*]-*wajūd al-ẓillī*, (sufi concept of shadowy existence) 66
Wālī al-Mabarrāt (title) 115
waqf (endowment) 15–17, 25, 62, 71, 93, 98, 100, 202, 224
Wārith Mulk Sulaymān (title) 115, 147–8
wazīr dūn dar sharq 143
wazīr-i-lashkar 220
Wazirpur-Beldanga inscription 88, 117
West Benegal 3, 6, 25n23, 27–9, 50, 54n38, 64–5, 75–6, 90–1, 97, 102–4, 106, 108, 113–14, 119n8, 120, 122, 131, 133–4, 140–3, 146, 150, 152, 161, 163–6, 175–6, 184, 189, 191, 193, 195–7, 200, 210, 213, 214, 223, 232–4, 236–8, 240n16, 247–8, 253
Wilāyat 'Alī, 'Abd al-Karīm ibn 56
Wise, Dr James 5
wuḍū (ablution) 47

Yāg̲h̲istān 55–6, 250; Yāg̲h̲istān-i-Qadīm 55; Riyāsat-hā'i-Yāg̲h̲istān 55
Yamīn Khalīfat-Allah (the right hand of the caliph of Allah) 79, 98, 104
Ya'qūb ibn Kals 76
Yavana (Sanskrit word meaning aliens) 36
Yazdani, Ghulam 5
yoga 66–7
Yoga-Qalandar 71n28
[ibn] Yūsuf, Ḥajjāj 77
Yūsuf Shāh, Sulṭān Shams al-Dunyā wa 'l-Dīn Abū 'l-Muẓaffar 193–211, 218; *see also* ibn Bārbak Shāh al-Sulṭān ibn Maḥmūd Shāh al-Sulṭān; Shams al-Dunyā wa 'l-Dīn Abū 'l-Muẓaffar Yūsuf Shāh al-Sulṭān
Yusufganj (village) 109, 215
Yūsufzai 55

zāda khayruhu (may his benevolence increase) 57
Ẓafar Khān Bahram Aytgīn Sulṭānī 24n6, 53, 76, 104–6, 108, 114–16, 151, 153, 232, 248
Zāhir Shāh (the last Afghan king) 80
Zā'ir al-Qadamayn (title assumed by Ḥājjī Bābā Ṣāliḥ) 39
[al]-Zamān alladhi Mulkuhu Mulku Sulaymān (Sulṭān) 75, 120
zamindars 65, 162
[ibn] Zamrak (wrote verses on the Rayḥān Court) 18–20
Zarrīn Dast 123–4
Zayedpuri, Sayed Ghulam Hussein Salim 4, 43, 218, 243; *see also Riyāḍ al-Salāṭīn*
Zayn al-'Abidīn 'Alī 229
Zenana Khanah 129–30
Ẓill-Allah fī 'l-'Ālam (title) 115
Ẓill-Allah fī 'l-Arḍayn (title) 104